CAST

lost and found in history

AWAY

For Leendert Hasenbosch:
Lost on Ascension Island, 1725

CAST *lost and found in history* AWAY

Epic true stories of shipwreck, piracy
and mutiny on the high seas

Joseph Cummins

PIER 9

Contents

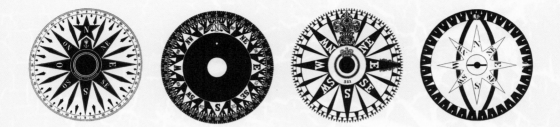

Introduction

Robinson Crusoe by Daniel Defoe, published in 1719, tells the story of a man who is cast away on a deserted island and spends twenty-eight years there until rescued. It is the most reprinted, translated and adapted book in the history of Western literature, but the reason for this is not to be found in Defoe's deathless prose style. Instead, it's because Defoe's novel tapped into a pre-existent human longing: the hunger for stories of those cast away.

What would it be like to sight Pitcairn Island, a dot in the ocean 5000 kilometres (3107 miles) from anywhere, with the original crew of *Bounty* mutineers? What must it feel like to find oneself thrashing through the jungle trying to escape from pirates, as Philip Ashton did on deserted Roatan Island off Honduras in 1722? And can we really envision the fate of Leendert Hasenbosch, a Dutch ship's officer who found himself alone on uninhabited Ascension Island, deep in the South Atlantic Ocean, in 1725—and who was, after a few months of near-starvation and thirst, literally haunted by ghosts?

We know this only from Leendert Hasenbosch's journal, discovered on a beach. Hasenbosch didn't make it, but many of the solitary souls in *Cast Away* do survive; and one of the great pleasures of reading about castaways is sharing in the vicarious thrill of their rescue. Alexander Selkirk, the model for Robinson Crusoe, found that when he saw a ship's boat nearing his island that he had forgotten how to speak his native language. Charles Barnard and his men, long cast away in the bleak Falklands in the early nineteenth century, fell to the ground and began weeping when they saw two whaling ships enter their desolate bay. In a sense, whatever the reason for being marooned, to be cast away is to be cleansed—to shed civilisation, to spend one's figurative forty days in the wilderness, and to come back a newly-minted person.

All of this philosophising is quite nice, of course, but how does one survive being cast away, especially in an inhospitable environment? Thirst was a serious issue for many of our castaways, including Leendert Hasenbosch, the survivors of the Dutch East Indies merchant ship *Batavia*, and the crew of the American vessel *Commerce*, which crashed into the west coast of Africa. If there is little ground water, rain will serve nicely, but without this liquid manna from heaven, survivors tried all sorts of liquids.

Drinking one's own urine was a favourite solution, although modern science tells us it only works in the short term. A healthy person's urine (and when castaways get to the point where they are ingesting their own pee they are none too healthy) is 95 per cent

pure, but contains 5 per cent toxins—among them calcium and potassium—which, after all, the kidneys have been trying to excrete. By drinking urine, one is placing these toxins back in the body. So if you find yourself at the point where you feel the need to drink your own waste products, figure you only have about two days left to live.

In the days of sail, almost every sailor avoided drinking sea water, and in the main they were right—it can easily dehydrate the body and cause a build-up of harmful salts. However, there has been some research to show that if fresh water is available, one can dilute it with 30 or 40 percent sea water and experience few if any side effects.

Blood was another big one, especially turtle blood and seal blood, since these creatures were readily available, but sometimes human blood—Daniel Foss chillingly describes lapping up the blood of his fellow shipwreck survivor who drew the wrong lot and slit his wrists. Blood is not the worst substitute for water—it has a high protein content and does give you needed fluids. But your body still needs water to digest protein and will sooner or later shut down on a steady diet of the red stuff.

As for food—you name it, castaways have eaten it. In these twenty-four stories alone, castaways eat frozen seal entrails, locusts, snakes, rats, seagulls, rotting bear meat, ground-up animal bones, their shoes and, of course, each other—cannibalism is an unavoidable part of the extreme castaway experience, as Daniel Foss, the English mariners huddled on Boon Island, and others can attest.

Moving from the frozen Arctic to the rolling Pacific, *Cast Away* satisfies *our* elemental hunger for stories which are by turns gripping, mysterious, unpredictable and exciting. If you want to know what it's like to be cast away—in all its horror and glory—turn the page.

Part One
THE STORMY
ATLANTIC

'Now would I give a thousand furlongs
of sea for an acre of barren ground.'
William Shakespeare, *The Tempest*, Act I, Scene I

The Wreck of the Sea Venture, 1609
Rescuers Cast Away

On 2 June 1609, a fleet of nine ships left Plymouth, England, and set sail across the Atlantic. The ships, carrying between 500 and 600 people, were led by the proud and sturdy flagship *Sea Venture*. Displacing some 300 tons, this vessel carried, in addition to 140 men and women, Sir George Somers, the fleet's admiral, and a penniless civil servant and poet named William Strachey, who was keeping one step ahead of debtor's prison.

The fleet might seem paltry, as fleets go, but as it scudded across the Atlantic that June, it was on a rescue mission of some importance. It was heading for Jamestown, the English colony struggling to survive in the wilds of Virginia, North America, whose very existence depended on the arrival of the vessels and the people and supplies they carried.

'The Sharp Pricke of Hunger'

Virginia. In the sixteenth and seventeenth centuries, this single word inflamed the minds of the English public as no other. It signified long sea voyages, hardship, incredible toil and painted savages. But it also meant the fantastic allure of the New World, where a man could find land, a modicum of freedom and, if he was lucky, a fortune.

Virginia was named after England's Virgin Queen, Queen Elizabeth I, and first applied to an area extending from Canada south to the present-day state of South Carolina. England's enemies Spain and France disputed the claim, but the explorations of English adventurers like John Cabot, who discovered the North American continent in 1497, and Richard Hore and Sir Humfrey Gilbert, who made early attempts at trading with the Indians they found there, gave England at least a toehold on the continent.

That toehold became an actual settlement when, in 1584, Sir Walter Raleigh received the Queen's patent to become 'Sir Walter Raleigh, Lord and Governor of Virginia', and established a settlement on Roanoke Island, in the future state of North Carolina. The colony had failed—indeed vanished, its inhabitants possibly massacred by Spanish or the local Roanoke Indians—but the English continued in their attempts. In 1606, three years after the death of Queen Elizabeth, the Virginia Company was formed to establish 'a colonie of sundrie of our people'. One branch of the company would send colonists to what is now New England. The other would deploy ships, goods and settlers to 'that parte of America' in more southerly climes but far enough up the eastern coastline to escape the Spanish raiding north from the Caribbean.

These 104 men, women and children arrived in the Chesapeake Bay area aboard three ships in early 1607, sailed west until they found the James River, and up that broad estuary until they found a readily defensible position. Within two weeks they had erected a fort and called their settlement Jamestown. For the two years the colony's very existence was uncertain. Re-supplied only haphazardly from England, feeling the continuous 'sharp pricke of hunger', as one colonist was to write, plagued by disease, bad water, a shortage of qualified workmen and sometimes treacherous relationships with the local Powhatan Indians, the colony hung on precariously.

It wasn't until 1609 that the *Sea Venture* and the other eight ships of its fleet set forth in the first major effort not only to re-supply the colony, but to bring able workmen, craftsmen and farmers—men whom the Virginia Company, under a new charter from King James I, lured to the enterprise by depicting Virginia as a 'paradise'. But for those who knew the real conditions in Jamestown, the question was: would the *Sea Venture* be too late? Would Jamestown be another vanished colony?

Tempest-tossed

As the *Sea Venture* crossed the Atlantic, it was operating on special instructions that differed from those given to ships that had previously made this voyage. Before they left port, Somers and Sir Thomas Gates, who would become the new governor of the Jamestown colony and who was also aboard the *Sea Venture*, had been warned by Virginia Company higher-ups to avoid the Caribbean 'lest you fall into ye hand of the Spaniard'. This meant they had to steer clear of the usual route, which was to head south for the Canary Islands, then across to the West Indies, and catch the northward-flowing Gulf Stream up the coast of America to Jamestown.

This fleet was to sail in a more direct line across the Atlantic, keeping well north of the Indies. At first this worked well, and William Strachey, who later wrote an account of the voyage, reported that the westerly winds blew the fleet along on a steady course for nearly two months. Despite the crowded conditions, where people intermingled with livestock and seasickness caused the decks to be slippery with vomit, the ships sailed along in 'friendly consort', and people's hopes were high. According to Strachey, the *Sea Venture* was only seven or eight days from making landfall in America when disaster struck. On Monday, 24 July, 'the clouds gathered thick upon us and the winds [began] singing and whistling most unusually'.

A four-day storm out of the northeast hit the little fleet, a 'dreadful storm and hideous', as Strachey put it. In the 'hell of darkness' that followed, terrified passengers were flung about the decks, some to be washed overboard. Others wept and prayed in the holds. Aboard the *Sea Venture*, Strachey watched as Somers ordered the pinnace *Virginia*, being towed by the *Sea Venture*, to be cut adrift lest it capsize and drag the *Sea Venture* with it. The twenty people on the *Virginia* were never seen again.

The *Sea Venture* was soon alone on the raging ocean, its captain having no idea of the whereabouts of the rest of the fleet. By the second day the ship's caulking had begun to leak, and passengers and crew crawled through the dark hold with candles held high, trying to plug the holes with beef meant as supplies for the starving settlers in Jamestown. The water kept rising, and Somers divided the men into three groups to man the ship's primitive pumps fore, aft and amidships; they pumped for their lives for three days.

By Friday, 28 July, many aboard the *Sea Venture* had begun to give up hope, to offer up 'their sinful souls' to God and the 'mercy of the sea'. One group of gentlemen broke out a hidden cache of wine and began to get drunk, toasting each other as giant waves slammed over the deck. But that afternoon, the skies cleared ever so slightly, and Admiral Somers, staring over the ocean, suddenly saw the unimaginable. '*Land!*' he screamed above the whistling wind.

Through prayer or simple fate, the *Sea Venture* had come upon Bermuda.

The existence of the uninhabited 150-island archipelago, now known as Bermuda or the Bermudas, was no secret in 1609. Situated roughly 960 kilometres (596½ miles) east of Virginia and some 5600 kilometres (3479½ miles) of England, the islands were a little too northerly to be discovered by Columbus as he coursed the Caribbean, but were finally sighted in 1503 by the Spanish sailor Juan de Bermúdez—although legend has it that an Irish saint found them centuries before (see **Saint Brendan in Bermuda**, page 17).

The islands had remained uninhabited because of the coral reefs and rocky shoals which surrounded them. In the two hundred years since Bermúdez sighted them, these treacherous rocks had claimed many a vessel, so many in fact that the islands had become known as the Devil's Islands, a place that, as one contemporary wrote, 'every navigator and mariner [should] avoid … as they would shun the Devil himself'.

But the mariners aboard the *Sea Venture* had no choice in the matter. If they did not find landfall here, all would die. With the winds abating somewhat, Somers brought the *Sea Venture* closer and closer to the nearest island, taking depth soundings all the while by tossing out a lump of lead attached to a knotted line. He was still about 1500 metres (almost 1 mile) from shore when he realised that the ocean was only six fathoms (11 metres, or 36 feet), deep. He could not anchor—the vessel, in its holed and leaking condition, would soon sink—but if he risked sailing closer to the wave-battered shoals it would be torn apart on the rocks.

Spotting a V-shaped opening in the offshore reef, Somers made the dangerous decision to crash the ship into it, hoping to wedge it firm among the rocks and get the passengers off before it broke apart. Incredibly, this doughty admiral—a man his contemporaries praised for 'the most memorable courage of his minde'—had made the right decision. The ship stuck fast, the longboats were lowered, and one by one brought crew, passengers and supplies ashore in a small cove. The men, women and children staggered onto land and fell to the ground, thanking God for their salvation.

Then they stood, clustered in small groups, and carefully looked around them. They were, after all, on Devil's Island. Almost anything could happen.

A Paradise for Real

In fact, the desperate people found themselves pleasantly surprised. The devil seemed entirely absent from surroundings which included broad beaches, azure waters teeming with fish so unwary the castaways could grab them from the water, a dozen different delicious fruits and berries, untold thousands of tropical birds, which could also be had for the taking, large green sea turtles which made delicious eating, and a healthy population of wild pigs, descendants, no doubt, of hogs set ashore from some earlier shipwreck.

The woods were full of cedar trees, perfect for shipbuilding, and palmetto trees whose fronds the castaways used to thatch the cabins they built. The mushy tops of the palmettos could even be roasted or boiled and eaten. According to Strachey, 'they [tasted] like cabbages, but not so offensively [gassy] on the stomach'.

By the middle of August they had built huts, planted seed brought from England, and set kettles of sea water boiling constantly in order to produce salt. They had landed on the island now known as St George's and their settlement faced what is now Gates's Bay (supposedly, when Sir Thomas splashed ashore, he shouted out 'Gates, his bay!'). This place had everything they needed, or so it seemed; according to one passenger, Bermuda was 'the richest, healthfullest and [most] pleasing land … as a man ever set foot upon'.

But however pleasant Bermuda might be, Admiral Somers and Sir Thomas Gates knew that the Virginia Company had hired them to arrive at Jamestown, and this they intended to do. And they could not afford to wait until they were rescued. They had no idea of the fate of the other ships in the fleet, aside from the pinnace they had been forced to cut loose, and had to presume they were lost in the storm. (Remarkably, all the other ships had arrived safely in Jamestown, although much the worse for wear.) Somers and Gates set about immediately to remedy their situation. The first thing they did was rig out one of the ship's boats with a sail and supplies and set her, along with six men led by a very brave master seaman named Henry Raven, to sail the 960 kilometres (596½ miles) to Virginia and bring back help. Raven set out in early September. About a month later, William Strachey would row every day to a small neighbouring island and build a fire on top of a hill to guide Raven and the rescue ship he would be leading back to St George's. But by late November he had abandoned the effort—it was apparent that Raven was not coming back. (He and his crew were never seen again and were probably lost at sea, although rumours persist that they made the American mainland only to be killed by Indians.)

Despite having sent Raven for help, Somers and Gates decided that the only certain way off the island was to build their own ship, and to this end in early October they started constructing a vessel on the beach, using part of the wreck and cedar trees cut from the island. Progress was painfully slow, for while they had a master shipbuilder named Richard Frobisher to direct the work, most of the men were untrained in the intricate and backbreaking business. Somers himself supervised the construction of another, smaller vessel, and life on the island was taken up with shipbuilding, the ringing of hammers and the shouts of the men vying with the cries of seabirds and the crash of waves.

Gates, now that they were on land, was in charge of the expedition, and governed the castaways firmly. Religious services were held morning and evening, led by a preacher, and those who did not attend were punished with extra labour. But there were lighter moments. Romance flourished—a lady's maid married a gentleman's cook—and two babies would be born, a boy and a girl, both named Bermuda. The girl—born to John Rolfe and his wife (Rolfe would later, as a widower, marry the Indian princess Pocahontas at Jamestown)—died soon after birth, as did the boy, but their names were a token of the gratitude with which the castaways viewed the former Devil's Island.

In fact, as the ships were being built, a group of passengers began to complain that there was no need to sail to Jamestown when they had all they needed right here.

'Let the Governor Kiss, etc.'

These men wondered, as Strachey recorded, why go to an uncertain future in Virginia when 'ease and pleasure' might be enjoyed in Bermuda? Finally, six castaways, all seamen, made a secret pact not to aid in the ship building; in fact, they decided to abscond to another island, there to live without interference from the likes of Gates. They convinced a blacksmith and a carpenter—both valuable members of the castaway community—to go with them, but before they could steal a boat and leave, their plot was discovered.

Gates sentenced the men to isolation on an island, but not the one of their choosing— they were put on a barren, rocky atoll, with just enough supplies to keep them alive.

vnd men als sich gesang do entschliessend sy vnd och die schifflut die
das schiff fuortend vnd liessend das schiff selber rinn vnd die munch
verdrossen sich ze selbs gar von ener stimen das sy nit wisten wenn
sy fuoren do traib sy das mer zu ainem berg der itel fuoren was
lesser dem lieff ain schwartzer man der rieff dem schiff der zu
das sy dor von erwachsten vn sprach zu men kerend her zu wie ich
wil iuch sagen wenn ze veren stillen

Saint Brendan in Bermuda

When the crew and passengers of the *Sea Venture* staggered ashore in 1609, they were the only human beings on the Bermudas, but they were not the first. In 1503, the archipelago was discovered by the Spanish seafarer Juan de Bermúdez, but even he was not the initial European visitor—at least according to legend. The very first may have been an Irish monk known as Brendan the Navigator.

Brendan was born around 454 AD in what is now County Kerry, Ireland, took holy orders in 513 and became abbot of a monastery on Ireland's west coast. In 530, he and a small group of his monks supposedly set sail from Dingle, braving the Atlantic in a skin boat. According to the ninth century manuscript, *The Voyages of St Brendan the Navigator*, Brendan and his fellows made their way to the Faroe Islands north of Ireland, and then west across the Atlantic to what Brendan called 'the Promised Land', or America.

Here the story becomes quite interesting. After touching the American coast, Brendan supposedly sailed south until he got to an island he called the 'Island of Delight', which had plenty of fruit, birds, water and trees. This sounds a lot like Bermuda, though Brendan should not to be taken too literally—he also claimed that a whale arose by their boat every Sunday so the monks could say Mass on its back, and that he found Judas chained in perpetual penance on a wet rock in the middle of the ocean, and that a demon carried off one of his sailors.

But one note about Brendan's 'Island of Delight' is intriguing: according to the legend, it was filled with thousands of a particular bird which, as the sun went down, would begin singing in unison, a loud inharmonious noise. As anyone from the *Sea Venture* could tell you, Bermuda has just such a bird: the cahow, or Bermuda petrel.

Life was so miserable there that somehow they managed to send Gates a note begging him to have mercy. Relenting, he let them return. Winter had set in, with cool, wet weather, and huge flocks of migrating birds passing overhead. More turtles migrated to the island, so many that the men took up to forty each day, to dry and salt away for the future.

Storms began to flail the islands in January and a storm of a different sort approached from an unlikely source, a man named Stephen Hopkins, a clerk to Reverend Bucke who held the island's religious services. Hopkins assisted at these services and sometimes took over when Bucke was indisposed. He was considered by most a pious and mild-mannered fellow, but the pleasures of Bermuda apparently got to him as well. According to Strachey, Hopkins argued that any authority Gates had over the castaways had ceased with the shipwreck and that they were under no obligation to do anything the Governor said. Gate quickly stifled this rebellion by sentencing Hopkins to death, only to remit the sentence when Hopkins and his family pleaded piteously for his life.

But soon a more serious threat arose, this time from a 'gentleman' (as opposed to a lowly seaman) named Henry Paine, who refused to go on guard duty one night. It appears he was part of a larger conspiracy of mutineers plotting to overthrow the camp, although Gates was probably unaware of this. When Paine was told that such insubordination, when it came to the attention of the Governor, would result in his execution, he replied, according to Strachey's rendering of the exchange, 'let the governor ... kiss, etc.'

Gates finally got serious. The next day, Paine was tried and sentenced to death. His pleas were to no avail, Gates acquiescing only to his final wish to be shot rather than hanged. As the day ended, Strachey wrote, '[Paine] had his desire, the sun and his life setting together.'

In the meantime, several other men involved in the plot, assuming Paine had confessed to their participation, ran into the woods and hid themselves.

'In Memory of Our Great Deliverance'

By the end of April, both vessels were completed—Frobisher's 12-metre (39-foot) sloop, the *Deliverance*, and Somer's 8.8-metre (29-foot) pinnace, the *Patience*. But there remained the matter of the mutineers who had fled. Many of them, faced with the prospect of being left behind as escape became a reality, relented and wrote a letter to Somers—whom they considered a fair and honest man—asking him to intercede on their behalf with Gates. He did so, and Gates promised not to punish them. One by one, they trickled out of hiding, except for two steadfast fugitives, Christopher Carter and Edward Waters. The rest of the survivors gathered on the beach on 10 May 1610 to board the ships.

Sir George Somers takes possession of the Bermudas on behalf of Britian.

Tempest-Tossed?

'A tempestuous noise of thunder and lightning heard.'

Thus reads the very first stage direction of Shakespeare's play *The Tempest* which, many literary scholars believe, owes a great deal to the wreck of the *Sea Venture*. First performed in the latter half of 1611, *The Tempest* tells the story of a fleet of ships carrying Alonso,

the King of Naples, which is battered by a horrible hurricane. Alonso and his vessel come to rest on the reef of a tropical island controlled by the sorcerer Prospero and his servant spirit Ariel. While *The Tempest* is definitely a work of fantasy and imagination, many scholars think that Shakespeare may have been inspired by William Strachey's account of the wreck of the *Sea Venture*, which was circulating in manuscript in London in 1610. If so, it marked the first time that events in America influenced the great playwright. Shakespeare makes reference to 'the still-vexed Bermoothes', a phrase from Strachey's story, and his characters' experiences echo those of the passengers of the *Sea Venture*: fighting through a horrible gale, tossing luggage and vital supplies overboard, sighting an island in the gloom and making for it and, finally, reaching shore before the ship splits apart on the reef.

This no doubt applies to other shipwrecks as well, but Shakespeare does weave in details from Strachey's account of the castaways' life on the island. With an eye on the tourist trade, present-day Bermuda has adopted *The Tempest*—there is a Prospero's Cave, a Caliban's Bar and an Ariel Sands Beach Club.

Before they left, they built a cross from the timbers of the *Sea Venture* and attached it to a tree. Underneath it was a piece of beaten copper, with an inscription which began: 'In memory of our great deliverance, both from a mighty storm and leak: wee have set up this to the honour of God. It is the spoil of an English ship called the *Sea Venture* ...'

They sailed away, carefully navigating the reefs under trimmed sails before letting the canvas billow in the open ocean as northerly winds pushed them toward Virginia. The vessels arrived in Jamestown twelve days later, expecting to see the colony thriving. Instead, they found what they thought was a deserted town. The gates were torn off the fort and there was no sign of life. But finally, when Gates ordered that a bell be rung, the colonists of Jamestown appeared looking, as one historian has written, 'like corpses held upright by unseen marionette strings'. They cried: 'We are starving! We are starving.'

Jamestown had undergone a horrible famine. Terrified of Indians and afraid to venture outside for long, the inhabitants had been forced to eat cats and dogs, shoe leather, and 'wylde and unkowne Rootes' from the forest. Those who died were buried in shallow graves; at night, the starving settlers would dig up the bodies and devour them.

Hundreds died during the famine, so that Gates and Somers were met by sixty colonists at most. Faced with this shocking situation Gates decided to evacuate the colony. Putting the colonists aboard the *Patience* and *Deliverance* and the few small vessels available at Jamestown, they set sail, only to be met by a small boat carrying great news—a new fleet would shortly arrive from England, carrying plentiful supplies and new settlers.

Delighted with this news, Gates turned his small, ragged flotilla back to the stinking, tumbledown fort of Jamestown. Two days later, three English ships arrived with new colonists and enough supplies for a year. Jamestown was saved and would begin to grow.

And what of the principals who had been aboard the *Sea Venture*? Sir Thomas Gates left Jamestown in April 1614, having fulfilled his duties to King James and the Virginia Company. Sir George Somers would return to Bermuda and die there, of natural causes, during an attempt to re-supply Jamestown in November 1610.

While Strachey stayed on in Virginia until 1611, he sent home a letter in July 1610 entitled 'A true repertory of the wrake and redemption' of the *Sea Venture*. It received wide circulation and a certain playwright named Shakespeare read it, drawn in particular to Strachey's depiction of 'a most dreadful Tempest'. Shakespeare's play *The Tempest* (see **Tempest-Tossed?**, opposite) appeared in November 1611. Strachey probably attended a performance. He almost certainly knew that his report of the wreck of the *Sea Venture* had been profitably used by Shakespeare. Strachey himself, however, still had difficulty turning a profit. Creditors hounded him and he died a pauper in England in 1621.

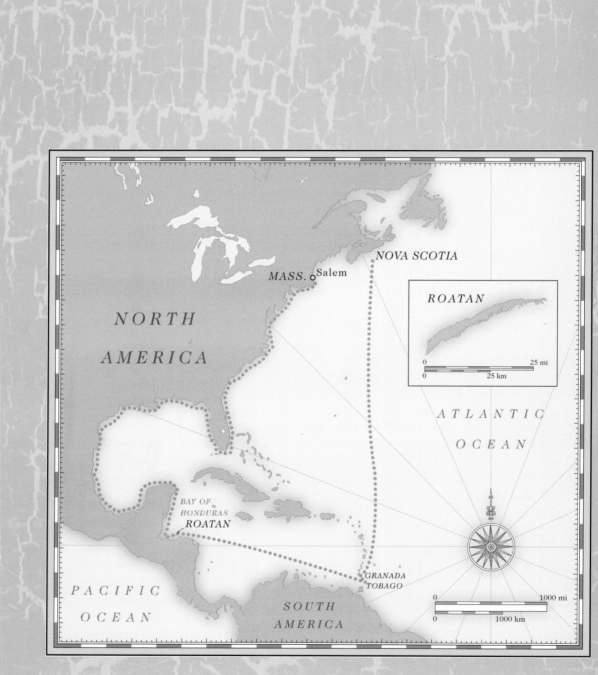

Philip Ashton, 1722–1725
Lost on Roatan Island

In March 1723, the 20-year-old North American colonist Philip Ashton found himself wandering breathless and alone through a tropical rainforest. A number of things confirmed for the terrified young man that he was no longer in the friendly confines of New England—the shovel-nose sharks that waited in the lagoon, for instance, or the strange, possibly poisonous, blood-red fruit that hung low from the trees he passed under.

But perhaps most frightening of all were the mossy logs that turned out to be alive. We'll let Ashton describe them:

> *Many serpents are on this and adjacent islands; one, about twelve or fourteen feet long, is as wide as a man's waist. When lying at length they look like old trunks of trees covered with short moss, although they more usually assume a circular position. The first time I saw one of these serpents I had approached very near before discovering it to be a living creature. It opened its mouth wide enough to have received a hat and breathed on me.*

Feeling a serpent's hot breath on his legs was not exactly what Ashton had bargained for when he set out on his fishing schooner nearly nine months and thousands of kilometres before to catch haddock and cod to bring to market. Human serpents in the form of pirates had brought him to this strange place and he now needed to learn the lessons that would let him live. The giant snake's hissed warning was enough, and he never again approached a seemingly fallen tree with the same lack of caution.

Taken by Pirates

We don't know a great deal about Philip Ashton beyond his own account of his adventures and an article that appeared in *The Boston News Letter* in July 1722. The newspaper story confirmed that Ashton, born in 1702 and a native of a Massachusetts fishing village, had disappeared in Nova Scotia, along with a number of other fishermen, taken by the pirate Ned Low. Ashton's account fleshes out the rest of the story. After a day of fishing, he had brought his schooner, with its crew of five men and a cabin boy, into Port Rossaway, Nova Scotia. It was Friday, 15 June, and Ashton intended to lay up and rest before returning to Massachusetts. There were numerous other fishing boats in port, along with a brigantine, a vessel known for being sleek and fast. The fact that pirates were quite fond of brigantines did not seem to make Ashton suspicious, nor the fact that port scuttlebutt had the ship just arrived from the West Indies, a notorious pirate haven.

Ashton and the others paid for their innocence when, about four o'clock that afternoon, 'a boat from the brigantine came alongside with four hands, who leaped on deck and, suddenly drawing out pistols and brandishing cutlasses, demanded the surrender both of ourselves and our vessel'. The unarmed fishermen could do little but comply—in fact, Ashton related, thirteen or fourteen fishing vessels suffered the same fate that evening.

'You Dog!'

Ashton and the other men were taken aboard the brigantine to find themselves in the presence of the infamous Ned Low (see **Notorious Ned Low**, opposite). While it may seem to those of us who have read *Peter Pan* and seen the crop of *Pirates of the Caribbean* movies (Ned Low, by the way, plays a part in these) that being captured by pirates was a romantic fate, it most certainly was not. The early eighteenth century has been called by some 'the golden age of piracy', but these sea-going muggers plagued the lives of ordinary citizens on the ocean and along seacoasts everywhere. Unlike movie pirates, real-life pirates shied away from bigger, better-armed prize ships (very few chests of gold were actually taken) and spent their time picking on poor fishermen or merchant vessels. The passengers and crew they captured were subject to death, torture, abandonment, rape, even forced to become pirates themselves.

This latter fate befell Philip Ashton. When Ned Low asked whether any of his captives were married, Ashton (who was single) could not think of the best reply. At first he refused to answer, which turned out to be a mistake when Low put a pistol to his head, cocked it and shouted: 'You dog, why don't you answer?' Terrified, Ashton replied truthfully that he was not wed. This, too, turned out to be a mistake—Low, while almost certainly a sociopath, had a reverence for family life (he also made his men take Sunday as a day of rest).

Within a few days, Low released all married men taken prisoner in Port Rossaway, keeping only Ashton and seven others. He tried to force them into signing the so-called 'articles of agreement' under which all pirates sailed. These documents were spurious contracts drawn up at the beginning of a voyage to which all the pirates affixed their mark or signature. Forcing the captives to sign made them part of the crew, or so the thinking went—if they were caught, they would all hang, a powerful incentive for any captive to work with a will.

Notorious Ned Low

'Of all the piratical crews,' Philip Ashton wrote of his captors, 'none of the English name came up to [these] in barbarity. Their mirth and their anger usually had the same effect, for both were usually gratified by the cries and groans of their prisoners … the unfortunate could never be assured of safety from them, for danger lurked in their very smiles.'

The leader of these demons was one of the most notorious pirates of his times, Edward 'Ned' Low. Born to a poor family in London around 1690, Low became a thief at an early age, but appears to have straightened out his life when he married, had children, and moved to Boston. He worked as a ship's rigger until his wife died in childbirth in 1719. Her death seems to have pushed Low over the edge. By late 1721, he had begun his career as a pirate and by the time Ashton met up with him he was already notorious, as much for boldness as for cruelty. His usual modus operandi was to sail into a safe harbour under a false flag then attack, either taking ships as prizes or stealing their cargoes and blowing them out of the water.

His captives faced horrible fates. The captain of a Nantucket whaler was forced to eat his own ears, fried and lightly salted, before he was killed. Low is reputed to have personally killed all 53 crewmen aboard a captured Spanish vessel with his cutlass, first making one ship's officer eat

The cruel captain Edward 'Ned' Low.

the heart of another. By these lights, his treatment of Philip Ashton was mild.

Low did not last long, but as his end neared he became ever more cruel. Hunted by a British man-of-war, he sailed north from the Caribbean in the summer of 1723, once again preying on fishing vessels. He decapitated the captain on one, and another time ordering such tortures that his crew refused to carry them out. In the end his crew mutinied and abandoned him. No one is quite certain how Low died. However the notorious Ned Low died, his legend lives on.

Philip Ashton, however, now showing the courage that he would later display in great quantity, refused to sign, despite another gun being put to his head, so the pirates forged his name. And now he was to prove even luckier than he was brave. Just before the pirate ship departed, two Marblehead men managed to escape, and Ashton was accused of being in league with them. An enraged pirate named Russel put a pistol to Ashton's head—the third time this particular nicety had been practised—and pulled the trigger. The gun misfired. He cocked the gun again and snapped the trigger three more times, with the same effect. Finally, the pirate aimed the gun overboard in disgust—and it fired. This so enraged him that he drew a cutlass and chased Ashton, who only managed to escape by jumping into the hold while the pirate was restrained by a few of his mates.

The Red Skeleton

Ned Low set sail for the Caribbean, fertile ground for marauders. The islands of the Caribbean Sea, stretching in a semi-circle from North to South America, were filled with prizes (merchant ships carrying sugar, rum and molasses, passenger vessels carrying wealthy English, French or Spanish settlers) as well as untold places to hide—atolls, cays, obscure islands where few men ever set foot. Flying his infamous flag—a red skeleton on a black background—Low took at least twenty prize ships, sailing from Tobago to Grenada. A typical capture technique was to sail into a port with most of his men hiding below decks, then surprise its inhabitants—as Low had Ashton and his fellows in Nova Scotia— and attack several ships. In Grenada, his vessel appeared so innocent that the mariners aboard a French sloop in port took it for a harmless smuggler and decided to take the ship themselves. Low turned the tables on them. In a flash, ninety pirates appeared on deck and eight cannon were trained on the sloop, which surrendered meekly.

The pirates took the nicely appointed sloop and, now with two vessels, sailed for the Spanish settlements in Central America. On the way, they made the mistake of approaching a large ship which turned out to be an English man-of-war. Not a smart idea. The man-of-war, in Ashton's nice phrase, 'showed off its great range of teeth' (rows of gleaming cannon) and gave chase. Ashton confessed 'that my terrors were equal to any I had previously suffered' (he assumed he would either be blown out of the water or hung as a pirate upon capture) but the ship he was on, while it became separated from Low's vessel, managed to escape.

The experience was even more frightening as the pirates aboard Ashton's vessel— captained by one Francis Farrington Spriggs, who was only marginally less a psychopath than Low—all got drunk during the pursuit, cocked their pistols, and 'swore that if they saw no possibility of escape to set foot to foot and blow each other's brains out'.

Wild Flight

Spriggs rejoined Low and the pirates cruised among the numerous small islands in the Bay of Honduras (see **The Bay of Honduras**, page 33), which were considered so overrun by these outlaws that even today, mainlanders on Honduras refer to islanders as 'pirates'. While the pirates took their ease and re-supplied at any number of islands, they were careful never to let Ashton ashore. Becoming more and more desperate, Ashton plotted with several other captives to seize the ship when the pirates were in one of their frequent drunken stupors, and make off with it. Somehow Spriggs got wind of this, and went to see Low, making, as Ashton put it, 'a furious declaration' against the would-be mutineers. But Low, possibly drunk, dismissed the report, and Spriggs returned to his own ship in a state of rage.

'You dog, Ashton, you deserve to be hanged up to the yardarm,' he shouted.

Ashton decided that his luck was going to run out fairly soon and that he had better make good his escape while he had the opportunity. One day the ship's cooper took six hands and went ashore on deserted Roatan Island to fill water barrels from its freshwater springs. Ashton begged to be taken along, saying that he had 'hitherto never been ashore and thought it hard to be so closely confined'. His plea worked well. When Ashton got to the beach, he set to work with a determined will, getting the casks out of the longboat and rolling them to the springs. His industry lulled the cooper and his work party and, ever so gradually, he began to wander down the beach. When he was about a musket shot away from the rest of the crew, he strolled with seeming casualness to the very fringe of the woods.

'What are you doing?' called the cooper.

'Getting some coconuts,' Ashton replied, with a wave.

Once out of sight in the coconut grove, Ashton raced wildly away, tearing through the forest, despite the fact that his feet were bare and the underbrush rough. He finally hid deep in a thicket and waited. Having filled the barrels, the cooper and his party came looking for him. They wandered close by in their search, but Ashton kept perfectly still. He could hear them talking. 'He has run away and won't come to us,' one said. The cooper replied that had he known Ashton was going to pull such a stunt, he would never have let him ashore. Then he called out to Ashton, not unkindly: 'If you do not come away presently, I shall go off and leave you alone.'

But nothing, as Ashton wrote, 'could induce me to discover myself'. Shortly afterward, the cooper and his men rowed back to the boat. Ashton found a vantage point from which he could secretly watch the pirate vessels. Five days later, he was overjoyed to see both sail away.

'This Melancholy Prospect'

It's easy to imagine the emotions that went through Ashton's mind when he finally walked down to the beach and surveyed the empty ocean. On the one hand, he was free—his tormentors had disappeared. Yet on the other, here he was wearing nothing but the clothes on his back (and without shoes), 'altogether destitute of provision, nor could [I] tell how my life was to be supported'. Ashton literally sat down on the beach and wept 'copious tears' at his 'melancholy prospect'. The picture is a truly pathetic one—a young (now barely 21) New Englander alone on a strange and forbidding island, weeping as the waves crash against the shore, the seabirds wheel overhead, and the black flies—for Ashton was beginning to realise Roatan was infested with these tiny, stinging bugs—pester and bite him.

However, Ashton was a religious man: 'As it had pleased God to grant my wishes in being liberated from those whose occupation was devising mischief against their neighbours, I resolved to account every hardship light.' Having thus given himself a pep talk, he walked the narrow island, which he estimated to be ten or eleven leagues long, roughly 50 kilometres (31 miles), which was almost exactly right (and it ranges in width from 1.5 to 10 kilometres, or from 1 to 6 miles). He noted the 'high hills and deep valleys' that characterised the place, and the abundance of fresh water and fruit trees from which hung figs, coconuts and the strange, reddish, oval-shaped fruit that he suspected was poisonous. It was on this same stroll that he nearly stepped on the hissing serpent—and came upon herds of ill-tempered wild hogs.

Ashton had hoped to find some friendly human habitation, but he was to be disappointed, except for 'some shreds of earthenware scattered around' (which probably were ancient evidence of the Paya Indians who had formerly inhabited the island). There was no one else.

It was March 1723 and his long marooning had begun.

'Not Very Savoury Food'

Ashton's first job was to find food and water. The island was certainly fertile, and for the first weeks he ate fruit (including the blood-red fruit, which he saw the wild hogs feed on without ill-effect). He devised a way to dig for the turtle eggs he knew were buried on the beach, walking along with a stick and poking it deep into the sand until he found particles of egg and yolk stuck to the end. The eggs made him gag, so he worked out a way of placing them on palmetto leaves in the boiling sun, which hardened them somewhat and made them more palatable. 'After all, they were not very savoury food,' Ashton comments, 'though one who had nothing but what fell from the trees behoved to be content.'

He longed to catch and eat a wild hog, but without even a knife he did not know how to go about it. He considered digging a deep pit and covering it with palmetto leaves, but having no shovel didn't think it could be managed. And then there was the matter of the flies. Although Ashton built rough lean-tos of branches near the beach to protect himself 'from the heat of the sun by day and the heavy dews by night', the flies were insatiable, biting him until he thought he would go mad. Finally he decided to swim to a small island nearby which appeared to be relatively barren of vegetation and swept by sea breezes. Admitting to being 'a very indifferent swimmer', Ashton searched until he found a large, hollow piece of bamboo, which he used as a flotation device, and set off for the cay, which was probably only a few hundred metres away. This in itself shows how desperate the flies had made him, for the waters were filled with sharks with strange shovel-shaped snouts (probably the fairly aggressive tiger shark, which can grow up to 7.5 metres, or 24½ feet, long), as well as alligators.

But he made the island safely and there found sweet relief. Perhaps only 160 metres (175 yards) in circumference, it was scoured by ocean breezes against which the insects could not make headway. Now Ashton had, as it were, two homes—Roatan, where he was obliged to spend much of the day searching for food—and this little island, where he could sleep in peace.

The Solitary Englishman

So Ashton managed until November 1723, growing skinnier on his diet of fruit, turtle eggs and fish he managed to scoop from the waters, but staying alive. Life was full of hazards, however. One evening, swimming to his little island, he was attacked by a shark. 'It struck me in the thigh, just as my foot could reach the bottom,' he wrote. Fortunately, the water was so shallow that the shark hit the bottom and Ashton got away, but he felt the blow for hours. Another time, on Roatan, he was attacked by a wild boar suddenly rushing him. With no means of defending himself, Ashton grabbed an overhanging branch and pulled himself up into the tree. 'The boar tore away my ragged trousers with his tusks and then left me,' he wrote. He fell gasping to the ground, thanking God for his deliverance.

A constant problem was the shape his feet were in; his bare soles were scored by so many deep wounds from the rough ground that it was agony to walk along the scorching sands. Sometimes he could barely move; at such moments he sat, exhausted and in fierce pain, 'my back leaning against a tree, looking out for a vessel'. His spirits sinking, he thought of his parents back in Marblehead and how they would weep at his death. He reminded himself to 'submit patiently to my misfortune'.

An eighteenth century portrait of a pirate.

And so day after day passed, running together, although he tried to keep a rough record of time passing by carving notches into the trunk of a tree. One day in November he saw a small canoe approaching, carrying a single person. Although frightened, Ashton resolved not to run away—he 'was incapable of resisting' an enemy in any event. But the canoe carried an elderly Englishman who was as astonished to see Ashton as Ashton was to see him. The man—'of a grave and venerable aspect and of a reserved temper'—claimed that he had lived for twenty years among the Spanish in Honduras, but now they had threatened to 'burn' him (possibly as a heretic, though Ashton thought it wiser not to ask for details). Therefore he had come with a dog, a gun, ammunition, a supply of pork, and flint to make a fire with (which Ashton has previously lacked) to live in solitude on one of the islands.

The man stayed for three days. Although he didn't talk much, he shared his food with the young New Englander and seemed companionable enough. On the third day, he invited Ashton to go with him to another island while he hunted wild deer. Ashton, comfortable by the fire and with his sore feet on the mend, decided against it. Perhaps his survival instincts, by now finely honed, were kicking in. The Englishman went off by himself, promising to return in a day or two. But within hours a tropical storm of ferocious intensity kicked up, and he never returned.

Ashton was deprived of companionship again, but his benefactor had left behind 'pork, a knife, a bottle of gunpowder, tobacco, tongs, and flint'. Simple things to us perhaps, but Ashton felt as if God had given him a new life. He could now have a fire in these cold and rainy winter months. 'I could cut up a tortoise and have [its] delicate, broiled meat,' he reports with an air of wonder. Through this 'blessing of God', Ashton began to grow stronger each day.

'We Will Give You Good Quarter!'

Two or three months after the Englishman's disappearance, Ashton found someone else's canoe washed up on the shore of Roatan. A stronger and more rested Ashton could now fulfil another human need: curiosity. 'I began to think myself admiral of the neighbouring seas as well as sole possessor and chief commander of the islands,' he wrote. He could journey to the islands he could see in the distance, 'partly to see how they were stored [with food] or inhabited and partly for the sake of amusement'.

However, his first 'excursion' ended dramatically and nearly tragically. Coming upon the island of Bonacco, about 25 kilometres (15½ miles) from Roatan, he saw a sloop at the far end of the island. Hope rose in him, but he knew he had to be cautious. He paddled to the other side of Bonacco and beached the canoe, intending to make his way on foot across the island to spy on the vessel. But his feet were still in such wretched shape that he had to crawl part of the way and it took him two days to cover the distance. When he finally got to the other side, to his great disappointment the sloop was no longer there. Exhausted, he fell asleep leaning against a large tree trunk.

He was jolted from deep slumber by gunshots. Before him were nine large canoes filled with men all firing muskets at him as fast as they could reload. As bullets struck the tree trunk and whizzed over his head Ashton darted into the woods and dived for cover, twigs breaking around him. The men were Spanish and cried out to him, 'O Englishman, we will give you good quarter!' but continued to fire randomly so that he dared not come out.

When at last they went away, he crept back to the beach and counted six or seven musket-balls embedded in the tree trunk, very close to where his head had rested. God had once again intervened in Philip Ashton's life, the castaway believed, but he decided to tempt fate no further, heading back to Roatan which, he commented wryly, now seemed 'a royal palace' compared to Bonacco. There he lived until June 1724 when, resting on the small island to escape the flies, he saw two canoes approach Roatan, drawn by the fire he had left. These men did not appear to be pirates or Spaniards and thus Ashton approached. They turned out to be English, living on plantations on another island in the Bay of Honduras, who periodically came to hide on Roatan when they heard rumours of threatened Spanish attacks.

They were amazed to see Ashton, who describes himself as he must have looked to them—'a poor, ragged, wild, forlorn, miserable object'. But one of them (whose name, fittingly enough, was John Hope—'an old man called Father Hope by his companions') embraced Ashton nonetheless and carried him down to the canoes. 'I was in an ecstasy of joy,' he writes, yet so weak that when Hope gave him 'a spoonful of rum', having been so long without alcohol he fainted. When he revived, the men took him back to their settlement on the island of Barbarat. They, like Ashton, actually spent much of their time on a barren nearby cay which they had sardonically nicknamed 'The Castle of Comfort'— its only virtue was that it was insect-free.

'One Risen from the Dead'

Ashton stayed six or seven months with these men. He appears to have become suspicious of their real occupation—'they were bad society,' he wrote, 'but it did not appear that they were now engaged in … any evil design'. In other words, it was quite possible they were

The Bay of Honduras

To be a pirate demanded certain essentials—a pistol, cutlass, a certain amount of cruelty, and, most of all, a good hideaway. The Bay of Honduras, where Philip Ashton was marooned, fits this last requirement quite nicely. The Bay's numerous islands were discovered by Christopher Columbus on his fourth voyage, at a time when they were peopled by the Paya Indians, whom Columbus described as 'a very robust people who adore idols and live mostly from a certain white grain from which they make fine bread and the most perfect beer'.

By the late seventeenth or early eighteenth century, however, most of the Indians had been killed by European diseases or driven to the mainland, and the islands in the Bay of Honduras had become the home of buccaneers from England, France and Holland. This was partially because they were perfectly situated—near the ports on the Spanish mainland of Central America, the pirates and privateers could raid Spanish shipping and then disappear into the islands, leading to reports of much buried treasure there (none of which has been found).

Roatan is the largest of the Bay islands and the one most frequented by pirates. After Ashton's stay there, the infamous Henry Morgan built a base at Port Royal, on the southeast coast, from whence he lured unwary ships onto the hidden reefs surrounding the harbour. Today the Bay islands are tourist paradises, with snorkelling, swimming and sailing much in evidence—but you'll also see men poring intently over metal detectors patrolling the beaches, hoping to find that elusive buried treasure from the golden age of piracy.

smugglers, but since they had not asked him to do anything illegal he had no problem remaining in their company while he regained his strength. However, returning from a hunting trip to Bonacco one evening, he and five companions saw the flash and heard the thunder of gunfire, cannon and musket, coming from the settlement. Barbarat was under attack by pirates. And not just any pirates—Ashton soon realised that they were led by none other than Francis Farrington Spriggs, Ned Low's former chief lieutenant, from whom he had escaped in March 1723. Spriggs had fought with Low and gone off on his own, freelancing as it were, and decided that these plantations were too rich a plum to pass up.

Ashton and his companions beached their canoes on the other side of Barbarat and hid in the thick underbrush for days, not daring to light a fire, while Spriggs and his men rampaged through the island, killing at least one man and beating the elderly Father Hope severely. When the pirates finally left, Father Hope and most of the other survivors fled further into the Bay of Honduras, now terrified of pirates more than the Spanish.

Nicholas Merritt, Pirate's Prisoner

During the attack on Port Rossaway, a cousin of Philip Ashton was also taken captive by Ned Low, which led to a strange adventure. Nicholas Merritt, born in the same year as Ashton, was transferred shortly into Low's voyage south to another vessel captured by the pirates, whose intention was to head for England to raid those shores. Due to shortages of food and water, the pirates were forced to put in at the Azores, where they were arrested and clapped in manacles almost as soon as they set foot in port. Poor Merritt was unable to convince the authorities that he was not a pirate—for he had signed articles of agreement—and was held in a dreadful gaol with the rest, living on one meal of day of thin soup, a mixture of bread, cabbage and foul water. He also suffered smallpox.

For three months he languished but was released by the authorities without a word of explanation, simply set on the street, penniless in a strange land. He managed to scrape together a few cents by doing odd jobs around the waterfront, until a Massachusetts vessel showed up. He convinced the captain to take him back to America. He arrived in Marblehead on 29 September 1723, having spent thirteen awful months away from home.

Ashton remained on Barbarat with a friend named John Symonds, with whom he spent the winter months of 1724–25. One fine day in early spring, two years after his marooning, Ashton and Symonds were hunting on Bonacco when they saw a ship approach and discharge three men in a lifeboat to take on water. Deciding they were friendly, Ashton approached them. Astonishingly, they were from a ship that originated from Salem, Massachusetts, just 5 kilometres (3 miles) from Ashton's home.

And by extraordinary chance—or providence—the trading vessel was commanded by one Captain Dove, whom Ashton knew, who received him 'with great civility ... and [promised] to take me into pay, having lost a seaman, whose place he wanted me to supply'. Taking tearful leave of Symonds, Ashton sailed in a little convoy of merchant ships protected by an English man-of-war. Parting company with the other vessels at Jamaica, they headed up the coast of North America, arriving in Salem on the first day of May—'two years, ten months and fifteen days after I was first taken by pirates', wrote Ashton.

And here is the last sentence of his memoirs, which were published the same year and entitled *The History of the Strange Adventures and Signal Deliverance of Mr. Philip Ashton*: 'That same evening I went to my father's house where I was received as one risen from the dead.'

The emotion buried in that simple sentence is extraordinary. We know little else about Philip Ashton's life, except that he published his story, married twice, and fathered six children. He went back to his occupation of fishing, but presumably kept a weather eye on suspicious brigantines, and perhaps even armed himself. But that simple sentence of homecoming is the picture that stays in our mind's eye—Ashton opening the door, the look on his father and mother's face, the embraces of astonished joy. There is perhaps nothing happier than the homecoming of a castaway.

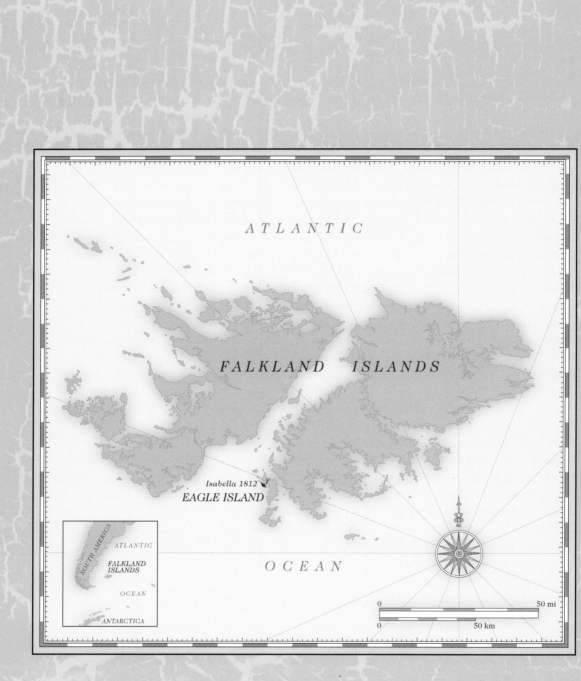

Charles Barnard, 1812–1814
The American Robinson Crusoe

The word 'remote' might have been invented to describe the desolate Falkland Islands, an archipelago in the stormy South Atlantic, over 1000 kilometres (621 miles) west of the coast of Argentina and about 380 kilometres (236 miles) north of the Straits of Magellan. The islands may have been inhabited by Patagonian Indians in the distant past, but when the first European sailed past—either the English explorer John Davis in 1592 or the Dutchman Sebald de Weert in 1600—they had not seen a human presence for some time.

Other Europeans passed that way as they ventured down the east coast of South America and sought to round Cape Horn. The descriptions they sent back would not exactly have brightened the pages of a tourist brochure. Captain James Cook, no stranger to uninviting shores, called the place 'savage and horrible'. The French explorer Louis Antoine de Bougainville rode into the harbour of East Falkland Island—along with West Falkland the main landmasses of the archipelago—one day in 1777 and sat down to pen a description that, over two centuries later, can still make the reader shudder:

> *We knew not what could prevail upon us to stay on this apparently barren ground: the horizon terminated by bald mountains, the land lacerated by the sea, which seems to claim empire over it ... a vast silence, now and then interrupted by the howls of marine monsters. We knew not what could prevail upon us to stay.*

But one man was prevailed upon to stay—by dint of being marooned in this inhospitable region after his betrayal by the shipwrecked group he had risked his life to rescue. The man was Charles Barnard, a Quaker sealing captain from New York, whose honesty, grace, toughness and resourcefulness make him seem like a character out of fiction.

A Seafaring Life

Charles Barnard was born in 1781, a member of a Massachusetts family. The Barnards were among the earliest settlers on Nantucket Island in the mid-seventeenth century, and Charles' father Valentine was a well-known whaling captain. Valentine Barnard and his wife left Nantucket in 1773 to move 190 kilometres (118 miles) up the Hudson River to the port village of Hudson, New York. Ironically, in light of what would later happen to his son, Valentine's move was prompted by fear that the British might confiscate the ships and property of the Nantucket seafarers in the looming Revolutionary War.

In Hudson, Barnard and other exiled Islanders helped establish a booming whaling port and Charles grew up, as it were, at sea: 'From boyhood,' he writes in the published account of his ordeal, 'I have loved and pursued a seafaring life.' Charles almost certainly shipped out as a cabin boy with his father, crewing on whaling voyages to many parts of the world. He grew into a young man with vast experience. Although a devout Quaker there is a record of his being 'disowned' by the Friends of his local meeting group for being 'outgoing in marriage' (marrying a non-Quaker).

The story of Barnard's desolate marooning begins, according to his later account, in a very routine way. In 1812, at the age of thirty-one, he signed an agreement with a New York shipping firm, John B. Murray & Son, to make a sealing expedition to the Falkland Islands. Murray would provide the 132-ton brig *Nanina* and all necessary supplies. Barnard would recruit the eleven-man crew—which included his 60-year-old father. The plan was to fill the hold with seal furs and rendered seal oil—for sealing had become as lucrative as whaling (see **The Slaughter of the Seals**, opposite)—and sail to China, where Barnard would sell both in the lucrative market in Canton. Murray & Son would receive 52 per cent of the profits. The rest, after paying his crew, would go to Barnard.

The Journey

A simple enough proposition—and it is evident by the way Barnard tells it that he had made the Falklands voyage a number of times before—but the geopolitical situation complicated matters greatly. In April 1812, Great Britain and the United States were very nearly at war; Congress was considering an embargo which would have, at least temporarily, kept all American shipping in port. This Barnard could not risk, so with the foresight which characterised him, he ordered the *Nanina* to leave New York Harbour on 6 April, without a full complement of crew, and lie off the coast of New Jersey, safely out of the reach of customs officials. When the full crew came aboard on 12 April, Barnard took his ship first to the Cape Verde Islands, to load up on fresh water, and salt for the curing sealskins. After crossing the Equator with the traditional toasts to Neptune, the *Nanina* fought its way through heavy gales and made it to the harbour on New Island in the Falklands on 7 September.

Here Barnard put together a prefabricated shallop, or sloop, he had brought along, and sailed among the islands, depositing small groups of men in various locales where they stayed for weeks, clubbing and skinning fur seals, shooting the giant elephant seals and rendering their blubber in huge try-pots. On 3 January 1813, with the men still engaged in

The Slaughter of the Seals

Charles Barnard, after leaving the Falklands, and finding his way to the South American coast, was nearly crushed to death by a huge herd of seals stampeding down a ravine to the ocean. He only saved his life, and that of his dog Cent, by diving behind a rock.

Although whaling is the pursuit that made American seamen of the early-to-mid-nineteenth century famous, sealing was an equally prosperous activity, at least for a time. While explorers like Captain James Cook, Louis Antoine de Bougainville and other had decried in published accounts the desolate aspect of the Falklands, they also noted that the archipelago teemed with sea lions and fur seals. Before long, sealers descended on the Magellan Straits, South Georgia Island (some 1300 kilometres, or 807½ miles, east of the Falklands) and the Falklands themselves. In the 1790s, it was estimated that 100 vessels with 3000 sailors were hunting seals south of the Equator. In 1800, seventeen American and British sealers took 120,000 skins from South Georgia Island alone.

It was bloody work. Spending as much as six months in shacks on any given island, sealers clubbed the fur seals to death (an experienced sealer could kill one a minute) and shot the huge elephant seals through the roof of the mouth with muskets. The fur seals were skinned, and the elephant seals' blubber rendered into oil in huge kettles. Since there was little fuel on the islands, the sealers also killed penguins by the hundreds of thousands, using their skins as material for the fires. The mass slaughter resembled the large-scale killing of buffalo in the American west—no thought was given to trying to keep the animal herds viable.

Fur-seal skins were valued in China, Barnard's intended destination on his fateful voyage, for their warmth as coats and for use as insulation, while a large elephant seal could produce three barrels of lubricating oil. Such profligate abuse of natural resources was bound to take its toll. By the time Barnard was sealing in the Falklands, seals were becoming scarcer. And by the 1830s, with sealers having to roam as far as Antarctica, the industry had declined considerably.

An unlikely depiction of an encounter between a sea lion and a sealer during the nineteenth century on the Falkland Islands.

these activities, the *Hope*, out of New York, arrived at New Island. Its master, Obed Chase, told Barnard that war had broken out between America and England that past June. Not only that, but he had a message from John B. Murray & Son: Barnard was to abort his mission and return to 'the first port in the United States' immediately, lest the ship and its contents and crew be captured as a prize of war by the British navy, or by English whalers furnished with the letters of marque which allowed them to act as privateers.

He refused to consider the order, knowing that he would lose everything he had invested, and moved ship and crew to a remote harbour where he was certain they would not be seen. There he stayed until April, filling the hold with thousands of sealskins.

Then, cruising the islands on 5 April, he saw smoke billowing up in the distance.

Barnard sailed the shallop to Eagle Island, to investigate, proceeding cautiously because it was possible the smoke came from fires lit by Spanish smugglers. Across the expanse of Eagle Island, Barnard saw what appeared to be topmasts. Soon afterward he saw a man on the beach, waving frantically, then ten more. A few wore the uniforms of British marines. Thus reassured, Barnard inquired who they were.

Their tale was a piteous one. They were from the brig *Isabella*, sailing from Australia to London when her captain steered too close to the Falkland reefs and on 8 February 1813 ran the ship aground. There were 47 men, women and children, slowly starving to death while their captain, George Highton, whose skills as a seaman Barnard found quite unimpressive, sought fruitlessly to build a small sloop to sail them away.

Three weeks before Barnard found the castaways, one Captain Brooks, a passenger on the *Isabella*, had bravely embarked in a longboat with a few crewmen in an attempt to sail 1600 kilometres (994 miles) to Brazil. There seemed little hope of surviving such a perilous journey and, had not Barnard happened upon them, the remaining passengers and crew might easily have died a lingering death. Given the kind of man Charles Barnard was, he could not abandon these people. But there was a problem. It was evident that they did not know that hostilities had started between America and Great Britain.

And so Barnard did the honourable thing. 'Lest they suspect us of having base motives', he later wrote, he told Captain Highton and his officers that their respective countries were at war, and asked them to sign an agreement that they would act as if this were not the case. In return, Barnard would 'relieve them of their suffering' by taking them to South America immediately—an immense hardship on his finances and crew. The agreement was signed forthwith by all parties, with the exception of Sir Henry Browne Hayes, a passenger on the *Isabella* (see **A Restless, Troublesome Character**, page 42).

'The Strongest Ties of Gratitude'

'I felt assured,' Barnard wrote, 'that rendering them this assistance would bind them to me by the strongest ties on of gratitude.' He would soon regret this. Winter gales blew for two weeks, delaying the *Nanina*'s departure. When the weather moderated, Barnard took four sailors in a longboat to Beaver Island, some distance away, to hunt wild pigs to provision the journey. Returning to the anchorage around ten o'clock that night, they discovered to their horror that the *Nanina* was nowhere to be seen. Huddled on the beach, the men awaited daylight with 'the most impatient and tormenting anxiety', hoping that morning would bring sight of the ship, or at least a message telling of its whereabouts.

But morning dawned cold, grey, desolate and empty, nothing in sight but the barren horizon and the rocky outlines of the other islands. It gradually became apparent that they had been marooned. Barnard could not believe it. 'To be reduced to this deplorable and almost hopeless state of wretchedness by the treachery and ingratitude of those for whose relief I had been labouring' was almost too much to take, as was the realisation that his ageing father and the rest of the crew had been taken along as prisoners.

'A Restless, Troublesome Character'

When Charles Barnard found the survivors of the *Isabella*, one of the first things he noticed was that Captain Highton seemed delusional and inept (his plan to build a boat to sail from the island, Barnard politely points out, was doomed to failure for lack of proper tools). He also noted that one of the passengers, the Irish nobleman Sir Henry Browne Hayes, seemed strangely adversarial toward both Highton and Barnard, his rescuer. Before Barnard arrived, Hayes had interfered with the attempts of Captain Brooks—even then sailing to Rio de Janeiro—to save the *Isabella*.

Captain Highton apparently told Barnard Hayes' story, but Barnard only mentions that Hayes was 'already infamous', although words like 'infamous' and even 'notorious' barely touch on his character. Born into a wealthy County Cork family in 1762, Hayes was knighted in 1790. About seven years later, he fell passionately in love with one Mary Pike, who would have nothing to do with him. Hayes' solution was to kidnap the poor woman and force her to 'marry' him in a ceremony conducted by a friend of his disguised as a priest.

It was Hayes' hope that Mary would the next morning consider herself so dishonoured that she would truly marry him. But Mary's screams during the 'marriage ceremony' brought rescue. Hayes took off, remaining in hiding for two years before giving himself up. He was sentenced to hang, but was granted a reprieve at the very last moment, and duly sentenced to transportation for life to Australia. (The reason he so hated Captain Brooks was that Brooks had been captain of the convict ship that carried him into exile.)

Hayes arrived in Sydney in 1802 and spent his time raising hell, constantly in trouble with the magistrates, who dubbed him 'a restless, troublesome character'. When Captain William Bligh (of *Bounty* fame) became governor of New South Wales and a mutiny arose, Hayes took his side. When the mutiny was finally put down, Hayes was pardoned, or so he said—however, some historians think he may have bribed his way out of his life sentence. In any event, considering the number of enemies he had made, Hayes thought it wise to book passage on the *Isabella* in 1812, only to be shipwrecked. Refusing to sign the agreement of non-interference, he may have been one of the chief plotters behind the plan to steal the *Nanina* and maroon Barnard.

One likes to think that a villain like Hayes would get his just deserts, but in fact he made it back to Cork, lived to the ripe old age of seventy and was buried in the crypt of the local church. Poor Mary Pike died the same year, having spent most of her life insane.

They had with them only the clothes on their backs, their boat, their knives, one blanket, and Barnard's faithful dog, Cent. The American crewman was Jacob Green, a black whaleman whom Barnard characterised as 'the most experienced black man I ever knew'. The three Britons were James Louder, Joseph Albrook and Sam Ansel.

That first morning, the four sailors began to panic, 'frequently exclaiming that they must perish'. Barnard knew that they 'looked to me for relief although [I was] suffering equally with themselves'. And so, using flint and steel, he lit a small fire of driftwood and made a breakfast of half-cooked pork.

'Pinch-Gut Camp'

The next day, Barnard had the men row to another island where he thought they might find better shelter and provisions. Here they stayed, using the overturned boat as shelter, drinking the fresh water Barnard discovered in an iced-over pond. For food, they forced down blubber and attempted to eat the tough tussock-grass which grew in the rocky soil— but the grass made them vomit, and even hallucinate. With the aid of Cent they brought down a few of the island's wild foxes whose flesh, Barnard wrote, was so gamey that 'nothing but the sauce of extreme hunger could force it down'.

It had begun to snow—20 centimetres (almost 8 inches) fell on their first day —and blustery gales blew through their camp as they shivered miserably. Sam Ansel, an illiterate bully who had spent the greater part of his life aboard British men-of-war (and was using an assumed name, for reasons Barnard never ascertained) was turning out to be a problem, berating himself because he had apparently known of the plan to capture the *Nanina* but had gone along on the hunting trip anyway. Angrily, Barnard told him: 'Then you are just where you ought to be; your guilty conscience troubles you; and you are tormented in your words.' This exchange presaged troubles that Barnard did not foresee.

In July, with the men slowly starving in what he called 'Pinch-Gut Camp', Barnard insisted that they move to New Island—the island where the *Nanina* had originally moored— where the chances of finding game or being rescued would be greater.

Twice Marooned

New Island proved somewhat better for the castaways, with more wild pigs to provide food. Here the loyal Cent was worth his weight in gold, hurling himself fiercely at the boars, being slashed repeatedly by their tusks but bringing down the animals which kept his masters alive. Under Barnard's direction, the men built a stone shelter to live in and, high on a hill, a stone sentry box (which still stands) from which to watch for passing ships. They replaced their tattered clothes with sealskins sewed together with a sail-needle and a ball of twine.

And when spring arrived, so did the birds—penguins, geese, herons, albatross—and from their rookeries the men procured a veritable cornucopia of eggs to vary their diet.

One day in October, Barnard went hunting for elephant seals. On his way back, he glimpsed the boat heading out to sea, with the four crewmen in it. He called, but they did not respond or even look in his direction. His heart pounding, he ran as fast as he could back to camp, only to find that they had cleaned the place of everything valuable: extra clothing, knives, food, flints. What hurt especially was that they had taken Cent.

Barnard was stunned. 'I gazed at the boat, whose sail was yet in sight, and said "go then, for you are all bad fellows!"' But the desertion of Green hurt deeply. As it turned out, Sam Ansel, using fist and club, had intimidated the others into abandoning Barnard and making their way to Eagle Island, where the wreck of the *Isabella* might provide supplies.

For the second time abandoned by the very men whose lives he had helped to save, Barnard set about with extraordinary ingenuity to save his own. Fire was his chief concern. He scoured the beach's thousands of rocks until he found one against which the steel of his knife would strike sparks. Discovering an ample supply of peat, he kept a fire banked at all times. A broken tin pot served as a frying-pan for the eggs he gathered.

This may have been when he began keeping his journal, written on the skins of elephant-seal pups that he had dried to parchment, using quills plucked from geese for pens, and charcoal mixed with plant juices for ink. Everyday he walked to the lookout and stared out at the endless horizon, thinking of Alexander Selkirk (Daniel Defoe's *Robinson Crusoe* had been published in 1719 and become an instant classic. See Alexander Selkirk, page 79). He mused bitterly on the poem William Cowper had written about Selkirk:

> *O, solitude! Where are thy charms*
> *That sages have seen in thy face?*
> *Better dwell in the midst of alarms,*
> *Then reign in this horrible place.*

It soon became clear to Barnard that although he could take care of his physical needs, the deep solitude might drive him crazy. Reaching his thirty-second birthday on 25 October, he prayed for the company of family and friends, of festive meals at home, of warmth and love. The memories were too much and he had to shake them from his head. He began to suffer paranoia, imagining that Ansel had returned and was sneaking up on him, perhaps aiming a musket from the tall tussock grass.

Whaling in the nineteenth century was a perilous business.

'A Sulky, Malicious Mood'

But one day toward the end of December, having now been alone for three months, he watched as a small boat hove into view carrying Green, Louder, Albrook and Ansel. They hovered offshore, begging to be allowed to return. They had made it to Eagle Island but had found very little salvage in the wreck. Ansel had threatened to kill anyone who disobeyed him but, nearing death from starvation, the others finally rebelled and forced him to join them in returning to Barnard. They brought gifts of a wild hog and some newspapers they had salvaged, hoping these small items would buy his forgiveness.

Barnard, desperate for company, allowed them back on the island, but only when Ansel promised to behave himself. That promise did not last long, for by the end of December the other three had told Barnard of Ansel's remark that he would like to kill him for his warm seal-fur coat. When Ansel began bullying one of the men into doing his work for him, Barnard had had enough. Ansel, he wrote, 'was in a sulky, malicious mood', capable of anything. When the others came to him with a plan to maroon Ansel on Swan Island, he approved. Green, Louder and Albrook took the bully to the island on the pretext of foraging for firewood in the interior. While he was so engaged, they raced down to the boat and left him there.

Thus began an almost halcyon period in the lives of the castaways, if that adjective could ever be applied to being marooned in the Falklands. Freed from 'apprehensions about our personal safety', as Barnard wrote, the men looked to their survival, hunting with the gallant Cent (who lost an eye to a boar's thrusting tusk) and trying to improve their situation. At the beginning of February 1814, Barnard set out with his men to check on Ansel. They found him in a deplorable state, living in a crude hut made of tussock-grass, reduced almost to a skeleton. He literally fell to his knees before Barnard, begging to be allowed to return.

A man such as Charles Barnard could not refuse this plea; he forgave Ansel, although making it clear that any further transgressions would be punished by permanent banishment on Swan Island.

Rescue

Over the next few months, life on New Island fell into a settled routine. The men built a stronger house to keep out the gales and snows of the coming winter. Green, Albrook and Louder returned to the wreck of the *Isabella* at one point to salvage more nails and wood, leaving Ansel alone with Barnard—possibly a dangerous move. But Ansel was a changed man. By firelight on their long nights together, Barnard taught him to read, using scraps of newspaper. Ever the leader and teacher, Barnard had the satisfaction one day of coming upon Ansel having an imaginary conversation with his mother.

'Mother, have you got a newspaper?'

'Pooh. What do you want with a newspaper? You can't read!'

And Sam told the old woman figuring so largely in his imagination that 'that American captain I was so long with had' taught him his letters.

On the morning of 26 November 1814, Barnard, Louder and Albrook headed for a hill to gather balsam bushes, whose leaves exuded a resinous substance the castaways used on cuts and insect bites. Louder climbed the hill in one direction, Albrook and Barnard in another. Within a few minutes, they heard Louder cry out, as if he had been 'suddenly and severely hurt'. Barnard and Albrook raced to his side to find him rolling on the ground and crying out. Barnard was sure that he had gone crazy when Albrook suddenly pointed off into the distance and turned pale. All he could whisper was 'Two ships, two ships!'

And so Charles Barnard turned around and viewed his salvation, two tall-masted brigs sailing into the harbour of New Island. All three fell to the ground and broke into tears.

'A Beard Eight Inches in Length'

The ships were British whalers, the *Asp* and the *Indispensable*. Barnard and his men rowed out, the Quaker presenting an unforgettable sight: 'The whole of my dress, with the exception of a piece of old checked shirt was comprised of skins and my face was almost entirely covered with a beard eight inches in length.' He wrote with irony that the ships' officers, who looked on with astonishment, must see him as a 'Crusonian representation'.

Four days later, the whalers took Barnard and his men off the island. Honourable to the end, Barnard answered in the negative when one of the captains asked if any of the British sailors had caused him any problems. Loyally protecting Ansel, Barnard replied that 'generally they had been attentive and obedient … and they had exerted themselves to render our situation as comfortable as the severity of our sufferings allowed'.

On this voyage, Barnard was to learn that the longboat from the *Isabella* captained by Brooks had indeed made the long voyage to Rio de Janeiro safely, and that another ship had been sent out to rescue the castaways of the *Isabella*. However, this ship had met the captured *Nanina* and taken the Yankee sealer as a prize of war. The captain had been told of the existence of Barnard's group, but made little effort to find them. Ironically, on the day they were rescued, the *Nanina* was being sold as a prize of war in England.

After a long, hard voyage home—relying on the vicissitudes of various whalers, and travelling by way of the Sandwich Islands and Canton—Barnard landed in Martha's Vineyard on 23 October 1816, four years after he left. That evening he set foot on American soil, experiencing 'the unspeakable happiness of finding myself on my native land'.

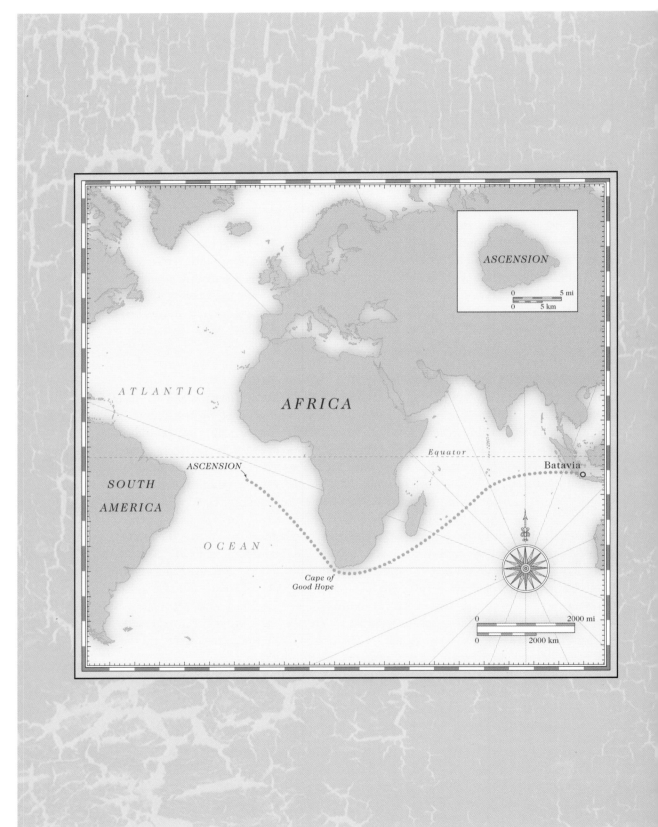

Leendert Hasenbosch, 1725–1726
The Prisoner of Ascension Island

> *It would be needless to write how often my Eyes are cast on the Sea to look for Shipping and every little Atom in the Sky I take to be a Sail; then look til my Eyes dazzle. And immediately the Object disappears.*
> Journal of Leendert Hasenbosch, 4 June 1725 (translated from the Dutch)

If one of the hazards (attractions?) of reading castaway stories is to make us feel cast away ourselves, then the story of Leendert Hasenbosch is the most effective of its genre. For Leendert Hasenbosch is the most haunted of all our poor castaways. Without the inner resources of a Philip Ashton or an Andrew Selkirk, he lasted just six months on one of the most forlorn and desolate islands on the planet, leaving behind only a tattered journal. Even his body has completely disappeared. In fact, until only a few years ago we didn't even know his name.

We did, however, know the crime for which the 30-year-old Dutchman was sentenced to be marooned on the unforgiving South Atlantic island of Ascension in 1725. For he wrote in his journal, alone with the screaming birds and the immensity of ocean and sky around him, 'my most heinous Crime [was] making use of my Fellow-Creatures to satisfy my lust, whom the Almighty creator had ordain'd another Sex for'.

In other words, he was homosexual.

The Unknown Man of Ascension Island

In January 1726, the *Compton*, a merchant vessel of the English East India Company, sailed from the British base on the South Atlantic island of St Helena (where Napoleon was to spend his final days a century later) but soon began taking on water. Although accompanied by a sister ship, the *James and Mary*, the captain of the *Compton* felt it wise to head for Ascension Island, some 1300 kilometres (807½ miles) to the southeast, to make repairs before sailing on to England.

Then, as now, not many people visited Ascension. Isolated in the South Atlantic, 1600 kilometres (994 miles) from the coast of Africa, the island was discovered in 1501 by the Portuguese explorer João de Nova, who did not see fit to report its existence. It was not until 1503 that another Portuguese mariner, Alfonso d'Albuquerque, sighted it on Ascension Day and gave it its name.

Ninety square kilometres (56 miles) in size, Ascension is the head and shoulders of an undersea volcano. Its interior is a dreary combination of hills, dead lava flows and cinder cones, although its beaches are made of superb white sand. Deep in the hills, in the fittingly named Breakneck Valley, there is a single, strong water source. Aside from that, the only water comes from a sporadic, rain-generated rock hollow called Dampier's Drip, after buccaneer William Dampier, who was shipwrecked on Ascension in 1701, along with sixty others, and managed to survive long enough to be rescued only by finding both water sources.

When the *James and Mary* and the *Compton* anchored off Ascension on 20 January 1726, men were sent ashore to capture the huge green turtles which abound on the island's beaches and whose flesh and eggs the seamen prized. The turtle-hunters made an extraordinary discovery, as described in the *Compton's* log:

> *We found a Tent a Shore in the Bay and Bedding in it, a Tea Kettle and Tea. Pipes, a Hatchet and Nails and several other things, with some Writeing Papers by which we found the Dutch Fleet the fifth of May … had put a Shore one of their Men for some Crime he had committed on board. His writeings continue to November but we have no Dutch enough amongst us to read them. We have searched several places to find the man or his body but could not and we doe believe he is not gon off the Island because his Paper and a great many Necessary are left in the Tent.*

On 22 January, the two vessels sailed away to England, carrying with them the unknown Dutchman's journal. Two years later, someone translated it into English and published it as *An Authentick Relation of the Many Hardships and Sufferings of a Dutch Sailor*. But the author was not known, and until 2002 (see **Michiel Koolbergen's Amazing Detective Work**, page 53) he was referred to as 'the unknown man of Ascension Island'.

Leendert Hasenbosch

Because of the scholarship of Michiel Koolbergen, and of Alex Ritsema who expanded on Koolbergen's work after the latter's death, we now have a name and at least a partial history for this unknown man. Leendert Hasenbosch was born in the Netherlands in 1695, the only son (he had four sisters, one of whom died in infancy) of Johannes Hasenbosch, probably a greengrocer, and his wife Maria. The family was Roman Catholic, but in Hasenbosch's youth converted to the Dutch Reformed (Calvinist) Church.

Maria Hasenbosch died in 1706 or 1707 and shortly thereafter Johannes moved to Batavia, Jakarta in modern Indonesia, headquarters of the Dutch East Indies Company's spice trade. There Johannes became sexton of a Dutch Reformed Church. He took his three surviving daughters with him. Leendert stayed in the Netherlands, and at the age of eighteen became a soldier for the Dutch East Indies Company, the Vereenigde Oostindische Compagnie (VOC). The Company, which would figure prominently in Hasenbosch's life (and death) was a powerful force in the Netherlands at the time. It was the world's first stock company (shareholders supplied operating capital) and had quasi-governmental powers, among them the ability to seize territory, wage war and punish miscreants.

As a part of the VOC's armed forces, Hasenbosch was sent to Batavia in 1714, where he was no doubt happy to see his family. From there he was sent to Fort Cochin, on the west coast of what would later become British India, and saw action in various conflicts against Indian native leaders, and English and Portuguese mercenaries. By the time he returned to Batavia in 1720, he had been made corporal, and the next year became a military clerk or bookkeeper.

From these years we have few clues to Hasenbosch's personality. Joining the VOC military was an odd move for someone of his background—the pay was poor, the treatment brutal (floggings and other draconian punishments were commonplace). It is known that while he was in Cochin, he donated two-thirds of his annual salary to the building of a shelter for lepers in India. And it is known that from Batavia in 1722 he signed over several years' accumulated pay to one Jan Backer in the Netherlands. The transaction was officially recorded with notaries; we just don't know why it occurred.

After his father died in 1723, Hasenbosch apparently became tired of the Dutch East Indies and decided to return to the Netherlands. In December 1724 he boarded the *Prattenberg*, one of a convoy of eleven VOC vessels. Hasenbosch was the ship's bookkeeper.

'Being a Villain'

We know a little about the voyage of the *Prattenberg*. Typhus broke out on board, causing at least twenty deaths on the way to Cape Town. Hasenbosch may have been spared because, as ship's bookkeeper he was considered a minor officer, and probably had a semi-private cabin and better food. Rounding the Cape of Good Hope, the *Prattenberg* stopped at Cape Town on 19 March 1725 for provisioning and refitting, and set sail again on 11 April, heading north with the rest of the fleet for the Netherlands.

And then … something happened. We don't quite know what. We do know that the Breede Raad (Broad Council), consisting of the VOC fleet's commodore (Ewout van

Ships of the Dutch East India Company.

Dishoeck) and all the ships' captains, tried Hasenbosch on 17 April—only six days after leaving Cape Town—and sentenced him 'to be set ashore, being a villain, on the island of Ascension or elsewhere, with confiscation of his outstanding salary'.

Given his journal entries, the most likely possibility is that Hasenbosch was caught in the act of sodomy on the vessel, perhaps with a cabin boy. Or perhaps this had occurred in Cape Town and only now been reported. No one will ever know. But the punishment for homosexuality at that time was severe (see **The Crime of 'Sodomie'**, page 55). If the act had occurred on board ship and Hasenbosch's partner was a seaman or soldier, that person was most likely thrown overboard. Hasenbosch, considered an officer, was spared that fate, but sentenced nonetheless to dire punishment: marooning on Ascension.

By 3 May, the *Prattenberg* had reached the isolated island. Hasenbosch was no doubt forced to watch for two days while the crew hunted for turtles ('turned' them, in the parlance, for by flipping the huge creatures on their backs they could be kept alive on board for months). On Saturday 5 May, Hasenbosch was set ashore.

Michiel Koolbergen's amazing detective work

For many years, as stories of castaways were told, Leendert Hasenbosch was referenced merely as 'the unknown man of Ascension Island'. After the *Compton* brought his journal back to England, it was translated and published in 1728 as *An Authentik Relation of the Many Hardships and Sufferings of a Dutch Sailor*. The fact that it was published by J. Roberts of London (Daniel Defoe's publisher) led many to believe the story was, if not fiction, at least exaggerated—some have even speculated that Daniel Defoe may have had a hand in dressing up the journal to make it more dramatic.

The original journal disappeared. In about 2000, Dutch author Michiel Koobergen became fascinated by the story and attempted to discover the identity of the poor castaway. He began by verifying details. The journal as published by Roberts states, in its first entry, that the Dutchman was cast away on Saturday, 5 May 1725. Sure enough, 5 May was a Saturday in 1725—for a Dutchman, that is, since the Netherlands used the modern or Gregorian calendar we use today (England was then eleven days behind, still using the old Julian calendar). It is unlikely that an English publisher would have been canny enough to make up this little detail.

Through further research, Koolbergen discovered that a VOC fleet did stop at Ascension Island on 3–5 May 1725.

Koolbergen searched in vain for minutes of the Breede Raad meeting which condemned Hasenbosch to his fate, eventually concluding that the nature of his 'crime' meant that no minutes had been recorded, or kept after the ship returned. But he discovered from a German author that the castaway was a bookkeeper. And every VOC ship had only one bookkeeper.

Koolbergen searched VOC archives to find that eighteen VOC ships had left Batavia in 1724–1725 bound for the Netherlands. He discovered the salary records of the bookkeepers on these vessels. And under the name Leendert Hasenbosch, bookkeeper of the vessel *Prattenberg*, he found this notation, written by a VOC clerk to explain why Hasenbosch was no longer on the rolls:

> *On 17 April 1725, on the Prattenberg, he was sentenced to be set ashore, being a villain, on the island of Ascension or elsewhere, with confiscation of his outstanding salary.*

And so Koolbergen solved the mystery of the unknown man's identity.

'I Hope Almighty God Will be my Protection'

What emotions did Hasenbosch suffer as he watched the ship disappear over the horizon? Anger, forlorn sadness, fear? The thirty years of his life had come down to this foreign place, this sere island, its shore beaten by raging breakers. There on the horizon, where the ship was disappearing, was life. Here was … what?

Hasenbosch's first journal entry was made that day:

> *By Order of the Commodore and Captains of the Dutch Fleet, I was set on Shore on the Island of Ascension, which gave me a great deal of Dissatisfaction, but I hope Almighty God will be my Protection. They put ashore with me a Cask of water, two Buckets, and an old Frying pan&c. I made my Tent on the Beach near a Rock, wherein I put some of my Clothes.*

In other words, the captains of the fleet were marooning him, but giving him the barest of chances with limited water, a few utensils, a little rice and some seeds for planting. He had apparently been told that there was a water source on the island. But the Dutch bookkeeper was not the most enterprising or hardy of castaways. The very next day, after wandering the hills 'to see if there were any Thing green' (and being disappointed) he writes: 'I sincerely wished some Accident would befall me, to finish these miserable days.' One gets the sense that Hasenbosch feels that his punishment is, if not deserved, then preordained, in the Calvinist sense. On the evening of 6 May, coming down from the hills, 'I walked to my Tent again, but could not very well find my way. I walked very melancholy along the Strand, praying to God Almighty to put a Period to my Days or help me off this desolate island'.

Hasenbosch set up a crude tent on the beach—a tarpaulin held up with sticks and weighted down with rocks—but misfortune befell him almost immediately. On 7 May he went to his water cask and tried to tap it, but botched the job and lost a good deal of water before he managed to turn the cask upright. He turned to searching for food. His main choices of sustenance would be the green turtles, wild goats (whose presence he had not yet realised) and seabirds such as boobies. (This name is derived either from the Spanish *bobo*, 'clown', or from the fact that English sailors considered them among the stupidest of creatures because they were so easy to catch—they would land on a man's outstretched arm.)

Hasenbosch killed three boobies, salted them, and put them in reserve. In the next few days he began to take steps to ensure his survival. Perhaps trying to be kind, his captain had told him that during this season ships passed by Ascension quite often. Hasenbosch therefore tied a white flag to his musket ('I had no Powder or Shot, which rendered the gun useless') and walked to the top of a high hill near the sea. On the way, he encountered a green turtle whose head he smashed in with the butt of the musket. He left it there while he planted his signal flag. The turtle was too heavy to move, but he cut flesh from its fins and took it back to his tent, broiling the meat over a low fire. Feeling somewhat better, he wrote: 'I would by no means be accessory to my own Death, still hoping that God will preserve me to see better Days.'

The Crime of 'Sodomie'

In the homophobic eighteenth century Netherlands, 'sodomie' was defined very loosely as any non-reproductive sexual act—it could be anal intercourse between a man and a woman, masturbation, even sex with an animal. But 'full sodomie', the term used in Hasenbosch's case, meant anal intercourse with ejaculation taking place inside the body. Unlike masturbation, which might receive corporal punishment or imprisonment, full sodomy was a capital offence.

Nowhere was sodomy more guarded against than on board VOC vessels during long voyages with no women. The sailors' food was dosed with saltpetre (potassium nitrate), which supposedly deadened their sex drive. A study by a modern historian of trials aboard VOC ships that passed through Cape Town in the eighteenth century found 44 cases of men accused of sodomy. Nine were sentenced to death. If such incidents happened aboard ship, the malefactors, if not officers like Hasenbosch, would be tied together and thrown overboard.

Sometimes that was the gentler execution. In a heartbreaking story, two years after Hasenbosch was marooned, two young boys aboard the VOC ship *Zeewyk*, wrecked on an island off the west coast of Australia, were seen by the marooned crew to be having sex together. Their names were Adriaen Spoor and Pieter Engels. The marooned crew decided to further maroon the boys for their offence and took them to separate islands in what are now known as the Mangrove Islands, mere outcroppings of coral, without even the scant food and water Hasenbosch was able to discover on Ascension. The boys died horrible deaths.

'My Life a Greater Burden'

Aware that his keg of water would soon run out, Hasenbosch began to range the island searching for the water source he'd been told of. Here his seemingly conflicted feelings about his own survival again came into play. While he needed water to live, on most days he gave up the search far too soon, returning to his tent to read his Bible or rest. His journal entries for the last few weeks of May are mundane, but reflect the fact that he had been unable to find water and that the boobies and turtles upon which he must subsist were not always plentiful:

> *14 May 1725*
> *In the Morning after I had prayed, I took my usual walk but found nothing new; so I returned again to my tent and mended my Banyan Coat and wrote in my Journal ...*

> *16 May 1725*
> *I looked out, as the Day past; only caught no Boobies.*

> *17 May 1725*
> *I was very much dejected that I found no Sustenance, and a Boobie that I kept alive [possibly as a pet] seven or eight Days now died.*

> *19 May 1725*
> *Nothing worthy of note.*

On 19 May, Hasenbosch went to a rock near the sea and fished for hours without a single bite. He then took 'a Melancholy walk to my [signal] flag' high on the hill, but could see no ships on the horizon. Returning to the beach, he saw smoke issuing from his tent. He raced there to find he had left his 'Tinderbox a-fire on my Quilt'. Fortunately there was not too much damage, but even this small setback made him despair: 'I entreat God Almighty to give me the patience of holy Job to bear with my Sufferings.'

Perhaps God answered his prayers temporarily, for on 25 May he caught several boobies sitting on their eggs, killed the birds and took them and the eggs back to his tent, where he gorged on the flesh and ate the eggs boiled. But by the end of the month he was forced to begin eating the birds he had salted and stored away for an emergency. And on 8 June he writes: 'My Water is so much reduced, that I had but two Quarts left, and that so thick as obliged me to strain it through a Handkerchief.' Frantically, the castaway

56

walked around the island digging pits in the sand, hoping to strike water. All he found was brackish mud.

'It is impossible to express my concern,' he writes. On 9 June he states, with a simple fatalism haunting in its intensity: 'Found nothing; past away the Day in Meditations on a future State.'

On 10 June, Hasenbosch spent the entire day roaming the hot, rocky, volcanic inner wastes of the island. 'The Heat of the Sun,' he wrote, 'made my Life a greater Burden that I was able to bear.'

And then, astonishingly, he found water:

> *Walking among the Rocks, God of his great Bounty led me to a Place where some Water run out of a hollow place in the Rock. It is impossible to express my great Joy and Satisfaction in finding of it, and thought I should have drunk til I burst.*

Haunted by Demons

Hasenbosch returned to his tent that night a far happier man, but he did not know that he had only found the so-called Dampier's Drip, which was not a perennial water source. It depended on rainwater leaking through porous clay into a rock hollow; because the rainy season had passed, the water would soon run out.

By 12 June, the solitude was starting to prey on Hasenbosch's mind. He wrote: 'I often think I am possessed with Things that I really want; but when I come to search [for them], find it only a Shadow.' As day after day passed with no ship, his bare subsistence living was beginning to get to him. His clothes were in tatters, as were his shoes: 'My shoes being worn out, the Rocks cut my feet to pieces; and I am often afraid of tumbling.'

'It makes me very melancholy,' he wrote on 13 June, 'to think that I have no hopes of getting off this unhappy island.'

And then, on the night of 16 June, Leendert Hasenbosch's whole world exploded. As he wrote the next day:

> *In the Night was surprised by a Noise round my Tent of Cursing and Swearing, and the most blasphemous Conversations that I ever heard. My Concern was so great that I thought I should have died with Fright. I did nothing but offer my Prayers to the Almighty to protect me from this miserable Circumstance; but my fright rendered me in a very bad Condition.*

What he was hearing outside his tent were screaming voices, men swearing, using 'the most libidinous Talk'. Huddled and shivering inside the tent, the terrified castaway speculated that 'the Devil had moved his Quarters, and was coming to keep Hell on Ascension. I was certain that there was no human Creature on the island but myself'. Even more surprising, among the raging voices he heard one that bore 'affinity of an intimate Acquaintance of mine; and I really thought that I was sometimes touched by an invisible Spirit'.

Hasenbosch finally fell asleep clutching his Bible, but when he woke in the early dawn there was still shrieking outside his tent. 'I took my Prayer Book, and read the Prayers proper for a Man in my Condition, and at the same time hear a Voice crying, "Bouger!" "Bouger!"' (which, in modern spelling would be 'bugger').

What was happening here? It's hard to know. The most likely answer is that Hasenbosch was hallucinating, either because of scurvy or some plant he had eaten, and that guilt and shame over his 'crime' had risen to the surface. It is also possible that this passage was enhanced or even entirely made up the unknown English translator of his journal, as a way of showing Hasenbosch being punished for the sin of his sexuality. The latter doesn't appear likely, however—genuine fear and grief show through here in an extraordinary way.

As Hasenbosch walked the beach after his sleepless and terrified night, 'an Apparition appeared to me in the similitude of a Man whom I perfectly knew; he conversed with me like a Human Creature, and touched me sensibly of the Sins of my Past Life ... and was such a terrible shock to me, that I wished it would kill me'. The next day, the apparition came again, as he was cutting up a tree that had washed ashore: 'His Name I am afraid to utter, fearing the Event. He [now] haunts me so often that I begin to grow accustomed to him.'

On the night of 20 June, spirits continue to haunt Hasenbosch as he cowers in his tent, even to the extent of hurling objects through the air. The apparition comes again, but this time Hasenbosch identifies him: 'The Person that I was formerly acquainted with spoke to me several times this Night: but I can't think he would do me any harm, for when he was in this world we were as great as two own brothers. He was a Soldier at Batavia.'

And it now becomes clear that Hasenbosch was seeing the ghost of a former lover. He writes: 'I only desire to make atonement for my Sins, which I believe my Comrade is damned for ... I spent all Day in Meditations and Prayers, and ate nothing. My strength decays, and my life becomes a great Burthen to me.'

For a time his hauntings gave Hasenbosch new energy. Deciding he was wasting time travelling between his water source and the beach, he moved his belongings to a rocky cave near Dampier's Drip. It was 27 June. The next day, 'I went upon the Hills and to no purpose looked out for Ships'. Afterward he descended to a beach he had not traversed before and 'discovered a piece of wood sticking in the Strand, which I first took for a Tree,

A desperate castaway prays for salvation in this eighteenth century etching.

but when I came to it I found it was a cross. I embraced it in my Arms and prayed to God Almighty to deliver me: I believe there was a man buried there from some ship'.

Only to a castaway as desperate as Hasenbosch could a grave be a source of hope. Not only was the cross a reminder that God was present, but the burial meant that ships *did* stop here. He *might* be saved.

Finding the grave was perhaps the last high point for Hasenbosch. For on 1 July, he found that the water in Dampier's Drip had dried up: 'there is now not one Drop and I am much in want of it.' Once again he set out on a desperate search for water. For the first time he saw a herd of goats, and chased them; they got away quite easily, but he realised that they had been gathered around a pit, where water probably collected in the rainy season. There was none there now, however— Hasenbosch dug deep, to no avail.

Continuing to follow herds of goats over the next few days, the castaway found, here and there, small quantities of rainwater preserved in rock hollows. But that was all. The goats probably spent most of their time in Breakneck Valley, a hidden ravine near the top of Ascension's largest mountain, which did contain a strong water source. Hasenbosch never found it, but it is possible that that source, too, had dried up in an unusually dry season, and that the goats were wandering the island, like Hasenbosch looking for water.

By mid-July, Hasenbosch is writing: 'I delayed no time to look for Water, unless when I prayed.' During one of his searches, he looked up to hear 'a very dismal Noise of Cursing and Swearing in my own Language', but saw, flying above him, such a huge flock of seabirds that 'intercepting between me and the Sky deprived me of some of its light'. Plagued by this sound—although he postulates it is the birds, he is not completely sure—he hunted restlessly for water, his body gradually weakening.

31 July 1725
My heart is so full that my Pen can't utter it. I now and then find a little Water which the Goats have left for me; I always scoop it up to the last Drop, and use it very sparingly.

'The Heavens All Around Me'

After drinking what was seemingly every drop of water, Hasenbosch began to dig deep holes in the beach, praying that it would rain and they would fill with water. He spent day after day staring up at the sky, 'at the Heavens all around me, to see if I could see the sky overcast, that might give me some Hopes of rain; but all, to my Sorrow, was very clear'.

On 21 August, Hasenbosch was forced to drink his urine. The next day, he killed a turtle and drank a quantity of its blood, mixed with his urine, but this dreadful concoction did not assuage his thirst; in fact, it gave him the flux, which further weakened him. He now resorted to the expedient of killing turtles and cutting out their bladders, the contents of which he drank mixed with blood, but this too made him ill, although he found that by boiling the mixture he could sometimes keep it down.

Frantically, as August ended, Hasenbosch went to all the pits he had dug, but found nothing. Lying down in his tent—he had moved back to the beach after Dampier's Drip dried up—he 'wished that it would rain, or that I should die before I rose'. But he did not die. The next day he awoke, found a living turtle, cut off its head with his razor and, lying on the sand, lapped up its blood. Then he went back to the tent he had begun referring to as 'home' and 'drank some boiled Piss mixed with Tea'.

In early September, for the first time, Hasenbosch drank sea water. 'I was so very ill after it,' he wrote, 'that I expected immediate death.' In actuality death was not far away. He continued to kill turtles and drink their blood but, he wrote, 'my Strength decays'.

He was gradually wasting away, fighting a holding action against death. On 9 September he wrote: 'I am so much decayed, that I am a perfect Skeleton, and can't write the Particulars, my Hand shakes so.'

His journal entries become short and sporadic:

17 September 1725
Lived as before. I'm in a declining condition.

6 October 1725
All as before.

7 October 1725
My Wood's all gone, so that I am forced to eat raw Flesh and salted fowls.
I can't live long and I hope the Lord will have mercy on my Soul.

8 October 1725
Drank my own urine and eat raw Flesh.

14 October 1725
All as before.

There are no more entries after this.

Leendert Hasenbosch's journal and other belongings were found by the crew of the *Compton*—the ship he had so vainly prayed for—three months later, but his body was not with them, not even his bones. Where did he spent his last moments? Did he crawl down to the ocean, to be swept away by the waves? Did he find his way to the hills one more time, to die in some rocky crevice? Could he have been rescued—found, just in time, and placed aboard a friendly ship?

This last is extremely unlikely—the crew of the *Compton* thought he would never have left all his belongings behind, especially the journal he had kept even in the direst extremity—but one devoutly wishes that happy fate for Leendert Hasenbosch. Many castaways have suffered greatly, but none were as wretched to their very souls as the 'unknown' man of Ascension Island.

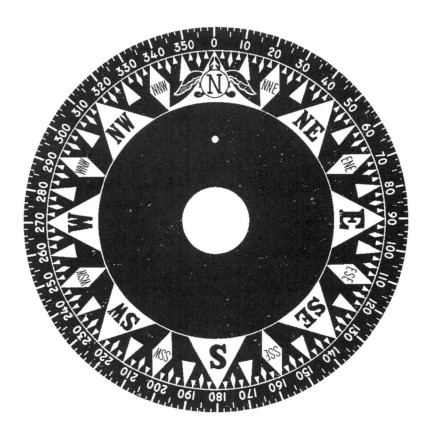

Part Two
IN FAR-OFF
SOUTHERN SEAS

*'I'd have nightmares of other islands
stretching away from mine, infinities
of islands, islands spawning islands ...'*
Elizabeth Bishop, *Crusoe in England* (1976)

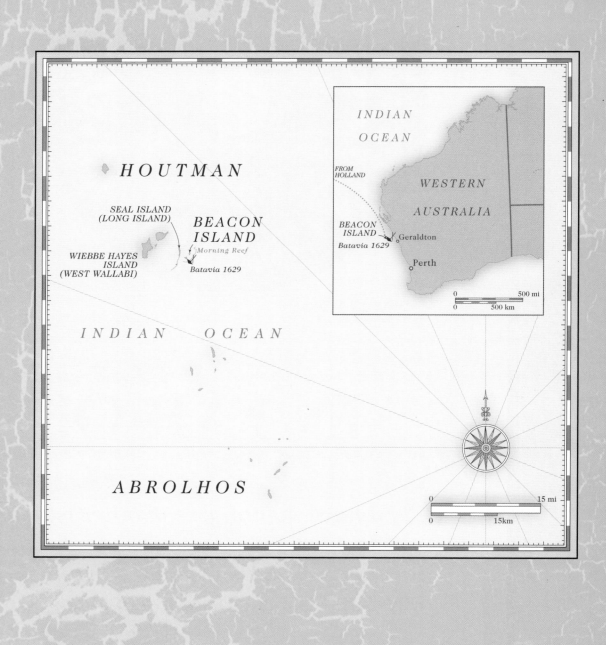

HOUTMAN

SEAL ISLAND
(LONG ISLAND)

BEACON
ISLAND

Morning Reef

WIEBBE HAYES
ISLAND
(WEST WALLABI)

Batavia 1629

INDIAN   OCEAN

ABROLHOS

INDIAN
OCEAN

FROM
HOLLAND

WESTERN
AUSTRALIA

BEACON
ISLAND
Batavia 1629   Geraldton

Perth

0   500 mi
0   500 km

0   15 mi
0   15km

The Wreck of the Batavia, 1629–1630
The Island of Slaughter

Before a fateful June morning in 1629, it is almost certain that the tiny island—460 metres (503 yards) long, 275 metres (300 yards) across—had never felt the footsteps of a human being. Made of coral rubble, slick from the guano left behind by thousands of seabirds, without a single tree, with no natural water except what rainfall might collect in crevices, the nameless atoll was part of an archipelago some 80 kilometres (49½ miles) from the western coast of Australia.

The windswept island kept its isolation for millennia, until the morning when 180 terrified men, women and children stumbled ashore through the shallows, thanking God to be alive. This most desolate of places was suddenly peopled by enough human beings to make a small village. For most castaways—solitude being one of the most difficult aspects of being marooned—there would be comfort and safety in such numbers. But not on this island. For among the survivors was a man who turned out to be one of the most murderous of sociopaths ever to find himself cast away. With the help of those he recruited, his horrendous actions would give this desolate pile of rubble a name: Batavia's Graveyard.

The Apothecary

Ironically, the homicidal castaway, Jeronimus Cornelisz, was an apothecary—his profession was treating the sick. Cornelisz was born in the Netherlands, probably in 1598, in the northern province of Friesland. Well educated and from a good family, he trained as an apothecary between 1615 and 1620. In those days an apothecary did not just fill prescriptions at a doctor's behest; they made diagnoses of everything from the common cold to tuberculosis, and provided healing potions. There were thousands of these concoctions, which could include roots and herbs, animal droppings, spiderwebs, and even ground human flesh (called 'mummy' because it was supposedly taken from Egyptian mummies, but more likely from the corpses of executed criminals).

An apothecary could make a good living and was a respected member of his community. His apprenticeship completed, Cornelisz set up shop in Haarlem, Holland, married, and set to work building up a practice. Unfortunately, his success was interrupted by great personal tragedy. His wife, Belijtgen, gave birth to a son in the winter of 1627, but fell ill and was unable to nurse him. A wet nurse was hired to feed the baby, but by February 1628 the boy was dead. Not only that, he had died of syphilis. It was clear to

Cornelisz and his wife (surviving court records seem to confirm this) that the wet-nurse was syphilitic, but the rumour spread that either Cornelisz or Belijtgen—who worked with her husband—was infected with the then-incurable disease. Business fell off to the point where an embittered Cornelisz, his reputation in tatters, was forced into bankruptcy.

Cornelisz was also a religious iconoclast, not hewing to the Calvinism which was becoming the state religion. In Haarlem he had fallen in with a group of heretical thinkers—gnostics, libertines, anabaptists—but seems to have developed a highly personalised way of thinking. As he explained to friends: 'All I do, God gave the same into my heart.' In other words, whatever he did, he could do no wrong, commit no sin.

As the Calvinist authorities began to crack down on heretical thinkers, and with his business on the skids, Cornelisz decided it was time to leave town. Abandoning his wife, he headed for the seaport of Amsterdam.

The *Batavia*

Amsterdam had become one of the richest cities in the world, thanks to the Dutch East Indies Company, or Vereenigde Oostindische Compagnie (VOC), a consortium of merchants who had joined forces to take advantage of the trading treasures of Indonesia and India. The first voyage of a VOC fleet, in 1602, had been an enormous success. By the mid-1620s the trade between Amsterdam and Batavia (present-day Jakarta) was well established and immensely profitable, and the VOC had become an all-powerful, quasi-governmental entity, employing thousands of people in positions from captain to merchant to lowly seaman and soldier.

Somehow the penniless, heretical and possibly unhinged Jeronimus Cornelisz was able to secure a position as under-merchant, the second most powerful VOC agent, on a new vessel bound for Batavia. This was probably testament to his youth, his eloquent manner and his education, although it may also have been because, as an apothecary, his familiarity with spices would stand the Company in good stead in the Indies. Thus, in the autumn of 1628, Cornelisz boarded the *Batavia* on its maiden voyage. She was the pride and joy of the VOC merchant fleet. With four decks, three masts and 130 guns, displacing 1200 tons and 49 metres (53.5 yards) in length, the *Batavia* was the largest ship in the fleet. She had a triple hull to protect against the pounding of the ocean waves and the depredations of sea-worms, and carried passengers as well as crew.

Her prime cargo outgoing, however, was an enormous sum of money, for the natives of India and the Indies cared little for European trade goods but a great deal for European silver. Thus, the *Batavia* had on board as much as 250,000 guilders

A 1647 engraving showing the Beacon Island massacre of survivors of the *Batavia* shipwreck.

(about $20 million in twenty-first century currency) stored in massive wooden chests weighing up to 225 kilograms (496 pounds) each, which were kept in a special cabin and guarded constantly.

'Very Beastly'

On 29 October 1628, the *Batavia* sailed from Amsterdam bound for her namesake city. She was accompanied by seven other vessels, including a warship, and carried some 340 passengers and crew. As she plied her way down the English Channel and into the open Atlantic, Jeronimus Cornelisz became friends with the captain, one Ariaen Jacobsz, an experienced seaman in his mid-forties who had piloted other VOC vessels. Jacobsz was not the ideal skipper for a vessel with civilians, however—he was known to drink a good deal and to have importuned female passengers.

And worse, the deadly ingredient in the witch's brew that was to come, Jacobsz hated Cornelisz's boss, Francisco Pelsaert, the upper-merchant, the senior VOC official on board.

Pelsaert's position meant that he could overrule Jacobsz on all matters, both nautical and commercial, an unusual situation, for the captain of a vessel was usually in complete command of his ship at sea. There is evidence that the gruff, decisive Jacobsz and the rather vacillating and hesitant Pelsaert had a pre-existing animosity when they came together on the *Batavia*, dating back to previous VOC service in the Indies. This did not bode well for a voyage that generally took about nine months and was only broken by one stop on land, at Cape Town, in what is now South Africa.

As the *Batavia* coursed southward, tensions increased when Jacobsz came to make passes at the young and beautiful Lucretia 'Creesje' Jans, sailing with her maid to join her husband. Creesje put him off, and the captain promptly switched his attentions to the maid, Zwaantie, with whom he pursued a torrid affair. Pelsaert disapproved of this unseemly behaviour, and had further cause to be critical of Jacobsz when the *Batavia* landed at Cape Town to take on provisions in April 1629, after seven months at sea. While Pelsaert negotiated with the local Hottentot people for sheep and cattle, Jacobsz went on a drinking jag, visiting the other vessels of the fleet at anchor and becoming, according to Pelsaert's log, 'very beastly with words and deeds'.

Pelsaert ordered Jacobsz to his cabin and severely scolded him 'over his arrogance and the deeds committed by him'. Naturally, Jacobsz did not take this well.

Mutiny Interrupted

The *Batavia* set sail again on 22 April, turning her massive bow to the east and ploughing through the high waves of the Southern Ocean. While most of the passengers and crew remained unaware of it, mutiny was quietly brewing. It began when Jacobsz confided to Cornelisz just how angry he was over his treatment by Pelsaert. 'I would treat that miserly dog so that he would not come out of his cabin for fourteen days,' he threatened. Cornelisz encouraged his anger and they began plotting. To begin with, they would turn the crew against Pelsaert, who was not popular, take over the ship with its vast treasure and then find some quiet port where they could divide it up. After that, perhaps they might become pirates, or join forces with the perennial enemies of the Dutch, the Portuguese, who were based in Malacca.

That the plot was far-fetched made it no less serious. Although Jacobsz first brought up the idea in his angry mutterings against Pelsaert, Cornelisz seems to have been the prime mover, driven by the seething resentment he felt against humankind after his infant son's death, combined with his strange belief in the morality of any action he might undertake. Jacobsz and Cornelisz decided that the way to spark a mutiny was to provoke

Pelsaert into an act of reprisal against the crew, and decided on a blatant assault against Creesje Jans. After dinner one night, the young woman was attacked on deck and knocked over. A mixture of tar and dung was smeared over her face, legs and genitals before her assailants disappeared into the shadows.

Jacobsz and Cornelisz waited for Pelsaert to react, to clap the suspected assailants in chains or have them flogged, but Pelsaert did nothing of the sort. He had become aware, as he wrote in his journal, 'that the Skipper had been the Author of [the attack]', and therefore chose to do nothing, yet. In fact, both Pelsaert and the mutineers were playing a waiting game—Cornelisz and Jacobsz sure that Pelsaert would soon act, Pelsaert waiting until they arrived in the Indies, in perhaps a month's time.

But fate would intervene. Or perhaps it was not fate. The usual route for a VOC ship was along the Southern Ocean until the longitude of Java was reached, and then north to its destination, with Australia—at this time almost completely unexplored and referred to as 'the South Land'—to starboard, or the east. But the *Batavia* sailed too far east, either through Jacobsz' inattention or because he wished to make sure the rest of the fleet was not with him during the mutiny. On 4 June, about three o'clock in the morning, the lookout cried out that there was white water ahead. Jacobsz dismissed this—it must be the moon shining on the waves, he said. He ordered the *Batavia* to proceed under full sail—and without warning she slammed into a coral reef which caught her up short, as if a deadly hand had grabbed her, and held fast. Passengers and crew tumbled out of their hammocks as a horrendous screeching tore through the ship—triple hull or not, the *Batavia* had been torn at the core. She was still 3200 kilometres (1988 miles) from her destination.

Houtman's Abrolhos

As dawn lightened the sky, it became apparent that the *Batavia* had grounded in the archipelago that the Dutch called Houtman's Abrolhos, after Frederik de Houtman, a VOC merchant who had nearly run aground there some thirteen years before. No one had ever explored the islands—there are some 200 small rocky outcroppings in all—and, had Jacobsz's navigation been correct, they should have passed some 500 kilometres (310½ miles) to their west. At Jacobsz's command, the sailors pushed overboard all the cannon—totalling some 30 tons—in an attempt to lighten the ship so she could float off the reef, but she was stuck fast.

Perched high on the stern that dawn, Pelsaert saw some islands in the near distance and decided to evacuate the panicked passengers. In the chaos, 'poor-hearted men' pushed to be the first on the ship's two boats, ahead of women and children, while others, refusing to wait as water poured into the hold, dived into the sea and drowned. As night fell, 120 people were still on the wreck, but a squall caused operations to be suspended for the hours of darkness. On board (all officers, with the exception of Cornelisz, had left) chaos reigned. Sailors tapped the casks of wine and brandy reserved for Pelsaert and his officers, and became raging drunk. Twelve chests full of VOC silver stood on deck, ready to be offloaded, but the sailors wrenched them open, filling their hands with coins. But, realising there was nothing they could do with such treasure, they began throwing coins at each other and tossing them overboard.

'It is rubbish,' one sailor shouted, 'even if it is worth so many thousands.'

'Deep Grief of Heart'

All the next day rescue operations continued. By nightfall, the 322 survivors were divided into three groups—180 on the island closest to the ship that would become known as Batavia's Graveyard; about 70 men still on the wreck, including Cornelisz; with Pelsaert, Jacobsz and about fifty sailors on a tiny island not far from the wreck. With this group were almost all the supplies taken from the ship, including food and water. More food and water remained on the *Batavia*, but Pelsaert had seen the chaotic conditions on the wreck—soldiers and sailors roaming drunk, wearing officers' clothes and hurling silver into the water—and refused to go aboard.

Pelsaert was in possession of both the ship's boats, which could hold forty people—a small yawl and a larger longboat—and had experienced sailors with him. After making one abortive attempt to bring water to Batavia's Graveyard, only to row quickly away when a crowd of survivors nearly swamped the longboat, he made a fruitless search of nearby islands for water. Now he was faced with a crucial decision. Should he share what he had with the other survivors, in which case the food and water would be gone in no time? Or should he take his experienced sailors, including Jacobsz, and attempt to sail directly to Batavia to get help? Pelsaert later wrote, 'It was better and more honest to die with them if we could not find water than to stay alive with deep grief of heart.'

But the sailors convinced him that the only course was to set sail for Java, and this Pelsaert did.

The New Commander

Over the course of the next few days, the survivors on Batavia's Graveyard realised that they had been abandoned, and named the small island where Pelsaert had sheltered Traitor's Island. Soon, however, their thirst made them forget everything else. It had rained during the first night, but no rain fell for the next four days and ten people died of thirst. Fortunately, on 9 June, a thunderstorm hit and enough water was saved in sailcloths to replenish supplies.

In the meantime, the sailors still on the *Batavia* clung to life as the wreck was slowly battered to pieces on the reef. On 12 June the ship's side burst open and water poured in. Numerous drunken sailors were swept away and drowned, others grabbed casks and hatchcovers and made it to shore. The last person aboard, Jeronimus Cornelisz, hung onto the bowsprit for another two days before that, too, crumbled, and he dropped into the water along with a mass of driftwood. As malign fate would have it, he washed ashore on Batavia's Graveyard and was welcomed and nursed back to health by the survivors— he was, after all the highest-ranking officer of the VOC on the island.

Finding the *Batavia*

For centuries after the *Batavia* disappeared beneath the waters of the Houtman Abrolhos, her exact location— and that of the islands—was lost.

Wreckage seen by Captain Stokes of HMS *Beagle*, charting the Abrolhos in the 1840s, was assumed to be the *Batavia*, but was probably the *Zeewyck*, another Dutch vessel wrecked in 1728. This misunderstanding caused the islands surrounding the wreckage to be named the Pelsaert Group.

In fact, *Batavia's* Graveyard (today's Beacon Island) was roughly 80 kilometres (49½ miles) to the north, in the islands known as the Wallabi Group. This location was first postulated by novelist Henrietta Drake-Brockman, who remembered that Pelsaert had described animals that had to be wallabies during his time in the Abrolhos.

In 1960, the wreck of the *Batavia* was discovered by a fisherman setting lobster pots; he dived to the wreck numerous times, finally sharing his find with another diver, who helped salvage a cannon bearing the markings of the VOC.

Since then, Batavia's Graveyard, Traitor Island, Seal Island, and Wiebbe Hayes' island have all been identified—on the latter, now West Wallabi Island, the rudimentary fort built by the Defenders still stands.

The *Batavia's* gigantic stern, salvaged in 1970, is held today in the Western Australian Maritime Museum, along with other artefacts, among them human remains. A replica of the *Batavia*, built in the Netherlands with traditional materials, is on display in Lelystad, attracting thousands of tourists each year.

On his recovery, Cornelisz was elected to the council of survivors which had been formed to help the castaways on Batavia's Graveyard eke out an existence until help came. As the leading VOC officer, he began to control proceedings, at first to the good. The little island was fortunately in the path of the flotsam and supplies from the now-sunken *Batavia*, and thus had received 2275 litres (601 gallons) each of water and wine, clothing, wood and other necessities. Cornelisz helped collect these invaluable goods to a central location, rationed them out, and set up a guard to protect them. He sent out hunting parties to nearby islands, for the people on Batavia's Graveyard had already killed and eaten thousands of seabirds and begun decimating the sea lion population—and seemed to take a deep interest in the wellbeing of those under his care.

It is questionable, however, whether any of this was genuine. Cornelisz appears to have been driven by two emotional forces. One was his pathology, that of psychopathic predator. The other was his so-called religion, his belief that, as one of the survivors would later relate, 'all he did, whether it was good or bad (as judged by others), [was moral]. For God was perfect in virtue and goodness, so was not able to send into the heart of men anything bad, because there was no evil and badness in himself'.

Cornelisz had also not given up his desire to turn pirate, when and if he left this wretched island. He could surmise that his co-plotter, Jacobsz, had left for Java with Pelsaert. Although there was a strong chance that their small boat would not survive the journey, there was also the chance that it would. If it did, a rescue boat would come to pick up the survivors—and arrest Cornelisz. Therefore, as he saw it, he had to act quickly. He and his chief lieutenant, Davidt Zeevanck, decided that they needed to reduce the population of Batavia's Graveyard by at least half if they were to survive on the limited supplies available and if they were to have any chance of seizing a rescue boat without being stopped by equally desperate survivors.

Exile

The first thing Cornelisz did was send mutineers to the islands they could see in the distance, ostensibly to find out if there was water and food. The men nailed together several rough skiffs from wreckage and driftwood and set forth. Returning, they reported privately that some of the islands had birds and seals, but none had the water necessary for survival. This was fine with Cornelisz. According to one survivor, 'the Merchant [Cornelisz] ordered [the mutineers] to say that there was water and good food for people' on the islands. Thus, forty men and women were taken to what they called Seal Island, and fifteen were placed on Traitor's Island—both within sight of Batavia's Graveyard.

Yet another group, this one consisting—not coincidentally—of the 'boldest soldiers' not allied with Cornelisz, was sent to a distant island that they called High Land. These men, led by a private named Wiebbe Hayes, were told to light signal fires if they found fresh water and Cornelisz would pick them up.

Of course, he had no intention of picking up anyone—his goal was that each little colony should die of thirst. By the first week in July, the number of people on Batavia's Graveyard had been reduced to about 130 or 140. Now it was time for the murders to begin.

'Kill!'

Cornelisz persuaded two dozen men (some of whom had already planned mutiny aboard the *Batavia*) to sign an oath of allegiance. Many were VOC soldiers and rough sailors whose behaviour had already begun to frighten the others. Cornelisz had begun wearing the ceremonial clothes belonging to Francisco Pelsaert, and allowed this group to dress in fancy clothes from the Company's chests and strut around the island. They had access to the wine supplies, which made them even more threatening.

On 5 July, Cornelisz abruptly dissolved the ruling council, proclaiming himself and a few lieutenants like Zeevanck and the soldier Jacop Pietersz in charge. Shortly thereafter, a man was executed for supposedly having stolen from the wine supply. People could understand this—discipline needed to be strict in such dire circumstances. Later the same day, two carpenters were accused of plotting to steal one of the homemade boats to escape and were summarily run through with swords. Although no one had any proof of the carpenters' crimes, this, too, was accepted without protest.

To keep the survivors from becoming too suspicious, Cornelisz varied his killing patterns. He issued an order that certain people be taken to High Island to aid in the search for water. As soon as the mutineers were out of sight, they tied these unfortunates' hands and feet and dumped them overboard. No one realised this until much later.

But on 9 July something quite unexpected happened. Wiebbe Hayes' men, crossing from High Land to a nearby island, found deep wells of water. They set up signal fires whose smoke could be readily seen on Batavia's Graveyard, Traitor's Island and Seal Island, and a group of men, women and children immediately set out from Traitor's toward High Land. They already understood that Cornelisz had abandoned them; now they were heading to the signal that meant water, and life. Cornelisz had to stop them and despatched a boatload of mutineers to intercept the Traitor's Island boat. They caught it in a deepwater channel, drowned three people and brought the others back to Batavia's Graveyard.

Zeevanck consulted with Cornelisz and returned to the beach shouting, 'Slaet doodt!' (Kill!') The boys and men who had landed were put to the sword where they stood; those still on the boat were taken out to deep water and thrown into the sea and left to drown.

A Time of Derangement

No one on Batavia's Graveyard could now fail to understand that they were dealing with men who would kill for almost any reason. In fear of their lives, many survivors joined with the mutineers, taking an oath of loyalty to Cornelisz—but they were tested. A young man named Andries de Vries was sent into the sick tent to strangle those on whom Cornelisz no longer wanted to waste rations. On his first few nights he killed sixteen men. Soldier Hans Harden made it known that he wanted to join the mutineers, but while he and his wife dined with Cornelisz, a mutineer slipped into Harden's tent and strangled his eight-year-old daughter. Three days later, the grief-stricken father swore the oath of loyalty, trying to protect his wife. There were numerous trade-offs of this type. Preacher Gijsbert Bastiaensz and his wife Maria had eight children, aged from 23 down to eight, all of whom had survived the shipwreck. On 21 July, the preacher and his oldest daughter Judick, who had been forced to 'marry' one of the mutineers, were invited to eat dinner with the apothecary. While they ate, his wife and the seven other children were murdered and dumped in a common grave.

The men who killed them now went around the island killing other survivors at random. The barber-surgeon Aris Jasz was taken down to the beach to be murdered, but he survived several sword blows, broke free of his would-be killers and hid in the darkness. When they had given up the search, Jasz stole one of the boats and struck out in the darkness for Wiebbe Hayes' island.

Throughout July and August, the reign of terror continued unabated. Men walked the island during the day, saying, 'Who wants their ears boxed?' (Who wants to die?) One deranged young mutineer was even more explicit, crying out, 'Who wants to be stabbed to death?' At night survivors huddled in terror in their tents as the murderers walked by with sharp knives in their hands. Cornelisz, who took care never to get his own hands bloody, spent his time in his tent with Creesje Jans, forcing her to become his lover under threat of death. (Other women were treated similarly by the mutineers.) Cornelisz even sent his killers to Seal Island to finish off the men and women marooned there.

Having reduced the population on Batavia's Graveyard to about seventy people, half of whom had sworn allegiance to him, Cornelisz turned his eyes to Hayes and his men.

The Mysterious Fate of Ariaen Jacobsz

What happened to the captain of the *Batavia* is a mystery. Arriving in Batavia with Pelsaert in July 1629, he was quickly thrown into prison on suspicion of having plotted with Cornelisz to mutiny against Pelsaert—when Pelsaert returned from the Abrolhos with Cornelisz's confession, things looked bleak.

But Jacobsz was stubborn. Despite being held in what was literally a dungeon deep within the confines of Castle Batavia, he refused to admit guilt. His VOC interrogators grew more and more frustrated. Part of the problem was that they believed that Pelsaert had lost control of the ship and that some of the blame could be cast on him. (Pelsaert, however, did not linger long enough to defend himself, dying of fever less than eleven months after rescuing the survivors.)

The last mention of Jacobsz in VOC records is the notation that the 'skipper of the wrecked ship *Batavia* is still imprisoned, although [he] has several times requested a relaxation and a return to the fatherland; on the strong indictment of his having had the intention to run off with the ship, [he] has been condemned to more acute examination' (a nice way of saying torture). And here this stubborn, angry man disappears from history. There is no record of his execution, nor yet of his being freed. It is possible he died in prison, but we'll never know for sure.

The Battle

But Wiebbe Hayes had been forewarned. Aris Jasz had managed to reach his island, along with a few survivors from Seal Island, and they all told the same tale—Cornelisz and his gang were wiping out everyone they could. It was only a matter of time before they came for Hayes and his men. And the mutineers possessed all the weaponry on the islands— swords, daggers, muskets and pikes.

But Hayes had a number of things going for him. To begin with, Cornelisz had inadvertently exiled this group to an island where they had access to abundant water, and food ranging from birds to wallabies and sea-life. Hayes had found deep pools just offshore where a man could catch 'forty fish as large as a cod' in an hour.

Secondly, Hayes, unlike the victims on Batavia's Graveyard, was a soldier who knew how to organise a defence. He and his men drove sharpened nails into sticks of wood and gathered piles of coral lumps, to be thrown or fired from large slingshots made of rope and wood. He also knew that Cornelisz could come at him only one way—across the mudflats that separated Batavia's Graveyard from High Land at low tide. As long as Hayes posted lookouts, there was little chance of his being surprised. He and his 45 men, who would become known as the Defenders, made their preparations and waited. The attack was not long in coming.

On 21 July, Cornelisz sent a young boy to Hayes with a note, trying to sow confusion by claiming that those who had warned Hayes were in fact 'evil-doers' who were themselves mutineers. Hayes did not buy this and held the young mutineer captive. Several days later, twenty mutineers led by Davidt Zeevanck made a frontal assault across the mudflats. Hayes' men raced down to the water's edge to meet them and beat them off. On 5 August the men returned with a larger, more determined group and again a battle was fought, 'up to their knees in water'. This assault, too, was driven off.

For nearly a month there was an uneasy truce. But as September neared Cornelisz realised that if a rescue ship were to come, it would come soon. He decided to open fake negotiations, 'under the cloak of friendship, [to] surprise them with treason at an opportune time'. Thus, on 2 September, Cornelisz and five of his main men landed on the island with blankets and shoes—two items the soldiers lacked. Cornelisz may have thought his plan was working when the soldiers gathered to open up the bales; gradually, his men circulated through Hayes' group, promising them money from the wreck of the *Batavia* if they would change sides. But Hayes' men were loyal, and took Cornelisz and the others captive.

When the remaining mutineers attacked across the open mudflats, Hayes made an instant decision. He could not fight and still guard his captives, so he had his men put Cornelisz' lieutenants, including Zeevanck, to the sword, while Cornelisz he imprisoned in a pit deeper in the island. The Defenders then drove off the men on the mudflats.

Rescue

The mutineers knew they had to subdue the Defenders if they were to survive being rescued. They elected as their new leader Wouter Loos, an experienced soldier, who explained that a frontal attack was the worst way to go. Under his direction, they dragged guns from the wreck of the *Batavia*, and early on 17 September began bombarding Hayes' island from the mudflats. As the morning wore on, four Defenders had been hit, one of them mortally, and it seemed as if the mutineers were gradually wearing down their defences.

And then—like a scene from a Hollywood movie—a sail appeared on the horizon. It was the *Sardam*, a rescue ship under the direction of none other than Francisco Pelsaert, who had made it back to Batavia. Both Hayes and Loos jumped into boats and made their way desperately toward her. If Hayes got there first, he could give warning of the mutineers. If Loos did, he and his men would swarm aboard and take over the vessel.

Hayes won by a nose, and explained to Pelsaert what happened just before the mutineers showed up, shouting that Hayes was a liar and not to be believed. But these men, armed to the teeth and ostentatiously uniformed, were obviously mutineers. Pelsaert trained the *Sardam*'s guns on them and forced them to drop their weapons overboard.

Thus the reign of Jeronimus Cornelisz ended. Pelsaert gathered the mutineers together under guard and over the next few days interrogated them, some under torture, and elicited confessions. Cornelisz was subjected to water torture, with vast quantities of water being poured down his throat until his belly became distended. He finally confessed, to both the killings on the island and the planned mutiny aboard the *Batavia*, and was sentenced to death. He would be hung, but not before his hands were cut off. Seven others would join him in death. Because Pelsaert did not want to transport these dangerous criminals back to Batavia, he decided to erect a gallows on Seal Island and execute them there.

On 1 October, Jeronimus Cornelisz was led to the gallows. He had previously raged that 'God will perform unto me … a miracle, so that I will not hang' but no miracle was forthcoming. He was confronted by Creesje Jans, who 'bitterly' reproached him for raping her. The other condemned men hurled imprecations at him, begging that he die first so they could watch. After his hands were torn off—some accounts say with hammer and chisel—Cornelisz was hanged, but not before shouting 'Revenge! Revenge!' at the jeering crowd.

Cornelisz' and his fellow mutineers' bodies were left hanging, to be eaten by birds, as the *Sardam* sailed away. Back in Batavia, others of the mutineers would be sentenced to mutilation, death by hanging or on the rack, or imprisonment. It seemed a small enough price to pay for one of the most horrible episodes in the history of castaways. Cornelisz's rampage had cost the lives of 216 men, women and children. Those who survived his murderous rage were no doubt scarred forever.

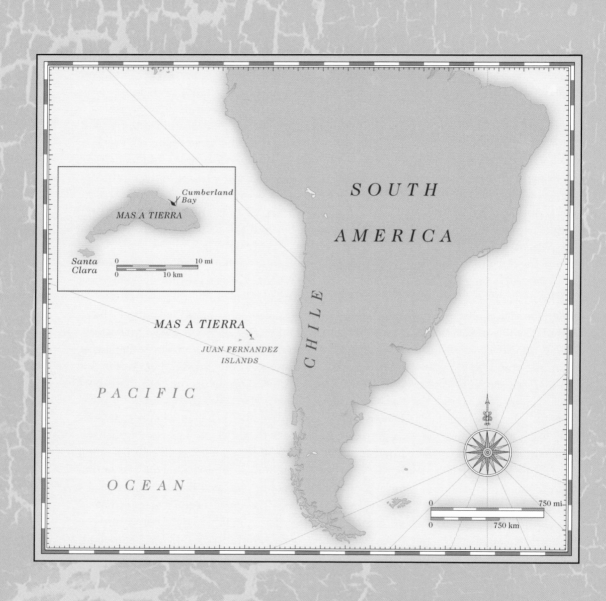

Alexander Selkirk, 1704–1709
The Most Famous of Them All

Alexander Selkirk, a talented but angry man given to physical violence, is not a convenient hero. He once attacked his own mother and father, and another time in a drunken rage— drink was a problem for him—nearly beat a man to death. Selkirk's passionate nature led him to spur-of-the-moment decisions which included running off to sea and being married to two women at once.

His most mercurial decision of all, however, turned out to be his most fortunate one. In a fit of anger one day in the Pacific Ocean off the coast of South America, he begged to be marooned—and his wish was granted by a captain who was heartily sick of him. He was set ashore on Isla Más a Tierra in the Juan Fernández group, 650 kilometres (about 400 miles) off the coast of Chile, on a September day in 1704, and left to his fate. Although he could not know it at the time, Selkirk's marooning would not only save his life, it would make his fortune. And because of his lonely sojourn, Robinson Crusoe, a hero for the ages, was born.

Más a Tierra

Although the Chilean government re-named the island Robinson Crusoe Island in 1966, as a tourism gimmick, it's hard to call it that with a straight face, since it is so very, very different from the fictional tropical atoll on which Daniel Defoe placed Robinson Crusoe (see **The Life and Strange Surprizing Adventures …**, page 89).

Más a Tierra means 'Nearer to Land' and was named by Juan Fernández, the Spanish navigator who discovered it in 1570. (Fernández was not exactly the most imaginative island-namer. Más a Tierra's counterpart 160 kilometres (99½ miles) to the west he named Más Afuera, or 'Farther Out to Sea'.) Making up in ego what he lacked in creativity, Fernández named the two islands, along with some small accompanying atolls, the Juan Fernández Islands.

Más a Tierra is the only habitable member of the group. Nineteen kilometres (12 miles) long, 6.5 kilometres (4 miles) wide, volcanic in origin, it is notable for its steep precipices, slashing ravines, high cliffs and a flat-topped mountain, some 915 metres (about 1000 yards) high, that Selkirk named The Anvil. But Más a Tierra supports life in profusion. In Selkirk's time its steep slopes were covered with sandalwood and pimento trees, streams cascaded through green, hidden valleys, and uncountable numbers of fur seals and sea lions appeared at mating season, as well as green turtles. The hills were populated by goats released by long-departed Spanish settlers, along with feral cats and rats. One could pluck black plums and eat wild berries. The surrounding sea boasted fish of all types, especially the huge and delicious crayfish, which in those days could be caught simply by reaching into the water.

On Más a Tierra's the average temperature is a mild 16° Celsius (60.8° Fahrenheit). The island receives about 100 millimetres (about 4 inches) of rain a year, as steady rain in winter (June to August) and thunderous storms in summer (which lasts from December to March). Winds sweep through the valleys and crash down into the one safe anchorage, Cumberland Bay, which the eighteenth century privateer Woodes Rogers, who rescued Selkirk, called Windy Bay. At higher elevations, dark clouds enshroud the mountains and fogs roll through the forests. It is an island given to sudden and dramatic changes, an island both fertile and vengeful, an island—not unlike Selkirk himself—whose face can change at any moment.

Seventh Son

Alexander Selkirk—his name was initially spelled Selcraig, or perhaps Selchraige, but it was later changed, possibly by an inattentive clerk—was born in 1680 in eastern Scotland, in the fishing village of Largo, the seventh and last son of cobbler John Selcraig and his wife Euphan. They were a strict Presbyterian family and Alexander was a 'wild and restless boy', so there was trouble almost from the beginning. Alexander wanted to go to sea; his father wanted him to stay home and be a cobbler. Euphan, however, saw that the boy, perhaps imbued with the fortunate power of a seventh son, could not be restrained and encouraged him to seek his destiny elsewhere. Or perhaps she just wanted to get the angry young man out of her home. At the age of fifteen, the Elder Council of his church accused him of 'Undecent Beaiviar in ye church'—no one knows quite what this means—but when he was called by the Elders to account for himself, it turned out he had already gone to sea.

Records are sketchy, but it appears Selkirk joined with privateers sailing through the Caribbean, perhaps first as a cabin boy who was tough and quick-witted and who soon learned how to navigate with sextant and stars. He may even have been a part of the ill-fated Scottish expedition to create a colony on the isthmus of Panama, often called the 'Darien Disaster', where 1200 Scottish emigrants sought their fortune and founded a settlement they called New Caledonia. Rather than fortune they found death through disease and Spanish steel. If Selkirk was among the 300 who survived this disaster, he returned home hardened by the fire of the experience.

Back in Largo in 1701, it was said that he was 'more reckless and boisterous than ever'. When his 'half-witted' brother Andrew gave him salt water to drink, as a prank, Selkirk became so enraged that he beat him badly, and wrestled his father into a headlock when the poor man tried to intercede. When his mother screamed 'Will you murder your father and my husband both?' he apparently struck her, causing, she told the authorities, 'a sore pain in her head'. These scandalous goings-on once again brought Selkirk up against the council of Elders at his church, where he 'promised amendment in the strength of the Lord and so was dismissed', but it was obvious that Largo was too small and mild a place to hold such a man.

Dampier's Voyage

In the spring of 1703, Alexander Selkirk left Largo behind and joined forces with the privateer William Dampier, who had been issued letters of marque by the British government to attack Spanish and French shipping in the Caribbean and South (or Pacific) Ocean. The War of Spanish Succession had begun, and these countries were at war with England.

Selkirk was sailing master aboard the 130-ton vessel, the *Cinque Ports*, which sailed with Dampier's ship, the *St George*. This meant that he was navigator of the vessel, at the ripe old age of 23, and he received high praise for his work—Dampier called him 'the best man on the *Cinque Ports*', and the ship's captain, William Pickering, called him 'a main Pillar of the Voyage'. They headed across the Atlantic and down the east coast of South America, aiming to round the Horn and reach the Pacific. But scurvy struck and men began to die, one by one, and thus the ships were forced to anchor at a small island off the coast of Brazil. There, Captain Pickering passed away and was replaced by his second-in-command, one Thomas Stradling.

There, too, it was discovered that the hulls of the ships, particularly the *Cinque Ports*, had not been properly sheathed with an extra layer of wood to protect against the fierce, boring sea-worms of the tropics. The bottom of the *Cinque Ports* was so porous there were places a man could put his fist through it.

Still, the ships headed southward, rounding the Horn in January 1704 in a fierce storm. The battered *Cinque Ports* reached Más a Tierra in early February (Dampier and the *St George* showed up a few weeks later). The island, while technically owned by Spain, had been abandoned after an abortive attempt at settlement in the early seventeenth century and was now used by British privateers to refit and replenish, although Spanish men-of-war made sporadic sweeps of the Juan Fernández Islands in attempts to root them out.

The *Cinque Ports* was down to forty two crew members out of an original complement of ninety, and there were many—Selkirk the most vocal—who felt Stradling was an inept and callous commander. The crew, in near mutiny, left the vessel to refresh themselves with fruit and crayfish and the sparkling waters of Más a Tierra 's mountain streams. When Dampier showed up, he calmed the men down, promising that rich prizes lay ahead, that he would listen to their grievances against Stradling—basically sweet-talking them into getting back on board the *Cinque Ports*. At the end of February, the two privateers fought a pitched battle with a French merchant ship off Más a Tierra, but failed to capture her. When they returned to the island, they found two French warships in Cumberland Bay. In their haste to evade them, they left eight men and important supplies—in particular, extra anchors and sails—on the island.

Two very dissatisfied buccaneer crews sailed down the coast of South America, attempting to take prizes. They had scant success, in part because Dampier seemed drunk most of the time and unwilling to get into a fight. After a failed attack on the Peruvian town of Santa Maria, Stradling and Dampier quarrelled, and by the time they reached the Bay of Panama the two captains had decided to part company, with Stradling headed back down the coast in search of prizes.

However, the *Cinque Ports* was now leaking so badly that he was forced to put in again at Más a Tierra to repair the hull. They arrived in September 1704.

Marooned

They discovered that two of the men they had left behind in February were still there—the other six had been killed or captured by the French, but these two had survived quite well. No doubt this was to influence Alexander Selkirk's decision. He had been fighting with Stradling for some time about the condition of the *Cinque Ports*, saying the vessel was going to sink if it were not re-hulled properly. But Stradling would not take the time to do this—he wanted merely to patch the hull, re-provision and get back to sea.

As provisioning was being completed, Selkirk and Stradling got into a final argument. Shouting at his captain and shaking his fist, Selkirk said he would rather stay on the island than go to the bottom when the ship went down. Stradling said that was just fine with him—he would put Selkirk ashore immediately. Selkirk apparently believed that other crew members would join him in his mutiny, but none did. According to eyewitnesses, he was somewhat stunned as his sea-chest and musket were loaded into the ship's boat.

But, unable to admit defeat, Selkirk was rowed to the shore of Cumberland Bay, where his belongings were put on the beach. Stradling himself was in the boat, and as it made its way back to the *Cinque Ports*, Selkirk had a sudden change of heart. He charged into the water after the retreating boat, flailing his arms, until he was chest-deep, yelling: 'I've changed my mind.'

And Stradling yelled back: 'Well, I have not changed mine. Stay where you are and may you starve!'

Alexander Selkirk is rescued by British sailors.

Deciding to Live

Like many another person deliberately marooned, Selkirk stood on the beach watching until the *Cinque Ports'* sails were the size of a butterfly on the horizon. He could not accept that Stradling would not come about and pick him up. Thus he did not immediately begin to take the steps necessary for survival—searching the island for food and water sources, building a strong shelter, creating a signal fire.

He had with him, Woodes Rogers writes, food for two meals, a small amount of rum, 'clothes and bedding, a flintlock, some powder, bullets, and tobacco, a hatchet, a knife, a kettle, a Bible, some practical pieces, and his mathematical [nautical] instruments and books'. The fact that Selkirk, no shrinking violet, had not fought for more food, powder and bullets indicates his surprise at Stradling calling his bluff, and his confidence that the *Cinque Ports* would shortly return.

Thus the Scotsman stayed on the beach. When the sun went down behind the cliffs above him, he went a little way into the woods that edged the beach, beside a stream that poured down through a valley, and camped there miserably in a makeshift sailcloth hut left behind by the earlier maroons. He spent a mainly sleepless night, terrified by the sounds that came at him in the darkness, for Más a Tierra had a cacophonous night: the wind howling down the ravines, trees rustling in the forest, and the baying and growling and barking of the thousands of sea lions and fur seals that had come ashore to mate in the early spring. He feared they might swarm his campsite while he slept and crush him.

In the morning he stared into the lightening horizon, but saw no sail.

'The Desire of Society'

For his first few weeks on the island, Selkirk lived in a grove close to shore, keeping a signal fire bright, waiting for his ship to return. He made no attempt to explore the interior, living off crayfish and turtles (there was an abundance of other sea-life, but he claimed he could not eat fish without either bread or salt). Gradually the realisation set in that his punishment was not to be rescinded. Richard Steele, a journalist who later interviewed Selkirk in a London tavern (most scholars accept that this happened, although there are some who claimed Steele never met him) wrote: 'The Necessities of Hunger and Thirst were his greatest Diversions from the Reflection on his lonely Condition. When there Appetites were satisfied, the Desire of Society became as strong a Call upon him ... he grew dejected, languid, and melancholy, scarcely able to refrain from doing himself Violence.'

According to Steele, it took nearly eighteen months (Woodes Rogers says only eight) for Selkirk to shake himself out of this mood. In an act that would have pleased the church elders in Largo, Selkirk began to read his Bible for consolation, focusing on passages familiar from services at home: 'Hear O Lord my Prayer, give ear to my Supplication, hear me in Thy Justice.' Gradually his depression lifted. It became his habit each morning as the sun touched him to rise and read the Bible out loud, according to Woodes Rogers, 'in order to keep up the faculties, and to utter himself with greater energy'.

Selkirk's natural vigour and liveliness returned. He began to explore the interior, musket in hand, discovering the plum and cabbage trees, the profusion of fresh water and, especially, the wild goats. The Spanish had left goats there during their attempt at colonising the island a century earlier, and now the animals flourished in the high rocky places. Goat became Selkirk's main sustenance, particularly after he became sick of turtle and crayfish.

It was the sea lions which drove him to create his permanent island home. To escape these 'Monsters of the Deep' whose howling 'seemed too terrible for human ears', he moved inland to a grove on a ridge about 1500 metres (1640 yards) from the beach. There he built two huts of pimento wood (which he also found excellent for making fires)—one a smokehouse and kitchen, the other his main habitation. He lined them with goatskin and stuffed the crevices with grass—they were warm enough, if sometimes leaky in the mild, rainy winters.

Selkirk found, however, that here he was plagued by voracious rats, which nibbled at his food and crawled over him at night, biting him. Clubbing them and setting traps for them did no good. He finally hit on a solution. The island was also home to feral cats, descendants of animals which like the rats had made their way ashore from ships at anchor, and Selkirk began to lure them with scraps of goat meat. The older cats remained suspicious, but kittens came to him readily and soon, Richard Steele wrote, 'hundreds [of cats] would lie about him', protecting him from the ravages of the rats, and following him everywhere.

Selkirk had, at last, found some company.

The Selkirk Diet

Soon Selkirk—who, it may be remembered, was only in his mid-twenties—grew into an extraordinarily fit and adaptable man. When his powder and shot ran out he began running down the goats to catch them, racing up and down the steep slopes with ease. The sea lions he had formerly feared so much he now found were quite easy to kill. He knew they had powerful jaws which could easily crush a man's limb. But now that he was 'unruffled in himself', as Woodes Rogers wrote, he saw that 'the animals [were] mighty slow in working themselves round [and so] he had nothing to do but place himself exactly opposite their middle and as close to them as possible, and he dispatched them with his hatchet, at will'. Their stiff whiskers, Selkirk later said, made excellent toothpicks.

Had diet books been the fad back in the early eighteenth century, Selkirk could have made a pretty penny writing one. Instead of tobacco, alcohol and heavily salted preserved meat, he was eating plums, turnips (introduced by a group of privateers), parsley, cabbage, shellfish and lean meat. He grew fast, strong and agile, the island's premier athlete, chasing down goats, climbing trees, cutting wood for his fire. He had one similarity with the fictional Robinson Crusoe, and that was ingenuity. He carved goat's horns into eating utensils, hollowed blocks of wood into bowls and cups, built a shovel from a log and hardened it in the embers of his fire. He washed himself in streams and waterfalls. When his shoes fell apart he didn't bother to replace them, and his feet became hardened, immune to the sharpest rock. When his clothes fell in tatters from his body, he replaced them with roughly tanned goatskins—hat, shirt, pants—sewn together using a nail as needle and thread from an unravelled sock.

As the years went by, Selkirk accepted this existence, even if he pined to be rescued, but he had two chief fears. One was that he would injure himself in some way and, unable to care for himself, die alone and be eaten by the very cats who had become his friends. This was not baseless apprehension. One day, chasing a goat along a high ridge, he went over a precipice hidden by brush. He and the goat tumbled a long way and Selkirk was knocked unconscious. When he awoke, badly battered, the goat lay dead beneath him. Had it not broken his fall, he would have died himself. It took an entire day to crawl back to his hut, and another ten days before he could venture forth again. After that experience, he took precautions. He chased down kids, lamed them by breaking their hind legs, and kept them in makeshift pens, feeding them the oats that also grew wild on the island.

Selkirk's other fear was that the hated Spanish might return to the island. And, one day, they did.

The Spanish

Selkirk had a lookout on a plateau some 600 metres (656 yards) above sea level, which gave him a clear view in all directions, but particularly to the east over Cumberland Bay, where a ship might most likely approach. Three times during his first years on the island, he saw sails. Three times he raced to Cumberland Bay to light signal fires. And three times the sails kept on going, disappearing in the blue vastness of the ocean.

But one morning at dawn, Selkirk descended from his camp to bathe in the ocean. As he got closer he saw something gleaming and white through the trees: to his astonishment, the whiteness turned out to be the sails of a large ship at anchor. Unable to believe that what he had hoped for so devoutly had arrived, he ran onto the beach. The ship had already disembarked small boats which were rowing in. Selkirk so forgot himself that he began shouting, realising too late that the vessel was flying the red and yellow flag of Spain. The men in the boats had pistols and began to take shots at him.

Turning, Selkirk raced back into the woods, hurling himself up the steep hills with the Spanish in close pursuit. He said later that he might have surrendered to the French, but never to the Spanish, who would either have killed him outright or put him to brutal labour in their silver mines. He was faster and knew where he was going, but outnumbered by men who began trying to herd him like a wild animal. He finally climbed a tall tree and hid in its thick branches. According to Rogers: 'At the foot of the tree [the Spanish] made water, and kill'd several Goats just by, but they went off again without discovering him.'

For two days the Spanish searched for Selkirk while he hid deep in the woods, unable to light a fire. Finally they left and he came cautiously out of hiding, fearful that a group of soldiers might have been left behind. The enemy had destroyed his camp, burned his huts, killed the kids he kept as food, but they had, indeed, left.

The island was his again; he could breathe a sigh of relief and rebuild. So that he would never be caught off-guard again, he built a hiding place deep in the most inaccessible part of the woods, a safe haven he could head to immediately should Spanish sailors arrive again.

'Marooned! Marooned!'

In one of those coincidences that abound in literature, but are less common in life, William Dampier, having circumnavigated the globe and seen many adventures after splitting up with the *Cinque Ports* in 1704—none of which made him rich, however—in 1708 set forth on yet another privateering expedition in search of Spanish gold. There were two vessels on this voyage, the *Duke* and the *Duchess*, the former captained by the well-respected privateer Woodes Rogers. They made the hardship-filled voyage around the Horn, with men dying of scurvy, and sailed north to Más a Tierra for the usual rest and re-supply stop. It was by now late January 1709.

Alexander Selkirk was cooking dinner at his camp late one afternoon when he looked up—and saw sails on the horizon. For some reason, he felt strongly that these ships were not Spanish. Racing down to the beach, dragging a burning log behind him, he built up a huge fire that he prayed might be seen.

Eighteenth century portrait of Daniel Defoe, author of *Robinson Crusoe*.

The Life and Strange Surprizing Adventures …

It can be said without exaggeration that Defoe created the castaway genre when he wrote *The Life and Strange Surprizing Adventures of Robinson Crusoe*. And in doing so he also created what is considered the first novel written in English.

Defoe, born in London in 1659 (possibly 1661), was nearly sixty when he wrote *Robinson Crusoe*. By that time he was already a well-known and successful writer, beginning as a political pamphleteer (although some of these writings got him pilloried and tossed in jail). He was always in debt and thus wrote fast, for money—1719 saw the publication of *Robinson Crusoe* and sixteen other books. (In his lifetime Defoe published some 560 books, pamphlets and journals.) In fact, he wrote *Robinson Crusoe* in four months, so quickly that readers complained of careless mistakes— Crusoe strips off his clothes to swim to his wrecked ship, for instance, then fills his non-existent pockets with biscuits. No matter. By the time Alexander Selkirk died in 1721, the book had gone through five editions. Defoe churned out a few sequels to the story, but it was *The Life and Strange Surprizing Adventures of Robinson Crusoe* that became a classic.

Did Defoe take *all* his story from the adventures of Alexander Selkirk? Probably much of it, garnered from the journal of Woodes Rogers, published under the title *A Cruising Voyage Around the World*, and from the article by journalist Richard Steele, who claimed to have interviewed Selkirk in a London tavern in 1711.

But Defoe also changed things quite significantly. The island of his maroon was far more tropical, located near the mouth of 'the Great River of Oroonoque' (the Orinoco River) which flows into the Caribbean off the coast of South America. Though he was writing fiction, Defoe wanted his readers to believe that this island actually existed and even gave its latitude. But it doesn't. What existed were many accounts of Caribbean islands that Defoe could draw on for other details, while information on Más a Tierra was sparse. In the glamorous Caribbean, however, which most of his readers would have read about, Defoe could depict an island struck by hurricanes, filled with lush tropical jungle, alive with chattering monkeys and slithering alligators, and plagued by frequent visits from pirates and the evil Spanish.

However, in the popular imagination, Selkirk is inextricably entwined with Defoe and Crusoe. *Robinson Crusoe* also opened the floodgates for other novels that Defoe wrote, including *Moll Flanders* and *A Journal of the Plague Year*.

Woodes Rogers had brought the *Duke* to within 20 kilometres (12½ miles) of the island, but, with heavy squalls blowing, was afraid to venture in closer. He sent out a ship's boat to investigate the anchorage. As the boat made its way to shore, night fell and Selkirk's fire became visible.

Frightened that the flames meant that the Spanish were on the island, the sailors beat a hasty retreat. Rogers could see the fire even from further out, and also believed it meant the presence of a Spanish garrison. But during the night he and his officers decided that the ships must land, even if it meant a fight—they needed fresh water, and greens to ward off scurvy. So the next morning the *Duke* and *Duchess* approached Cumberland Bay. The *Duchess* flew a French flag, in the hope that confusion might keep the Spanish from reacting quickly. Because the bay was so windy, Rogers sent a small boat toward shore, its sailors heavily armed.

Selkirk, who had spent the night in fearful anticipation, built up his fire and began to roast two goats with fresh herbs, knowing how hungry the sailors would be. As the boat came closer, he tied a white rag to a stick and waved it frantically in the air as he ran along the shore. The boat hit the beach, the men leaped out, rifles at the ready, and surrounded Selkirk, firing questions. Who was he? Was he Spanish? Was there anyone else here?

Selkirk could only say one word, over and over again: 'Marooned! Marooned! Marooned!' His language had deteriorated to such an extent that the men could barely understand him—in fact, dressed in goatskins, with wild beard and tangled hair, he seemed more beast than human. But he gave them food and gradually they realised that he was friendly, and a fellow Briton.

The men invited Selkirk back to the ship, but at first he refused, trying to make them understand that he would not set foot on the vessel if Stradling, his old captain, was present. They assured him he was not. And so Selkirk finally boarded the *Duke*. There he was brought before Woodes Rogers and William Dampier. The latter remembered his former sailing master, but was astonished at the changes wrought in him. He could barely speak—Rogers would write that Selkirk 'had so much forgot his Language for want of Use, that we could scarce understand him, for he seem'd to speak his words by halves'—and when they gave him food he reacted in disgust, for it was too salty. Alcohol burned his throat. Shoes made his feet swell up and he immediately took them off, while regular clothes constricted him.

Even so, Selkirk was overjoyed to see fellow human beings. For two weeks the ships remained at anchor and Selkirk treated their crews like honoured guests. He was proud of what he had learned on the island. He helped nurse men sick with scurvy back to health and ran down goats, much to the astonishment of Rogers and his crew, over the most rugged terrain, returning with the animals tossed across his back. And when the *Duke* and *Duchess* were ready to leave, on 13 February 1709, Selkirk accepted a position as sailing master and sailed away from Más a Tierra. He had been on the island, alone, four years and four months.

'The Tranquillity of His Solitude'

What did Selkirk think as he looked back at the island, his home for so long, fast disappearing on the horizon? Selkirk, unlike many castaways, left no personal record or journal, so we do not know. Certainly his life on the island wrought changes in him, but just as certainly these changes did not last when he returned to civilisation.

Selkirk performed admirably during the two years that remained of Dampier's successful expedition. He must have felt both satisfaction and horror when he learned that, a month after he was abandoned, the *Cinque Ports* did indeed sink from worm damage off Peru. Stradling and a few others were marooned on a barren island and forced to drink tortoise blood before the Spanish found them and imprisoned them. Most of the men died, but Stradling escaped and four years later returned to England, sick and destitute.

Which was not the way Selkirk returned. Rogers and Dampier circumnavigated the globe and their fleet, with the addition of some rich Spanish prizes, arrived back in England on 14 October 1711. Selkirk walked down the gangplank wearing a new coat and shoes with scarlet laces. His share of the voyage was £800, although it took him almost two years to claim the money—there were court battles going on over shares of the profits—years spent drinking in the bars of Bristol. After he beat a young sailor badly in a brawl, he decided it best to return to Largo, where he supposedly arrived one morning in the spring of 1713, wearing gold-edged clothing. His mother 'gave a cry of joy' to see him, but things quickly deteriorated. He could not live in a house after all this time, and built a kind of cave in the hills beyond the city. Drinking again, he got into another fight and this time nearly killed his opponent.

He fled again, back to London, married a 16-year-old girl—some accounts have it that they were not officially wed—but abandoned her and in Plymouth wed a tavern owner. Still restless, he went to sea again in 1720, as first mate aboard a British warship patrolling the west coast of Africa. On 13 December 1721, at 8 p.m., it was recorded in the ship's log that Alexander Selkirk had died of yellow fever and been buried at sea.

While Selkirk had wanted with all his heart to be rescued, it was probably the worst thing that ever happened to him. As Richard Steele wrote, his 'return to the world' could not, even with £800, red shoelaces and gold-frilled clothing, 'restore him to the tranquillity of his solitude'.

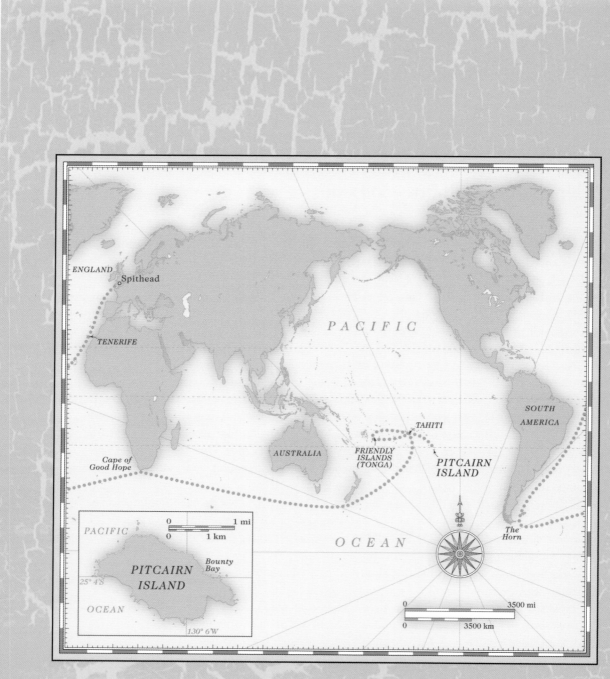

The Bounty *Mutineers,* 1790–1808
Paradise on Pitcairn Island

There were twenty-seven men, women and a small child aboard the vessel, and they had been at sea for two months. They had first headed south, deep into the unknown wastes of the Pacific, then east, pushed by westerly trade winds, and finally north again. These people were in search of an island—an island that had been once been found and now was lost.

Nine of the men wanted to be lost themselves. They were English sailors running as far as they could from the power of the British navy. The other six men, the eleven women and the baby were Tahitian, a number of them kidnapped. For these people any land at all would be welcome.

The ship was the soon-to-be notorious *Bounty*. On the evening of 15 January 1790, the disparate mix of men, women and cultures it carried sighted a lone island that looked, from a distance, like a huge humpback whale. They sailed closer the next day, but were forced by rough seas to stand off for three more days, which gave them time to closely observe the island. It was about 1600 metres (almost a mile) wide and twice as long. Rocky, heavily-wooded cliffs rose to 330 metres (361 yards), and seabirds wheeled and called. There was no obvious sign of human habitation, but the Englishmen were careful. When the seas finally calmed, they lowered a boat and eight of the men went ashore, fanning out along the ridges and hidden places of the island.

There was no one to be found. They were on their own. And thus began the saga of Pitcairn Island.

The *Bounty*

The story of the *Bounty* and the most famous mutiny in maritime history has been told over and over again in popular culture, since early in the nineteenth century. At least four romantic twentieth century films have furthered the legend, but without adding anything significant in the way of accuracy or insight. Simply told, the *Bounty* set sail from England on 23 December 1787, on a mission to the island of Otaheite—Tahiti, we call it now—to collect breadfruit plants to be transported to the West Indies, where they would be used as a cheap source of food for the slaves who laboured on the British sugar plantations.

The *Bounty*—a relatively small vessel which had been converted from a collier, or coal ship—was skippered by 35-year-old Lieutenant William Bligh, an experienced seaman who at the age of twenty-three had sailed with Captain James Cook aboard the *Resolution* on the latter's third and last voyage to the South Seas. Bligh was sailing master, or navigator, on that trip and had acquitted himself well—and when Cook was murdered by Hawaiian islanders, Bligh navigated the *Resolution* back home. But his subsequent career was not as successful as he might have liked and by 1787 he was still not a captain, although he had been promised his promotion on successful completion of the *Bounty* mission. This may have contributed to his general ill-humour during the voyage.

The initial leg took the *Bounty* generally southwest to the tip of South America, where Bligh attempted to round Cape Horn into the Pacific. After battling fierce gales for twenty-five days, Bligh was forced to turn back east for the longer but less stormy route south of Africa's tip. The *Bounty* coursed the Southern Ocean, stopping briefly in Van Diemen's Land (Tasmania) before heading north through the Pacific to Tahiti, reaching the island on 26 October 1788.

Tahiti

It's hard to overestimate the island's effect on the *Bounty*'s crew. They had sailed over 43,000 kilometres (26,718 miles), subsisting on salt-pork and hard biscuits for ten months, fighting both gales and doldrums, to end up in a paradise on earth. Still relatively untouched since its discovery by the British in 1767, Tahiti was a land of waterfalls, where fresh fruits, vegetables and meats abounded, and where the inhabitants seemed, to the delighted sailors' eyes, to be obsessed with sex. As the *Bounty* dropped anchor, bare-breasted women paddled out to meet her, and when nightfall came there were so many women on board that Bligh complained he could scarcely see his crew.

Ironically, given his later reputation, Bligh's problem in Tahiti was that he was too lenient. He needed to stay on the island for about six months to let the breadfruit plants they were collecting take root and grow sturdier, and during that time allowed his crew to 'go native'. Each man had his 'Peggy', or girlfriend, and set up house among the islanders, even undergoing elaborate tattooing around their buttocks and thighs which made them look as though they were wearing swimming trunks.

Thus when Bligh summoned the men back to the ship to sail away from this paradise, away from women (some of them pregnant) with whom they had formed strong attachments, there was not unnaturally a good deal of disappointment, not to say resentment. On 6 April 1789, the *Bounty* set sail with 1000 breadfruit plants and a volatile and angry crew.

Nearly three weeks later they called in at Nomuka Island in the Tonga Group to take on water and victuals. Here the natives were not friendly like those in Tahiti—in fact, they

A village on Pitcairn Island in the early nineteenth century.

were distinctly threatening—but Bligh refused to allow the crew to use their guns, perhaps afraid of provoking an incident.

The tension induced by a day spent surrounded by threatening natives menacingly clacking rocks together brought out the worst in Bligh, who even at the best of times could be short-tempered. No one knows quite what happened, but some lack of skill or failure of performance caused him to insult his sailing master, Fletcher Christian, calling him a 'cowardly rascal' in front of the crew and later accusing him (and others) of stealing coconuts from the ship's stores. Oddly, not only was Christian Bligh's second-in-command, but the two had a personal relationship, Bligh having acted as Christian's mentor on earlier voyages. Christian had even been to Bligh's home and enjoyed his hospitality.

Bligh's Incredible Voyage

Whatever history may record as the final verdict regarding William Bligh's responsibility for the mutiny onboard the *Bounty*—and the debate still rages—he is universally acclaimed for his extraordinary 4300 kilometre (2672 mile) voyage across the South Pacific in a 10.5 metre (34½ foot) open boat.

On 29 April 1789, Blight and eighteen seamen were set adrift in the *Bounty*'s yawl by the mutineers. They had four cutlasses, a five-day supply of food and water, a quadrant, a broken sextant and a pocket watch, but no charts. Essentially, they had been sentenced to death. And death would have been their fate in the hands of a lesser seaman and navigator than Bligh. But as the *Bounty* sailed out of sight, Blight said to his men in a loud, firm voice: 'Never fear, my lads: I'll do you justice if I ever reach England!'

At the time, fulfilling such a promise must have seemed almost impossible. The boat was so weighted down that its gunwales rode only a few centimetres (a couple of inches) above the water. Nonetheless, Bligh set sail for the nearby island of Tofua to search for food and water. There, however, they were attacked by hostile natives and one man was killed as they hastily beat a retreat. Now wary of landing anywhere in the South Pacific islands, Bligh set a course past Fiji and the New Hebrides, across the Coral Sea to the Great Barrier Reef off the east coast of Australia, along which he sailed until he found a channel which allowed the vessel to pass through and head north. By this time, the men were existing only on rainwater, seabirds, and a spoonful of rum a day.

Bligh had some familiarity with these waters from his voyage with Captain Cook, but now was navigating without charts, using only a quadrant and a pocket watch. He sailed through the treacherous waters of Endeavour (now Torres) Strait, between Australia and New Guinea, and across another 1750 kilometres (1087 miles) of open sea to Timor in the Dutch East Indies. They arrived there on 14 June 1789, having been at sea for forty-eight days. All the men (except the sailor killed on Tofua) were alive, although, as Bligh described it in his log, 'their limbs [were] full of sores and their bodies nothing but skin and Bones habitated in rags.'

Bligh made his way to England, arriving there in March 1790, where he set out to bring justice to the mutineers.

Bligh apparently thought nothing of his intemperate remarks, and the two men continued to dine together each evening as they sailed on. But the insults seemed to drive Christian into a state bordering on nervous breakdown. Twenty-four years old, Christian was strong, handsome and popular with the crew, but high-strung and brooding as well. He told one shipmate that he was going to tie a lead weight around his neck and jump overboard. To another he confided that he was going to build a raft, slip off the ship and go back to Tahiti.

Both improbable schemes. But what Christian did do, with the help of other sailors enraged by Bligh's outbursts, was break into the arms chest, seizing muskets and cutlasses, and sneak into the captain's cabin late on the night of 28 April 1789. The startled Bligh was dragged out of bed in his nightshirt, his hands tied behind his back, and brought on deck. There Christian told the assembled crew that anyone who wanted to could join Bligh in an open boat. Eighteen men decided to go with him. Four others were forced to remain with the mutineers for lack of space in the boat.

Just before Christian set him adrift (see **Bligh's Incredible Voyage**, opposite), Bligh remonstrated with him: 'I have a wife and four children in England and you have danced my children upon your knee!'

And Christian replied: 'It is too late, Captain Bligh. I have been forced through hell these past three weeks.'

And so the *Bounty* sailed off, with the mutineers yelling 'Huzzah for Otaheite!' and throwing the carefully cultivated breadfruit plants into the ocean.

The Search for Pitcairn

Christian, elected captain by the twenty-four men left aboard, turned the *Bounty* to the east and headed back in the direction from whence they had come. While Tahiti was an undeniably attractive destination, it would be the first place British men-of-war would look for the mutineers, so Christian decided that they should settle on the island of Tubuai, some 650 kilometres (404 miles) to the south. But Tubuai was inhabited by hostile natives with whom the mutineers were forced to fight two pitched battles. After several weeks it was obvious they could never live there in peace.

Most of the crew wanted to return to Tahiti, but Fletcher and eight others desired a new island to live on. A deal was worked out whereby most of the mutineers (and the men loyal to Bligh) would be taken back to Tahiti, given guns and supplies and left on the beach. It was late September 1789. Fletcher Christian shouted down to the longboats that took the men ashore that he would stay for a few more days.

But in the middle of the night, the *Bounty* weighed anchor and set sail. Many of the women who had come on board during the day protested violently when they realised what was happening—some dived overboard; six others, mainly older women, were put off at a nearby island. The rest disappeared with the *Bounty*.

The British man-of-war *Pandora* was sent in 1791 to capture the mutineers on Tahiti and search for the *Bounty*. After three fruitless months the *Pandora* ran aground and was wrecked, losing four of the fourteen mutineers found on Tahiti and thirty-one of her crew. The eighty-nine surviving crew and ten mutineers, like Bligh, eventually reached Timor in the ship's four small boats. For years people in England wondered what had happened to Fletcher Christian and the other mutineers, but gradually interest waned and it was assumed the *Bounty* had been lost at sea.

But Fletcher Christian got lucky. Searching Bligh's books for an island to put in at, he found mention of Pitcairn, spotted in 1767 by an English ship and named after the 15-year-old lookout who made the sighting. No one had sighted Pitcairn since, leading Christian to surmise that its position had been incorrectly charted. And he was right—Pitcairn Island was over 300 kilometres (186½ miles) from where it was marked on Admiralty charts.

Pitcairn would be the perfect haven. Or so the mutineers decided.

First Days on Pitcairn

Deciding it was safe to land, Christian slipped the *Bounty* into the bay during a rare respite from the high seas that usually batter the island. The crew made haste to offload as many supplies as possible, and the animals—they had pigs, goats and chickens on board, and dogs and cats—and stripped the boat of anything they could possibly find useful. Climbing the face of the steep cliff that bore down on the beach, they found a level plateau, perfect for building houses.

The next problem was what to do with the *Bounty*. Not only could it be sighted from the ocean (the mutineers were in such fear of discovery that they soon killed the dogs, in case their barking might carry out to sea and be heard) but it could be used to escape if any of the group became dissatisfied with their new existence. According to the account of Jenny, one of the Tahitian women, Christian wanted to keep the vessel, but Matthew Quintal, another mutineer, did not. Matthew Quintal and a few others boarded the *Bounty* and set it on fire.

Not only is this an early sign of dissension arising, but Christian's desire to keep the *Bounty* is interesting. One senses that the impulsive young man who had radically changed his life perhaps hoped there was a way to undo it. But now there was no going back.

In those first days, Pitcairn's new inhabitants wandered the rough interior. They found statues like those on Easter Island, although much smaller, and very old stone tools, signs that the island was once inhabited. (Archaeologists think Pitcairn was home to a Polynesian group for perhaps three or four hundred years, as late as the fifteenth century. Possibly it was abandoned when the population grew too large for the island's resources to support.) One has to be a nimble as a goat on Pitcairn, which has a razorback ridge along its west side, and steep slopes everywhere.

The new islanders spent their first year building huts of wood and sailcloth on the plateau above what would be called Bounty Bay, clearing the brush and trees—although they left some as a screen between them and the ocean—and planting melons, yams, breadfruit and sweet potatoes; they fished, made salt, collected bird's eggs.

It might have been an idyllic existence had the Tahitians and the mutineers shared common goals. But they were soon to be divided against each other, with violent results.

The First Murders

Much of what the world finally learned of the fate of the mutineers on Pitcairn came from John Adams, the last survivor, whose veracity is suspect. But Trevor Lummis' masterly book, *Life and Death in Eden*, published in 1997, reconstructs the hair-raising tale of the next few years, using both Adams' account and Tahitian sources. Essentially, the island was consumed in a violence that was racial and sexual in origin. In the end it was simply survival of the fittest—not evolution but devolution, in its rawest form.

When they arrived, the sailors each asserted what they felt was the prerogative of European 'superiority' by taking a Tahitian woman as wife, leaving only two with the six Tahitian men. But when mutineer John Williams' wife died of disease, he began to complain it wasn't fair that he have no woman at all. His complaints were so intemperate that his compatriots took the precaution of destroying their small boats lest he attempt to escape back to Tahiti.

But then Adams' wife Paurai died in a fall from a cliff while collecting birds' eggs and he, too, felt he should have a replacement wife. Adams is an interesting character. One hundred and 60 centimetres (5 feet, 3 inches) tall, severely pockmarked by smallpox, he had signed on under the name Alexander Smith, perhaps hiding a criminal past. However, he was the ultimate survivor. Although he was later to gloss over it, he took one of the women still with the Tahitian men, and John Williams, emboldened, took the other.

The Tahitian men's reaction, not surprisingly, was to attempt to murder the white men, but Fletcher Christian was warned of their plot by Prudence, John Adams' new wife, and he confronted them, forcing two to flee into the woods. The mutineers clamped the other Tahitians in irons, deciding they must be part of the plot. This they denied, but the Englishmen would only let them go if they hunted down the fugitives and killed them as proof of their loyalty. Finding the men hiding in the forest, they lured them by pretending friendship, and murdered them in cold blood.

Hands and Heads

All was relatively peaceful for the next few years. The community grew, babies were born, and sailcloth huts turned into more substantial dwellings. But, as Lummis writes, 'the four remaining Tahitian men had been brought to the point of virtual slavery' by the mutineers, and in 1793 they rebelled, violently. It is a sign of how contemptuous the Englishmen were of the Tahitians' ability to fight that they allowed them to carry guns for hunting birds. The revolt took place in broad daylight. One can picture the sun pouring down, the ocean pounding against the island, toddlers crawling among the women in their huts. John Williams was tilling his garden and the Tahitians simply walked up and shot him. Fletcher Christian was next. He, too, was working the soil; the Tahitians shot him in the back, then hit him over the head with an axe.

Christian's dying moans were heard by John Mills and William McKoy. Mills was the next to die, but McKoy managed to get away, meeting up with Matthew Quintal, with whom he fled into the woods. Then Isaac Martin and William Brown were shot and killed. John Adams heard the commotion and also fled to the woods, leaving behind only Edward Young, who was apparently protected by the women.

There were now four Tahitian men and four European men. John Adams attempted to sneak into the settlement that night and was shot and severely wounded but, remarkably, the Tahitians nursed him back to health. To make matters even more complex, the Tahitian called Menalee was so disliked by the others that he went off to live in the woods with McKoy and Quintal. As time passed, the women whose English husbands had been killed apparently made the pragmatic decision that the only way to bring peace to Pitcairn was to eliminate the remaining Tahitian men. Meeting with McKoy and Quintal, they convinced them to kill Menalee, and then helped Edward Young murder the others.

All this slaughter took about a month. Adams, recovered and now taking the role previously held by Christian, met with Quintal and McKoy, who agreed to come in from the woods and make peace—but only after seeing the heads and hands of the slaughtered Tahitians.

Fletcher Christian's Escape?

Just as Captain Bligh's reputation in history as a tyrant is misleading, so is Fletcher Christian's legacy as a romantic hero. Christian has been portrayed in numerous Hollywood movies by such leading men as Errol Flynn, Clark Gable, Marlon Brando and Mel Gibson as a man of action who—although perhaps overwrought at times—was protecting his men from the actions of a petty dictator.

People were so fascinated by the character of Fletcher Christian that for over 200 years rumours have persisted that he did not, in fact, die on Pitcairn Island. The stories began to circulate as early as 1809—just after Pitcairn was rediscovered by the whaler *Topaz*—and they came from Peter Heywood, a young mutineer left on Tahiti who had been granted a royal pardon, and later rose through the ranks to become a British naval captain. Heywood swore that one day in 1808 or 1809, as he was walking the streets of a town in England's Lake District, he found himself behind someone who resembled Fletcher Christian; he chased this man, who eluded him.

Is this possible? Just—but unlikely. In her book *The Bounty*, Caroline Alexander reveals that the logs of whalers in the late eighteenth and early nineteenth centuries show how close many of them came to Pitcairn, and suggests that it is possible that one of them might have taken a disaffected Christian off the island and given him passage elsewhere. She also notes that none of the money known to have been aboard the *Bounty* has ever been recovered, although it seems unlikely that the mutineers, who salvaged all they could from the vessel, would let it simply sink into the ocean.

The likelihood of such an escape is very low. Heywood was haunted by the mutiny all his life, and no doubt saw his old comrade in a stranger's face. One effect of the rumours, however, is that they are said to have inspired Samuel Taylor Coleridge's great poem, *The Rime of the Ancient Mariner*.

The Last Murder

In the four years since the mutineers and the Tahitians had landed on Pitcairn, violence had wracked the island—of the twenty-seven people who had come ashore, six Tahitians and five Englishmen had been murdered. Peace had apparently been made—but Pitcairn was not a place where peace remained for long. Despite siding with the four white men, the women—now in the majority—were tired of the men's interference with Tahitian customs, which included keeping the skulls of dead loved ones in their huts (Fletcher Christian's skull, kept by his wife, was apparently one of these). Within a year, they were plotting to kill the men while they slept. There is also evidence that some of the women tried to construct a raft to escape.

Things gradually settled down, with some of the women simply deciding to live apart. There was a scare of a different sort in 1795 when the islanders awoke to find a ship in Bounty Bay—it had apparently moored there very early in the morning. They hid until it sailed away, and later found a jack-knife on the rocks by the water—a sign that someone had come ashore. They waited anxiously for a year for other vessels to come by, but none did.

Six or seven more children were born. William McKoy, who had formerly worked in a Scottish distillery, learned to make rum from the roots of an island plant, and soon spent much of his time inebriated. In 1798, he committed suicide by tying a rock around his neck and leaping to his death from a precipice into the ocean. A year later, Matthew Quintal's wife, Sarah—whose ear a drunken Quintal had bitten off in a rage—fell while hunting for eggs high along a ridge and died.

Quintal—also drunk much of the time—now tried to claim a new wife by making approaches to both John Adams' and Edward Young's wives. The two men confronted him and—in front of a five-year-old girl who lived to be ninety and remembered the scene all her life—chopped him to death with hatchets. This left Adams and Young the only men alive; two years later, Young was to die of what was probably asthma, leaving Adams as the patriarch of an island of women and children.

'At Present a Worthy Man'

American whalers were plying their trade with increasing frequency in the Pacific and in September 1808, the *Topaz*, out of Massachusetts, rounding Cape Horn and heading west, spotted an island where no island should be. Her captain, Mayhew Folger, was fascinated, and anchored offshore. In the morning he was startled to see an outrigger canoe launched into the rough surf, carrying two strapping, handsome young men in native clothing. They were so dark, Folger said, that they appeared Spanish, yet once on board they were found to speak English. When the two youths began talking of Captain Bligh and the *Bounty*, Folger put two and two together—this was where the *Bounty* mutineers had gone. Eighteen years on, their hiding place had been discovered.

Landing on Pitcairn, Folger was astonished. He found a neat village full of handsome children who could read, write and sing hymns, all apparently taught to them by John Adams who, in a complete turnaround from his previous violent ways, had banned alcohol and set about creating a model society. Adams, although nervous that his whereabouts were now known, was happy to hear that Captain Bligh and his crew had made it safely across the ocean so many years ago.

Returning to his ship, Folger wrote in his log: 'Whatever may have been the errors or crimes of [Adams], in times back, he is at present a worthy man.' Folger was not privy to the full and bloody history of Pitcairn, of course, for Adams had given him a highly sanitised version of events, but as it turned out most of the world would assume the same forgiving attitude. Adams was to live until 1829, and instead of clapping him in chains, the British government offered him amnesty and accepted the island as a British possession.

By 1856, with the population nearing 200, Pitcairn resources were unable to support such numbers, and the islanders were taken to Norfolk Island, some 4300 kilometres (2672 miles) to the west. But Pitcairn exercises a deep hold on those who live there. Unable to stay away, seventeen islanders returned in 1864, to take up residence among ghosts.

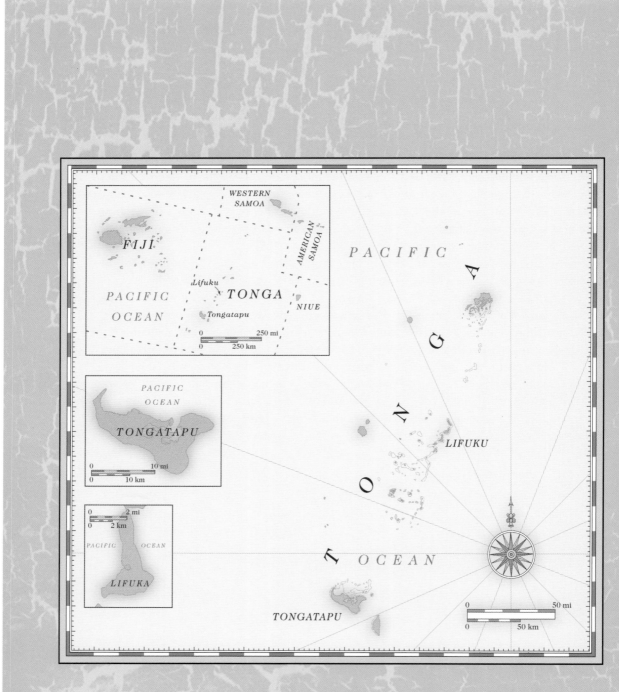

William Mariner, 1806–1810
Boy Chief of Tonga

On 20 October 1853, a 62-year-old man stood on the bank of the Grand Surrey Canal, in south London, staring at his reflection in its greyish waters. He was the very picture of a successful English businessman, a stockbroker, long-married, the father of eleven children, but a business scandal had stained his reputation, and he was now contemplating ending his life.

The balding, portly gentleman's name was William Mariner. It is tempting to wonder, as he stared fixedly at the sluggish flow, whether he thought of other, brighter and clearer waters, whether, in his imagination, the waft of island breezes replaced the smell of sewage in the notoriously dirty canal, and even if, for just a moment, his reflection brightened into that of his 16-year-old self, prince of a savage nation, leading war canoes into pitched battle.

Probably not. That's a fanciful ending, not a real one. Although … there is much in William Mariner's life that reads like the most incredible adventure novel.

Yet it's all true.

What's in a Name?

No self-respecting novelist would dare name a seafaring family Mariner, yet that was the name of this illustrious London clan. Magnus Mariner, William Mariner's father, was a wealthy shipbuilder who had skippered a vessel during the War of American Independence. William, born in 1791, grew up around London's docks seeing sailors embarking for foreign lands, especially the Pacific, which Captain Cook had opened up to the British during three epic voyages of exploration before being killed and eaten by Hawaiian islanders in 1779. By the age of thirteen, William had decided that he wanted to follow the family tradition of going to sea; while he was supported in this by his father, his mother thought he was too young and insisted that he be engaged as an apprentice to a London solicitor.

Fate, as in any good adventure, intervened in the person of one Captain Duck (another name no self-respecting novelist would touch). Duck had formerly been under Magnus Mariner's command and had stopped by the Mariner house to bid farewell, as he was taking his privateer, the *Port au Prince*, to plunder Spanish shipping in the Atlantic and do a spot of whaling in the Pacific. To the Mariners, *père et fils*, the opportunity seemed too good to pass up and so, overcoming the objections of his mother, William signed aboard the *Port au Prince* as cabin boy. The ship left England on 12 February 1805.

King Kamehameha I, King of Hawaii, standing in a Western suit, surrounded by his subjects wearing traditional dress.

The Incompetent Captain

The *Port au Prince* was a large ship—500 tons, three-masted, with an extra crew contingent whose job it would be to sail any Spanish prizes pounded into submission by her formidable array of thirty cannon. The privateer headed down the east coat of South America, where she found no targets, and rounded the Horn into the Pacific. Here tempting Spanish vessels began to appear, and Mariner heard the sounds of cannon fired in anger and helped board captured prizes and take them in tow. The *Port au Prince* also attacked the Peruvian coastal town of Ilo, the crew looting its church of silver crucifixes and candlesticks before reducing the city to ashes.

When the *Port au Prince* reached the Equator, Duck faced a conundrum. His charter was clear: he was to stop taking Spanish shipping and start whaling, but there were few whales about, and plenty of vulnerable Spaniards. He and the crew wanted to go on attacking Spanish vessels, but the whaling master, James Brown, had been given authority in this matter by the ship's backers. And Brown insisted they start whaling. Very soon afterward, Duck died from a bout of malaria.

It was August 1806 when the ship came under the command of a man one historian has called 'as incompetent a captain as ever to sail the Pacific'. Brown was a poor leader, ruthless to his men, and an abysmal navigator. As the *Port au Prince* headed deeper into the Pacific on a fruitless whale hunt, it began to leak badly, and Brown sailed to Hawaii for repairs. As the ship entered Honolulu harbour, young Mariner was enthralled by the dreamlike natural beauty of the island. Unfortunately, the king of Hawaii, Kamehameha I, would not let the English sailors land, as sailors from an American ship carrying the measles virus had recently spread the disease throughout Hawaii, killing hundreds.

The king himself was willing to make numerous visits to the ship, however, and young Mariner—blond-haired, quick-witted and eager to please—caught his eye. He offered the youth the chance to leave the ship and live in his palace as his personal secretary. The offer was tempting—with Captain Duck gone, Mariner owed no allegiance to the new skipper—but he turned it down, something he soon had reason to regret.

The Friendly Islands

After taking on provisions and hiring a number of Hawaiians to help crew the vessel, Brown left Honolulu on 26 October, making for Tahiti, where he would do more extensive repairs to the *Port au Prince*. His navigation was so poor that he overshot that island completely; when he realised this, he decided to head for the Tongan archipelago. These 170 islands east of Fiji and south of Samoa (Tonga means 'south') had been inhabited for perhaps 3000 years when

'Contracting the Fiji Habit'

Cannibalism was a relatively recent innovation on the Tongan islands when Mariner arrived. Although occasional ritual human (often infant) sacrifice and cannibalism took place, regularly eating their enemies was something the Tongans learned from their near neighbours, the Fijians—Mariner called it 'contracting the Fiji habit'—who were famous for their feasts of 'long pig'. (There is some question as to exactly how much cannibalism went on in Fiji—dramatic missionary accounts of kings eating hundreds of people a year are

not to be credited.) The practice certainly was exported to Tonga sometime in the late eighteenth century and took hold during the years of famine brought on by the civil wars that raged through the islands.

Mariner was aghast when Finau's warriors ate their dead enemies on Tongatabu and raved about the best part of the meal, supposedly the hands (smoked fingers were carried around for munching on the go, like beef jerky sticks). He found the practice unsavoury in the extreme and did not partake, and was glad to know that the Tongans believed that eating white people caused food poisoning—apparently, several visiting Englishman had earlier been killed and eaten, and those who ate them had become ill.

Articles reporting the eating of white men and women, especially missionaries, continued to be written as late as 1910, when the *New York Times* reported that the Reverends Horatio Hopkins and Hector McPherson had both found their way into a Tongan stewpot. But since these missionaries were supposedly carried on litters to the 'top of a volcano', where savage dancing took place before the poor Christians were dispatched, there may be reason to call this report into question.

they were discovered by Captain Cook in the mid-1770s. The Tongas were the very picture of tropical paradise, with palm trees, gleaming lagoons and glittering beaches. Cook was amazed at how cultivated the land was. 'I thought I was transported into one of the most fertile plains in Europe,' he wrote of the island of Lifuka. Agriculture was king, with plantations divided into land parcels by reed enclosures, and producing plantains and yams in orderly rows.

The people seemed so welcoming that Cook named their land the Friendly Islands. Unfortunately for the many sailors who stopped there subsequently, this was far from the truth. Cook was feted for three days when he visited Lifuka. What he did not know was that the chiefs were planning on killing him and his entire crew and seizing their ship.

The plot never came off, for reasons unknown, but the Tongas might better have been named the Deadly Islands, as those aboard the *Port au Prince* were to discover when she anchored in the harbour of Lifuka on Saturday 29 November 1806. At first things seemed quite amicable. What Mariner called 'a number of Indian chiefs' came aboard that evening, bringing with them a gift of yams and a Hawaiian native who spoke a little English. This man made a point of telling the crew that the Tongans were friendly, but the Hawaiians crewing on the vessel knew better. They nervously told Captain Brown that the Tongans had hostile intentions.

Brown dismissed this and the next day ordered his men to set about making repairs, but here he nearly faced a mutiny. The crew was not about to start careening the vessel on a Sunday in a tropical paradise. One sailor pulled a knife and challenged Brown to stop him from going ashore. Fifteen others followed, leaving the ship shorthanded and Brown in an even shorter temper, and seemingly oblivious to the fact that more and more Tongan warriors, armed with spears and clubs, were wandering around his vessel.

William Mariner went to Brown below decks, where he was meeting with two chieftains, to warn him of this. Brown was at first disinclined to pay attention but finally, with some impatience, came on deck. Mariner later recorded that the two chiefs with the captain 'turned pale'—they thought their plot to capture the ship had been revealed. All Brown did was ask the Tongans to leave, taking their arms with them—and then order the crew to stow all muskets and pikes below as a token of good faith.

The Fatal Morning

Then came, as Mariner was to write, 'the fatal morning' of 1 December 1806. Around eight o'clock Tongans began to climb aboard, chatting in a friendly fashion but all armed to the teeth. By 10 a.m., Mariner estimated there were nearly 300 warriors swarming over the vessel. At this point, the Hawaiian who lived with the Tongans invited Brown on a sightseeing tour of the island, which invitation the clueless Brown, unarmed, accepted willingly. A short time later Mariner, who was writing up the log in the hold, moved into to a shaft of light beaming down through the open hatch to better make repairs on the pen he was using. He happened to look up to see the first mate standing on a cannon, waving his arms and shouting that no more Tongans should come on board.

At that moment there came a loud collective shout from the Tongans. One of them knocked the mate off the cannon and clubbed him senseless. Mariner turned and raced through the ship, heading for the armoury. A warrior grabbed at him, but he dodged away. Further down the twisted passageways, he ran into the cooper, cowering in terror, and together they made for the powder magazine. Hearing bloodcurdling screams and horrible dull *thumps* from above, they were certain a massacre was occurring. It would be only a matter of time until their turn came.

So they decided on a desperate measure. They would blow up the powder magazine and 'sacrifice themselves and their enemies together'. Since they lacked flint to create a spark, Mariner ran to the armoury, only to find the pikes Brown had ordered stowed piled on top of the arms chest. The noise from the deck had stopped, replaced by an ominous silence. Afraid that if he moved the pikes the clatter would be heard, Mariner returned to the magazine and convinced the cooper that their only recourse was surrender—anything, even dying, was better than waiting to be discovered.

'To Thrill the Stoutest Heart'

Stealing down the passageway with Mariner in the lead, they came to the captain's cabin, which a group of warriors was tearing apart. Mariner raised his arms in surrender. To the surprise of both, they were not immediately killed, but taken on deck where they saw a sight, as Mariner later told it, horrible enough 'to thrill the stoutest heart':

> A short squat naked figure, about fifty years of age, was seated with a seaman's jacket soaked in blood thrown over one shoulder, on the other rested his ironwood club, spattered with blood and brains ... the frightfulness of his appearance was increased by a constant blinking with one eye and a horrible convulsive motion on one side of his mouth.

On the foredeck lay the corpses of twenty-two members of the *Port au Prince*'s crew, 'perfectly naked and arranged side by side in regular order'. They were so battered about the face and head that Mariner could recognise only a few of the men.

Tongan canoes with outriggers and lateen sails.

In a state of shock, Mariner allowed himself to be placed in a dugout canoe and taken ashore (the cooper was kept on board). On the beach he was stripped of his clothes and forced to walk along the shore. Coming upon the bodies of Brown and the three crewmen who had accompanied him, one of the Tongans pointed to the captain and asked Mariner if they had 'done right' by killing him, since he was a bad man. When Mariner did not reply, the warrior raised his club threateningly, but others restrained him. Naked and broiling in the sun, Mariner was marched for hours to a village in the northern part of Lifuka. Numerous Tongans came up to feel his white skin blistering in the sun (he later found out they were comparing him to a hog whose bristles had been scraped off). Some spat on him and threw coconut shells at him, although a woman gave him an apron of leaves with which to cover himself.

The Art of Tatatau

With his usual careful habits of observation, William Mariner was able to give a very detailed account of tatatau—the art of tattooing— in Tonga:

The instrument used for the purpose of this operation somewhat resembles a small-tooth comb. They have several kinds, of different degrees of breadth, from six up to fifty or sixty teeth. They are made of

the bone of the wing of the wild duck. Being dipped in a mixture of soot and water, the outline of the tatau [tatatau] is first marked off before the operator begins the puncture, which he afterwards does by striking in the points of the instrument with a small stick cut out of a green branch of the cocoa-nut tree. When the skin begins to bleed, the operator occasionally washes off the blood with cold water, and repeatedly goes over the same places. As this is a very painful process, but a small portion of it is done at once, giving the recipient intervals of three or four days rest, so that it is frequently two months before it is completely finished. The parts tattooed are from within two inches of the knees up to about three inches above the umbilicus. There are certain patterns or forms of the tatau, known by distinct names, and the individual may choose which he likes … It is considered very unmanly not to be tattooed, so that there is nobody but what submits to it as soon as he is grown up … The men would think it very indecent not to be tattooed, because though in battle they wear nothing but the mahi [traditional loincloth], they appear by this means to be dressed, without having the incumbrance of clothing.

The beauty and neatness of the tatau far exceeded my expectations.

Finau, the Great Chief

Several hours after reaching the village, a man came to take Mariner to the hut of the high chief, Finau Ulukalala II, who had planned the assault on the ship. In his mid-fifties, Finau was over 183 centimetres (6 feet) tall, with curly black hair, bladed cheekbones, and a pugnacious jaw, but he treated Mariner kindly, putting his nose to the youth's forehead in a sign of greeting between equals. Seeing that Mariner was dirty, he ordered a woman attendant to bathe him in a pool and anoint his sunburned skin with soothing oils.

Finau, seeing the 15-year-old aboard the *Port au Prince* while first meeting with Captain Brown, and thinking he was the captain's son, had been immediately taken with him, just as King Kamehameha had. Mariner was certainly brave and resourceful, but there must have been something else about him that made these men instantly want to mentor him. Mariner was young, possessed of a novel blondness, innocent yet ready for experience; he was a blank slate upon which Finau could inscribe himself. As well, Finau had apparently lost a son who had been around Mariner's age.

Now Mariner was allowed to lie down on a mat at the far end of the king's hut, where he collapsed into exhausted sleep, later to be awakened by a woman bearing yams and pork. Thinking the pork was human flesh, Mariner ate only the yams. The next morning, on leaving the hut, he was extremely happy to meet other crew members who had survived the massacre—mainly men who had been ashore at the time. In all, twenty-six had died, but an equal number had survived. To Mariner's surprise, the Tongans, who had shaved their heads as a sign of mourning, buried the dead sailors, tossing Spanish silver coins— booty from the *Port au Prince*'s privateering—over the mounded earth.

Over the next several days, Mariner and the other sailors were forced to strip the *Port au Prince* of everything valuable, particularly iron, much prized in the islands, and the ship's cannon, for which Finau had a special plan and which may have been his chief goal in attacking the vessel. This task completed, all but Mariner were taken off to different atolls to work as slaves.

Mariner's fate was to be quite different.

The Education of a Prince

In the beginning, Mariner lived in the royal compound; Finau did not want him walking around the island because, until he was accepted into the community, it was possible someone might club him to death as an outsider. He and Finau began to teach each other things. Mariner showed the king and his attendants how a watch worked, which made them exclaim: 'It is an animal or a plant?' When he drew a rough diagram in the sand to describe the passing of hours in relation to the sun and showed them how it compared to the watch, Finau let out a shout of delight. 'What an ingenious people,' he exclaimed.

But he liked other European customs less. Mariner was uncertain, watching the Tongans eat, whether he should join them, since an invitation was never issued. Finau told him that in Tonga, anyone could go 'into any house where eating was going forward, sit himself down without invitation, and partake of the company'. He found the English habit of keeping food to oneself selfish in the extreme. Mariner, for his part, marvelled at the elaborate tattoos of the Tongans, which extended from navel to shin (see **The Art of Tatatau**, page 112). He accompanied the king on his hunting exhibitions, learning the art of shooting bows and arrows.

Most importantly, Finau entrusted Mariner's care to Mafi Habi, one of his wives, who would act as his mother. Mafi Habi taught Mariner everything—the customs, taboos, dress and language of her people. Under her tutelage he began to wear his hair tied in a topknot and to dress in the *vala*, the tight-fitting skirt of tapa cloth. A few months later, Finau formerly adopted Mariner and made him a chief, naming him Iron Axe, after his dead son.

This was an incredible act of generosity, but Finau wanted something in return. And one day he sat Mariner down and explained what it was.

War

Finau told his adopted son that only a few years before, the islands had been ruled by the tyrannical chief Tuku-aho, who forced the other chieftains to pay tribute. The relatively peaceful agrarian society that Cook had seen in the 1770s was a result of this dictatorship, but gradually the tribute-payers, including Finau, grew restless. A number had visited the Fiji Islands and come back favouring the brutal customs of Fiji, which included cannibalism and ritual murder (see **Contracting the Fiji Habit**, page 108). In 1799 Finau and a group of chieftains assassinated Tuku-aho. Soon, however, these same chieftains began attacking each other, throwing the Tongan archipelago into civil war. Farms lay fallow as people huddled in palisaded villages, hiding from cannibalistic war parties.

'What madness!' Finau exclaimed to Mariner, bemoaning what had happened. But now he was ready to bring stability back to the islands. He had thirty cannon and a large amount of powder and ball, the only chief with such weaponry. He wanted Mariner to help him mount an attack on his most powerful enemies, wiping them out once and for all so he could bring order to Tonga. Mariner had little option but to comply. In the spring of 1807, he watched as Finau's warriors stockpiled huge quantities of stones, spears, and bows and arrows. Mariner instructed them to mount the cannon on wooden carriages, which could be placed on specially reinforced outrigger canoes, and requested, and was given, many of the enslaved sailors from the *Port au Prince*. These men, along with a group of warriors, he drilled in musketry.

By the beginning of summer, all was in readiness for an attack against Tongatapu, the largest island in the Tonga chain, some 110 kilometres (68 miles) distant. Finau's army numbered up to 5000 men and 200 war canoes. Wearing only their loincloths—the fighting man's dress—yet appearing to be clothed from the waist down because of their elaborate tattoos, the warriors blackened their faces to show that they brought death and destruction.

What must Mariner have thought as he looked back over the rolling, shining Pacific at this strange and awesome fleet? Spears flashing in the sun, chants echoing across the sea, lateen sails bent to the wind, carrying thirty cannon, it must have seemed an irresistible and powerful force, yet dreamlike, as if any moment the 16-year-old from London might waken in his bed beneath the eaves of his father's house.

The Bloody Battle

There was nothing dreamlike about what followed, however. The invasion force landed on Tongatapu, whose inhabitants had set themselves up in a huge fortified village, surrounded by a moat, with palisades 3 metres (over 3 yards) high concealing platforms from which their enemy could hurl destruction on the invaders.

A conch shell sounded and Finau's warriors charged. They were met by several hundred defenders, who raced out to do battle shouting war cries, but Mariner had trained the warriors to form into a British battle square from which they fired volley after volley at their attackers, driving them back. Then Mariner set up the cannon and ordered his British gunners to bombard the fort. Shot after shot penetrated the palisades, leaving round holes which disappointed Finau until Mariner explained that the cannonballs were causing great destruction behind the walls.

Finally, Finau ordered his men to attack the fort. They raced to the shattered palisades, tossing torches to set them ablaze, and after a couple of hours were able to break through. Inside they found wholesale destruction, for the cannonballs had torn off heads and limbs, which lay everywhere on the ground. Mariner was aghast at the brutality displayed by the warriors, who ran into every hut and dragged out women and children, shattering their skulls with wooden clubs. When the fighting ended, almost 400 people lay dead and Finau was undisputed chief of the island.

That night, fifteen captives were clubbed to death, then roasted in clay ovens for the triumphal feast. Mariner was so horrified by this that he went hungry for three days until canoes bearing supplies came from Lifuka. Nonetheless, he counselled Finau to continue the war, to strike against his other enemies and destroy them in one continuous campaign. This is, no doubt, what a European commander would do. But not Finau. Saying that he had to consult with his priests, he brought his bloodstained invasion fleet home.

'I am an Englishman'

Over the next three years, with Mariner as his chief lieutenant, Finau realised his dream of conquering most of Tonga. Mariner was given large landholdings on the island of Vava'u and literally held the power of life and death over the thirteen men and woman who were his servants. He became friendly with Finau's son and heir, Moenga, and like two Renaissance princes they hunted together, wrestled and womanised.

Unfortunately, like the despotic ruler he had overthrown, Finau became corrupted by his absolute power. His six-year-old daughter died of an illness and it is possible he went mad—at one point, he insisted that 1500 women fight each other in a bloody combat that left scores dead. He began to argue with the religious ceremonies presided over by the all-powerful priests; they in turn told the people that he was cursed, which caused Finau to murder a high priest. Perhaps the gods did begin to look with disfavour upon this once glorious chief; he died a few days after the priest, of a strange fever.

Moenga took over, and his rule was benevolent. He ordered a return to farming, and relaxed some of the harsher strictures Finau had put in place in his later years. Mariner, still Moenga's boon companion, could roam anywhere he liked in the archipelago. And, one evening toward the end of 1810, he was travelling back to Vava'u from another island when he spotted a ship silhouetted against the sinking sun. Making a split-second decision, he ordered his paddlers to take him to the vessel, but they cowered and refused—Moenga, they said, would kill them if he knew they helped Iron Axe escape. But Mariner—acting now like a true Tongan prince—said: 'Do I not have the power of life and death over you?'

He took his musket, its barrel by now worn to a sharp point, and jabbed one of the men in the stomach, seriously injuring him. Then he ordered the other two to paddle—hard. As the sun sank lower on the horizon, the canoe slammed up and down through the waves and eventually reached the ship. Mariner grabbed a rope and began to climb aboard as a sentry aimed a musket at him.

'I am an Englishman, formerly of the ship *Port au Prince*,' shouted Mariner. 'Let me come aboard.'

The ship was the American merchantman *Favorite*, bound for China. Its captain was astonished to find that the person they had mistaken for a young Tongan warrior was English. The *Favorite* anchored off Vava'u for three days while Mariner sent messages to the other sailors scattered around the islands; half a dozen of them managed to make their way to the *Favorite*. Mariner would not go ashore, but Moenga visited the ship, imploring him to reconsider. Mariner would not. Moenga loved him so much that offered to go to England too, and Mariner had to convince him that this was an extremely bad idea.

'I Cannot Wipe Away the Stain'

Following a circuitous route, Mariner made it back to England in June 1811, six years after he had left. To his horror, a few moments after he set foot on British soil he was captured by a pressgang seeking manpower for the navy. It was fully a week before Magnus was able to bail him out using his connections.

William Mariner was now almost twenty-one years old. With enough adventure under his belt to last a lifetime, he stayed put. He married Margaret Roberts, the daughter of a banker, fathered nearly a score of offspring, and became a successful stockbroker. He did not speak much about his life on Tonga, although he did collaborate on a book about his experiences with Dr John Martin, who had a mainly anthropological interest in the Pacific islands. But even Mariner's children knew little about his time as a princely captive.

In 1841, the reputation of Mariner and his business partners was blemished by a financial scandal. Although Mariner's name was cleared, an investigation found that he had not been sufficiently cautious in his financial oversight of the firm. Mariner took this hard. 'I cannot wipe away the stain the Commission has thrown upon me,' he wrote. He was never the same afterward, and the business began to fall apart. He took to wandering along the banks of the Grand Surrey Canal, which brings us to that autumn day in 1853, when he brooded upon his reflection in its discoloured waters. His ending would not be fanciful or adventurous; there would be no narrow escape into bright, if savage, sunlight. William Mariner leaped into the canal and drowned. A few days later, his body was found floating near where the Grand Surrey entered the Thames.

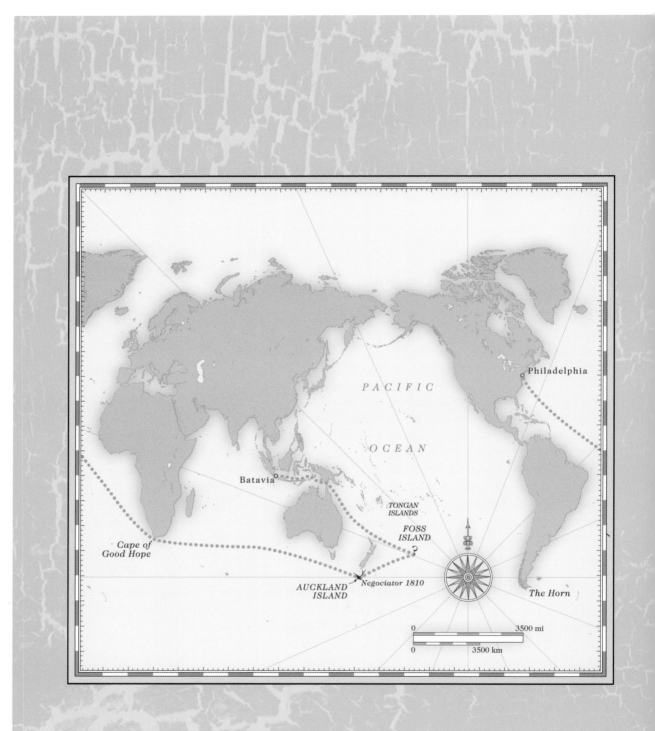

Daniel Foss, 1810–1815
'A Horrible Confinement'

Being a solitary castaway is always a bleakly existential experience—your entire being is focused merely on survival, your life and death plain before your eyes like a newspaper you pick up and read each morning. The headlines trumpet: WILL YOU GO STARK RAVING MAD TODAY? And in smaller type: *Castaway reaches second year living on edge of despair; no help in sight.*

Things are bad enough when one has relatively ample supplies of food and water, as was the case for Alexander Selkirk (see page 79) and some of our other maroons. But when you're stuck on what is literally a tiny rock in an expanse of wild ocean, with nothing but rain to drink and seal to eat, with your clothes literally shredding on your back, the question becomes not how you stay alive but, really, why.

A Native of Elkton, Maryland

The most famous story of a castaway reduced to such an elemental circumstances is that of the American sailor Daniel Foss, who hailed from the tiny village of Elkton, Maryland, on the banks of the Elk River, which flows into Chesapeake Bay. We don't know much else about Foss beyond what he tell us in his memoir *A Journal of the Shipwreck and Sufferings of Daniel Foss, a Native of Elkton, Maryland*, which was published in 1816.

In the beginning of September 1809, Foss set sail from Philadelphia 'in the capacity of Mariner' aboard the brig *Negociator*, which was, Foss relates, 'bound for the northwest coast on a sealing voyage'. This leads one to assume the *Negociator* was intending a voyage to America's Pacific Northwest, where seals abounded, and then possibly on to China to sell or trade the sealskins. In this case, the ship would have rounded the Horn into the Pacific. But in the next breath Foss speaks of rounding the Cape of Good Hope and heading for the Friendly Islands (Tonga). There are several possibilities here— perhaps the *Negociator*'s captain, one James Nicoll, was unable to buck the gale-force winds of the stormy Horn and was forced to double the calmer waters of the Cape, as did Captain William Bligh in 1788 (see page 93). There also remains the chance that an editor had mistranscribed Foss's story, and that the Friendlies, not the Pacific Northwest, was where the ship was headed all along.

This confusion makes it hard to pinpoint the location of what happened next. By 20 October of that year—another confusing point, as the voyage south through the

Negotiating through icebergs was fraught with danger, as Foss was to discover when the *Negociator* went to the bottom after being struck by an 'island of ice'.

Atlantic should have taken at least four to six months—the *Negociator* had rounded the Cape and was on its way to the Friendlies. Captain Nicoll apparently piloted his ship too far south, into sub-Antarctic waters, for soon the *Negociator* passed 'several islands of ice, some of them nearly three miles in circuit and sixty or seventy feet in height'. Foss goes on to relate his awe of these giant icebergs: 'They exhibited a view which for a few moments was pleasing to the eye, but when we reflected on the danger, the mind was filled with horror, for were a ship to get on the weather side of one of these [icebergs] when the sea runs high she would be dashed to pieces in a moment.'

'The Preservation of Our Lives'

Unfortunately, this is exactly what happened. As the *Negociator* sailed among these stately but horrifying creations of nature, a severe snowstorm arose that covered the ship's sails and rigging with icicles. In the middle of the night, her crew blinded by the blizzard, the *Negociator* struck an iceberg, 'creating a scene of horror past description', Foss writes. The ship was sinking fast and no man could survive more than a few moments in the water in the appalling cold, so the twenty-one crew members and the captain grabbed what food and water they could and took to the ship's open boat. 'Some [of us] were without jackets, hats or shoes,' Foss relates, 'myself having on only one thin jacket and a pair of trousers.'

Five minutes after they abandoned ship, the *Negociator* went to the bottom, the shivering men watching in horror as their only home was sucked down in a whirlpool into the black and frigid deep. When dawn came, they took stock of their situation: twenty-two men, 20 kilograms (44 pounds) of beef, half a barrel of salt pork, a barrel of water and a keg of beer. 'We made such arrangements for the preservation of our lives as our miserable situation would admit of,' Foss writes, relating how each man was allotted only a mouthful of food and water a day. But the men began to die of exposure as they desperately headed in search of more temperate waters. Within nine days, there were only eight men left. Of those still alive, four 'were so severely frostbitten as to be unable to stand on their feet'. To make matters even worse, their water froze into a solid cake of ice, forcing them to chip pieces off and suck at them.

The Custom of the Sea

By mid-January the ship's boat had reached warmer latitudes, but now only three of the crew remained alive, and they had eaten their last scrap of salt pork. For five days they remained without food, vainly hoping that a ship might appear on the horizon or a flying fish leap into their boat. They cut their shoes into small pieces which, after soaking in water, 'they devoured with the keenest appetite'.

Finally, staring at each other with hollow eyes, they decided to follow a practice which sailors called 'the custom of the sea'. In direst extremity, it was considered morally permissible to draw lots to decide which surviving member of a shipwrecked or castaway group might be killed to provide food for the others (see **The Strange Case of the *Mignonette*, page 122**).

It was desperately hard for Foss and his two fellow survivors to consider this option, but they really had no choice in the matter. Foss was chosen to make the lots: 'Having cut a small piece of my jacket into three small detached pieces, one of which was marked with a brown thread, they were deposited in a hat, from which each with a trembling hand drew a piece.'

The Strange Case of the *Mignonette*

The 'custom of the sea'—drawing lots to see who would be killed and eaten in a desperate life or death situation—was considered morally acceptable by most seamen, but was fraught with problems, for very often the lottery was rigged to do away with an outsider among the survivors, or someone of a despised ethnic group.

Authorities attempted to prosecute castaways or shipwreck survivors who admitted to such murder and cannibalism, but public sympathy for these poor wretches usually kept such prosecutions from being successful. This was not so in one case in England, however. In 1883, the English yacht *Mignonette* was purchased by an Australian lawyer who

hired an English crew to sail her to Sydney—not an easy undertaking, for the ship was rather small to be going on such a lengthy voyage. Nonetheless, Captain Tom Dudley and three crewmen—Edmund Brooks, Edmund Stephens and 17-year-old Richard Parker—set sail in 1884 to make the attempt.

While still in the South Atlantic, the yacht was hit by a rogue wave and sank, leaving the men with few provisions in a leaky lifeboat. This was 5 July. They ate a turtle they managed to catch, and the few tins of turnips they had saved, but within a few weeks were drinking their own urine. Parker began to sicken, probably from drinking sea water, and on 23 July went into a coma. Captain Dudley told the others that Parker should die in order to feed them, and that it was better he be killed so they could drink his blood while it was fresh. Brooks could not agree to this, but Stephens went along with it, so Dudley jabbed a knife into the unconscious Parker's throat. However, Brooks joined the others in eating the body.

The men were rescued by a passing ship on 29 July. After they told their story, Dudley and Stephens were arrested by the British government, charged with murder, found guilty and sentenced to death. Public opinion was so outraged, however, that their sentences were commuted to six months in prison.

The man who drew the fatal lot was the ship's surgeon, whom Foss said seemed 'perfectly resigned to his fate'. He asked for a few moments to prepare himself for death, then made a short speech: 'I am a native of Norfolk, Virginia, where I have a wife and three children living. The only favour that I have to request of you is that should it please God to deliver either of you from our perilous situation and should you be so fortunate as to reach once more your native land that you would acquaint my unfortunate family with my wretched fate.'

Being a surgeon, this brave man knew just how to end his life with dispatch. Taking a knife, he made a swift incision in his left wrist, severing the arteries. As blood poured from his soon-to-be-lifeless body, Foss and his companion scrambled to lap at it. When the surgeon was dead, they cut his flesh into small slices and dried it in the sun.

The Island

This meat sustained the two survivors for a month or so, while fairly frequent rains kept them from dying of thirst. Still, Foss and his companion 'grew so feeble as to be unable to support ourselves long on our legs'. Chafed by the sea water and constant exposure to the sun, as well as suffering from malnutrition, they began to develop huge open sores.

Finally, one evening they spied, about 9 kilometres (5½ miles) distant, the sight of waves breaking. With all their might they rowed toward the spot and saw 'a small island bordered with high, craggy rocks against which the sea broke with a thunderous roar'. All that night they held their position off the island, and in the morning attempted to find some way to land. To their immense frustration they found an uninterrupted line of rocks along the beach, against which their boat was sure to be shattered. In desperation, about four o'clock that afternoon, they aimed at a rocky point and attempted to surf the vessel in, hoping they might be thrown up on land. But within 100 metres (109 yards) of their target the waves overturned the boat.

According to Foss: 'At this critical juncture I was so fortunate as to seize an oar, with which I was enabled to buoy myself up until the swell of the sea carried me within reach of a shelving rock, which I ascended before the return of another sea.' He rested there before dragging himself up the rocks to a high point above the water. 'Having at last reached the summit, I looked around for my unfortunate companion, but alas nothing was discernible but broken fragments of the boat, which had been dashed into a hundred pieces by the surf and which were now floating upon the foaming waves.'

'Barren of Everything'

Thus began Daniel Foss's lonely battle for survival. The first thing he did after the shock of discovering that his companion was gone was to stumble over his new home, looking for water. The island, he discovered to his horror, was about 600 metres (656 yards) long and 300 metres (328 yards) in breadth, and 'barren of everything that could serve to gratify the cravings of exhausted nature—not a shrub or plant did it produce, of any kind, nor was there any appearance of springs of fresh water'.

It seemed that fate had played a cruel trick upon Foss, bringing him through such great hardships only to cast him up on the shores of an island that was as lifeless as a tomb. That first night he lay shivering under the shelter of a great rock; a rain squall passed over and he lay flat on his back with his mouth wide open, drinking in moisture from the skies. The next day he again wandered his rocky islet and found a few small shellfish the size of snails, which were barely edible but which he chewed to moisten his mouth. Unfortunately, the rainwater which had collected in rock crevices was brackish from the constant assault of the sea and could not be drunk.

By now Foss had been without food for three days. 'To add to my misery,' he writes, 'my legs began to swell and my whole body became so bloated that, notwithstanding the little flesh I had left, my fingers with the smallest impression of my skin sunk to the depth of an inch, and the impression remained for some moments afterwards.'

That night, Foss took to his cold and lonely bed beneath the rocks and had a dream of his home and his parents, which made him melancholy yet also gave him a strange sense of comfort. For the first time since he arrived on the island, he experienced a short period of deep sleep, and he awoke in a strangely altered state. He felt refreshed, 'free from delirium', as he puts it, yet 'painfully alive to the horrors that surrounded me'.

Orgy of Slaughter

The morning of the dream, the sun came out and shone warmly, which revived Foss enough to send him on another search for food. This time he struck paydirt in the form of the rotting carcass of a seal, which he discovered lodged in the cavity of a rock near the sea. 'Although in quite a putrid state,' Foss writes, the discovery of this animal was crucial. Without it, 'I must inevitably have perished'.

Even so, he found he had to eat the rotting meat sparingly, due 'to the debilitated state to which my stomach was reduced'. That night, a kind Providence provided even further—thunderstorms raged for hours, and when Foss awoke, he found fresh rainwater had collected in the depressions in the rocks. Since the seas were not quite as thunderous, this water turned out to be potable. Foss took the precaution of covering the pools that remained with flat slabs of rock to keep the salt water out and slow the process of evaporation.

With his pantry full, as it were, Foss attempted to improve his rudimentary shelter. There was seaweed washing along the rocks, and he gathered a large bundle, dried it out and used it as a mattress. The night he passed was a restless one but early the next morning, he awoke to a cacophonous uproar, which his experienced ears soon identified as the barking sounds of seals. Limping from his rocky alcove, he found to his tearful delight that the island was nearly covered in the creatures, which apparently came there during the mating season. Almost delirious with joy, he took his oar—the only weapon he had—and stumbled to the beach, where he set about slaughtering the animals. 'For the space of quarter of an hour,' Foss wrote, 'I had fine sport, when they all (as if by signal of their leader) instantly disappeared.'

Nonetheless, he now had the means for survival. He cut the throats of the seals and drank their blood 'as it oozed from their wounds and thought it most delicious'. He discovered that he had, in his frenzy, killed 100 seals. This orgy of slaughter was wasteful— for Foss could not possibly eat all this meat before it began to go bad—but understandable in a man at the edge of sanity. He admits it: 'So valuable did I esteem the acquisition of … provisions at this critical moment that had the stay of the seals and my strength admitted of it, it is probable that I should not have spared one of them. Indeed, I never made use of an eighth part of the number of them destroyed.'

The Oar

With food and water fairly assured, Foss sat down and thought hard about his situation. He 'despaired of ever meeting with the opportunity that should enable me to quit this dreary island'. Every castaway in such desperate conditions eventually makes that most existential of decisions—to strive mightily to live or to die little by little. Daniel Foss promised himself that, despite the hopelessness of his situation, he would do all in his power to survive. In order to do so, he needed better shelter. Accordingly, 'he now projected a scheme of forming for myself as tolerable a dwelling as my situation and the materials for building would admit of.' He decided on a spot on the highest part of the island, away from the reach of the stormy waves, and gradually built a hut of rocks which contained three apartments: 'one for the deposit of provision, one to lodge in, and another an occasional retreat from foul weather or the heat of the sun. It was built in the form of a sugar loaf, the walls of which were three feet thick, the whole of which I covered with dry rock weed'.

The Star Rover: Jack London and Daniel Foss

The American author Jack London (1876–1916) is famous for his stories of adventure on land and sea, of man fighting alone against savage nature, with nature almost always coming out on top.

In 1915, a year before his early death, London published an unusual novel called *The Star Rover*. It tells the story of a university professor named Darrell Standing who is serving a life sentence for murder at San Quentin prison in California. There, prison officials try to break his will by tightly encasing him in a straightjacket which cuts off his respiration. Standing discovers that the only way to survive this torture is to enter a kind of trance state, where he literally 'walks among the stars' before experiencing parts of the past lives of others in history, usually men in extremity.

One of these men is Daniel Foss. Suddenly the reader finds himself aboard the *Negociator* on that stormy November night deep in the frozen ocean. 'The moon, bursting through a crack of cloud, showed a bleak and savage picture. Everywhere was wrecked gear and everywhere ice.' Standing/Foss manages to get on board the open boat with the rest of the crew and captain, when they are faced with the monumental task of 'finding our way through an uncharted ocean with no knowledge of any near land'.

With a few differences from Foss's actual manuscript—London has the crew steering the lifeboat north-east, where Foss says south-west, but north-east would have been the probable direction if warmer weather was being sought—Jack London follows Foss's fate through the death of the surgeon and onto the rocky island. For the twenty-first century reader, it is interesting to watch London struggle with the same discrepancies, for at one point he has Standing say: 'One vexed point, however, I never did succeed in clearing up: Was this island situated in the far South Pacific or the far South Atlantic?'

Probably, he concludes—and we might agree—the South Pacific. There are other details—such as Foss becoming poisoned by tobacco immediately after being rescued by the *Neptune*, at which point he swears off the evil weed for good—that might be fictionalised, but could also be due to the fact that London may have had a rare copy of the manuscript of Foss's memoirs, which told a fuller story. He says at the end of the chapter that Foss's story had been published by the Boston house N. Coverly, Jr., which did exist in the nineteenth century, and published an 1834 edition of the tale which may have had more particulars.

This project took him a month. His next job was to find a way to mark the passing of time, for without this he 'should lose all knowledge of the day of the week and not be enabled to distinguish one from another'. Foss hit upon the idea of taking his knife and notching the days on the flat blade of his oar, for 'even though I was doomed to spend my days in solitude' he wanted to observe the Sabbath.

Foss's oar became for him an almost totemic object. It had saved him from drowning, was employed as a weapon in the great slaughter of the seals, and now marked the passage of days. As the months passed into a year, he began to painstakingly inscribe a message on the wooden instrument, making ready for the day when he should die alone and some passing vessel might find his remains. It read:

> *This is to acquaint the person into whose hands this oar may fall that Daniel Foss, a native of Elkton, in Maryland, one of the United States of America, and who sailed from the port of Philadelphia in 1809 on board the brig Negociator, bound to the Friendly Islands, was cast upon this desolate island the February following [actually March] where he erected a hut and lived a number of years, subsisting on seals—he being the last who survived of a crew of said brig, which ran foul of an island of ice and foundered on the 26th November, 1809.*
>
> *Said Foss earnestly requests that information of his fate and that of his Shipmates may be made known to their friends in America.*

This was not only a message, but an obituary and a forecast. For although Foss wrote it early in his stay, he did indeed live on the island for 'some years', day in, day out, carving his notches, eating seal meat, and drinking rainwater. Modern historians debate how he was able to survive without contracting scurvy (his earlier description of the indentations he could make in his skin are one sign of that disease) but it is possible he eventually decided to eat seaweed, which, depending on the type, can be an anti-scorbutic.

Deliverance

Foss's oar did double duty as a sentinel, placed upon the highest rock on the island, covered with sealskins, with part of his tattered shirt attached to it as a flag. Five years had passed since Foss arrived on the island and he had become, essentially, a cackling hermit, talking to himself and marking the time by great events in his life—such as the huge tempest that came during his fourth year and washed giant waves over the island, but did not knock down his sturdy structure and even deposited a treasure trove of flopping flying fish upon the rocks. (Foss's survival is all the more remarkable when we remember that he had no fire, and was forced to eat everything either raw or dried in the sun.) The same storm also washed ashore 'an enormous dead whale', in whose innards, Foss was delighted to discover, was part of a harpoon with 'a few fathoms of new line attached thereto'.

These treasures were added to the small store in his hut. Despite his self-sufficiency, he did not give up climbing to the highest rock by his oar flagpole and scanning the horizon for ships and once even saw one, far in the distance, which sailed out of sight but gave him hope. One morning, feeling ill, Foss slept late, and did not arrive at his lookout post until almost noon when, lifting his weary eyes to the horizon, he saw a ship, 'with topsails aback, nearly within hail of the island'. He couldn't believe his eyes and began jumping up and down like a madman.

Foss writes: 'I made every motion I possibly could indicative of my distressed situation, which [the ship's crew] answered by pointing to an extreme point of the island.' Racing down the hill, oar in hand, he found that the vessel had already launched a boat, which was attempting to land. 'But after making several unsuccessful attempts, by their motions they signified to me that they must return to the ship without being enabled to effect their object!' Filled with horror at the notion of being abandoned when rescue was so close, Foss refused to let it happen. Once again, his oar was his salvation: 'I seized my oar and with it plunged headlong through the foaming surf and was unaccountably successful in reaching the boat, which conveyed me immediately on board the ship.'

'The Inspection of the Curious'

Daniel Foss had found rescue. The captain of the ship, the *Neptune*, told him that it was only because of his oar flagpole that he had stopped by the island, since he correctly interpreted it as a distress symbol. The *Neptune*, out of New York, was on its way to the Dutch East Indies. Foss at this point was a scarecrow, with a beard over 30 centimetres (12 inches) in length. The crew cared for him and helped nurse him back to health on the way to Batavia. Foss clung to his precious oar throughout the voyage home, and when it was over and he was back in Maryland, he 'presented it to the keeper of the Philadelphia Museum, where it is lodged for the inspection of the curious'.

Unfortunately the oar disappeared from history, as did Daniel Foss, of whom we know nothing else. One hopes that he grew old, but we'll never know. His story stands as a tribute to what a man can do alone if he is determined to survive.

The Poor Englishman

A classic story in the castaway genre, and one which prefigures that of Daniel Foss, is the tale of the unnamed Poor Englishman who was supposedly marooned on a desolate islet off the coast of Scotland around 1615, after his ship was captured by pirates.

The Poor Englishmen and a few others were set adrift in a small boat with only some sugar to eat and their own urine to drink. Gradually everyone died except the Poor Englishman and one companion, who made it to a deserted island—essentially a large rock—far out in the Atlantic. As with Foss, the Poor Englishman's island contained no plant life or water, and the two men were forced to live off birds' eggs, seals and rainwater. One day the Poor Englishman woke up to find his companion gone—he presumed he had either died a suicide or from falling into the ocean while trying to collect eggs.

A year passed. The Poor Englishman's clothes rotted off his back and he went around essentially naked in the sometimes snowy winter. He lost his knife and was forced to use an old nail for killing birds. And then 'gracious Providence' sent a ship, blown there accidentally by a storm, and piloted by a Flemish captain named Pickman. Pickman sent some men ashore to gather birds' eggs, where they glimpsed a frightening and shaggy creature in the distance. Terrified, they rowed off, and the figure appeared again, on a cliff top, 'making signs with his hands lifted up, entreating them to come nearer'.

Landing cautiously, the men found the Poor Englishman 'more like a ghost than a living person, a body: stark naked, black and hairy, a meagre and deformed countenance with hollow and disfigured eyes'. Now deeply sympathetic, they took him on board and brought him to the coast of Ireland, where people took pity on him and raised enough money for his return to England. The story of the Poor Englishman was first told in the *Voyages and Travels of J. Albert de Mandelslo* in 1662. Whether true or not, it was a staple of the growing body of castaway fiction of the day.

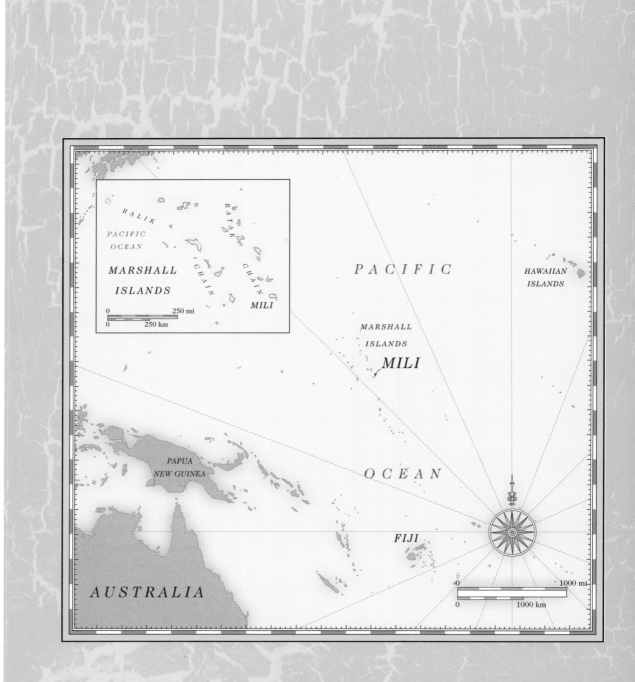

Munity on the Globe, 1824
Murder Most Foul

Being a whaler in the nineteenth century was not a life for those easily daunted by danger and hardship. Taking part on journeys which routinely lasted three or four years, fighting through vast seas hunting the largest mammal on earth with handheld iron harpoons, facing aggressive tribes on wild and unknown islands—none of this was for the faint of heart. Yet the ordinary whaling seaman made very little money—his 'lay', or share of the profits, was tiny compared to what the ship's officers and owners received—and draconian treatment on board was more often than not his lot.

Mutinies, or the threat of them, were common aboard whalers, so much so that one historian has said that 'before the development of labor unions … [the mutinies] represented a kind of labor movement that threatened to destroy the very foundations of the organizational structure of the workplace'—in other words, the ship. Despite the fact that many mutinies were justified by terrible working conditions and despotic captains, courts back in America invariably sided with the owners. Mutineers, if caught, were executed promptly.

For a sailor to mutiny, therefore, he needed literally to be desperate beyond reason—in other words, to have been driven crazy. But Samuel Comstock (whose closest relation among castaway mutineers would have to be Jeronimus Cornelisz of *Batavia* ill fame, see page 64), leader of a bloody mutiny on the whaler *Globe* in 1824, had not been treated so badly that he'd lost his mind. He arrived on the *Globe* a steely sociopath (with all the awful charm his breed can exude) and struck violently out of nowhere after being treated with great kindness, which why his mutiny and subsequent murderous arrival on a remote Pacific island is considered one of the most terrifying episodes in American whaling history.

The Downtowners

Samuel Comstock—the 'Terrible Whaleman', as he was later termed in a biography by his brother William—was born into a family of Nantucket, Massachusetts, Quakers in 1802. He had two younger brothers, William and George; his father, Nathan, had been a teacher, and a cashier at a bank, but moved to New York in 1811 and rapidly became a wealthy merchant of whaling products—oil, whalebone corset stays, ambergris, and the like. Samuel was nine years old at the time and soon fell in with one of New York's numerous violent youth gangs, the Downtowners, who spent much time battling a rival gang. Samuel began to alarm his Quaker parents by coming home 'late at night, bloody and bruised'. Following a rather typical pattern among well-to-do parents with troubled children, Samuel's mother and father sent him off to a strict Long Island boarding school, but this had little effect on his behaviour. By the time he had reached his early teens, he was 'executing' dogs and cats during the course of war games and had begun to arm himself with knives and pistols before going out on the streets of New York.

Finally, Nathan Comstock decided that the best antidote for his son's behaviour was to send him off to sea; and through his business connections found him a job as cabin boy aboard an American merchantman, the *Edward*, which regularly plied the waters between Liverpool and New York. Samuel was all of thirteen. While his father may have meant well, sending a nascent sociopath like Samuel to sea at this tender age only hardened his tendencies towards dehumanisation and violence. By the time he returned four months later, he had become a hardened seaman who spent a good deal of time dallying with local girls. 'I do not know if he was particularly susceptible of pure disinterested affection,' his brother William wrote astutely. But girls liked Samuel Comstock enough to be badly hurt when he walked away.

'Nothing Left in His Eyes'

Very shortly, Samuel went back to sea, this time aboard the famous trader John Jacob Astor's *Beaver*, which was actually on a secret mission to provide arms to Chilean rebels. The ship was seized in Chile, where Samuel and his crewmates spent five months in gaol. The story goes that the lenient Chilean authorities would occasionally let the sailors out on day furlough; when it was Samuel's turn, he offended so many people by his behaviour that he was stoned and had to run for his life back to gaol.

The *Beaver* was finally allowed to depart, but Samuel Comstock was not on board. He had decided to ship out on a Nantucket whaler, the *George*, which had stopped in the Chilean port on its way home to Nantucket after a successful voyage. Despite his previous experiences at sea, Samuel had not understood how hard a whaler's life was until he shipped out on the *George*. Still, in 1819, he sailed with another whaler, the *Foster*, out of Nantucket, and was away for three years, crisscrossing the Atlantic and the Pacific in search of sperm whales. When he returned to his family home, his brother William wrote in *The Terrible Whaleman*, 'his face and neck [were] nearly as black as an indian's, while there was nothing left in his eyes ...'.

There is very little knowledge available about Samuel Comstock's *Foster* voyage; in his book *Mutiny on the Globe*, Thomas Earl Heffernan writes that he was apparently seen wandering around the vessel during storms talking to himself. During the voyage, he also suggested to friends that the first mate be seized and flogged. Would they care to join him? That Comstock would even consider this is a sign of how detached he had become from reality.

And one more thing. The now 19-year-old Samuel confided to his brother William that he wanted to become king of a Pacific island, a white man lording it over natives. And the way he would do that would be to seize a whaling vessel, murder its officers, and force the crew to take him to a likely island refuge. Once there, Samuel told the disbelieving William, he would murder the rest of the crew and take his ease in Paradise.

The *Globe*

In December 1822, Samuel Comstock sailed on the Nantucket whaler the *Globe*, his youngest brother, 14-year-old George, also on board. The twenty-man crew of the *Globe* was quite young—half of them, like George, were teenagers (Samuel was now twenty years old). The captain, Thomas Worth, was the oldest person on board at twenty-nine. Although the crew was perhaps a bit on the young side, this was not too unusual—whaling, like war, was not a pursuit for older men—but their youthfulness perhaps made these teenage sailors a trifle more malleable in the face of what was to occur.

The *Globe* was considered a lucky ship, having now made three voyages and becoming the first whaler, in 1818, to fill its holds with over 2000 barrels of oil from the fabled Off-Shore Ground west of Peru, which teemed with whales and soon became a favourite hunting area of the American whalers. The *Globe*'s previous captain had left her and Thomas Worth was a new skipper. He was tough but in the main fair, although he could be harsh in his discipline. Interestingly, Samuel Comstock was a favourite of his, having even been entertained by Worth and his wife before the *Globe* sailed. It soon became apparent that Comstock was something of a 'captain's pet', for he got away with things, with Worth coming to his defence in numerous incidents, once clapping a man in irons 'for differing with Comstock', according to a seaman's later testimony. The rest of the crew began to resent Comstock as much as they started to resent their captain.

The *Globe* left harbour with her usual good luck, weathering a severe storm flawlessly and then sailing east toward the Azores and Cape Verde islands, where whalers generally found the north-east trade winds which would blow them down the Atlantic to

Men at work on a whaler, cutting whale blubber into small pieces ready for rendering.

Cape Horn. The grumbling started almost immediately, however, when Worth refused to stop at the Cape Verde for supplies—the usual practice, which also allowed the seamen some liberty—probably because they had got off a slightly late start to the whaling season. In the south Atlantic, the *Globe* killed her first sperm whale, from which her crew tried down 75 barrels of oil, but Samuel Comstock began to complain that 'contact with the whale oil caused [him] great distress ... filling him with biles and inflaming his flesh', an affliction which apparently had not shown up until now. He began to stalk angrily about the ship.

Mounting Tension

In March 1823, the *Globe* rounded the Horn and headed for the Off-Shore Ground, but did not call in at Valparaiso first, as whalers often did, further infuriating the crew. To make matters worse, they had little luck in finding whales. Finally, in May, Worth brought the ship to harbour in Oahu, Hawaii. The men had not been ashore in five months and were desperate for liberty in this lush tropical paradise. But Captain Worth had provisions brought on board, rather than going ashore for them. He did allow women to visit the sailors on the ship, but forbade them to spend the night. Samuel Comstock apparently managed to flout this edict—the next morning, according to his brother William, a young Hawaiian woman 'emerged from steerage, with an air of great dignity, dressed in a new Scotch bonnet'.

Comstock escorted the woman his brother sarcastically called 'Lady Comstock' to a waiting outrigger and the crew waited for Worth to react. He failed to issue even a strong word, further proving that Comstock had been singled out for special treatment.

The *Globe* spent the summer months hunting in the rich whaling grounds near Japan, but her spate of bad luck continued. There is no evidence that Worth knew quite how much the situation was deteriorating around him. The crew complained bitterly about not being given enough meat and about the favouritism shown to Comstock—and at one point, Worth struck the cook because he had quarrelled with his favourite. To make matters worse, they met five or six other Nantucket whalers returning home with holds filled with whale oil—bad luck was plaguing only the *Globe*, it seemed.

When the *Globe* returned to Hawaii that autumn and the crew was at last allowed liberty, six of them immediately jumped ship, forcing Worth to replace them with 'a rough set of cruel beings', as George Comstock was to write, five of whom would eventually join Comstock in his mutiny. The *Globe* left Hawaii on 9 December 1823, heading back for the Equator to seek her luck.

'So Fatal a Deed'

'There is but one eye that sees the hearts of wretches who put so fatal a deed into execution,' wrote George Comstock in his account of the bloody mutiny that his own brother was about to put into motion, meaning that only God could see into the centre of evil impenetrable to ordinary men like himself. But there were clues as to what was coming. On the way south, Worth flogged Joseph Thomas, one of the riff-raff he had brought on board in Hawaii, and Samuel Comstock used this as an incident around which to organise his revolt. Meeting with Thomas and four other conspirators, Comstock laid out his plans. On the night of

Roger Starbuck and *The Golden Harpoon*

The Comstocks, apart from Samuel, were quite a creative group. William Comstock produced a biography of his brother's life and went on to a career as journalist and author. And Samuel's other brother, George, produced a journal which horrifyingly relates an eyewitness account of the events that night of the mutiny.

William's son, Augustus, would have as adventurous a life as any a Comstock, and become the best-known writer of the group, although he laboured under the pen name Roger Starbuck. Augustus was born

in Massachusetts in 1837, but left school at the age of fourteen to set type in a newspaper office. After this, he studied law for a time, but this was far too tame a pursuit for a Comstock, and he went to sea, making several whaling voyages. He returned to New York in the late 1850s and began writing whaling yarns in the popular dime novel format of the time. These cheap, mass-produced softcovers appealed to a wide audience and Roger Starbuck—Augustus had taken the name of one of the most famous of Nantucket whaling families—had a loyal following. His most famous book, *The Golden Harpoon*, features a mutiny aboard a whaler, although these mutineers are Maori whalemen, tattooed cannibals whose leader Comstock calls 'a blue-skinned devil'. The story is racist, focusing on the attempt of the white hero to save the life of a damsel in distress ('the flesh of that gal is tender', the hero muses to himself, 'and them fellows are cannibals and like good grub!'), but in spite (or because) of this was quite popular.

During a prolific career—which saw him take time out to serve with the Union Army in the Civil War, where he was badly wounded—'Roger Starbuck' churned out at least fifty novels about whaling and, increasingly as the whaling industry fell into decline, the American West. The date of his death is not known, but he was alive as late as 1907, and still writing.

26 January 1824, George Comstock was helming the ship on the midnight watch when his brother sneaked up on him and demanded in a fierce whisper that George 'keep the ship a good full'—to keep her sails full of wind and not allow them to luff. Comstock told George that if he made 'the least D—d bit of noise he would send me to h—l'.

If the sails were not full of wind, the sound of their flapping and rattling might awaken the captain or the mates, and obviously Comstock did not want that. With the ship as silent as possible, he crept into Worth's cabin and brought down an axe so hard that he nearly decapitated the sleeping skipper, who died without ever knowing how wrong he had been to place his faith in Comstock. Another conspirator stabbed the first mate, and Comstock finished the job by bashing in his head with the axe. He then took a musket and shot the second mate, a man named Fisher, through the mouth, wounding him severely. The third mate, Lumbert, was able to wrestle the gun away, but Comstock promised to spare him if he relinquished it. As soon as he gave it up, Comstock ran him through several times with the bayonet.

Comstock now administered the *coup de grâce* to Fisher by shooting him in the head, and had him tossed overboard, along with the captain and the first mate. Lumbert, still alive, was dragged to the side of the boat, begging for his life. Comstock pushed him over but Lumbert clung to the gunwales until Comstock smashed his fingers in with his boots. Lumbert fell into the ocean with a splash and according to the terrified George's account, 'swam very quick' toward the lights of a sister whaler, the *Lyra*, which could be seen in the distance. He never made it, dying alone in the dark waters.

Mili Atoll

Samuel Comstock now gathered the rest of the crew around him, told them there had been a mutiny, and revealed that they were sailing west, away from the *Lyra*. He forced those who had not taken part in events to clean up the mess of blood and brains left on the decks, and produced new ship's articles appointing him the captain and his fellow mutineers the mates. The ten who had not taken part in the mutiny all signed, terrified they would be butchered if they refused.

Comstock was not yet done with killing. He claimed that a black sailor named Humphreys had conspired to re-take the ship from the mutineers. This was certainly a manufactured charge. William Comstock would later write that Samuel 'was much averse to having a black man on board—he always felt a strong dislike to coloured persons'. After a 'jury' found Humphreys guilty, he was hanged from a yardarm, his last pathetic words being 'when I was born, I did not think I would come to this'.

Two weeks later, the *Globe* reached the Gilbert Islands. Comstock ordered a boat landed, but after a fracas with the inhabitants which resulted in the death of at least one of them, he sailed on in a northwesterly direction. It was apparent that he was seeking the island of his twisted dreams. On 12 February he found Mili Atoll, at the southern tip of the Ratak (meaning 'sunrise') chain of the Marshall Islands. The Marshalls were first sighted by a Spanish explorer in 1529, but named after the English navigator John Marshall, who visited them about twenty-five years before the *Globe* arrived. Mili Atoll consists of about twenty-two low-lying small islands along a coral chain, islands with brilliant white beaches and waving palm trees.

The *Globe* anchored off Mili, one of the largest of these sandy islets, and the next morning began unloading supplies. The Milians watched from within the jungle with surprise and unease. The islands had been settled as much as 2000 years earlier, during the great wave of Polynesian migration, but were seldom visited, being off the major European trade and whaling routes. When white men did come ashore, they stayed only a short time, to trade for provisions. But the growing mound of supplies on the beach showed that these white men were up to something entirely different.

The Death of Comstock

The mad Comstock began to pace the broad beach with one of his fellow mutineers, tracing the outlines of his proposed village in the sand. The first building he laid out, according to George Comstock, was a church. But Comstock did something else as well. As the Milians carefully approached his growing camp, he welcomed them with open arms and gave them gifts—in particular, the best clothes from the ship's chests. This largesse, of course, had reason in a man incapable of 'pure disinterested affection'. Comstock wanted the natives to kill the white men who had landed on the beach, with the exception of himself, of course, so he could begin living his dream as their king.

The absurdity of this boggles the mind. Comstock was able to explain things to the Milians only with signs and gestures, so it's doubtful that they understood what he was talking about. And did he really expect them to install as their new king a stranger who had only hours before waded ashore? Part of this was Comstock's own particular form of madness, and part the racial superiority that most white whaling men of the day felt towards Pacific Islanders. His lavish gifts were to have dire consequences for him, however, for they infuriated Silas Payne, his chief co-conspirator, who felt Comstock was being too generous and figured something must be up. He and Comstock got into a heated argument, at which point Comstock armed himself with a cutlass and headed off into the bush.

Afraid that he was going to come back accompanied by a native army, Payne rounded up the other mutineers and armed them with muskets. When Comstock emerged from the jungle, alone, he saw this firing squad waiting for him. He shouted 'Don't shoot me!' but it was too late. A volley cut him down, then Payne took an axe and decapitated him, an eerie echo of the death of Captain Worth.

It was 17 February and they buried Samuel Comstock on the beach. That evening, Gilbert Smith, sent back to the *Globe* by Payne to unload more stores, carefully plotted with the few others on board—men who were innocent of mutiny, including George Comstock—to steal the ship and take her back out to sea. As dusk fell, they suddenly unfurled the sails, cut the anchor cable, and headed past the coral reefs to the open sea. The sailors left on shore, four mutineers and five innocent men, were powerless to stop her.

Bikini Atoll

At the northwest tip of the Ralik chain of the Marshalls, 320 kilometres (199 miles) to the north of Mili Atoll, lies Bikini Atoll, which became famous due to a bomb and a swimming costume.

Bikini was the site, between 1946 and 1958, of twenty-three nuclear explosions as American scientists tested the effects of atomic blasts on derelict World War II ships. The largest explosion took place on 1 March 1954, when a H-bomb was set off; the explosion was larger than predicted and caused far-flung contamination. The Bikini population of 200 had been moved before testing began; the United States declared the atoll habitable again in 1968, and began moving the islanders back home, but within ten years it was realised that Bikini remained radioactive, with women miscarrying or suffering a high incidence of stillborn children and children with birth defects. The islanders were once again forced to move, this time permanently, while America paid up to $150 million in damages and was forced to clear over a foot of radioactive topsoil from the island.

On a more frivolous note, the modern bikini swimsuit was invented by a French fashion designer in the 1950s and given the name 'bikini' since it was thought that the excitement of seeing women in such a revealing garment would cause the equivalent of a nuclear blast.

And Then There Were Two

For a week these men lived at peace with the Milians until Silas Payne, infuriated when some tools were stolen from their camp, put one of the natives in shackles until the implements were returned. That was enough for the Milians. The next day, they attacked the camp with stones and clubs and spears. A young seaman named William Lay watched a 60-year-old woman spear and club to death one of his friends, and saw a group leading Payne away to a spot where he was executed by smashing his brains in with a rock. Other seamen were murdered in like fashion. Lay was saved, curiously, because two elderly Milians had come to him just as the massacre was beginning, made him lie down out of sight, and then placed their own bodies on top of his.

When the killing was over, he saw that his friend Cyrus Hussey was also alive; they were the only two to survive, and only because both had been deliberately protected. The next day, Hussey and Lay were forced to bury the dreadfully disfigured corpses of their former shipmates before they were taken to meet the *iroojlaplap*, or chief of chiefs of the island, a man named Luttoun. He decreed that Lay should be given to the old couple who had saved him (although, since they were too old to support an extra mouth, his ownership was soon transferred to a man named Ludjuan). Hussey was to be adopted by an *irooj*, or chief, named Lugoma.

Thus began an extraordinary 21-month castaway period for these two young whalers. They were never really to understand why they were chosen to live. By April 1824, Hussey had been taken 40 kilometres (25 miles) away to the island of Lukenor, while Lay remained on Mili. At first Lay was lonely and dispirited, unable to stomach the local food and wary of his captors, who had destroyed his Bible because they felt it contained evil spirits. Gradually, however, he became friends with the son-in-law of his master and was allowed to Hussey's island, where he and his former shipmate had a short-lived but emotional reunion.

'The Chiefs Are Going to Kill William'

Lay, in particular, was a quick learner and had soon mastered the language of the Milians and even learned something of their supreme god, Anit, who controlled even the smallest daily decisions. At work harvesting breadfruit one day, he heard a boy say: 'The chiefs are going to kill William.' When Lay's master saw that he understood, he tried to reassure him that it was not true, but Lay heard the comment again, with Hussey's name added—both the Americans were to die.

Lay couldn't understand why the Milians were planning their execution, but finally pieced it together—a mysterious sickness had broken out on the island, causing people's faces and extremities to swell up like balloons. No one had yet died, but such a shocking illness had to be the fault of Hussey and Lay, and so the high priest had commanded that they both die. Hussey and Lay were brought together again to be executed, but Lay made an impassioned speech in their defence, as did Hussey's master, and they were reprieved. But it was a close call and underscored to both men how foreign the culture of the Milians was to their own. Sometimes this could be endearing—the Milians constantly entreated Hussey and Lay to allow them to pierce their ear-lobes in Milian fashion, inserting pieces of wood that caused the lobe to dangle to the shoulder.

Other times, though, cultural disconnect could be quite dangerous. When a severe drought hit the islands later in the year, many Milians thought Anit had sent it because they had not yet killed the Americans, while others thought it was a punishment for having murdered the other seven sailors. This was debated back and forth, at great length. It was not until four months later, when the rains came at last, that the dangerous discussions ceased.

The *Dolphin*

While Hussey and Lay were living by their wits on Mili Atoll, the skeleton crew which had re-taken the *Globe* managed to sail her over 11,000 kilometres (6,835 miles) across the Pacific to Valparaiso in Chile. They reported the mutiny and that there were crewmen (and mutineers) still alive in the Marshall Islands. In August 1825, at the behest of President John Quincy Adams, the United States navy sent a warship from Peru to search for these men—to save the innocent and punish the guilty. The *Dolphin* was commanded by Captain John Percival; his senior lieutenant was Hiram Paulding, who kept a journal of this unique voyage. Three months later, the *Dolphin* reached Mili Atoll and began cruising the islands looking for any sign of crew members of the *Globe*.

At first, all they found was an old whaler's lance and a few pieces of canvas, which might or might not have come from the *Globe*. The Milians who gathered around this new American presence, taking care not to steal anything and to act with great politeness, were in reality spies. They were alarmed to realise that these sailors—who were heavily armed and whose vessels had many cannon—were methodically combing the islands with search parties.

Lay and Hussey were very aware of the presence of the warship, but were kept hidden in huts when the Americans neared. Still, Paulding wrote, the searchers knew something was happening because the islanders' faces would grow blank and they would edge away when asked if they knew of the presence of any Americans on the islands. At the beginning of December, Paulding's search party of thirteen sailors landed on Mili, to find a large group of warriors assembled there—perhaps 200 in all. Paulding knew this population was too great for the island and suspected that the Milians were there for a special reason.

He was right—the Milians had decided to overwhelm the party and kill them. But Paulding was not intimidated. He prepared to disembark his men on the island, with muskets cocked, to search the huts he could see. But just at that point a figure arose from the group of Milians and came towards the sailors. He had his hair in a topknot and his skin was quite dark, so they mistook him for a native until he said: 'The Indians are going to kill you; don't come on shore unless you are prepared to fight.'

The man identified himself as William Lay, whom Paulding knew to be one of the innocent crewmen who had remained on Mili. He told Lay to come aboard the longboats, but Lay said he could not—that the Milians would stone him to death if he did so. He had only been allowed near Paulding's men to lure them into thinking all was well. Paulding was having none of this. He told his men to fire their muskets in the air, for psychological effect, and reload quickly, then told Lay to tell the natives that the first man among them who threw a stone would be killed.

Lay, nearly hysterical with both fear and relief, tried to shout out this warning, but both English and Milian failed him and his words came out garbled. He kept saying, 'They are going to kill me! They are going to kill me!' but it wasn't certain to Paulding who 'they' were, nor if Lay really knew whether he was still American or a Milian. Finally, an old man approached, the man who had protected Lay during the massacre on the beach. He put his hand in Lay's and asked if the people in the boats—Paulding's men—were going to hurt him. And Lay, breaking into tears, answered no—they were going to take him home.

With that, Lay was allowed to depart in safety, and led Paulding straight to Hussey's island, where no protecting warriors appeared. Hussey was in the woods and some women yelled for him as the Americans approached. He came out, as Paulding wrote, 'with his fine yellow hair hanging in ringlets about his shoulders, and his person quite naked, with the exception of a piece of blanket, tied around his waist'.

Hussey's 'family' cried as he left, and Paulding was forced to promise that Hussey would come back and visit 'if his mother consented to his return'.

The Young Mutineer

Cyrus Hussey's mother never did agree to his return and in any event, he was to die of illness aboard another Nantucket whaler in 1829, when he was all of 24 years of age. In 1828, he and William Lay had ghost-written for them a memoir called *A Narrative of the Mutiny on Board the Ship Globe of Nantucket*, which chronicled their terror-filled days on ship and curious existence on Mili Atoll. Twelve years later, William Comstock was to write *The Life of Samuel Comstock, The Terrible Whaleman*, which told the story of Samuel Comstock's bloody life and death from an insider's point of view—although even William was hard put to understand why his older brother acted the way he did. Ultimately, neither defending nor exonerating his brother, he ends up quoting a poem written by Henry Glover of Nantucket, a childhood friend of the Comstock brothers. 'The Young Mutineer' was first been published in a Nantucket paper shortly after word of Samuel Comstock's bloody actions spread like wildfire through the seafaring village.

He lies on the beach—with a heart-rending yell,
Horrid and despairing, he sunk down to Hell,
His glazed eyes in horror were turned up to Heaven,
His last yell to the skies, in wild echo was given—
In vain it ascended, no mercy was there,
To cheer the dark dying of the young Mutineer.

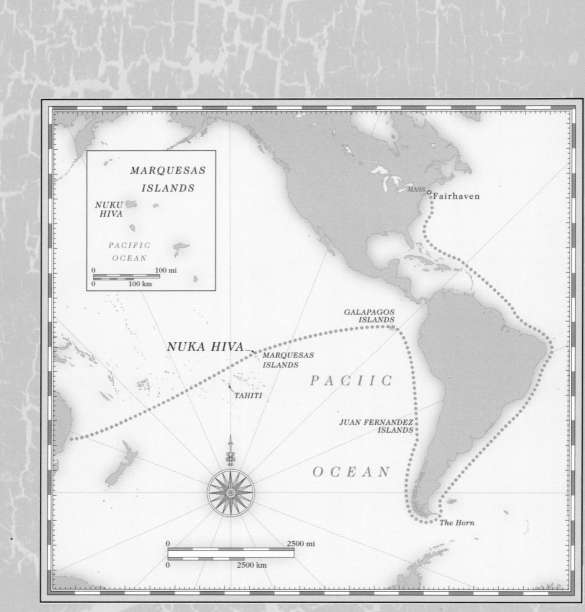

MARQUESAS
ISLANDS

NUKU
HIVA

PACIFIC
OCEAN

0   100 mi
0   100 km

MASS. ○ Fairhaven

GALAPAGOS
ISLANDS

NUKA HIVA

MARQUESAS
ISLANDS

PACIIC

TAHITI

JUAN FERNANDEZ
ISLANDS

OCEAN

The Horn

0   2500 mi
0   2500 km

Herman Melville in the Marquesas, 1842
The Making of a Writer

On 23 June 1842, a young American seaman stood in the rigging of the whaler *Acushnet* as it slowly entered harbour on the island of Nuku Hiva, one of the ten atolls of the Marquesas Islands. 'No description can do justice to its beauty', he was to write later, and indeed the Marquesas are among the loveliest of South Pacific islands, with steep cliffs, deep valleys, and rainbow-shrouded waterfalls—'as if shot forward from a fairy cavern'—which cascade through lush forest landscapes.

But even more beautiful to this enraptured seaman's eyes were the women of Nuku Hiva, who swam out to meet the *Acushnet*, holding their wraps of soft tapa bark with one arm above the water:

> *As they drew nearer, and I watched the rising and sinking of their forms and beheld the uplifted right arm bearing above the water the girdle of tapa and their long dark hair trailing behind them as they swam, I almost fancied they could be nothing else than so many mermaids ...*

Herman Melville—for that was the seaman's name—watched these young woman climb aboard his vessel, seizing chains and ropes and pulling themselves up with extraordinary agility. They laughed and shook out their hair and advanced with inviting smiles towards the stunned crewmen, who had been at sea for a year and a half. 'The [*Acushnet*] was fairly captured,' wrote Melville. 'And never I will say was a vessel carried before by such a dashing and irresistible party of boarders.'

Never a vessel—and never a man, either. For Herman Melville himself was captured. The experiences of the next month or so would stay with him all his life and eventually lead to the creation of some of the masterpieces of nineteenth century American literature.

'Unshored Harborless Immensities'

Melville was born Herman Melvill in New York City on 1 August 1819, the son of Allan Melvill, a well-to-do merchant. The young Melvill had ties far into America's past—his paternal grandfather took part in the Boston Tea Party while his mother's father, Peter Gansevoort, was a hero of the Battle of Saratoga during the War of American Independence. More tellingly, his uncle, Thomas Melvill, had been a midshipman in the United States Navy, and entertained young Herman with tales of sailing the Pacific Ocean—and in particular of visiting the Marquesas, of their lush beauty, willing females and brutal cannibals.

In 1832, young Melvill's world fell apart—his father went bankrupt in the depression gripping the country, caught pneumonia and died, raving. To separate her eight children from the stain of their father's failed business dealings, his widow, Maria, added an 'e' to the family name. After several more years of schooling, young Herman, despite his ambitions of being a writer, took a position as a bank clerk. But with few if any in the way of prospects in a country gripped by financial panic, he decided to ship out as a cabin boy in the spring of 1839, when he was nineteen. The ship was the *St Lawrence*, a small, three-masted merchant vessel bound for Liverpool. The *St Lawrence*'s register wrongly had Melville's first name as 'Norman', but the voyage opened up a whole new world for the young man, who, harking back to the stories of his Uncle Thomas, decided that he next wanted to see what he called 'the unshored harborless immensities' of the great Pacific Ocean.

The best way for a young American to do that, in the 1830s and 1840s, was aboard a whaling ship. America's whaling fleet had over 630 vessels, compared to just 230 in total from other countries. Sperm oil was worth $1.70 a gallon (almost 4 litres), while whalebone—used to make corset stays and hoop-frames for skirts—had risen to 97 cents a pound (almost 500 grams) in 1840. Enormous fortunes were there to be made by shipowners, although not by sailors like Melville.

But rich adventures were there for the taking.

Aboard the *Acushnet*

In late 1840, Herman Melville, 21 years old, broad-shouldered, open-faced and red-haired, signed up as an ordinary crewman aboard a new whaling vessel, the *Acushnet*. The ship was 359 tons, square-rigged with three masts (each with a crow's nest for the spotters), and was built broad-beamed for strength, stability and endurance rather than speed. The *Acushnet*'s first whaling cruise was to last four years, about average for the time, and Melville was given an advance of $84, which he was forced to use to buy the clothes, pillows, blankets, mattress, knives, soap, needle and thread, and other items he would need on board. If he ran out, he would have to purchase goods from the ship's stores at inflated prices—many a whaleman came back from a long voyage actually owing money to the owners.

The *Acushnet* set sail from Fairhaven, Massachusetts, on 3 January 1841, under the command of Captain Valentine Pease. Pease, who would later form the basis of Melville's portrait of Captain Ahab, the haunted and driven protagonist of *Moby Dick*, was a cruel master who made the lives of his men hell. Melville later wrote that 'we left both law and equity on the other side of the Cape [Horn]' and that Pease settled disputes with 'the butt-end of a handspike, so convincingly administered as effectually to silence the aggrieved party'.

The life of an ordinary seaman aboard a whaler was difficult enough without a tyrant for a captain. He ate 'salt horse' or salted beef (which, aboard the *Acushnet*, had often rotted) and drank a loathsome concoction of coffee, tea and molasses called 'longlick' if he did not want to drink dreadful water from the mouldy barrels in the hold.

But there were consolations, especially for a young and romantic would-be writer like Melville. Off the coast of Brazil, he took part in his first whale hunt, seeing 'a gigantic Sperm Whale ... rolling in the water like the capsized hull of a frigate', and leaping into a small boat to chase down the creature, watching the harpooner, standing in the bow, lean back with all his might and throw his hooked lance into the creature's back.

Herman Melville as a young man.

A whale so harpooned would speed off, tied to the boat by the line attached to the harpoon (and one had to be careful not to in any way touch the rapidly unreeling line, which could take an arm off), careening across the ocean. If the whalers were lucky, the whale would finally tire, broach, and could be dealt the *coup de grâce*. If fortune was on the side of the whale, the harpoon would fall out and the crew would be left to row an often considerable distance back to the ship with nothing to show for their labours.

The Marquesas

The voyage was at first quite successful. Heading down to the South Atlantic, rounding Cape Horn and moving up the west coat of South America into the Pacific, they found and killed sperm whales aplenty. Even before they turned west for the killing grounds of the central Pacific they had 'tried down' 700 barrels of oil out of a hoped-for 2000. But then their luck changed. 'Cruising the Line'—tacking back and forth across the Equator—they saw no whales for several months. Melville spent hours aloft in the crow's nest, watching 'the long, measured, dirge-like swell' of the Pacific, but seeing none of the tell-tale forward spouting of the sperm whale (other whales spout straight up in the air).

In the spring of 1842, the *Acushnet* headed further south. On the way they encountered another whaler, the *Lima*, and had a 'gam'—a much-longed-for mid-ocean meeting, in which crews boarded each other's vessels and exchanged news and gossip. It was during the *Lima* gam that Melville met young William Henry Chase, son of Owen Chase, whose adventures aboard the whaleship *Essex* (see **Stove by a Whale**, page 151) would form the nucleus of *Moby Dick*.

Soon, however, it was back to business. Lacking fresh food and water, and with a weary, angry, restless crew, Pease decided to stop in at Nuku Hiva, one of the largest of the Marquesas, to re-provision.

Although Melville's paradisiacal description of Nuku Hiva as the *Acushnet* entered the harbour in June 1842 held true (and to some extent is true today), these remote islands were already changing. The Marquesas were one of the first Polynesian groups to be settled—their Polynesian name, Te Henua Enata, means 'Land of Men'—probably 2000 years ago. It was from here that courageous mariners struck out on voyages of exploration that took them to Easter Island, to Hawaii, and as far as New Zealand. The Marquesan people, or Hivans, developed into a warlike society which built giant religious and ceremonial structures and practised headhunting and ritual cannibalism.

But then, inevitably, the Europeans arrived, in the form of the Spanish explorer Álvaro de Mandaña, in 1595. He named the islands for the wife of his patron, the viceroy of Peru, then fought a pitched battle with the inhabitants, killing some 200 Hivans. He and his men raped numerous women before they departed. The Marquesas were left in peace for nearly two centuries—though now ravaged by syphilis—until Captain Cook rediscovered them in 1774. American Admiral David Porter, sweeping the Pacific free of British warships during the War of 1812, claimed them for the United States, but the government never acted on the claim.

Thus, when the *Acushnet* rode into harbour that day in 1842, several French frigates has just arrived and—much to the surprise of both the Americans and the Marquesans—staged a small ceremony on the beach and claimed the islands for France. As one historian has written, the French brought 'guns, liquor and Bibles'. They also brought diseases like smallpox, measles, tuberculosis and leprosy to add to the syphilis brought by the Spanish. The beginning of the nineteenth century saw a Marquesan population estimated at 100,000. The first census, in 1887, counted just 5246 people.

Escape

So Herman Melville arrived at Nuku Hiva at a cusp in time, as a once-mighty culture was about to be transformed, and was soon to see much of the original Marquesan way of life. Like his friend and fellow crew member, Richard Tobias 'Toby' Greene, Melville was thoroughly sick of the dictatorial treatment meted out by Captain Pease and had determined to jump ship at the first opportunity. On one of their few trips ashore he and Toby hid supplies of cotton and tobacco (for trading) in the jungle, and awaited their opportunity. It came on 9 July. The *Acushnet* was about to set sail when, under cover of a driving rainstorm, Greene and Melville slid down a hawser and swam to shore. They headed straight into the jungle and made an arduous climb to the summit of a steep hill overlooking the harbour, from where they kept careful watch.

The *Acushnet* departed, but when Pease realised the two young men had disappeared, he sailed back and came ashore in a longboat, trying to recruit replacements from the other whalers at anchor. However, he was so widely known as a terrible skipper to sail under that no one would go with him. (Like Alexander Selkirk, Melville and Greene were fortunate in choosing to jump ship, for the *Acushnet* was ill-fated. She eventually limped back to Massachusetts with just eleven men, for by then half the crew had deserted, one had committed suicide, and two others had died of venereal disease.)

Watching the ship set sail, Melville and Greene felt giddy at the prospect of freedom and adventure, a giddiness soon dispelled when they found that there was little food to be had at their higher elevation. After a few days spent scrambling around the cliffs, with Melville hurting his leg at one point, they became completely lost. They wandered through the jungle, chilled to the bone by frequent rainshowers, Melville shaking with fever from his infected leg. Then, as Melville describes it:

> *I chanced to push aside a branch, and by so doing disclosed to my view a scene which even now I can recall with all the vividness of the first impression ... From the spot where I lay transfixed with surprise and delight, I looked down into the bosom of a valley, which swept away in long wavy undulations to the blue water in the distance. Midway toward the sea, and peering here and there amidst the foliage, might be seen the palmetto-thatched houses of its inhabitants, glistening in the sun that had bleached them to a dazzling whiteness.*

It was the valley of Ti Pai, or Typee, as Melville calls it in his book of the same name about his adventures. The two young Americans were aware of the Marquesans' reputation as

Stove by a Whale

Herman Melville based his famous novel *Moby Dick* on several different sources, including the tall tale (published in *Knickerbocker* magazine in 1839) of a monstrous white whale known as 'Mocha-Dick', which supposedly cruised the Pacific, wreaking havoc on any whaler who might attack it.

But one of the main inspirations for his novel was the incredible experience of the whaler *Essex*, which set sail from Nantucket in 1819, the year of Melville's birth. Captained by George Pollard, with Owen Chase as first mate, it headed for the not yet fully explored whaling grounds of the Central Pacific, taking in as many as 800 barrels of oil on the way. On 20 November 1820, the *Essex* gave chase to a sperm whale, which Chase harpooned but did not kill. The whale's gigantic tail smashed a hole in the longboat, which returned to the *Essex* for repairs.

As the boat was being repaired on deck, a crewman looked up to see a giant bull sperm whale, perhaps 27 metres (29½ yards) in length, charging straight at the ship. The creature struck the boat a tremendous blow forward, stoving in the hull, then lay as if stunned in the water before slowly sinking. As Chase ordered the *Essex* pumped out, the whale rose to the surface, convulsing, and attacked the ship again, this time doing so much damage that the *Essex* had to be abandoned.

Three small boats now bobbed on the surface, 1600 kilometres (994 miles) away from the nearest landfall, Tahiti. Afraid to land either there or on the Marquesas (because of the perceived threat of cannibals), the sailors headed for Chile, a journey of some 7200 kilometres (4474 miles). Incredibly, both Pollard's and Chase's boats made it, although only five men in total survived, being forced to resort to murder, and ironically, cannibalism along the way.

When Melville began his voyage on the *Acushnet* he had not read the account that Chase published of his adventures, but the whaler's second mate had served with Chase on later voyages and told Melville the story. Then, incredibly enough, during the gam with the *Lima*, Melville met Chase's son, William Henry, and was able to borrow a copy of Chase Sr.'s narrative.

The rest is literary history.

cannibals, but they were also starving. Feeling they had no choice, Greene and Melville stepped out of the jungle to walk toward the first village. Almost immediately, they spotted two figures almost hidden among the trees, a boy and a girl transfixed by the sight of them. Making signs of friendship to overcome their alarm, Melville and Greene approached, and the children took them to their village.

'Domestic Felicity'

The people they now met—the Typees—treated the two seamen with great affection and respect. Melville—whose probable bisexuality has been debated by American scholars of literature for the last fifty years—was especially taken with the handsome Marquesan men, who wore earrings, leaves in their hair, and decorations of whale's teeth. Their tight skirts of patterned tapa cloth gave their walk fluidity and emphasised rather than minimised their genitals. The women, bare-breasted, wearing the same type of tapa garb, were lovely. Melville was astonished at the open sexuality he observed, for the adults had little inhibition about making love or fondling each other in public. Melville, fortunately, was no prude. He saw the way of life in the valley of Typee as one with a 'buoyant sense of healthful physical existence'. Men outnumbered woman and polyandry was practised, with the women having two or more husbands or lovers in a way that, according to Melville anyway, resulted in much 'domestic felicity'.

The Americans were objects of great curiosity, for few white men had penetrated this far into the interior of Nuku Hiva. The Typees took off their rain-soaked garb and felt their skin 'in the way that a silk mercer would handle a remarkably fine piece of satin'. They were introduced to Mehevi, the all-powerful chief of the valley, a tall, well-built man whose body was covered with tattoos and who carried a 4.5 metre (15 foot) paddle spear, one end pointed, the other a canoe paddle. Melville, no fool, decided to 'secure ... the good will of this individual'. Mehevi was not loath to have these Americans among his tribe, and soon Greene and Melville were wearing native clothing, eating the abundant fruits, fish and vegetables of the valley, which was blessed with a small lake and numerous streams. Melville became close to Mehevi's daughter, Fayaway, a classic South Seas beauty who taught him her language and with whom he may have had a daughter, according to Marquesan tradition and gossip. (Their names, and many others Melville noted, he may have invented, or possibly misheard.)

With Fayaway, Melville explored the valley, marvelling at the temple ruins and stone statues, or tikis (miniature versions of those found on Easter Island), hidden deep in the forests, evidence of an ancient past. He learned about the generosity of the Typees and their sense of community—if one person lacked food or shelter, others readily gave it. Children were raised communally and happily. Food was there for the taking. After a few weeks, Melville began to think that perhaps he might live here forever. He had reached, he later said, 'a higher estimate of human nature than [he] had ever before entertained'.

The Valley of the Man-Eaters

Melville claimed that Typee meant 'the Valley of the Man-Eaters' but, although the meaning is obscure, there is little evidence for his translation. Nonetheless, Typee warriors (and other groups in the Marquesas) did practise cannibalism, and Melville and Greene began to wonder if they, too, might end up in the cooking pot. Battles were fought with tribes in neighbouring valleys; one day, Melville saw bloodstained warriors returning to the village with dripping packages of tapa cloth containing human flesh, and heard the pounding drums which signalled ceremonial feasting on the enemies' remains. He had been warned by Mehevi to stay away, but on the third day of the celebration, while the warriors were enjoying the sleep of the well fed, he went to the large central hut where he opened a wooden box and found a human skeleton, flesh hanging in rags from its bones, themselves stained red.

Melville began to have nightmares: 'Was I destined to perish, to be devoured and my head to be preserved as a fearful memento of the event?' He realised that everywhere he went in the valley, even when he was accompanied by Fayaway, he was trailed by a warrior sent by Mehevi. He was beginning to believe that he and Greene were 'indulgent captives', highly prized and treated well, but prisoners nonetheless.

There are a few versions of what now happened to Greene. In *Typee*, Melville claimed that Greene escaped from the valley, abandoning him. In Greene's account of the adventure (see **Romancing the Truth?**, page 154), he said that he left Typee to find help for Melville's injured leg—although Melville claimed he had been cured by native medicine—met up with an Irish seaman named Jimmy Fitz and told him of Melville's plight. Fitz promised to help him, and Toby—rather cavalierly, it's true—shipped off the island on the next whaler.

From Melville's point of view, deep in the forest with a cannibal tribe (however kindly they might be), it certainly seemed as if he had been deserted, and he began to cast around for a way out. One presented itself when the Australian whaler *Lucy Ann* appeared at Nuku Hiva. Its captain, whose name was Ventom, needed another seaman and sent bearers with trade goods deep into the Typee valley to ransom Melville. At least, this is how Melville tells it. It's possible that the mysterious Jimmy Fitz was a whaling recruiter and had told Ventom of Melville's presence in the valley.

Romancing the Truth?

When Melville's travel memoir *Typee* was published in 1846, it became an overnight bestseller, but was viewed with great disapproval by many prudish persons who did not approve of the (for the time) sexually graphic depictions of the islanders (one review called the book 'a panegyric on cannibal delights') and Melville's obvious anti-European, anti-missionary stance.

A further cause for disapproval was what some felt was the imagined nature of the narrative. Many questioned what one reader called 'the sober veracity' of what Melville was labelling 'a true narrative of events which actually occurred'. Another suggested he was 'romancing' the facts. The outcry was so great that Melville's publisher wanted him to alter some of the more 'outlandish' descriptions of cannibalism and sexual licentiousness. But just as this pressure was being brought to bear, support appeared from an unexpected quarter—Melville's companion in the Typee valley, Richard Greene (Toby of the book), now living in Buffalo, New York, published a letter saying: 'I am the true and veritable "Toby" yet living, and I am happy to testify to the entire accuracy of the work, so long as I was with Melville ...'

But the modern reader is still left with the question—what is truth, what is fiction, in Melville's account? He obviously changed the timeframe. *Typee* has him on the island for four months; in reality he was there for three or four weeks. Melville has Toby deserting him, which was not quite true. Greene's own account says he left to get help for Melville's infected leg, fell in with Jimmy Fitz, who promised to get aid to Melville, at which point Toby departed the island on a whaler.

In Melville's account, he escapes to an Australian whaler but only by dint of burying a boathook in the neck of a native trying to keep him there. Some historians suspect that Fitz merely brokered a quiet deal and that Melville went aboard the *Lucy Ann* in a much more peaceable way.

Interestingly, however, an oral history gathered in Nuku Hiva by a Columbia University anthropologist in the 1950s seems to support Melville's version of his 'indulgent captivity' and escape, saying that the red-headed white man had been given a wife called Pe-ue (Fayaway, in Melville's account) and treated as a valued guest because he was thought to bring good luck. But when he escaped aboard a ship, he was showered with stones.

We will never know to what extent *Typee* is embellished, but the core of Melville's account—the open sexuality of the people, the fact of cannibalism (although it is doubtful cannibalistic intentions were aimed at Melville) and the sense of an earthly paradise about to be ruined by the intrusion of the white man—is verifiable by other sources.

The trade goods did the trick, and Fayaway, Mehevi escorted Melville to the coast. When the whaler sent in a longboat, Mehevi suddenly changed his mind, wanting more for his prized guest. The whalers refused his demands and began rowing back to the ship. Desperate, Melville broke away and raced for the longboat, diving into the surf and swimming with all his might. He reached the boat and was hauled in by the seamen just as a warrior grabbed him. Paradise or not, this was too much—Melville snatched a boathook and buried it in the man's neck.

'The Art of Book Craft'

Melville did not have much luck with whaling captains. Take away the 't' from Captain Ventom's name and you have some idea of how poisonous a skipper he was. Almost a third of the *Lucy Ann*'s crew, including all three mates, had deserted by the time Melville joined her, and almost everyone on board was drunk much of the time. When the *Lucy Ann* arrived in Tahiti the crew, in an alcohol-fuelled fury, rioted. Although Melville had taken no part in the affray, he was clapped in irons along with eight others and put to forced labour by British authorities. The *Lucy Ann* left without them. Six weeks later, Melville was released and found passage on an American whaler which took him to Hawaii; from there, he boarded an American naval frigate, the USS *United States*, which landed him in Boston on 14 October 1844, almost four years after his departure.

Having had his adventures, it was time for Herman Melville to practise what he called 'the art of book craft'. Writing at fever pitch, he produced *A Narrative of Four Months' Residence among the Natives of a Valley of the Marquesas Islands*. It was rejected by the American publisher Harper Brothers, who felt it was too fantastic to be true, but was published in London by Wiley & Putnam in January 1846, where it immediately became a bestseller. A month later, the publisher brought out an American edition more invitingly titled *Typee: A Peep at Polynesian Life*, and Melville became something of an overnight sensation. He was to quickly write two more books on sea-faring, *Redburn* and *White-Jacket*, before settling down in Massachusetts' Berkshire Mountains to produce *Moby Dick*, now considered the greatest novel produced in nineteenth century America.

Unfortunately when it was published in 1851 *Moby Dick* was poorly received, and Melville was forced to take a position as a deputy inspector of customs for the Port of New York, which he held for nineteen years. He still wrote poetry, but was mainly forgotten.

Herman Melville died on 28 September 1891, at the age of seventy-two. His place in posterity was assured, a literary journey that began in a valley hidden deep beneath the cascading falls and vertiginous slopes of Nuku Hiva.

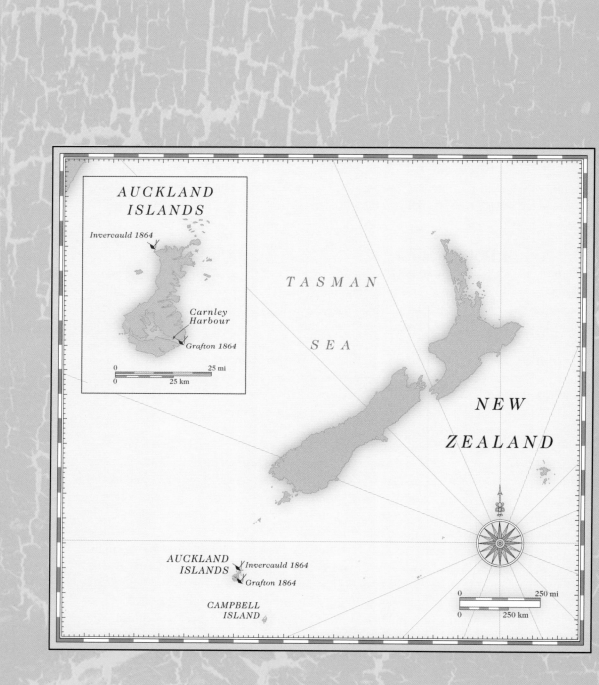

AUCKLAND
ISLANDS

Invercauld 1864

Carnley
Harbour

Grafton 1864

0   25 mi
0   25 km

TASMAN

SEA

NEW

ZEALAND

AUCKLAND
ISLANDS   Invercauld 1864

Grafton 1864

CAMPBELL
ISLAND

0   250 mi
0   250 km

The Grafton *and the* Invercauld, 1864–1866
Lost on Auckland Island

The remote and uninhabited Auckland Islands were notorious in the age of sail for gobbling ships whole and spitting them out well-chewed. Swept by gales, shrouded by fog and snow, this dangerous archipelago some 500 kilometres (310½ miles) south of New Zealand would appear suddenly out of a dark night, cliffs looming hundreds of metres high. If you were caught on a lee shore, with the wind blasting your sails full, you might easily meet your maker on these apocalyptic coasts.

There were eleven known shipwrecks in the Aucklands between 1833 and 1908. Of these, nine left castaways. Astonishingly enough, two wrecks, those of the *Grafton* and the *Invercauld*, occurred within months of one another and left survivors marooned on the opposite ends of Auckland Island itself. These men, fighting for their lives, had no inkling that the other group existed just 30 kilometres (18½ miles) away.

How one band of men lived—and the way in which the other mainly perished—is a lesson in group dynamics from which we can learn a great deal.

The *Grafton* Sets Sail

On 12 November 1863, a former collier known as the *Grafton*—a sturdy, two-masted schooner which displaced 75 tons—set sail from Sydney with a crew of five men. She was off on a risky mission—to sail hundreds of kilometres to Campbell Island, a mountainous sub-Antarctic island of volcanic origin which had been a prime base for sealing earlier in the century until the seals were nearly exterminated. It was not seals the *Grafton* sought, however, but something far more valuable—a rumoured vein of argentiferous tin—tin containing silver—which would bring a great deal of money on the market, if only it could be dug out.

The two men leading this expedition were Captain Thomas Musgrave and François Raynal. Musgrave was 31 years old and an experienced sea captain. He had plied the Liverpool–Australia route since he was sixteen, eventually being given command, and ultimately marrying and settling in Sydney, where he was employed sailing merchant vessels back and forth to New Zealand. However, by 1863 he had lost his job and was looking for a new venture to take its place.

His partner Raynal, in his mid-thirties, was a man with an interesting history. Originally from France, where he had trained as a scientist and engineer, he had come to

Australia in the 1850s, lured by the gold fields of New South Wales. He had failed to make a go of prospecting, in part because of recurring ill health, which included dysentery and a disease that made him go blind for nine days and nearly drove him to suicide. Finally a tunnel collapsed on him, forcing him into eight months of recuperation. When he recovered, he sought about for work that was *anywhere* but the gold mines.

By chance, Thomas Musgrave's uncle, who worked in the drapery business, had a partner who was an old friend of Raynal's. It was these two men who heard the rumour about the valuable tin on Campbell Island and introduced Musgrave and Raynal to each other. A deal was struck: Musgrave and Raynal would lead an expedition to the island which the two clothiers would finance.

Campbell Island

Raynal and Musgrave were both serious, intelligent men whose straitened circumstances led them to decide on the wild trip to Campbell Island—a trip that Raynal admitted they should have thought out more seriously first. The expedition was fated from the start. Shortly after leaving Sydney, they were hit by a storm of formidable force, which nearly rolled the ship. They were caught in it for days and when it finally blew itself out they found themselves some 250 kilometres (155 miles) off course.

Fortunately, Musgrave was an experienced captain and he had picked a good, if eclectic, crew. Aside from Raynal, the *Grafton* was manned by a 20-year-old English seaman named George Harris and a 28-year-old Norwegian named Alexander Maclaren, whom they called Alick, a strong person who seldom said a word. The fifth member of the crew was perhaps the most exotic, a Portuguese sailor from the Azores who introduced himself by the obviously invented name of Brown, and finally admitted that his real name was Henry Forges. Forges apparently had leprosy, or some disfiguring disease which had eaten away most of his nose, but his resume included (if he was to be believed) working aboard an American whaler and living in Samoa among the natives.

This disparate group helped bring the ship safely to harbour at Campbell Island on 2 December 1863, in the sunny, warmish weather of the far southern summer. The next day Raynal and Musgrave starting roaming the tussock-filled slopes of the island, searching for tin. They climbed a tall mountain they called the Dome for the awe-inspiring view—they were truly at the ends of the earth, and the ocean stretched away forever, to Antarctica—but they found no tin. The next day, Raynal fell ill with a fever and was unable to prospect. Alick searched in his place with Musgrave, but they found no tin either. With Raynal now delirious, Musgrave, hoping to salvage something from the voyage, decided to make his way to the Auckland Islands to see if the seal population was stronger there; perhaps a bit of sealing would make the trip worthwhile in the end.

Auckland Island

On 1 January 1864, according to the ship's log kept by Musgrave, which later formed part of his published narrative, *Castaway on the Auckland Islands*, the *Grafton* arrived off Auckland Island, the largest of the archipelago's seven major islands. On the west side of the island, which Musgrave sailed around, the cliffs present an unbroken wall. He marvelled at the surf crashing against these precipitous cliffs, but kept his distance, lest the ship be driven ashore. On the southeast side he found Carnley Harbour, protected by high headlands, and the *Grafton* sailed in. To their great relief, they saw sea lions and fur seals basking on the rocks. Musgrave and Raynal, who was gradually recovering from his illness, came to a decision. They would land, kill enough seals to fill a few barrels with oil, return quickly to Sydney and raise a proper sealing expedition—perhaps thirty men, with the right equipment and another ship—and come back to make their fortune.

Unfortunately, Auckland Island was not about to let them have such an easy time of it. The Aucklands had been discovered only relatively recently, in 1806, by an English whaling captain, although some evidence has since been found of Polynesian settlement as early as 1200 or so. Sealers had come here in the 1820s and 1830s but, as on Campbell Island, had eliminated much of the seal population. There had even been an attempt to settle Auckland Island, in the northeastern part near Port Ross, but this had been abandoned in 1849 after only a few years. The soils were poor; it rained twenty-seven days out of every month; overall the Aucklands had a well-deserved reputation as a godforsaken, gale-driven place offering scant shelter among their twisted volcanic rock formations and stunted dwarf forests.

Driven Ashore

The *Grafton*'s problems began immediately on reaching harbour, and were due to financial shortsightedness on the part of Musgrave's backers. Wanting to finance the expedition on the cheap, they had refused to allow Musgrave to purchase anchor cables of the proper length and thus he was forced to anchor the ship in about 30 fathoms, quite close to shore. 'There is hardly room for her [the *Grafton*] to swing clear of the rocks should the wind come from the S.W.,' Musgrave wrote. It was New Year's Day but there was no celebrating.

The gale Musgrave was worried about came up and soon the ship was 'jerking and straining at her chains'.

All the next day the gale blew 'with the most terrific violence' and the men on board watched the anchor chains with deep concern. And, 'precisely at midnight', Musgrave wrote, one of the chains snapped and the ship hit the rocks side-on with a terrifying scraping sound. The men clung to whatever they could as wave after wave pounded over the decks. By morning it was clear that the *Grafton* could not survive—'water was rushing into her like a boiling spring', Musgrave wrote—and they decided to abandon ship.

And here was the first instance of the instinct for group—rather than individual— survival that was to characterise the efforts of the *Grafton* survivors. Rather than battle their way to shore, every man for himself, they rigged up a pulley system by which the ship's boat, carrying precious supplies, could be tugged through the treacherous surf. The men swung themselves to shore the same way, with François Raynal, still weak, tied to Musgrave's back.

On the shore they huddled under a sail as shelter from the rain and took stock. They had a barrel of hardtack, a little over 20 kilograms (44 pounds) of flour, 1 kilogram (over 2 pounds) of tea and 1.5 kilograms (over 3 pounds) of coffee, a little tobacco, the rifle which Raynal had providentially brought along, and the clothes on their backs.

'The Vessel Leaves Her Bones Here'

For a week, the men were assailed by steady gales and downpours—and this was summertime. It was discouraging, to say the least. Forays that Musgrave and Alick took through the hills showed the formidable nature of the winds—there was not one tree on the island beyond a certain height that remained unbent. Climbing to the top of a mountain, Musgrave saw nothing around him but rocky crags, steep precipices and the raging ocean. He wrote in his log: 'Mine appears a hard fate. After getting to where I might have made up what was lost [through sealing in lieu of finding tin] I lose the means of doing so. The vessel leaves her bones here and God only know whether we are all to leave our bones here, also.'

Fortunately for the group, Raynal had recovered, and his sturdy optimism and engineer's knowhow offset Mulgrave's pessimism. Realising that in all probability they were going to be on Auckland for a while, Raynal set about guiding them in building a cabin, picking a place up the slope from the beach where, as Musgrave put it, 'There is plenty of timber and also a beautiful creek of clear water.' They levelled a rectangle of ground, dug deep holes in the corners, placed stones in the holes as anchors, and used

A two-masted schooner similar to the *Grafton*.

sections of mast salvaged from the vessel, which had not completely broken up, as corner posts. They notched the tops and placed other parts of the masts between the posts to create a framework, and used the bowsprit as the ridgepole. Rafters were cut from the straightest trees they could find and the roof was thatched with some 5000 bundles of the local vegetation. Slowly but surely they built a proper house.

The most extraordinary thing about this house was its fireplace. Because the island's peaty soil would catch on fire, they had to dig a pit for the fireplace and line it with stones. They had no mortar to bind the stones together, so Raynal made his own. He made a fire, placed a large quantity of seashells on it and covered it. When the shells burned down, he was left with calcium oxide, or lime. Normally this would be mixed with clay, but since there was none to be had, he mixed the hot calcium oxide with fine gravel and sand from the beach—burning his hands badly—and came up with a sturdy base for the fireplace which would not collapse when heated. The chimney was built of stones and lined with copper stripped from the *Grafton*'s hull.

It was now early February and the men had a proper house, where they slept on stretchers made of sail canvas and poles, slung 2 metres (6 feet) above their heads so they could walk around more easily in the day. Their mattresses were dried moss, their blankets sealskins.

Coming Together

Still, the *Grafton* castaways had a difficult time of it. They all missed their families and homes—'What is to become of my poor unprotected family?' wrote Musgrave. 'It drives me mad to think of it.' They were constantly bitten by small flies which meant that their faces and hands were always red and puffy. The seals were their mainstay. They followed the sea lions, shooting or clubbing them to death for their skins, and killing the pups, finding these the easiest eating—'a great deal like lamb', Musgrave wrote. The huge male sea lions did not take this sitting down and on several occasions attacked the castaways, once nearly stoving in their ship's boat.

There were pigs, rabbits and goats, left on the island by others who had come ashore, but they were nearly impossible to catch in the dense undergrowth. They once saw a dog and attempted to capture it to help them hunt, but it eluded them and they never saw it again.

Seal meat sustained the men but alone would not have prevented scurvy, luckily Raynal found a plant now known as Macquarie Island cabbage, *Stilbocarpa polaris*, which was edible and nutritious. He grated the roots, which he made into cakes, fried in seal oil and served piping hot, to the men's delectation, but did not realise that the stems and leaves were also edible.

Raynal made another, highly important contribution to their welfare. As their stay on the island lengthened, Raynal and Musgrave noted that the others were not quite as ready to obey the captain's orders as they had been on the ship. The gruff Musgrave wrote that he thought the men should be grateful to him for using the bounty of the wrecked ship to keep them alive, 'but [one] might as well look for the grace of God in a Highmanland's log as gratitude in a sailor'.

Seeing dissension brewing and knowing it could lead to disaster, Raynal hit on a solution. He proposed that they elect a leader—a 'head' or 'chief of family'—who would guide them. The men agreed, with the caveat that they should be able to fire anyone not doing a good job. A contract was drawn up on a blank endpage of Musgrave's Bible and signed by all, then Raynal nominated Musgrave for the job. He was unanimously elected, and all, including Musgrave, were happy. They even held a competition to name the house, which Musgrave won with the name Epigwaitt, which he claimed was an American Indian word meaning 'near the great waters'.

A well-timed dose of democracy had kept the men from descending into the chaos that plagued many groups of castaways—and would plague an unfortunate group of sailors even now being dashed ashore, 30 kilometres (18½ miles) to the north.

The Wreck of the *Invercauld*

On 3 May 1864, the Scottish freighter *Invercauld* left Melbourne en route to South America, carrying a crew of twenty-five. On 10 May she approached the Aucklands in a blinding snowstorm. When a dark coastline appeared through the snow the captain, George Dalgarno, thought he was seeing Adams Island, at the southern tip of Auckland Island. In fact he was looking at the northern part of Auckland itself, so that when he tacked to the right to clear land, he actually headed directly for it. With Dalgarno realising his error and frantically shouting orders, the crew tried to bring the ship about to clear the black cliffs rising above them, but it was too late. The *Invercauld* struck the rocks under full sail, her upper masts snapping off against the cliffs.

Unlike the *Grafton*, the *Invercauld* broke up very quickly and her crew was washed overboard by the huge waves that crashed down upon the ruined vessel. The survivors crawled up on the stone beach and huddled in the overhang of the cliffs. When a grey dawn finally glimmered, it was seen that nineteen out of the twenty-five had lived, including the captain, the first mate, Andrew Smith, the second mate, James Mahoney, and a common seaman, the young Englishman Robert Holding.

These men were in terrible shape, much worse off than the crew of the *Grafton*. For one thing, their ship had been completely destroyed and their only food was 1 kilogram (2 pounds) of wet biscuit and 1 kilogram of pork. For another, they were in a far more precarious position, surrounded by 100 metre (109 yard) cliffs on a tiny beach. But they also lacked leadership. Captain Dalgarno, according to the memoir written later by Robert Holding, was in an almost catatonic state, unable to help himself or the crew, incapable even of organising the most rudimentary search for food and water.

After five days of shellfish and rainwater, Robert Holding had had enough. He climbed to the top of the cliffs, gaining footholds in fissures in the rock and hanging onto tussock grass. When he arrived at the windswept summit, he could see land sloping down gently to bays in the northeast—a more promising prospect than the rocky beach. The next day he climbed down and prodded the other survivors into getting moving.

Thus began a miserable trek across the island, with Holding attempting to lead the way and the captain and the others dragging miserably behind. After three days of this crawling pace, Holding got tired of trying to force the others along. Leaving them

Jules Verne, François Raynal and *The Mysterious Island*

François Raynal also wrote a memoir, *Wrecked on a Reef*, of his experiences on Auckland Island. It appeared in 1870. While Musgrave's *Castaway on the Auckland Islands* focuses largely on his black depressions and his battle not to give up hope, Raynal's book is a tale of resourcefulness. Always with modesty, the French engineer describes his triumphs in building a house, making soap from seal blubber, creating the all-important forge, and ultimately building the ship which would take them off the island.

Jules Verne (1828–1905).

The author Jules Verne, who had written such famous early tales of science fiction and adventure as *20,000 Leagues Under the Sea* and *Round the World in Eighty Days*, almost certainly found himself inspired by Raynal's bestselling book, which was illustrated by Alphonse de Neuville, also the illustrator of several of Verne's books. Raynal and Verne were both members of the Geographical Society of Paris, where in 1868 Raynal delivered a paper on his experiences. So it probably isn't any coincidence that when Verne published his novel *The Mysterious Island* in 1874 it bore striking resemblances to Raynal's real life story.

In *The Mysterious Island*, five men escape from a Confederate prisoner of war camp in the United States by means of a hot air balloon (a favourite conveyance of Verne's), are blown westward into the Pacific, and crash on an unknown island. Their leader, an engineer named Cyrus Smith, is, like Raynal, in poor health, but believes (like Raynal) that 'God helps those who help themselves'. And so he makes soap and candles from seal fat and bellows from sealskin, builds a house for his men, and generally makes things so comfortable for everyone that when the chance for rescue comes, four years later, they don't want to leave.

near a rocky cairn, he headed back to the wreck to see if there was anything to be salvaged. The veteran boatswain went with him. Along the way, they came upon the body of the cook, who had fallen behind and died of exposure. At the bottom of the cliff where the *Invercauld* was wrecked, they found the corpse of a sailor who had stayed behind.

The next day, four men joined them from the group at the cairn. They discovered the rotting carcass of the ship's pig stuck in a rocky crevice and devoured the putrid meat. Then the boatswain declared that they were obviously starving to death and that they should draw lots to see who should die so that the others might eat him. Holding declared that he would never become either killer or cannibal—and then realised that his statement made him the most likely first victim. He lay awake in terror all that night and in the morning climbed the cliff and ran across the headlands as if pursued by ghosts.

Civilisation?

Holding wandered the cliff tops for a few days, eventually finding his way down into one of the bays he had sighted, and discovered not only seals—which he had no way of killing—but also limpets, clinging to tidal rocks, which he was able to scrape off with his knife and eat. He filled his pockets and brought them back to the group near the cairn. They were as he had left them, eating roots and wasting away, as if unable to help themselves without his presence. He did not tell them about his brush with cannibalism—and the four would-be cannibals were never heard from again, so presumably they died.

It was now May—the southern winter—and aside from suffering from malnutrition, many of the seamen were barefoot, having cast away their heavy boots when they leapt from the boat. Over the next few days, several died, until there were perhaps ten left. Holding led five of these survivors on a desperate search for sustenance which caused them to make a surprising discovery: a ruined village, with one house and an outbuilding partially intact. The village was the remnant of the failed settlement on the island, which had been abandoned some seventeen years before, but the men had at last found shelter, of sorts.

Strangely, a common hallucination now took hold of all the castaways save Holding. They did little to improve their lot in this ruined village, and Holding realised that they were waiting for its inhabitants to come back, even though it was obvious that this would never be the case. A feral cat which showed up caused great excitement—perhaps its owner would now return to retrieve it.

'I Cannot Call It Living'

In the meantime, the survivors of the *Grafton*, with no idea of the *Invercauld* group leading such a wretched existence, were leading a calm, orderly, almost domestic life to the south, with each man assigned to his daily chores and Musgrave leading them in evening teaching sessions and prayers on Sunday. Still, the spectre of starvation shadowed even these resourceful men, for their lives depended the ebb and flow of the seal population as the creatures came to shore to mate, give birth and raise their pups, then slipped into the water out of their reach.

There was no sign of a ship. Raynal and Musgrave thought it possible that their partners would send a rescue vessel, or that a sealer would stop by the island, and waited hopefully until October or November, the season when a ship would most likely appear. Musgrave's journal records the tedium of their lives: 'I think I have never described our precise mode of dragging out this miserable existence, for I cannot call it living. Breakfast—seal stewed down to soup, fried roots, boiled seal, with water. Dinner—Ditto ditto. Supper—Ditto ditto.'

In September, the seals began to migrate to new feeding grounds and they were reduced to eating more roots and any birds they could shoot. October came. 'The long looked for month has arrived at last (God send relief before it passes),' wrote Musgrave. But no sails were evident on the horizon. They had been on the island nine months and it was becoming clear that there was little hope of rescue. 'Our friends,' Musgrave wrote bitterly, meaning his uncle and his uncle's partner, 'have been, to say the least, wanting in energy.'

He began referring to Epigwaitt in his journal as his 'prison-house'. Christmas 1864 came and went, with no sign of a boat.

Three Only

In the abandoned village on the other side of the island, the illusion of rescue also disappeared as the men died one by one. When the second mate, James Mahoney, died, the others simply left his body rotting in his bunk. There were now only three—George Dalgarno, Adam Smith and Robert Holding. Holding recognised that while the ruined village provided an illusion of safety, to stay there any longer without a proper source of food was madness. Under his direction they made a raft, which they took across to a small island which Holding dubbed Rabbit Island because of the number of the animals there.

Unfortunately, the rabbits proved hard to catch in the thick undergrowth and had eaten most of the Macquarie Island cabbage which the *Invercauld* survivors had also learned to subsist on. Holding took to climbing the cliffs to pluck baby birds from their nests, but he was aware that the three of them were slowly starving to death.

Then the impossible happened. On 22 May 1865, Holding was gathering wood when he heard Dalgarno screaming at the top of his lungs: 'A SHIP—A SHIP—A SHIP!'

The men ran to the beach. The ship had disappeared behind a point, and they waited with bated breath for it to reappear. They hurriedly built a signal fire, throwing green branches on it when the ship came in sight again to make it smoke. The vessel fired a gun to let them know they had been seen, and lowered a boat.

The castaways' existence had changed in a split second. As the longboat approached, Dalgarno turned to Holding and snapped: 'Don't *you* speak to them. *I* will be the one who speaks!', belatedly assuming the authority he had abandoned. It mattered little, however, as the sailors from the Spanish ship *Julian* spoke almost no English. The ship was on her way from China to Callao in Peru, with a cargo of Chinese coolies, and was stopping in for fresh water. Even though there was some kind of deadly illness raging on the ship, the castaways boarded gratefully and she set sail for South America, unaware of the other group's existence.

The Forge and Boat

On their side of the island, the *Grafton* castaways were equally unaware of the *Julian*. They were engaged in the labour of building a boat, for by now they understood that they could not depend on outside help—they must get themselves off the island. Musgrave wrote that his hair was falling out and that he was covered with boils, both, no doubt, signs of malnutrition. He had decided that they should sail to New Zealand, the nearest landfall, some 500 kilometres (310½ miles) distant over a notoriously difficult stretch of water. The ever-resourceful Raynal was able to make a bellows out of sealskin and forge a crude anvil and tongs. With these he fashioned nails from bolts from the hull of the *Grafton*. When the attempt to build a boat from scratch resulted in an unstable, leaky craft, Raynal and the others set about strengthening the ship's dinghy.

This boat could not hold all five men, and finally it was decided—with the equitableness that had marked all these castaways' dealings—that George Harris and Henry Forges would be left behind, since, as Musgrave wrote, 'the two had always agreed very well and the latter had evinced a strong disinclination to going in the boat at all'. The plan was for Musgrave, Raynal and Alick to reach safety and send a rescue ship back for the other two.

On the morning of 19 July 1865—a morning which 'broke fine and promising'—the three men said goodbye to Harris and Forges, boarded their little vessel—most hopefully named *Rescue*—and steered a course out of the harbour. The minute they hit the open sea they were assailed by icy winds. They were running ahead of a gale which, by the time night fell and the Aucklands had disappeared behind them, turned into winds so strong that the *Rescue* was riding huge waves in a dizzying roller-coaster fashion. Raynal had built an improvised pump for bailing out the boat, and the three men took turns, working it constantly. For five days, their passage remained a miserable one, as Musgrave wrote: 'I stood upon my feet holding a rope with one hand and pumping with the other.' None of them was able to eat.

On the morning of the sixth day they spotted Stewart Island, just south of New Zealand, and made for Port Adventure. They were exhausted. 'I had not eaten an ounce of food since the time of our leaving,' Musgrave wrote, 'yet I felt no fatigue until the night before we landed', at which point he realised he was near collapse, with rescue so close. The people of the town near where they landed came rushing down to the bay to help.

Robert Holding's Colourful Life

Although newspapermen in their native Scotland were to interview Dalgarno and Smith from the *Invercauld* (and Smith would later write his own account, published in 1866), Robert Holding, being but a humble seaman, was never asked to recount his exploits on Auckland Island. Not only that, instead of being given a ticket home by the British consulate when the *Julian* set them ashore in Callao, as Dalgarno and Smith were, he was sent to a boarding house for seamen and left to his own devices.

Holding existed on handouts from other sailors until he managed to work his way back to Europe on a vessel rounding the Horn, finally getting home to England in October 1865. After visiting his family he went to back to sea. Some twenty years later he gave up the ocean-going life and migrated to Canada, where he worked as a machinist in Toronto before heading to the gold fields of West Shiningtree, Ontario. He apparently did well enough to start his own hotel in the area, which he managed until his death in 1933 at the age of ninety-three.

Holding wrote his memoir of his awful sojourn on Auckland Island in the end, typing it, at the age of eighty-six, on an old Remington typewriter. The manuscript remained in the family until Holding's great-granddaughter, Madelene Ferguson Allen, discovered it and, with additional chronology and details gleaned from her own research and trips to Auckland Island, published it in 1997 under the title *Wake of the Invercauld*.

Alick passed out in their arms and Musgrave and Raynal could barely speak. Warmed and fed, they collapsed into sleep for a full twenty-four hours.

Although Musgrave was anxious to get back to Sydney and his family, he knew that it was his duty to guide a rescue vessel back to Auckland Island, and this he did. The government official he spoke to showed a terrible bureaucratic indifference, but a brave fisherman named Tom Cross offered to take his cutter, the *Flying Scud*, to the island to pick up Harris and Forges. They sailed on 29 July but, forced to return to port because of a faulty compass, it was not until 24 August that they entered Carnley Harbour. Cross and Musgrave landed and raced to Epigwaitt, where they found the two men near death—they had been reduced to catching and eating mice.

Aboard the *Flying Scud* and given a proper meal of fish and potatoes, Harris and Forges collapsed, exhausted. Because Cross thought he had seen smoke from a fire on the northeast part of the island, they now sailed in that direction and landed in Port Ross—near where the *Invercauld* castaways had been tossed ashore—seeking other possible castaways. The smoke turned out to have been a mere wisp of fog but, coming ashore nonetheless, Musgrave discovered the abandoned village and discovered, too, the corpse of James Mahoney, still lying in his bunk. Having no knowledge of the *Invercauld* wreck, he could only surmise where this man had come from.

It was the dead man, rather than the living survivors, that stirred government action. After Musgrave, Harris and Forges had finally returned with their story, it was decided that the Aucklands must be provisioned—by releasing live animals—and erecting signposts which pointed the way to stores of food and to the *Grafton* castaways' hut. The indefatigable Musgrave accompanied the first ship to make such a voyage, rounding Auckland Island and firing guns to alert possible castaways. But the island met them with silence. It was only in November 1865 that Musgrave and Raynal, both back in Sydney, learned that the *Invercauld* had been wrecked on the island at the same time as the *Grafton*.

Musgrave published his memoirs, became a harbour pilot in Sydney and finally a lighthouse keeper, dying in 1891 at the age of fifty-nine. Raynal also published his Auckland memoirs (see **Jules Verne, François Raynal and *The Mysterious Island***, page 164), which became a bestseller in France, and was to die just two years before Musgrave, at the age of sixty-eight. Neither of these men ever met Robert Holding (see **Robert Holding's Colourful Life**, opposite), but if they had they would have recognised a kindred spirit.

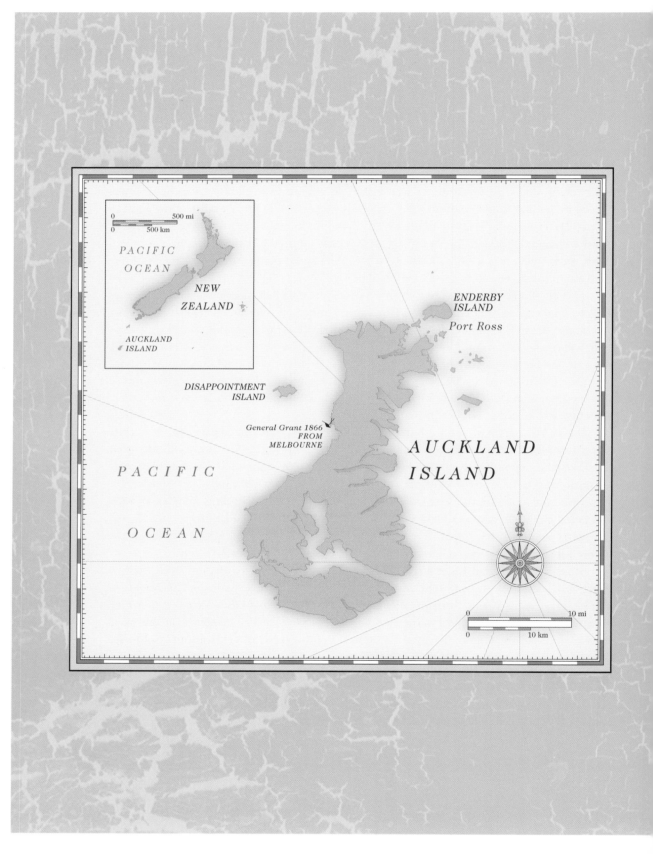

The Loss of the General Grant, 1866–1869
The Ship of Gold

On 3 May 1866—barely ten months after the exhausted survivors of the *Grafton* had returned to safety—a proud three-masted American-built cargo ship with 83 people on board set sail from Melbourne's Port Phillip Bay, heading for London. Fully laden with a cargo of wool, hides, timber and, fatefully, 73 kilograms (2576 ounces) of gold, the *General Grant* weighed almost 1100 tons. The vessel was captained by the experienced mariner William Loughlin, in charge of a crew of twenty-four hardened sailors. The *General Grant* was one of many ships plying what had come to be called the Great Circle Route, pioneered by the clipper ships which had brought fortune-hunters by the thousands to Australia and New Zealand as soon as gold was discovered in the 1850s. A ship on the Great Circle Route, taking advantage of prevailing westerly winds, would sweep southeast from Australia below New Zealand, and head down to the latitudes known as the Furious Fifties before striking east across the Pacific, around Cape Horn, and then through the Atlantic to England or America.

The *General Grant* was no swift clipper like the famous *Lightning*, which had made the run to England in sixty-three days, but certainly she was expected to arrive in England in under three months. As the ship headed south in clear weather, the passengers attempted to make themselves at home. There were forty-one people in the forward steerage area, including four women and thirteen children. The ship's more exclusive aft cabins carried fifteen, including four children. Many of the passengers were miners returning after years of prospecting in Australia; some of them almost certainly had hidden stashes of gold, while others were barely able to pay their way. Whatever their financial status, all longed for one thing: to be home again.

Fog and Fear

As the ship passed through the Roaring Forties, the fine weather, predictably, began to disappear, replaced by thick fog. Captain Loughlin knew he was nearing the Auckland Islands—was aware of the experiences of the *Grafton* and the *Invercauld* and other vessels—and so set a careful lookout. The fog was so thick, one sailor later reported, that one could barely see the jib-boom. Around ten o'clock on the night of Sunday 13 May, with the weather clearing slightly, the lookout cried 'Land … land ahead to the port bow!'

Racing on deck, Loughlin saw cliffs in the distance, white water breaking. Assuming he was seeing Enderby Island, the most northerly of the Aucklands group, he ordered the

A vivid depiction of the sea cave described by a survivor as 'the horrible cavern'.

ship to tack to the north, away from danger. But, like Captain Dalgarno before him, he had miscalculated his position. He was not as far south as he thought. The land he saw to his left was Disappointment Island, which lies 13 kilometres (8 miles) to the west of Auckland Island. By steering north, he was heading straight into dire straits.

The good captain discovered this soon enough, for within an hour the lookout spotted land again, this time to starboard, 5 or 6 kilometres (3 or 4 miles) away. Realising their mistake, they knew they were looking at the main island of the Aucklands, but as that realisation set in, the wind suddenly dropped. With the shore appearing closer and closer, Loughlin saw that the *General Grant* was drifting towards her doom.

The Horrible Cavern

'A breeze, ever so slight, might save the ship and allow her to run between [Disappointment and Auckland islands],' one survivor later wrote. Desperately, Loughlin ordered every inch of sail set, hoping to catch the puff of air that would help push them away from the looming cliffs of Auckland's precipitous west shore. Soundings were taken to see whether the ship could be anchored, but the bottom could not be found. The passengers were now all awake and on deck. One crewman reported seeing miners tying up gold in blankets.

Despite the fact that Loughlin and his officers went into a huddle, trying to find a solution, a paralysis of leadership seems to have set in. It is one thing to find oneself, as the *Invercauld* did, dashed on shore in an instant in the midst of raging seas and a fierce storm. It is quite another to drift slowly to one's doom. It was as if Loughlin could not quite believe what was happening, and thus did not put his passengers aboard the ship's boats, or make any attempt to tow it with those boats, or to clubhaul it—drag the lee, or shoreward, anchor, in an attempt to pivot the vessel away from the cliffs. Loughlin and all the rest watched as the *General Grant* drifted inexorably, straight at the cliffs. At about one in the morning of 14 May, a shoreward current caught the ship and began to push her at speed. With the passengers screaming, the ship hit a rocky promontory, then literally ricocheted into another one, timbers shattering. And then, as if in some terrible nightmare, the cliff face opened up.

For a moment, this stunned the passengers into silence. But then they began to scream anew. The bow, dashing against the cliff face, suddenly rammed straight forward into the blackness of what one survivor would call 'the horrible cavern'. For a moment, the forward motion was braked by the mainmast, which was pressed against the very top of the entrance to the cavern, but as the waves and current thrust against the ship, the mast gave a horrible groan and snapped, tumbling down across the decks, sending rocks from the cliff hurtling into the panicked mass of humanity. A shroud of ruined sails and rigging now covered the *General Grant*.

Abandoning Ship

Captain Loughlin ordered lanterns lit, and crew and passengers stared up at the precipitous walls. James Teer, an Irish miner returning home, wrote that 'there was no place where a bird could rest'—no foothold where a man could haul himself up the cliffs. Because the ship seemed relatively stable for the moment, its forward progress halted, Loughlin decided against launching the boats, something for which he would later be criticised. He apparently did not fully understand that with the ship jolting up and down within the cavern, the base of the mainmast was slowly breaking through the hull. Water was also beginning to gush into the *General Grant* from a huge gash on her side.

Astonishingly, there had so far been just one serious injury. Only the forward part of the vessel was actually within the cave, and it would have been possible to launch the ship's boats in relatively good order, but Laughlin decided to wait until dawn. As the faintest light broke in the sky, the wind came up, jamming the ship over and over into the cavern, causing the mainmast to drive into the hull like a battering ram. Belatedly, Loughlin ordered the boats to be readied, and pandemonium swept over the passengers who had waited so patiently for so long. They jostled for positions on the three 7 metre (23 feet) longboats, carrying their luggage with them.

One boat was launched and rowed by three seamen to the entrance of the cove in which the cave lay, where it could pull the other boats via a line through the treacherous waters. Another boat was lowered to take the women and children, but to get into it each person had to have a rope tied around their waist and be dangled over the turbulent waters. Only Mary Ann Jewell, the young wife of able seaman Richard Jewell, would hazard this.

At this point the mainmast broke all the way through the hull and true panic set in, for the ship was indeed sinking. Water swept over the deck as men pushed women and children aside and dived for the one boat still on the deck. Passenger Nicholas Allen left his wife and two children behind to perish as he found himself a place. Miners dived into the sea, weighed down by gold, and sank. The longboat floated off the deck and overturned, drowning the women and children wearing voluminous skirts and heavy clothing. Allen survived and swam to one of the other boats. As the crews manning these boats pulled away, they could see Captain Loughlin, high in the crosstrees of the *General Grant*, waving a white handkerchief in farewell—he was going down with his ship.

In only a few moments the screams were silenced, and the two boats floated alone on the choppy seas under the cliffs. There were fifteen survivors, fourteen men and the one woman who been able to bring herself to be lowered into a boat. Sixty-eight lives had been lost.

James Teer

In almost every multiple castaway situation, someone must take charge or the group will perish. The *Grafton* had Musgrave and Raynal, the *Invercauld* Robert Holding. The shattered survivors of the *General Grant* had James Teer. Although seven of the fifteen were crew members—one of them the ship's chief officer, Bart Brown—passenger Teer became the natural leader. A tall, powerful man about forty years old, he had emigrated from Ireland at the age of eighteen and spent over twenty years in the gold fields. Now he and his friend Patrick Caughey, from the same fishing village on the west coast of Ireland, had booked passage home together (Caughey, too, was one of the survivors).

But with Brown apparently in a state of shock, Teer stepped in. He divided the survivors more evenly between the two longboats, when it was decided that they should make for Disappointment Island, some 10 kilometres (6 miles) away. With wind and current against them—and with seven in Teer's boat, eight in the other—it was a near impossible task. At one point, Teer would write in the journal he kept on sealskin, using charcoal as a writing implement, the boats were 'all but full' of water, despite constant bailing. As last, as night was falling, they made it to a lone rock standing in the water (now known as Needle Rock) about 2 kilometres (over 1 mile) from Disappointment.

There the survivors tied up and spent a miserable evening, being forced, as Teer would write, 'to keep on our oars all night to prevent our being blown off the land'. When day dawned, they decided to row around the north end of Auckland Island to Port Ross, but stiff winds opposed them and they eventually headed back to Disappointment. That afternoon they found water, and shared what provisions they had, which was a little salt pork and a few tins of beef stew.

Gold-seekers

The gold that was supposedly aboard the *General Grant* when she went down has lured many a treasure hunter to that island's inhospitable west shore.

In March 1868, shortly after his rescue, survivor James Teer returned with a steam-tug, the *Southland*, to pinpoint the cave, but the weather was so bad and the seas so dangerous that the expedition was unsuccessful. Teer never returned. Survivor David Ashworth took his turn with an expedition in 1870. Ashworth and four others set out in a whaleboat to circumnavigate the island, looking for the cave, and never returned—presumably lost in the stormy seas. The cavern where the *General Grant* went down was identified in 1916—when the searchers dived directly to the bottom without finding any sign of gold.

Salvaging any gold today is unlikely, but there have been more than twenty-five attempts. There is much controversy as to how much gold was on the ship, with estimates ranging from US$150,000 to $5 million. The ship's manifest claimed 73 kilograms (2576 ounces), which would be US$2.4 million at current prices, but it is unclear if this is accurate—rumours have spread that more gold was in a safe where many miners placed their bullion. With the passage of time—and with access to the Aucklands limited—the treasure may never be found.

The next day the wind lessened and they tried once again to round the north end of the island, finally reaching Port Ross and coming ashore near the site of the abandoned settlement where the *Invercauld* survivors had sheltered. Here, they decided to stay.

'We Obtained Fire'

Now came one of the most pivotal moments of the castaways' lives on Auckland. They were ashore and they were alive, but would need fire to keep them from dying of exposure in the approaching winter. James Teer was the only one who had any matches with him, which he now put in his hair to dry. A dispute broke out, with several of the castaways wanting to light a fire before Teer thought the matches were fully dried out. Finally, Bart Brown grabbed a match and tried to light it but, Teer wrote tersely, 'as we had no dry grass or brush in readiness, it was wasted'. What Teer did not say, but other castaways attested to, was that he then struck Brown and knocked him down.

Not at all bothered by this type of violence—a fairly common way of settling arguments on the gold fields—Teer now made the survivors gather dry brush and place it in a pile. Then, he knelt and carefully struck his last match against a piece of metal. It flared, and flames leaped from the brush. They were saved. 'From this one match,' wrote Teer, 'we obtained fire, which, by constant care, we never allowed to go out.'

After eating a meal of albatross and limpets, the castaways sat by the fire and pondered their fate. They knew that the chances of another ship calling in just now were slim and that they needed to settle in for the long haul. They had one advantage over the crews of the *Grafton* and the *Invercauld*—Teer and Brown knew that animals had been placed ashore the previous autumn by the expedition led by Musgrave. A bottle was found containing the information that pigs, goats and chickens had been released but not, unfortunately, the important point that a cache of food and tools had been stored nearby (a cache the *General Grant*'s survivors never found). Also, and even more unfortunately, the message did not provide the coordinates for navigation to New Zealand.

With Brown in charge of the camp at Port Ross, Teer led four seamen on a search, for Musgrave's hut at Carnley Harbour. Suffering from dysentery, they fell short of their destination and were forced to return to the camp where everyone was also sick—reduced to 'mere skeletons', as Teer wrote. A second expedition was undertaken, this time led by Brown, since Teer was still ill. With the help of a sail they had made from sealskin, Brown and his men found the hut, but were disappointed in their hopes of discovering tools or better shelter. All they found were ruins and old sails which they used to patch clothing that was becoming increasingly torn.

Clippers docked at the Port of Melbourne during the nineteenth century gold rush.

Clothes were a problem, and here once again Teer's ingenuity came into play. Discovering a way of properly curing sealskin by scraping off the hair, softening it, and scraping again, he and the others were able to turn out suits, blankets and coats. Teer was able to make moccasins as well, and showed the others how to do it.

Mary Ann Jewell, the only woman, contributed greatly, taking part in all the physical labour. Despite the presence of her husband, Richard, the attractive 21-year-old drew the attentions of a seaman named Bill Scott that first winter on the island. Scott apparently made untoward remarks towards her and eventually got into a fight with Teer, who knew that this kind of tension could destroy the camp. Although Scott was no lightweight, Teer smashed him to the ground repeatedly until Scott gave up.

When Brown returned from Musgrave's hut with his disappointing news, he had found Teer and his group in terrible physical shape, suffering from scurvy, with its telltale symptoms of swelling legs and loose teeth. One survivor later reported that the illness was so severe that 'in closing our mouths our teeth would project straight out, flattening against each other'. The effects of scurvy eventually passed as they added roots and grass to their diet, but the health of several of the castaways remained precarious, especially that of David McClellan, at sixty-one the oldest of the group.

In October, while hunting rabbits on Rose Island (which both Teer's group and Robert Holding had independently named Rabbit Island), a sail was spotted—a ship was passing only a few kilometres (some 3 miles) away. Signal fires were lit and Teer and others piled into one of the boats to give chase, but the ship sailed on, despite the fact, as Teer wrote disconsolately, that 'she must have seen the smoke'. They rowed home in 'low spirits'.

Brown's Voyage

Brown, as chief officer and the best navigator on the island, made the decision to undertake what Musgrave had done before him—take a small group of seamen in an open boat and make for New Zealand. Numerous trips were made to Musgrave's old camp to salvage what timber and nails could be found, and one of the boats was fitted up to make the long passage. On 22 January 1867, Brown, along with Bill Scott (Mary Ann Jewell's unwanted admirer), Andrew Morrison and Peter McNevin, set sail on a boat partially closed in with sealskin. According to Teer, 'they carried 30 gallons [114 litres] of water in seal gullets, and some seal's meat, and the flesh of three goats, and twenty dozen eggs—all cooked'.

But, Teer wrote, 'they had no compass or nautical instrument of any sort'. Brown thought that the course to set for New Zealand was east-north-east, but the actual course was north or a little west of north. This is where the correct compass coordinates could have saved lives if they had been left on the island; for instead of going in the right direction, Brown set a course for the vast South Pacific. They were never seen or heard from again.

The ten remaining castaways kept watch for weeks, hoping that Brown might return with a ship, but after two months of disappointment, many of the group began to act strangely. Some gave up hope entirely. Others were certain that Brown had reached New Zealand but had failed to send anyone to help them. The castaways broke into factions, one faction defending Brown, the other cursing his name.

Shortly after Brown's departure, Patrick Caughey reported a dream in which his mother had appeared to him and said: 'My son, you will be rescued in January and the vessel will be sighted during your cooking week.' The others laughed at him, and as January passed into February and then into March and on to May, the dream was forgotten. By now the survivors of the *General Grant* had been on the island for a year.

'Upon a Sandy Hill'

To keep themselves busy, the castaways carved small toy boats, masterpieces of ingenuity which were weighted down and had messages carved on them ('WANT RELIEF: Ship Gen. Grant Wrkd Auckland Island May 14 1866 10 Survivors') and set floating out to sea in the hope that someone might find them. In the meantime, the ingenious Teer continued to work to improve their lot. The pigs that had been let loose on Auckland had bred and were plentiful, but almost impossible to kill without firearms. Teer now contrived a hook made out of sharpened iron bolts tempered by fire. He attached it to the end of a long pole with a flaxen rope, crept up on the pigs, jammed the hook into their backs, and then dispatched them. Cruel, perhaps, but the castaways were literally dying for the animal protein.

Teer was able to capture pigs by this method without killing them, which allowed the castaways to keep a group of pigs penned up against the possibility of hard times. He also decreed that they should move to Enderby Island, just across the channel from Port Ross, where they had kept a lookout post for some time. It made sense, since here they would be able to signal passing ships more readily. On Enderby the castaways, who now had plenty to eat, alleviated the boredom of their situation by playing football with inflated sea-lion bladders and making pets of pigs, rabbits and even a young hawk they had captured.

But the seriousness of their situation was driven home again when David McClelland died, probably of sepsis, on 3 September 1867. His passing was unexpected. As Teer wrote: 'This sad event, owing to its suddenness, and which by many of us was unexpected, cast a feeling of deep gloom upon us. He was buried upon a sandy hill on Enderby Island.'

19 November 1867

For the castaways on Enderby, 19 November began as just another day, with some hunting for seals, and others preparing meals. High on a hill, the lookout, whose name was Bill Ferguson, suddenly began shouting: 'Sail ho! A sail to the east!' He ran down into camp yelling 'A sail! A sail! A sail!' His excitement was so great that he had forgotten to light the signal fire, so Teer and several others, grabbing brands from the always burning campfire, raced up the hill and set the pile of dry brush blazing. To their frustration the strong wind forced the smoke close to ground and the ship sailed on without spotting it.

With the adrenaline still pumping through their veins, the castaways watched the vessel disappear. In fact, it was the cutter *Fanny*, headed for Carnley Harbour on a sealing expedition—they could have followed her there, had they but known. However, they decided, if one ship came so close, there might be others, and so they stayed where they were. Two days later, the whaler *Amherst*, commanded by the legendary Irish skipper Paddy Gilroy, was on its way to the Aucklands on a sealing expedition when the lookout

Memories and a Wooden Spoon

Mary Ann Jewell was the pretty and plucky sole female survivor of the wreck of the *General Grant*, who proved her worth several times over on the island, even if her presence did provoke jealousy and at least one bout of fisticuffs.

After she and her husband Richard made it back to Australia, they embarked on a lecture tour, speaking to large audiences about their experiences as castaways and wearing their homemade sealskin clothing. Mary Ann supposedly earned about $600, quite a large sum at the time, from talking and selling photographs of herself and her husband.

She then disappears from the record except for one glimpse. In his 1974 book, *The Wreck of the General Grant*, Keith Eunson describes a letter he received from a great-nephew of James Teer, who had met her in Sydney probably about 1920, when she would have been in her seventies. Mary Ann was living in impoverished circumstances, her husband having died years before, but still clung to memories of her Auckland Island sojourn, which included her sealskin coat and a wooden spoon she had carved on the island.

spotted something out of the ordinary. Gilroy's log reads: 'On sighting Enderby Island, the man at the mast noticed a sail coming out from the beach towards the vessel.'

It was Teer, with five other men, waving and shouting frantically. At first Gilroy was suspicious of these rough-looking types, but finally agreed to let Teer come on board by himself. Teer was able to stifle his excitement enough to explain who they were, and that three more men and a woman were on the island. After giving the castaways tea, coffee and tobacco ('No Persian monarch ever enjoyed such a treat as we,' one reported), Gilroy took his ship in close to Enderby and brought off the others. He offered to head back to New Zealand with them immediately, but the castaways insisted he finish his seal hunt. Heading south, they ran into the *Fanny*, which had seen messages left behind by the *General Grant* crew in Carnley Harbour and was sailing north to rescue them.

They spent the next six weeks with the *Amherst* while Gilroy finished his seal hunt. Returning to Enderby they paid a final farewell to David McClelland's grave, carved a stone to the memory of Brown and his men, lost at sea, and departed.

It was January 1868—the month Caughey's mother had predicted in his dream.

'The Curse of the Widow and the Fatherless'

The castaways were taken to Invercargill, where they were received enthusiastically and subjected to much media attention. A court of inquiry found that the wreck of the *General Grant* was 'an accident, attributable to no one' (although there were whisperings that Captain Loughlin had not done all he could, but his brave death stifled open criticism).

Later some of the survivors (see **Memories and a Wooden Spoon**, opposite) would become short-lived sensations on the lecture trail. Others, like Richard Teer and his fellow castaway David Ashworth, would seek to find the gold that the *General Grant* had spilled into the deep (see **Gold-seekers**, page 175). Ashworth would die in his attempt. Teer would survive—as he always did—living almost as a hermit on the west coast of New Zealand, eking out a living as boatman and prospector. He never did return to his village in Ireland, dying in 1887.

Their rescuer, Paddy Gilroy, returned to the Aucklands. Unable to stand the thought that any more castaways should be stranded there, he placed more caches of stores on Enderby and Auckland islands, marked by huge beacons. He also provided compass headings to New Zealand. And on the lids of the caches he left behind, he inscribed a warning:

The curse of the widow and the fatherless light upon the man who breaks open this box whilst he has a ship at his back.

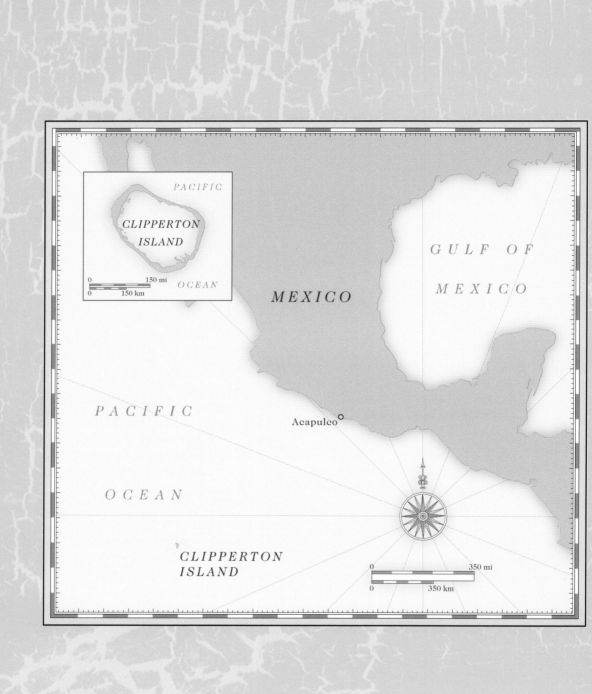

Clipperton Island, 1910–1917
The Murderous Castaway King

Some islands are fascinating for their beauty, others for their history, still others for their inhabitants. Clipperton Island, however, is fascinating for its sheer hideousness. This skull-shaped coral atoll sitting in the Pacific Ocean in the middle of nowhere, about 1200 kilometres (745 miles) south-west of Mexico, with a land area of about 6 square kilometres (4 square miles), gives people the heebie-jeebies for a number of reasons. The dead lagoon that lies within the atoll's narrow ring of land reeks of naturally occurring ammonia and sulphuric acid. The island is home to many thousands of seabirds—terns, boobies, gulls—whose guano at one time formed Clipperton's only viable industry and whose screeching, along with the pounding of the ocean waves, causes shouting to be the normal method of discourse.

Fist-sized orange land-crabs blanket the place, so that its surface, observed from offshore, seems literally to be crawling. These crabs tend to get on the nerves of visitors. In the early twentieth century, a journalist happened past Clipperton on a sailing voyage and decided to stop off for a visit. He left very quickly, later writing:

> *The land crab which literally infests the island, diabolical in appearance and persistent in activity, is a source of continued wonder ... It gives one an uncanny feeling to see this little red crustacean gazing on him with malignant stare and causing him to wonder if some demon of the deep were watching him and waiting to drag him down the depths and make a meal of his flesh.*

Speaking of demons of the deep, the waters off Clipperton abound with them. An old sailing manual, every bit as true today as in the nineteenth century, says: 'The water is infested with sharks which are of a ferocious variety and swarm in great numbers close to the island.' There are at least six types of shark, including the great white. Perhaps even scarier are the tangled masses of poisonous yellow-bellied sea-snakes which thrive in their thousands in the reefs surrounding Clipperton. These are joined by moray eels, which hunt for land crabs in the shallow water near the beaches and have been known to take a snap or two at human beings foolish enought to go wading.

The Murderer's Castle

Although Clipperton has a humid tropical climate and receives a considerable amount of rain each year (mostly from May to October), there is no fresh water. The island tends to be in the path of tropical hurricanes, which can send waves 6 metres (19½ feet) high washing across the entire atoll, most of which is no more than 2 metres (6½ feet) above sea level. It is also directly in the path of a 'drift line'—as sort of ocean corridor in which surface currents converge to carry along thousands of items of flotsam and jetsam. Clipperton's most distinctive feature is the Rock, a massive volcanic outcropping 21 metres high, 90 metres long and 6 metres wide (23 yards high, 98 yards long and 6½ yards wide), which from a distance resembles a ship in full sail. The Rock shines white in the sun, beckoning the foolish to come closer.

Men checking the quality of guano on an island off the coast of South America.

Clipperton is surrounded by treacherous reefs and gives little warning of its approach—the water is many fathoms deep only a short distance from shore—and so in 1906 the Mexican government decided to put a lighthouse atop the Rock to warn unwary sailors. And a lighthouse, of course, needs a lighthouse keeper. Being lighthouse keeper on Clipperton carries with it numerous occupational hazards, chief among them going crazy. The first lighthouse keeper went insane and had to be taken off the island. So did the second, known only as Álvarez, who Jimmy M. Skaggs, Clipperton's chief historian, calls 'a mysterious and somewhat sinister person'. Álvarez, however, was not taken off Clipperton. His existence had been completely forgotten—along with the existence of a small and terrified group of women and children marooned with him for two years—by a Mexican government embroiled in civil war. King of his Rock castle, Álvarez embarked on an orgy of rape and murder which, even on as ominous an isle as Clipperton, stands out as truly evil.

L'Île de Passion

Before we get to Álvarez and the courageous women of Clipperton, a bit of the island's chequered history. It was probably first sighted by Ferdinand Magellan during his circumnavigation of the world in 1521 but he had little reason to stop. Two centuries later John Clipperton, the English pirate for whom the island is named, supposedly used it as a regular stopping place to bury treasure, circa 1705, but there is little evidence that this was the case, and the few treasure-hunters who have dug on the beaches found nothing. The first actual documentation of the island's existence was made on Easter Sunday, 1711, when a French merchantman sailed by. Its captain noted in his log 'the large, tooth-shaped rock [that] projects off the south point of this low-lying land'—in other words, the Rock. 'In the middle of the island,' the captain goes on to say, 'is a great lake that appears to be marginally connected to the sea.' (Today, Clipperton's lagoon is completely enclosed.)

No attempt was made to go ashore because of the fringing reefs, dangerous anchorage and high surf, but passengers aboard the merchantman called the atoll *L'Île de Passion*, after the Passion of Christ. The name—perhaps a better one than Clipperton, given the bloody torments and martyrdoms which later occurred there—never stuck, and the island stayed on the charts as Clipperton's Rock. The first documented evidence of anyone setting foot on shore came in August 1825, when an American whaler and explorer named Benjamin Morrell sailed by. Morrell was not easily intimidated and sent a party ashore to capture the few sea lions and green turtles which could be found (never present in great numbers, both had disappeared from Clipperton by the mid-nineteenth century).

Guano

Today we take fertiliser for granted, but this was not the case in the nineteenth century, especially in Europe and the eastern United States, where land had been farmed for hundreds upon hundreds of years, to the point where declining crop yields were the norm. But help was on the way, for around 1804 scientists noted that bird droppings contained high level of nitrates and phosphates which worked wonders on depleted soil.

By the 1840s, shiploads of guano from South America were reaching Europe and America and producing crops that appeared like miracles. The guano craze was on, with prices doubling and then doubling again, so that the stinking ships entering port filled to the gunwales with bird poop were literally treasure ships. As prices got higher, England, France and America began to look for guano islands, particularly in the Pacific, where South American countries would not control distribution. Naturally, with its oppressive blanket of clamorous seabirds, remote Clipperton was high on the list.

The question, however, was who owned the island. Many countries, including Mexico, assumed it belonged to Mexico, but France decided it was theirs. Emperor Napoleon III instructed the French navy to 'take possession of the island in the name of the Emperor', not out of any excess of patriotism but so that he could sell the guano mining rights. It was not worth the cost of sending a fully crewed naval ship, however. A lone lieutenant would do, one Victor le Coat de Kerveguen, who sailed on the merchant vessel *L'Amiral* and became only the second man, after Benjamin Morrell, to set foot on the island. What he found was 'stony white coral, devoid of vegetation', although 'littered with bird droppings'. Closer inspection, however, revealed that Clipperton's guano, while plentiful, wasn't of very good quality. The copious rainfall washed out the calcium phosphate, the richest part of the fertiliser. And, as Lieutenant Kerveguen noted, getting the stuff off the island was going to be difficult. There was no safe anchorage—ships had to stand offshore and send in longboats through thunderous surf.

But Kerveguen knew his duty. He formally took possession of Clipperton in the name of 'His Majesty the Emperor Napoleon III, and his heirs and successors in perpetuity'.

Pig Heaven

France may have annexed Clipperton, but the United States did not recognise the fact. The Guano Islands Act, passed by Congress in 1856, basically gave America (or any American citizen) the right—as far as the Americans were concerned, that is—to claim any fertiliser-rich 'island, rock, or key'. In 1861, Clipperton was visited by an American prospector named John Griswold, who spent twenty-seven days there collecting samples for study, but as he was killed almost a year later during the American Civil War, he was unable to follow up on his ideas for guano mining.

Twenty years passed with no one developing any further interest in the island. Clipperton is the kind of place that tends to be discovered, forgotten and rediscovered. This is what happened in 1881, when another American, Captain Frederick W. Permien, sailed by, saw, as he wrote, that the island had 'millions of birds [hovering] over it ... and I [supposed it] to be rich in guano'. Permien landed, planted the American flag at the highest point on the Rock—conveniently enough, it happened to be the Fourth of July—returned to the United States and filed claim under the Guano Islands Act.

Interestingly, no action was ever taken by the United States in response to this claim, perhaps because by this time they had discovered that France also claimed the island. Ignoring this rebuff, Permien proceeded as if he owned Clipperton and sold 'his' mining rights to the Oceanic Phosphate Company of San Francisco. Oceanic began the first true occupation of Clipperton Island in 1893. Two men were sent to live there; they built a hut and daily hauled loads of guano to the nearest beach. Mining guano, at best a horrid occupation—with miners risking lung diseases, and ailments like histoplasmosis and shigellosis, gastrointestinal complaints caused by ingesting bird droppings—was even worse on Clipperton, with the awful heat, the stink, and the constant depredations of the land-crabs—but these two hardy souls managed to bring off about 50 tons of the stuff.

Oceanic Phosphate mined the island until 1897, but the quality of the guano was poor and the market for it declining in any event. During those years, the main thing that happened on Clipperton was that another species was introduced—the pig—when a schooner called the *Kinkora* was shipwrecked there. These hardy swine discovered—to the pleasure of the island's few human occupants—that the orange land-crabs made a nice dinner, and so the little island's ecosystem began to change (see **Pigging Out**, page 188).

'Days Are All Alike'

By the early 1900s, Clipperton had a small settlement—several huts and a more or less permanent workforce. The American flag still flew over the island, an insult which was finally noticed by the Mexican government, recognising neither American nor French claims, in 1897. It sent a gunboat to take the trespassers off. One Oceanic employee, a German-born engineer named Theodore Gussman, who had a powerful sense of duty, literally leapt off the gunboat and swam back through the shark-infested waters, lying quietly on the beach until the Mexicans, thinking he had drowned, departed. He thus became Clipperton's first solitary castaway. The journal he kept gives a sense of just how appalling that experience was. 'Days are all alike to me,' he wrote. 'I don't know Sunday from Monday, and sometimes think it is all a dream that I will wake out of very soon.'

The monotony, replete with the 'breakers' roar and the seabirds' scream', made him think he was going mad: 'The days go on and the sun rises and sets, but life is at a standstill.' A ship finally arrived, having spotted his signal fire, and took him off about ten months later, but he appears to have been permanently affected by the experience. Soon after this, Mexico landed a garrison of troops as final refutation of any foreign claim, and in 1906 employed the Pacific Island Company, belonging to Great Britain, to mine the guano. Pacific Island made great improvements to the settlement, erecting buildings made of sheet metal (the only substance the voracious crabs would not eat) and building a small railtrack with a hopper car to transport the guano.

Existence on Clipperton was not pleasant for the men—or the women, for some of the garrison soldiers had brought wives, girlfriends and maids—but they learned how to make the best of it. They created huge vegetable boxes on stilts to foil the crabs, and thus were able to cultivate tomatoes and corn. For relaxation they rowed around the lagoon,

Pigging Out

The accidental introduction of pigs to Clipperton after the schooner *Kinkora* was shipwrecked in the 1890s proved a turning point in the island's ecology. Before this, the place had been largely barren, since almost everything that grew was eaten by the crabs. But the pigs discovered that crabs made a hearty meal.

In 1958, Clipperton was visited by a scientific expedition wishing to study its ecology. They had read descriptions of the island as barren and, from examining the droppings of the pigs, knew that the

creatures ate crabs. The scientists, in particular ornithologist Kenneth Stager, also noted an absence of the birds that supposedly flocked to the island, and mistakenly assumed that the pigs had reduced the bird population (in fact, the birds usually waited until the hurricane season was over in order to roost in large numbers).

The scientists decided that the pigs must be eradicated. And so Stager shot all fifty-eight pigs. Since that time, the crabs have been resurgent and the vegetation has again diminished.

pretending it was a lovely lake and not a noxious dead pond. And at night they watched the pulsing of the light that had been built atop the Rock, a 2 metre (6½ feet) high glass cylinder with a 10,000 candlepower oil lamp. A set of wooden ladders provided access to this precarious spot for the light's keeper, who lived in a hut at the foot of the Rock.

No one knows the name of the first lighthouse keeper, but he appears to have become insane and to have been taken off the island by the boat that came from Acapulco every two months with supplies. In 1912, a man named Álvarez came to take over the job.

Abandoned

By this time, mining had ceased—the poor quality of the guano and the invention of artificial fertilisers had ended the guano craze, and the Pacific Island Company's men departed. But Mexico maintained what one author has called 'one of history's most isolated military posts' there. There were eleven men and two officers, one of them Captain Ramón Arnaud, a Mexican of French origin, who enjoyed the title of military governor of Clipperton. When he arrived in 1908, he brought with him his new wife, 20-year-old Alicia, whose patrician birth disguised a steely will. She soon learned that her fancy dresses and jewels were of little use to her here, but bore four children to her husband in conditions which can only be imagined. There were other women, including Alicia's maid, Altagracia Quiroz; and Tirza Randón, the lover of Arnaud's second-in-command, Lieutenant Cardona.

The Mexican government, which was undergoing the chaos of threatened revolution and civil war, refused to pay for the upkeep of the Clipperton lighthouse, ordering the light extinguished in 1914. For some reason, however, Álvarez the keeper did not leave. Perhaps he had no place to go. In any event, he lived in his hut by the Rock a good 3 kilometres (almost 2 miles) away from where Arnaud, the soldiers, and the island's women and children lived in the old mining settlement. His job kept him chiefly nocturnal and the garrison had little contact with him.

Normally, the island received its crucial supplies of food, fresh water and medicines from a Mexican gunboat, the *Tampico*. But these were not normal times. Revolution had broken out in Mexico and the government of dictator Porfirio Díaz had fallen. On 16 June 1914, the *Tampico* was captured by rebels and spirited out to sea (or so the rebels thought). But it was followed by a federal ship and sent to the bottom. The Mexican Civil War degenerated into a faction fight, with numerous rebel leaders, including Pancho Villa, Emiliano Zapata and Venustiano Carranza, all vying for leadership.

In the chaos, no one thought to send another gunboat to Clipperton Island. Its inhabitants—fourteen men, six women and six children—were simply forgotten.

Madness

By the beginning of 1915, Clipperton had been without re-supply for over six months and food had run out. Used to being regularly supplied, the garrison had stopped cultivating the garden boxes set up by the Pacific Island Company, and these had fallen into disrepair and been consumed by the crabs. There were a few stunted coconut palms that produced, perhaps, several coconuts a week which, by order of Commander Arnaud, were given to the children. The adults, living on seabirds and fish, began to die of scurvy.

Within nine months, fifteen had died, most of them soldiers. Ramón Arnaud, Jr., the Commander's son, recalled them 'dying little by little. Then they got progressively worse'. And then, their limbs swollen, their teeth falling out, they died. Those who remained buried the corpses deep, to protect them. In the midst of this horror, however, new life was created, with Tirza Randón giving birth and Alicia Arnaud becoming pregnant.

By September 1915, it appears that Commander Arnaud had, like others before him, begun to go insane, a madness brought on by the lack of food, the constant noise of surf and seabirds and, as Jimmy M. Skaggs writes, by 'the unrelenting gaze of beady-eyed crabs that stood ready to eat the dead, the dying, and the weak'. One day Arnaud cracked. Seeing what he imagined to be a ship on the horizon, he demanded that the remaining men—with the significant exception of the lighthouse keeper—launch the island's small boat to try to reach it.

The only problem was, as one survivor said, 'the ship existed only in [the Commander's] imagination'. There was nothing but sea, sharks and writhing eels and sea-snakes. The women and children watched in horror as the men in the lifeboat, realising after the initial excitement that there was no vessel to be seen, fought with Arnaud. The wild struggle caused the lifeboat to overturn and the men were pitched into the ocean. They were never seen again. And as if the fates were piling disaster upon disaster, a hurricane swept over the atoll a few hours afterward. The women sheltered in Alicia Arnaud's house, the sturdiest on the island, as wave after wave crashed across Clipperton, sweeping belongings out to sea. Just as the storm ended, Alicia gave birth to a son, whom she named Ángel.

As the dazed women staggered from their shelter, distraught and in a state of shock, they encountered Álvarez, now the last man on the island. He had already gone to the barracks and thrown all the guns into the lagoon, keeping only one Mauser for himself. Now he turned to the women and declared himself 'the King of Clipperton Island'.

The King of Clipperton

In what follows, we have the testimony of the surviving women and children old enough to remember, especially Ramón Arnaud, Jr. Perhaps Álvarez had sat at night in his hut for years, brooding on his aloneness and the perceived happiness of the soldiers. He may even have suffered racist slights, since he was black. But really there can be no reason for what happened next except pure madness. Right after the hurricane, Álvarez 'brutally demanded the services of the women', and shot and killed one mother and daughter who refused to accommodate him. Having made his point, he dragged Altagracia Quiroz to his hut by the Rock. When he tired of her, he brought her back and took with him 13-year-old Rosalia Nava. After some months, he came back again, this time for Tirza Randón. Tirza seethed with rage during her kidnapping and brutalisation, and vowed that she would kill Álvarez if given half the chance. When he tired of Tirza, he went back and got Altagracia again, then Rosalia, and finally Tirza. The cycle went on and on—the only woman he spared was Alicia Arnaud, whose patrician airs may have intimidated him. He did, however, tell her that he would kill her the minute a ship appeared off the island. At night she would wake to find him standing over her with a dagger in his hand, as if contemplating cutting her throat. Then he would disappear into the darkness.

This cycle of rape and violence went on for twenty-two months. Everyone was existing at bare subsistence level. There were no more deaths from scurvy, although the children, malnourished, were stunted in their growth and the baby, Ángel, developed rickets.

Death of the Lighthouse Keeper

In the middle of July 1917, according to the testimony of the surviving women, Álvarez grew tired of Tirza Randón. He brought her back and told Alicia Arnaud: 'You are going to live with me.' She was to pack her belongings and come to his hut the next morning.

When he left, Tirza told Alicia, 'Now is the time.'

The next morning, 18 July, Alicia, her son Ramón and Tirza went to Álvarez's hut. Álvarez was roasting a gull, and when he saw Tirza demanded: 'What are you doing here?' She refused to reply, going instead into his hut and getting a large hammer she knew he kept. With Alicia distracting Álvarez, Tirza crept up behind him and brought the hammer down on his head, twice. Ramón Arnaud, Jr., takes up the story: '[Álvarez] fell. My mother shoved me away. I started to go inside, and then again he was standing. He took an axe and went at my mother. My mother grabbed him and held on. She yelled at me: "The Mauser!"'

Ramón raced inside to grab the gun, but by the time he returned Tirza had hit Álvarez with such force that part of his skull was caved in and had set upon him with a knife, slashing him repeatedly and hysterically, carving up his face, until finally Alicia pulled her off the corpse. Then, according to Ramón: 'My mother yelled at me to go to the other side of the hut and bring petrol to burn Álvarez, but when I got there I saw a ship ...'

Rescue

In the absolutely astonishing way of things on Clipperton Island, just as the women's murderous frenzy ended in the death of their tormentor, an American naval gunboat, the USS *Yorktown*, arrived on the scene. The *Yorktown* was on patrol off Central America and Mexico, on assignment to discover whether Germany had established any radio bases on the small islands in the region, for World War I was now raging. The *Yorktown*'s skipper, Harlan Perrill, decided to send in a boat to check that the lighthouse was still working. As he watched the boat approach the beach he saw two women 'making frantic signals'. They were Tirza Randón and Alicia Arnaud, begging the men to land and take them off.

With the boat was a lieutenant who inspected the scene of the murder and saw Álvarez's mutilated body. At first the women lied and said he had died of natural causes, but since this was transparently not the case they broke down and told the whole story—the months of torment and abuse culminating in the final revenge which had turned Álvarez's face, according to the lieutenant, 'into a perfect sieve'. The survivors were brought on board the *Yorktown*: three women (Tirza, Alicia and Altagracia), the 15-year-old Rosalia Nava and seven children. The ship's doctor examined them and found them relatively healthy, considering their ordeal, although Ángel could not walk due to rickets.

Alicia Arnaud, Perrill wrote later, 'was twenty-nine and looked forty'. After hearing their story, Perrill went on to wonder: 'What if we had been an hour earlier? It is almost certain that the man [Álvarez] would have killed Senora Arnaud.' Tirza Randón told Perrill that she felt no remorse for killing Álvarez—she was 'simply the instrument employed to carry out the wishes of some Higher Power'. But because he was concerned about the repercussions for Tirza, Perrill took an extraordinary step—he did not write the killing into the ship's log, and he and his crew kept the story secret for almost twenty years.

The *Yorktown* took the survivors to Santa Cruz, where most had relatives. On the way, the crew observed that the children did not know what candy was, or even how to open a box. They would not eat the ship's food, demanding 'bo-bo', or boobies, the food they had grown accustomed to, although the adults told Perrill they hoped 'they would never have to eat another gull again as long as they lived'. The ragged band of survivors landed in Santa Cruz on 22 July 1917, and dispersed to their waiting families. Despite the fact that Perrill kept the story a secret, it was soon 'freely told in towns up and down the Mexican coast between Santa Cruz and Acapulco'.

For the next twenty-five years, no one visited Clipperton. The island—before ultimately reverting to French ownership—was briefly surveyed by the United States and Britain for use as a possible refuelling stop for aircraft crossing the Pacific during World War II, but the difficulties of building an airstrip proved too daunting. An Australian pilot named Patrick Taylor visited the island in 1944 and survived a hurricane there, as well as attacks by a shark and a moray eel while fishing. One day, Taylor found:

> *an iron cross, apparently marking a grave. Looking across the bare rim of the island to the gaunt Rock, I had an impression of utter desolation, and I wondered why anybody should have been buried in such a place. Perhaps it was the grave of the lighthouse keeper, hurriedly put down in the sand.*

But Álvarez's body had been left to rot where it lay, long since consumed by the voracious crabs. Perhaps this was the grave of one of the dead of the Mexican garrison. Or perhaps it marked the final resting place of someone whose fate we will never know, for Clipperton, a grave itself, keeps its secrets well.

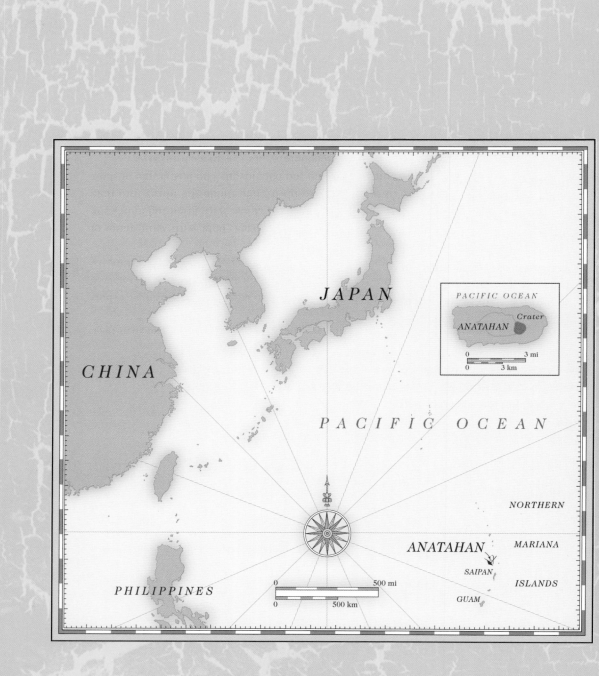

Japanese Castaways on Anatahan, 1944–1951
'The War Is Not Over'

The island of Anatahan in the northern part of the Marianas chain—it lies about 120 kilometres (74½ miles) north of its larger and more famous neighbour, Saipan—is only 9 kilometres long and 3 kilometres wide (3½ miles long and 2 miles wide), yet it contains two huge volcanic peaks soaring to 760 metres (½ mile). Between them lies a grassy plateau where rests the wreckage of a United States B-29 Superfortress which crashed on its return from a bombing mission to Japan in 1944. Everyone aboard was killed. For many years after the war, people could climb arduously to the tops of the mountains and view this relic of the past, but no longer. In 2003, one of these supposedly dormant volcanoes erupted (see **The Mountain that Roared**, page 196), sending a plume of ash and smoke 12,000 metres (7½ miles) into the air, lava cascading down its sides, a cloud of ash far to the west across the Pacific.

Not only does no one live on Anatahan anymore, but the B-29 may well be buried forever under the flood of lava. Which is a shame, really, because it was due to the loss of this bomber that one of the stranger stories of World War II came to light. In February 1945, a group of Chamorro scouts from Saipan, working for the US Marines, landed on the island to begin the sad process of retrieving the bodies of those who died in the crash. Anatahan had formerly had a tiny Japanese presence but was thought to now be uninhabited, although the Chamorros were taking no chances—they came heavily armed. As they trekked the ravines and gullies of the island, they became aware that other eyes were on them. They heard rustlings in the jungle and came upon hastily-doused campfires.

Cautiously completing their mission, the Chamorros brought the dogtags of the dead American aviators back to Saipan and some news: there were Japanese men on the island, in numbers greater than anyone had thought.

In the Backwater of War

Men and one woman, actually, a 21-year-old Okinawan named Kazuko Higa, who had come to the island with her husband Shoichi in 1942. He was a representative of the Japanese South Seas Development Company, set up by the government in 1935, after Japan withdrew from the League of Nations and began to fortify islands in the Marianas chain and elsewhere in the Pacific. The ostensible purpose of the South Seas Development Company was to help the islanders develop crops such as pineapples, bananas, sugar, coffee and copra for export to improve their economies, but in reality the company took much of what was grown for consumption in Japan and used its employees in order to exert control over the islands.

Kazuko, her husband, and her husband's boss, Kikuichiro Higa, who oddly had the same family name, were the only three Japanese on Anatahan, living among perhaps fifty Chamorros in the tiny village of Sonson on the northwest tip of the island. Duty on Anatahan was not easy. Food was scarce—the only real crop was coconuts—and the landscape inhospitable, broken by steep, grass-filled ravines and marred by large swamps which were home to swarming black flies, mosquitoes, fire ants and a particularly nasty species of yellow wasp. This is not to mention the scorpions that attained a length of 18 centimetres (7 inches) and left a vicious welt when they bit, and a most unpleasant type of beetle which had an unsettling propensity for crawling into your drink when you weren't looking and secreting a poison that could leave you near death.

As the war progressed, though, they began to consider themselves well off compared to the large garrison on Saipan Island, visible in the distance. For by late 1943, wave after wave of American bombers were bombing Saipan. They would sweep low over Anatahan as they made their runs, shaking the earth and bending the coconut palms, but they left

The Mountain that Roared

The Mariana Islands are the tops of fifteen undersea volcanoes poking up to the sky. Anatahan, despite its tiny land area, has two such peaks. The volcanoes were thought to be extinct—although close examination never really took place until 1990, when geologists visited and saw evidence of ancient explosions and lava flows. The first historical eruption on Anatahan took place in May 2003, a fierce blast which sent a tower of volcanic ash and gas 12,000 metres (7½ miles) above sea level and a cloud of ash far to the west across the Pacific.

The island's small population had been evacuated as a precaution after some weeks of warning signs, but a team of geologists had visited the island only four days before and seen no evidence that a major eruption was imminent. Eruptions continued for the next few months, lessening in intensity, and there have been only minor eruptions since, but there is always the danger of an explosion of even greater intensity, for scientists believe that the two magma chambers of Anatahan are gradually coalescing. There is little chance the island will ever be habitable again.

the island alone. By the late spring of 1944, the raids had increased in intensity and it was apparent that the Americans intended to invade Saipan—in fact, the American high command had targeted the island because the new B-29 Superfortress bomber, launched from a captured Saipan, would have the range to bomb Tokyo.

Kazuko's husband was worried about his sister, a civilian employee on Saipan, and so decided, on 9 June, to go there and, if possible, bring her back to Anatahan. It was but a day's journey there and back by motor launch, but by 12 June he had not returned. And that was the day the war came very directly to Anatahan.

Castaways

Early on that morning Kazuko and Kikuichiro, at the copra plantation deep in the jungle, heard the sound of bombers and assumed them to be on their way to Saipan. But then they heard the whistle of bombs falling and the chatter of machine guns close at hand. The Chamorro employees of South Seas immediately dropped their machetes and ran off into the jungle, but Kazuko and Kikuichiro raced to a high ledge on one of the mountains. From there they could see twin-engined dive-bombers attacking two small Japanese ships attempting to shelter against the mountainous coast. As the dive-bombers poured fire on the smoking, flaming vessels, Kazuko could see their crewmen diving overboard and attempting to swim to shore. While Kikuichiro ventured further down to get a closer look, Kazuko stayed where she was, hidden on the ledge. The next day she saw two more Japanese vessels near the island, and watched as the US Air Force sank them in their turn as more desperate sailors struggled to shore. That afternoon Kikuichiro brought Kazuko the news that about thirty Japanese sailors had been cast away on Anatahan and were making their way into the jungle.

The bombing of Saipan increased. On 15 June, a huge US naval fleet arrived offshore and, following an intense bombardment, launched an invasion that would ultimately take the lives of 22,000 Japanese civilians and 30,000 Japanese troops on the island. There was no chance now that Kazuko's husband and sister would return to Anatahan.

Alone on the Island

Petty Officer Second Class Junji Inoue of the Japanese Imperial Navy, 36 years old, now found himself the ranking officer on Anatahan. He commanded a rag-tag group of castaways, including twenty-two merchant seamen, several army privates and six navy men like himself. Several of the men were wounded and he immediately organised their care by transporting them to the little settlement at Sorbon.

Kikuichiro and Kazuko remained hidden. There is conflicting testimony as to why this was, but it appears that they had become lovers (or continued an existing relationship) after Kazuko's husband left the island, and that Kikuichiro wanted to keep Kazuko away from the sailors, who might try to harm her. But eventually the Chamorros told Inoue about them. The search parties he sent out bumped into Kikuichiro and Kazuko on a jungle trail and brought them to where Inoue's men were hiding near the beach.

It is a sign of how desperate things were at this stage in the war, of how discipline had broken down in the Japanese armed forces, that both Kikuichiro and Kazuko felt almost as if they had been captured by the enemy. Kazuko was particularly disturbed by the way some of the men were eyeing her, and by the fact that Inoue seemed to have only the loosest hold over them. In part this was because of his lowly rank, and in part because most of the men had never seen him before. But these were also men who were reaching the end of their tether. The sight of bombers pounding Saipan daily, and the increased presence of US vessels patrolling the surrounding waters with impunity, had driven home the fact that the castaways were completely isolated from any aid or reinforcements.

The next thing that happened was that the Chamorros vanished. One day they were there, the next they were nowhere to be found. At first the Japanese assumed they were in hiding, but assiduous searches showed that they had taken their wooden sailing craft and left the island. Now the Japanese were truly alone, and trouble was about to begin.

Marriages

Later, in Japan, Higa would say that Junji Inoue had insisted she form sexual relationships with at least five of his men—'marriages', he called them—to keep them from fighting over her. The problem with this story is that the men had fought over Kazuko almost from the start. Although at first it was recognised that she was with Kikuichiro, their adulterous affair, which soon became common knowledge, may have given the others reason to see her as 'available'. Or it might simply have been that, given the state of lawlessness, nothing could have kept them from fighting. By the autumn of 1944, another soldier was sharing a hut with Kikuichiro and Kazuko and, apparently, sharing Kazuko's favours.

It has never been clear what degree of coercion was involved in this and other liaisons in which Kazuko became involved, but she was certainly never in a position to refuse a man's advances and be certain of her safety. This predatory behaviour on the part of the survivors is rather amazing, given the circumstances they found themselves in. The energy involved in just finding food on this mainly inhospitable atoll was enough to occupy most people full time. The Chamorros had left behind gardens of beans, yams and tapioca, but

U.S. Airforce B-29 Superfortresses similar to the one that crashed on Anatahan in 1944.

the crops were poor and soon depleted. The men learned to track coconut crabs to their nocturnal dens and yank them out with long sticks with hooks attached, but this involved a great deal of labour for one small meal. They also killed the iguanas, some over a metre (a yard) long and managed to down their unpalatable flesh.

They also began to make meals of the huge flying foxes, bats with wingspans of 1.5 metres (almost 5 feet), which swooped low in the night skies. With great ingenuity the castaways pounded a certain type of tree bark into fibre, then made the fibres into nets which they would bait with rotted fruit, something the bats loved. The last staple of their diet was fish, caught with improvised hooks and generally ate raw in sashimi style.

The First Murder

All this created a diet that was enough to live on, but not enough to ever fully satisfy. Attempting to find some degree of pleasure, the men smoked crushed, dried papaya leaves wrapped in banana leaves and drank *tuba*, a highly intoxicating wine they made from fermented coconut sap. By the beginning of 1945, despite Inoue's crude attempts at discipline (he often beat the men), the castaways had started to scatter to different points on the island, living separately or in twos and threes in huts made of palm fronds.

One night in January 1945, Kazuko and the men with her in their hut higher up the mountain heard a huge crash during a blinding thunderstorm. They did not realise it at the time, but this was the B-29 Superfortress, gone astray on its way back to Saipan, hitting the side of the volcano. Shortly thereafter, the Chamorro patrols arrived. Since the Japanese did not know the B-29 had crashed, they thought Anatahan was being invaded and hid deep in the jungle. When they emerged several days later, the patrols were gone.

Also at the beginning of 1945, the first murder took place. At least, Inoue suspected murder. Goro Nakayama and Tadao Takao had gone off to fish one day, and Goro returned, seemingly crestfallen, with the news that Tadao had fallen off a reef and been devoured by lurking sharks. No trace of his remains was ever discovered, so the others could not be certain what had happened, but most thought that Goro had killed Tadao, his rival for Kazuko's affections. In any event, Kazuko shortly thereafter moved into Goro's hut.

During 1945 several men disappeared like this—Kazuko later said that their deaths had nothing to do with her, that they 'were swallowed by waves while fishing', or had died of illness. While it is true that some men died from tropical diseases, there is also evidence that eventually eleven were murdered because of their desire to be Kazuko's latest lover.

The Year of Victory

The Americans, hearing from the patrols that there was a stronger Japanese presence on the island than had been suspected, began to bomb Anatahan several times a week. These bombing runs never hurt anyone, partly because the Japanese were so widely dispersed, and partly because the planes arrived, predictable as clockwork, at noon every day. They were even looked forward to as a kind of excitement, a break from the deadly daily routine. But in the middle of August 1945 the bombing runs stopped abruptly, and the skies began to clear of the omnipresent planes on their way elsewhere.

On 15 September, the sound of put-putting engines was heard. The castaways peered out of the jungle to see a small American patrol boat making its way around the island. They were startled to hear a message in Japanese coming over a loudspeaker:

Japanese troops! All Japanese troops! The war is over. On August 15, his Imperial Highness proclaimed the surrender. Now you can return to your homes. I am Lieutenant Commander Sato Shyo of the Pagan Headquarters.

The message was repeated four times as the boat circumnavigated the island. The Japanese voice told them that all they had to do was come down to the beach with their hands empty and the patrol boat would pick them up. But none of the castaways believed that Japan had surrendered—they were certain this was an American trick and that they would be killed if they ventured onto the beach. In addition, the Japanese soldier's code did not allow for surrender. When the Americans returned another day and left gifts of cigarettes and candy on the beach, they took them gladly, smoked and ate greedily, but were quite certain they were bribes for the unwary.

Briefly, Inoue was able to reunite his men and their spirits rose. He told them he was certain they were playing a vital role in the war effort by diverting American resources to their tiny island, resources which might otherwise be used to attack the Japanese. As 1945 came to an end, he told the men he was proclaiming 1946 the 'Year of Victory'. The men marked the coming of New Year's Day with a celebration feast and a great deal of *tuba*, and tried to convince themselves that their future was bright.

The Plane

In the autumn of 1946, Kazuko Higa casually mentioned to Inoue the explosion that she had heard during the thunderstorm the year before. Inoue thought its source was worth investigation. A group of castaways began to ascend the taller peak, which rose to a height of 785 metres (½ mile). After five hours of arduous climbing, when they had nearly reached the top, they saw, off in a corner of the grassy plateau that separated the peaks, a glimmer of metal. As fast as they could they descended the jungle-covered rocks to find a huge airplane, the biggest any of them had ever seen. The B-29 Superfortress was about 30 metres long, 9 metres high (98 feet long, 30 feet high), had four huge engines and was armed with eight .50 calibre machine guns. It provided a bonanza in the way of supplies—the men salvaged rations, paper, charts, tools and a first-aid kit. They also dismantled several machine guns and brought them down the mountain to use in their defence of the island.

More importantly in the short run, two seamen, Tsuguo Naito and Ichiro Yanagawa, discovered two .45 calibre pistols and about 100 rounds of ammunition. The balance of power on the island was about to change. They swaggered back with the guns, with Naito

A Japanese naval vessel lies half-submerged, sunk by the U.S. Navy in 1942.

calling out: 'It's easy to see now who has the power around here!' On 11 November, Naito was hunting crabs when another sailor named Sato accused him of poaching crabs from 'his' territory. Naito replied by putting a bullet through Sato's head. Inoue protested—but he didn't dare protest too much, because he thought he might be next.

The murder foreshadowed what was to come in 1947, which would prove to be the bloodiest year on the island. After Sato's death, Naito and Yanagawa decided it would be expedient to move away from the scene of the crime, and built a small hut near that of Kazuko and Kikuichiro, who were back together again, at least briefly. But Naito and another man got into a fight over Kazuko, and Naito slashed this man across the face, nearly killing him. Now Yanagawa decided that Naito was losing his mind, that he might turn on almost any of them, so one evening, as the flying foxes swooped through the purple dusk, he walked into Naito's hut and shot him twice through the chest.

At this point, Kazuko voiced for the first time something she had been thinking for a while. She told Kikuichiro and Yanagawa that it was time to surrender to the naval patrols that still circled the island every few months, calling for the Japanese to come out. Yanagawa refused and threatened to beat her—or shoot Kikuichi—if she tried it. The three of them settled into an uneasy truce until September 1947, when Kikuichiro and Yanagawa went fishing together. Later that day, Kikuichiro came back alone. Yanagawa had fallen into the water, he told Kazuko, and been taken away by the sea.

Kazuko didn't believe him but had long ago realised that her main chance of survival was to keep her opinions to herself. This was especially true a few months later, when she heard a loud bang inside the hut. A man named Yoshida, who had been cleaning the .45 pistols while Kikuichiro was repairing the hut, walked out, his shirt stained with blood. He had shot Kikuichiro accidentally, he said, and now Kazuko's lover was dead. Could she ever forgive him?

Operation Removal

In a state of shock, Kazuko buried her lover and decided to keep the cause of his death secret, lest she be blamed for it. In the next two years, several more men were killed as a result of fighting over Kazuko. Junji Inoue had by now completely lost control; one of the men even beat him up in a fist fight, humiliating him in front of the rest. He tried to launch an investigation into the death of Kikuichiro, but the men just laughed at him.

In the meantime, the United States was stepping up its efforts to get the Japanese off the island. Aerial reconnaissance showed that Inoue had set up trenches and machine-gun nests, using the guns from the B-29. No American commander was willing to risk troops landing there, now that the war was over, and so a concerted peaceful effort, labelled Operation Removal, was planned. Aircraft overflew the island, dropping leaflets showing pictures of Emperor Hirohito and General Douglas MacArthur shaking hands. Other pictures showed American soldiers walking past familiar Japanese landmarks.

The US Navy combed records to find out which Japanese ships had been sunk in the waters off Anatahan, and contacted the families of the men who had been on those vessels, convincing them to write letters to their loved ones. This was a touchy task, because the Americans obviously could not know which sailors had survived and which had perished, and did not want to provide false hope. Yet the letters were written, copies made, and they too were dropped on Anatahan.

The response, for two more years, was a resounding silence. The Americans were astonished—surely the Japanese would grow tired of subsisting on lizards and coconuts and surrender? But those on the island remained certain it was all a trick—the photographs doctored, the letters from families coerced.

For her part, Kazuko was secretly convinced that the American appeals were real—that the war was over. She didn't mention these thoughts, partly because for most of 1948 and 1949 she had been in a fairly stable 'marriage' with a young sailor and the other men had left her alone. But her 'husband' was killed on 11 September 1949, and Kazuko was forced into a relationship with his murderer, whose name was Kuba. In early June 1950, Kuba got drunk, beat Kazuko, and passed out. When he awoke the next morning, she was nowhere to be found, nor was she to be found the next day, or the next.

Kazuko, her heart pounding, had stolen away to a remote corner of the island, near the coast, where she waited, hidden in the jungle, until 28 June. That morning the island was visited by an American patrol boat under the command of Lieutenant Commander James B. Johnson, in charge of Operation Removal. As Johnson inspected the shore through his binoculars, he was astonished to see a Japanese woman run down to the water's edge, wearing what appeared to be a dress made out of sailcloth. At first he thought it was a trap, something to lure the patrol boat closer so that it might be ambushed, but then he realised that the woman was terrified and was trying to swim out to them.

Rather than expose her to the shark-infested waters any longer, Johnson took a chance and sent a boat for her. Kazuko Higa was pulled aboard, saying to a Japanese translator: 'They'll kill me. They'll kill me if they see me trying to get away.' Soon she was on the patrol boat, on the way back to Japan, where she spilled out her incredible story.

'Living Robinson Crusoes'

Finally realising that Kazuko had defected to the enemy, the castaways on Anatahan prepared for the Americans to bomb them. Inoue regained discipline over the men by trying Kuba for shooting Kazuko's 'husband' and having him beheaded with an aluminium sword made from the wing of the B-29. By now, the Japanese government was begging the Americans to get these men out, calling them 'doomed and living Robinson Crusoes … living a primitive life on an uninhabited island'.

When Kazuko returned to Japan, the names of the surviving men became known and their families pressured the government and the Americans to step up their efforts. More leaflets were dropped, and gradually the men on Anatahan began to believe them. One received a letter from his wife telling him how much he was missing—that his children were in primary school, that his brother had died. It was time for him to come home.

Inoue himself became convinced that the war was over. He retreated from the rest of the men, refusing to act as their chief officer, and brooded in the jungle. Finally, in June 1951, a year after Kazuko got off the island, Inoue told a few of the men that he was planning on surrendering the next time the Americans came. On 9 June he walked down to the beach, a small white flag in hand, and gave himself up. A few weeks later, the nineteen surviving castaways of Anatahan Island decided to join him in surrender. For these Robinson Crusoes the war was over, although others would remain in the jungles of the Pacific for a very long time (see **Returning**, below).

Within a month the men were back in Japan trying to pick up their lives. For Kazuko, however, it was not easy. The press was titillated by her role as a 'castaway seductress', and published headlines like: 'I Had Five Husbands! The Secrets of Anatahan'. For a while Kazuko, whose husband had indeed been killed on Saipan, attempted to embrace her unwanted notoriety by going on a lecture tour. She insisted she was forced by Inoue to 'marry', that she had nothing to do with the deaths of eleven sailors. But no one listened. She returned to Okinawa, where she ran a tea-house for the American occupiers.

Returning

After the Anatahan survivors returned to Japan, other soldiers trickled back from the jungles, other men who had been lost in time. In the early 1970s a soldier was discovered on Guam, and another on Lubang (in the Philippines), each of whom had spent almost thirty years in the jungle believing the war was still ongoing. Their stories were incredible. Yokoi Shoichi, found on Guam in 1972, was the last survivor of a suicidal charge against American forces in 1944. He had lived in a burrow, coming out only at night.

Onoda Hiro, who emerged from the jungles of Lubang in 1974, had been waging a guerrilla war against local authorities, killing some thirty people, preparing for the time when Japanese forces would return to retake the island. He finally allowed himself to be caught by a young Japanese student who had gone to Lubang specifically to look for him. Even then, the only way Onoda would surrender was when his former commanding officer flew to Lubang and ordered him to lay down his arms. Onoda was repatriated to Japan and still lives there today.

Probably the last Japanese holdouts from the war in the Pacific were two soldiers in their eighties who were discovered in Indonesia in 1989. Kiyoaki Tanaka and Shigeyuki Hashimoto had fought with Communist guerrillas at the war's end and were aware that Japan had been defeated, but were afraid to surrender as they thought they would be punished.

Part Three
UPON A
FAR COAST
*'To this Island we gave the name
the Island of Ill-Fate.'*
Álvar Núñez Cabeza de Vaca

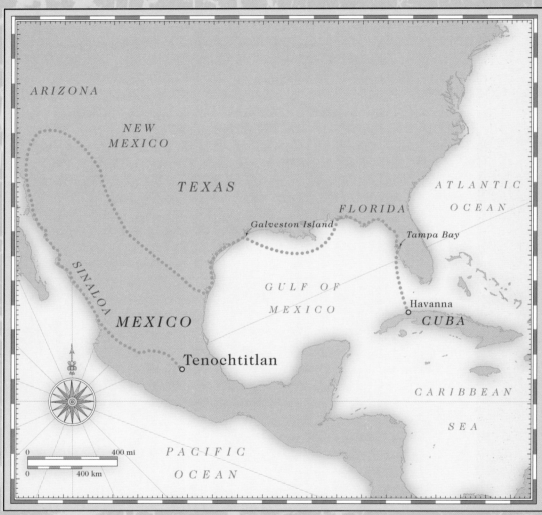

Álvar Núñez Cabeza de Vaca, 1527–1536
'A Tree Aflame'

On 6 November 1528, Álvar Núñez Cabeza de Vaca, adrift in a makeshift boat on stormy waters, came crashing ashore on an island he would name Malhado, the 'Island of Doom'. Malhado would become modern-day Galveston Island, off the coast of Texas in the Gulf of Mexico, but to Cabeza de Vaca it spelled the end to his dreams of glory. Cabeza and the 45 conquistadors who staggered ashore that dreary winter day were the sole remnants of a proud 600-man expedition which had left Cuba the year before with the intention of conquering Florida. Now they were, as Cabeza de Vaca later wrote in his *relación*, or narrative, 'as naked as the day we were born and had lost everything we had … We were the picture of death'.

They were in such a miserable state that the Karankawa Indians who found them sat down on the shore and wept for them. This disturbed Cabeza de Vaca: 'Seeing that these crude and untutored people, who were more like brutes, grieved so much for us, caused me and the others in my company to suffer more and think more about our misfortune.'

In other words, things were *really* bad when even 'crude and untutored people' like these could feel sorry for you. The future would soon bring extraordinary change to Cabeza de Vaca. He would be cast away, as it were, into a raging cross-current of Native American cultures thousands of years old. In the next seven years, as slave, free man and finally healer, Cabeza de Vaca would walk 'lost and naked through many strange lands' and undergo a transformation no other European had experienced.

Head of a Cow

Álvar Núñez Cabeza de Vaca was born in 1490 in provincial Andalusia in Spain. There is a probably apocryphal story that the name Cabeza de Vaca (which means 'head of a cow') was bestowed upon a humble shepherd ancestor of de Vaca's mother when he placed a cow's head at a mountain pass, thus guiding King Alfonso VIII of Castille to victory over the Moors at the Battle of Las Navas de Tolosa in 1212. But certainly Cabeza came from a distinguished military lineage; his grandfather was one of the conquerors of the Canary Islands. A soldier and adventurer, Cabeza de Vaca fought the French in the Battle of Ravenna in 1512, where he was decorated for bravery. Shortly thereafter the young man, who had the knack of making powerful friends, entered the service of the Duke of Medina Sidonia and fought on behalf of King Charles I (later Holy Roman Emperor Charles V) when a rebellion arose against him in Spain.

All this stood him in good stead when the jinxed, one-eyed conquistador Pánfilo de Narváez (see **Pánfilo de Narváez: The Unlucky Conquistador**, page 212) was appointed by Charles to take an expedition to the Spanish Indies in 1527, with a patent to conquer and settle Florida, which was understood to mean not just the peninsula which juts down from the southeast corner of the present-day United States but all the land across the Gulf Coast as far as New Spain (Mexico). Now about forty years old, Cabeza de Vaca was made treasurer of this expedition, effectively second in command.

The expedition sailed from Spain on 17 June 1527, with five ships and 600 men. They arrived in Cuba in the early autumn, just in time for the hurricane season, and had to wait out a terrific storm which battered the fleet so badly that Narváez was forced to remain there until April 1528 to refit. Finally the flotilla set sail for Florida and, after a month of fighting contrary gales, on Easter Sunday arrived on the west coast of the peninsula, probably in the vicinity of modern-day Sarasota, in Tampa Bay.

'Travelling Mute'

Pánfilo Narváez took possession of the land on behalf of the King of Spain, despite the local Indians making 'signs and threatening gestures' which seemed to indicate they wanted the Spanish to leave. On travelling a short distance inland they found a tribe which told them that, far to the north, there was another tribe, the Apalachees, who had 'very great quantities of everything we held in esteem', especially gold. This seems like a fairly transparent attempt by the locals to pass the Spanish on to an enemy further up the road, but Narváez fell for it, and in doing so made a fatal mistake. Assuming that the Rio de las Palmes in eastern Mexico (south of the Rio Grande) was only a short distance away rather than 2400 kilometres (1491 miles), he ordered his ships to sail there while he led 300 men overland to find the Apalachees. Cabeza de Vaca protested greatly against this decision: 'I responded that by no means should he leave the ships as [the pilots] ... did not know where they were' and that the army would be 'travelling mute, that is, without interpreters [through] a land about which we had no information' but Narváez insisted and in the end Cabeza accompanied him.

Their journey north was disastrous. The ships quickly disappeared from sight, forced out to sea by shallow coastal waters and contrary winds, while the expedition plunged into dense jungle. The conquistadors lived on the salt pork they had brought with them; when that ran out, they fed themselves on whatever they could scrounge along the way. During forty days of travel, they captured four Indians and forced them to become guides, wandering through a land with many rivers where there were 'very great forests, with trees wondrously tall', although many of the trees had been knocked down in storms, making travel difficult. They finally arrived in the land of the Apalachees, where Narváez ordered Cabeza to attack a village. The assault was easy, since the men were absent, but when they returned they attacked the Spanish and killed one of their horses.

Thus began three threadbare months in the land of the Apalachees, where the Indians—who lived in poverty and had no gold or other precious metals—launched arrows with deadly accuracy from their 2-metre (2-yard) bows, picking off the conquistadors one by one before melting away into the woods. Finally, even Narváez could take it no more and decided to make his way back to the coast.

'Each of Us Should Do What Seemed Best'

The conquistadors had lost about fifty of their number by this time, to Indians, starvation and disease, and of course had no ships—the vessels Narváez had sent to Rio de las Palmes had been unable to find it and eventually returned to Cuba. So Narváez and his men had to improvise. First they slaughtered their horses for meat (and turned the skins of their legs into water-bottles). Then they cut down trees, sawed them into rough planks, and fashioned boats which they caulked with pine resin. Their sails were made from deerskins. Piling aboard five of these craft, the remaining 250 conquistadors set sail from what they named the Bay of Horses, eventually finding their way through inland waterways to the open ocean. They headed west, towards Mexico, still underestimating the distance they had to cross. After about thirty days at sea, their horse-hide water-bottles began to rot, leaving them desperate for water. By this time, they had reached the broad mouth of the Mississippi River where they attempted to replenish, but each time were driven back by hostile Indians, who wounded Narváez.

A storm arose, separating the boats and blowing them far out to sea. The last Cabeza de Vaca saw of Narváez was during the night when their vessels neared each other. Cabeza begged Narváez to throw him a line and tow him toward shore, since Narváez' boat seemed more stable. Narváez answered that it was all he could to save himself—he couldn't take a chance towing others—and: 'Each of us should do what seemed best to save his life.'

His boat disappeared in the darkness and was never seen again.

Malhado

Several days later, when the men with Cabeza de Vaca were so weak that they had 'passed out, one on top of the other, so near death that few of them were conscious and fewer than five were still upright', a huge breaker 'cast the boat out of the water as far as a horseshoe can be tossed' and the exhausted conquistadors found themselves on the island they would name Malhado. They left their craft half-walking, half-crawling. The Karankawas appeared almost immediately and the next day brought food but, despite their apparent sympathy for the Spaniards' plight, Cabeza was concerned. There were a hundred of them, with bows and arrows, and 'our fear made them seem like giants', no matter what their real stature was.

The Indians wanted to take the Spaniards to their houses, which concerned those who had served in New Spain because they felt the Karankawas 'would sacrifice us to their idols' as the Aztecs had done. But desperate and starving, the men had no choice, and soon found themselves scattered among several villages. The winter of 1528–1529 was harsh, and by spring only fifteen Spaniards had survived disease and malnutrition. It was here that Cabeza de Vaca, having lived with the Indians for five months, began his transformation. The reason modern scholars think of him as an ethnologist becomes clear in his *narración*; despite the situation he found himself in, the explorer was able to observe the customs of the Karankawas with a clear eye. He tells us that their houses 'are

Pánfilo de Narváez: The Unlucky Conquistador

Pánfilo de Narváez, the tall, red-bearded, one-eyed commander of the doomed expedition which brought Cabeza de Vaca to America, had everything going for him in life, it would seem. Born in 1470 of a noble family, he married well and became a favourite of Charles I, King of Spain. He took part in the conquest of Jamaica in 1509 and was later awarded several large plantations in Cuba by Governor Diego Velázquez de Cuéllar. In 1520, Velázquez sent Narváez to Mexico with 800 armed men to rein in Hernán Cortés, who had set off to conquer the Aztec kingdom on his own. In a pitched battle near Vera Cruz in May of that year, Narváez lost an eye to the pike of one of Cortés' men and was defeated, with many of his own soldiers turning against him.

Imprisoned by Cortés in Mexico for three years, Narváez was eventually released and went to Spain, where he petitioned Charles for redress. The King responded by giving him patent to Florida, at which point Narváez raised the army which included Cabeza de Vaca. But, plagued both by storms and his arrogant treatment of the native inhabitants, Narváez finally met his end aboard a raft somewhere in the Gulf of Mexico, probably not long after he had refused de Vaca's plea for help.

An Aztec ceremony, with the victim sacrificed to the gods.

built of woven reeds on top of beds of oyster shells', that they sleep on animal skins, that in the spring they go to the mainland to pick blackberries, and that they love their children more than any people he had ever known, so that when a child dies, 'in the household in which the death occurs, they cease to seek food for three months' and would starve to death were they not fed by friends and neighbours.

During that dark winter the Karankawas 'tried to make us their physicians', Cabeza wrote. The Karankawas cured illness by blowing on the sick person to 'expel the disease from him'. Cabeza and the others laughed at this practice, but the Indians took their food away until they agreed to try it. Of all the Spanish, it seems that Cabeza was the most successful as a healer. His practice was to whisper prayers, make the sign of the cross, and blow gently on the patient's forehead and about his body.

The Trader

Successful as he was as a healer of others, Cabeza de Vaca was unable to heal himself. On the mainland that spring he came down with 'a great sickness' which made him so ill that a rumour spread that he had died. The other conquistadors, with the exception of two who remained on Malhado, decided to take their chances by striking along the coast toward Mexico. Cabeza was left behind. He lived for another year on Malhado, but the Karankawas began to treat him almost as a slave, working him hard and giving him little food. Finally, in 1530 he fled to the mainland and found shelter among a tribe he called the Charruco, who lived in the forests of the Gulf Coast.

Cabeza decided that his best hope of staying alive was to become a trader, carrying valuable goods between the tribes. The reasoning behind this was what he describes as 'continual warfare' between the tribes on the coast which made it hard for members of any tribe to travel. But Cabeza was allowed to move from tribe to tribe on a route that covered about 50 leagues (a Spanish league being about 4 kilometres, or 2½ miles). He carried with him animal hides, red ochre for face-painting, conch shells, 'beads of the sea' (pearls), flints, fly-tassels made of deer hair and the like.

Cabeza de Vaca's choice of profession was inspired, for the people he met treated him as an important figure, and he grew to understand their languages and customs—it also gave him a chance to explore the lay of the land, in the hope of finding a route to New Spain. He did not yet try to make his way to Mexico. He 'stayed in his land, as naked as [the Indians]' in an attempt to save the life of Lope de Oviedo, one of the two who had remained on Malhado (the other had died). Every year he returned to the island to try to convince the timid Lope to escape, and every year until early in 1533 he was rebuffed.

The Four

Travelling the Gulf Coast was a challenge, since Lope de Oviedo couldn't swim and there were numerous rivers to cross—at some points, Cabeza carried his friend. After a time they ran into a group of Indians who told them that ahead were 'three men like us', three Spaniards from the party of thirteen or so that left Malhado in 1529. When Cabeza asked after the other ten, the Indians told him that most had died of cold or hunger, although they had killed some 'for amusement' and at least one because 'of a dream they had dreamed'.

The Indians taunted the two men, putting arrows to their chests and saying that they would 'kill us as they had killed our other companions'. This was too much for Lope, who decided to return to Malhado with some women from the group, despite Cabeza's pleas. The intrepid explorer went forward and met his three former comrades, with whom he

'They Would Eat Stones'

De Vaca's portrait of the Yguazes Indians among whom he lived for so long is a classic study, the reason so many scholars describe him as America's first anthropologist. Despite the fact that the people were 'well-built' and crack shots with bow and arrow, they didn't seem to have much to eat. They lived mainly on what de Vaca describe as 'two or three roots', which 'took two days to roast'. Even then, 'the men who eat them bloat'. Although the Yguazes would sometimes shoot a deer, they basically lived on 'spiders and ant eggs and worms and salamanders and snakes and vipers that kill men when they strike, and they eat earth and wood and deer excrement and other things that I refrain from mentioning'.

The Yguazes also kept the bones of everything they ate grinding them into an edible powder. Although de Vaca frowns on some of their practices, including infanticide and sodomy, and while he tells us that mosquitoes so plagued this poor people that 'it seems that they have the sickness of St Lazarus [leprosy]', he claims that the Yguazes were 'a very happy people'. Even when everyone had gone hungry for three or four days, they would cheer him up by saying that the prickly pear festival would soon be coming up, and then everyone would eat their fill. De Vaca then writes, with impatience and a grudging admiration for their unquenchable spirit: 'And from the time they told us this until the prickly pears were ready to eat, was five or six months.'

would complete his journey. They were Andrés Dorantes de Carranza, Alonso del Castillo Maldonado and Estevanico, described by Cabeza as 'an Arabic-speaking black man, a native of Azamor' on the northwest coast of Africa. Estevanico was Andrés Dorantes' slave and is considered the first African-born person to have set foot on continental North America.

The three were astonished to see Cabeza alive and their reunion was a happy one— 'we thanked God very much for being together'. Agreeing on escape, they decided their best bet was to wait six months for the prickly pear festival, when several tribes met farther south, nearer New Mexico, to gorge themselves for three straight months on the delicious fruit. Cabeza was given as a slave to the Marianes Indians, who owned Dorantes; the others were owned by the neighbouring Yguazes. Once again Cabeza chronicled the strange customs of his hosts—the Marianes routinely killed their infant daughters to keep them from marrying into enemy tribes and producing sons who would fight against them. They also believed strongly in dreams—one of the larger group of conquistadors had been killed before Cabeza's arrival because a woman had dreamed that he killed her son.

Both tribes were so harried by mosquitoes that they burned damp wood for its smoke when they tried to sleep. 'All night long we did nothing but weep from the smoke that got into our eyes,' wrote Cabeza, yet even when they got to sleep they were often awakened with kicks and blows and told to gather more wood. Sometimes the Indians were so plagued by the insects that they would set fire to entire pastures and forests, simply to drive the creatures away, a circumstance that led to their being in starvation condition most of the time (see **They Would Eat Stones**, page 215).

'A Tree Aflame'

Six months passed and the castaways were planning to make good their escape at the prickly pear festival when their masters got into a dispute and marched them all in different directions, unwittingly foiling the plan. Isolated from his friends, Cabeza de Vaca underwent a period of great hardship: 'During this time I endured a very bad life, as much because of my great hunger as because of the bad treatment I received from the Indians, which was such that I had to flee three times.'

Each time he was recaptured, beaten and threatened with death. But finally the prickly pear festival came around again, in September 1534; and through what the four Spanish men termed 'God's will', they were all brought to it by their masters. They waited until the Indians were sated with feasting and then, filling sacks with prickly pear fruit, headed off into the wilderness of what is now southern Texas, looking fearfully behind them for signs of pursuit. They found themselves in an utterly alien landscape of endless, arid plains, but soon met up with another tribe, the Avaveres, who allowed them to live among them as free men. With winter approaching, the men decided to stay rather than try to make it to Mexico.

During this period Cabeza had an extraordinary, almost mystical experience. Out searching for food in the freezing cold, he became separated from his Indian and European companions and wandered for five days as hypothermia set in, 'as naked as the day I was born'. One day, off in the distance he saw a fire. Racing towards it, he found a burning tree—'a tree aflame', as he wrote—that must have been struck by lightning.

The warmth from the flames saved his life, and soon he was able to reunite with his companions.

The Great Shaman

Andrés Dorantes de Carranza, Alonso del Castillo Maldonado, Estevanico and Cabeza de Vaca left the Avaveres and headed in the general direction of Mexico, with Castillo also gaining a reputation as a healer along the way. But he was, as Cabeza puts it, 'a very cautious physician, particularly when the cures were threatening and dangerous', and gradually Cabeza took over most of the healing, becoming known as a great medicine man or shaman. At one point, he claimed, he saved the life of an Indian 'whose eyes rolled back in his head and [who was] without any pulse' by making the sign of the cross on him and blowing on him. The man suffered, says Cabeza, from 'sleeping sickness', which afflicted a great many of the Indians, so that he was kept busy going from hut to hut, curing them. This suggests some sort of group hysteria among the Indians or perhaps a deep psychosomatic desire to be 'cured' by the Spanish shaman but, whatever the truth, Cabeza de Vaca was soon followed wherever he roamed by large groups who sought him out.

All the Spanish performed cures, but Cabeza, or so he claimed, was 'most notable among them'. He goes on: 'And we never cured anyone who did not say that he was better, and they had so much confidence that they would be cured if we performed the cures, that they believed that as long as we were there they would never die.'

At one point the cures became something more than faith healing, however. An Indian with an arrowhead stuck in his chest, close to his heart, was brought to Cabeza. Using a knife, Cabeza opened up the man's chest, extracted the flint arrowhead and stitched the wound closed with a sharpened deer bone and animal sinew. The man was healed within a few days. (Cabeza's surgery was, much later, written up in the *New England Journal of Medicine*.)

De Vaca and his men trek across American terrain early in their journey.

Heading Homeward

Finally leaving the Avarares and their neighbouring tribes behind, Cabeza de Vaca and his companions crossed the Rio Grande into what is now Mexico, still moving along the coastal lands of the Gulf of Mexico. They were, finally, only 160 kilometres (99½ miles) or so from the Rio de las Palmes and Spanish settlements on the Mexican east coast, but on local Indians telling them that 'the people of the coast are very bad', they opted to turn inland and traverse northern Mexico. Once again they could have had no real idea of the geography involved, for the journey they made took them hundreds of kilometres out of their way. Crossing northern Mexico, they found themselves back in Texas, where they came across the first farmers they were to see on the trip, people who lived in settled villages. Cabeza called them the 'cow people' because they went once a year on a bison hunt. He and his fellow travellers were the first Europeans to see the massive bison herds that inhabited the North American plains.

Reaching the Rio Grande and following it upriver, Cabeza and his friends finally entered western Mexico, having described a wide semicircle from their previous position on the Gulf Coast. They were trailed by a silent horde hoping for cures, people who brought presents of deer and rabbit which they roasted in makeshift ovens. The Indians could be thought of as disciples, or acolytes, for they refused any food unless it came from the hands of the Spanish. Their belief in Cabeza's mystical powers was heightened at one point during this journey when he became angry at their refusal to guide him into a certain area. Shortly thereafter, eight Indians died, probably through some epidemic, but the others attributed it to the wrath of Cabeza's god.

In late December 1535, Cabeza de Vaca and his companions crossed the Rio Yaqui in the western part of the Mexican state of Sonora. There were by now hundreds of Indians following them, with more joining every day. In order to maintain their air of authority, Cabeza wrote, 'we [Spaniards] spoke very little to them'. 'The black', as Cabeza habitually refers to Estevanico, talked with them to find which route should be taken and where they might find food. In one village they were given a present of 600 deer hearts, in another six brilliant green arrowheads, probably made of malachite, although Cabeza refers to them as emeralds.

'People of No Luck'

One day Cabeza noticed an Indian wearing an amulet attached to a leather thong around his neck. Peering closer, he realised it was the belt buckle from a scabbard. Through the buckle was a horseshoe nail. It was the first sign of anything Spanish he had seen in eight years. Shortly thereafter, near the Spanish trading post of Cullucan on the Pacific coast, Cabeza, walking ahead with Estevanico, came upon 'four Christians on horseback'. These men 'stared at him speechless', seeing a Spaniard in strange animal skins and soon followed by a dusty crowd of Indians.

It is usual in stories like these to tell of those being rescued falling to the ground and weeping with relief, but Cabeza did not. He requested to be taken to the leader of the four men, who turned out to be on an expedition to capture Indians and enslave them. The expedition members were starving because the local people had disappeared into the foothills of the Sierra Madre, taking with them all the food they could carry. Seeing Cabeza's hold over his Indian followers, the commander asked him to order the local people to return. But far from turning over these 'crude and untutored people', Cabeza de Vaca had 'many and bitter quarrels' with the slave-traders over this request. The traders told the Indians, through their interpreter, that Cabeza and his companions

The Fountain of Youth

Explorer Juan Ponce de León.

Early Spanish explorers expected a good deal of North America—not just gold and riches and exotic Indians, but mythic creatures. According to one historian, rumours spread soon after Columbus's 1492 voyage that one could expect to find 'giants, dwarfs, Amazon women, white-haired boys, human beings with tails, headless folk with an eye in their navel, and trumpet-blowing apes'. This is not to mention the stories of the fabled Seven Cities of Gold or the Pearls of the Jumanos, a so-called 'river of pearls' to be found among the Jumanos Indians in present-day Texas.

No rumour was more persistent or famous than that of the Fountain of Youth. This did not begin with the New World, of course, for the story of a legendary spring which restores youthful vigour has been around at least since the time of ancient Greece, and similar fables were known in the Middle East. And perhaps such tales were told in the New World as well, since the Spanish claimed that the Arawak Indians of Cuba and Hispaniola spoke of an island called Beimeni or Bimini where life-giving waters spouted from the ground.

Add another legend: the Spanish explorer Juan Ponce de León is famous for having gone to Florida to hunt for the Fountain of Youth, but while de León was certainly familiar with the fable, it was not why he went to Florida. Governor of Puerto Rico until he clashed with the Spanish Crown, de León decided to explore the unknown landmass to the north of Cuba and travelled through Florida in 1513, probably the first European to reach the area. He returned on a second visit in 1521, bringing with him colonists, but was wounded by a poisonous arrow during a skirmish with Indians and died the following year. The persistent legend of de León and the Fountain of Youth only arose after his death, when a political enemy claimed that what the former Governor had really been after in Florida was a cure for his impotence.

'were of their own [Spanish] race but had gone astray for a long while and were people of no luck and little heart, whereas they were the lords of the land, whom [the Indians] should obey'.

Cabeza de Vaca had come a long way, literally and figuratively. He was so transformed—had gone so far 'astray'—that his own countrymen disowned him. The Indians knew who to trust, however—Cabeza, they said, 'cured the sick, while the others killed the healthy'. Cabeza 'went naked and shoeless, while the others wore clothes and went on horseback and with lances'.

The Indians knew Cabeza de Vaca as one of their own. When he finally left them, they were weeping.

Back in Spain

Cabeza and his companions reached Tenochtitlán (now renamed Mexico City) on 24 July 1536, receiving a warm welcome from the viceroy of New Spain, who listened carefully to the tales of their travels. He was particularly interested in the story of the five 'emerald' arrowheads, and the rumour arose that they had originated in the fabled Seven Cities of Gold, in northern Mexico. An expedition was quickly raised, but none of the three Spaniards would go back into the wilderness. (Estevanico, being a slave, was forced to go, and was killed by Zuni Indians.) But he and the other three men were to become legendary in history. They had travelled 4000 kilometres (2485½ miles) on foot since leaving the Island of Doom and, through their own courage and resourcefulness, had survived.

Cabeza de Vaca left New Spain and arrived back home in 1537, where he penned his *relación*. In 1540 Charles V made him governor of the area around the Rio de Plata in South America. Making his last voyage to the New World, Cabeza landed on the coast of Brazil and marched his men 1600 kilometres (994 miles) through the wilderness to the settlement of Asunción in present-day Paraguay. Amazingly, he lost only two men during this trek. As Governor, Cabeza pursued a more liberal policy towards the Indians than most Spanish, refusing to allow them to be mistreated or sold into prostitution. It was probably this, rather than the corruption with which he was officially charged, which caused the citizens of Asunción to rebel against him and send him back to Spain in chains in 1545.

Found guilty of several charges, Cabeza de Vaca was forbidden to set foot again in the Americas. He died in 1559, having wandered enough wildernesses for two lifetimes.

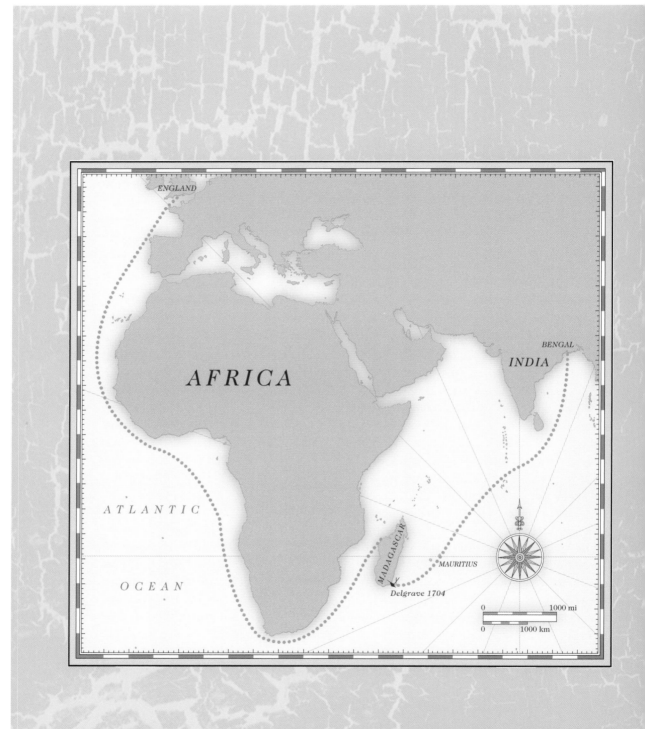

Robert Drury, 1703–1718
Marooned on Madagascar

If, in the 1730s, you happened to be visiting Old Tom's Coffee-house in Birchin Lane, London—a place frequented by poets, adventurers and rogues as well as ordinary citizens—you would almost certainly have the chance to speak with a fortyish gentleman named Robert Drury who had a colourful tale to tell—of how he had been cast away on the exotic, little-known island of Madagascar and lived there among savages for fifteen years, taking part in their wars, escaping, being recaptured and ultimately rescued in an unlikely fashion.

Drury—who made his a living as a humble porter at India House, the East India Company's headquarters—had told the same tale in a book called *Madagascar: Or Robert Drury's Journal During Fifteen Years of Captivity On That Island*, published in 1729, which ended with an open invitation. 'I am every day to be spoken with at Old Tom's Coffee-house on Birchin Lane,' he had written, 'where I shall be ready to gratify any gentleman with a further account [of my adventures].'

One can imagine him gesticulating in front of the fire in the smoky room, describing arid wastes, strange, lost forests, peculiar animals and bloodthirsty men with spears 2 metres (over 2 yards) long who, as a sign of obeisance, licked their rulers' feet. Sipping his coffee, he might even have begun his tale the way he began his *Journal*: 'I, Robert Drury, was born on the 24th of July, in the year 1687, in Crutched Friars, London ...'

To Sea

Drury was the son of a well-to-do innkeeper who ran a public house called The King's Head; he was raised in middle-class surroundings and sent to school. Despite these privileges, as he wrote, 'I could not be brought to think of any art, science, trade, business or profession of any kind whatsoever besides going to sea'. Therefore, in 1701, his father obligingly pulled some strings to get the 13-year-old boy a position as cabin boy on the *Degrave*, a 700-ton East Indiaman. The *Degrave* set sail in February of that year for India and arrived safely in Bengal, where ship and crew remained for many months. Drury put his time there to good use, learning to drink arrack (a potent alcohol made from fermented fruit or sugar cane) and to swim, a skill which was soon to come in handy.

Early in 1703, the *Degrave*, with a cargo of textiles and carrying 160 passengers (including two women) and crew, began the return voyage to England. The ship had the bad luck to run aground on a sandbar as it came down the Ganges River from Bengal;

it was floated off, apparently undamaged, but partway across the Indian Ocean began to take on water. Captain Younge—son of the previous captain, who had died while the *Degrave* was in India—decided to put in at the Dutch-held island of Mauritius for repairs. They stayed there two months, unloading the vessel with backbreaking labour, storing the cargo on the beach, but they were unable to find the where the hull had been damaged.

Captain Younge, whom Drury describes as inexperienced, was anxious to resume the voyage, and so ordered the vessel reloaded and set sail for the Cape of Good Hope. This turned out to be a fatal error, for once on the high seas the *Degrave* began leaking again, this time so badly that the pumps could not keep up with the inflow and the sailors became exhausted from bailing for half the night as well. Younge was adamant that the vessel could make it at least to the Cape; the crew were equally convinced that they would all drown in mid-ocean—that the vessel, as they said, could no longer 'swim'. They finally convinced Younge to put about and head for Madagascar, off the east coast of Africa, about 500 kilometres (310.5 miles) to the north.

'Our Utter Ruin'

It was a sign of how desperate the sailors were that they were willing to put into Madagascar, for the place had a strange and fearsome reputation. The fourth largest island in the world—it's about the size of France—Madagascar had remained free of human habitation until perhaps 200 AD, when it was settled by seafarers in outrigger canoes from Southeast Asia—a voyage of some 6000 kilometres (3728 miles). Africans, despite the fact that Madagascar is only 1300 kilometres (808 miles) from the east coast of that continent, arrived rather later and settled the southern portion of the island, where Robert Drury was shortly to find himself, bringing with them their obsession with animist gods.

By the fifteenth century Europeans had arrived, both the English and French, but diseases endemic to the island, the harsh landscape and hostile tribes kept settlement to small trading posts. Much of the time the Malagasy tribes warred with each other, either for power or for slaves, who were sold to Arab and European traders or to the pirates who made the island a regular port of call. Madagascar was rich in flora and fauna, home to some 250,000 species (70 per cent of which, due to isolation, are known nowhere else on the planet—see **The Elephant Bird**, page 226) and had, in Drury's time, a densely forested interior. The island is divided by central highlands, with tropical rainforests on the eastern coast and arid plateaus and deserts in the west and south. It is a land where one can, literally, travel from one climate zone to another in a matter of moments.

An eighteenth century engraving showing the native inhabitants of Madagascar.

The Elephant Bird

One of the strangest and most exotic creatures in a strange and exotic land, the elephant bird became extinct on Madagascar long before Drury arrived there, but at one time it ruled the island.

Judging from bone remnants and a few fossilised eggs (some of which contain skeletal embryos), the heavy-set elephant bird was 3 metres (over 3 yards) tall and weighed around 450 kilograms (99 pounds). It was flightless, like the ostrich and emu, and wandered large parts of the island, carefully laying its eggs—which measured up to 33 centimetres (13 inches) in length and held over 9 litres (304 fluid ounces) of liquid—in very secluded spots.

Scientists are unsure why the elephant bird became extinct, but it was almost certainly because of human beings. The Malagasy hunted the bird, but probably had more luck eating its eggs—which were large enough to provide meals for entire families—for remains of the eggshells have been found around fireplaces in archaeological digs. The Malagasy may have had a taboo against killing the actual bird— a formidable creature, in any event, with large, curved claw-like feet—which they called *vorompatra*, a name which suggests that it mainly frequented the Androy region of southern Madagascar, once known as Ampatre, where Drury was held captive. He would not have seen one— the last noted, at least by a European, was in 1649—but he certainly heard tales of the giant creatures.

As the *Degrave* moved sluggishly toward this mystery-shrouded island, Robert Drury was sent aloft to the crow's nest with orders to shout when he spotted land. 'At length,' he writes, 'I plainly discovered a white cliff and smoke at a distance from the cliff. I then cried out: Land! Land!'

Even the captain leaped into the rigging to see the island slowly rise over the heaving swell of the ocean. When they got closer, one of the sailors said they were near Port Dauphine, where there had been a small French settlement and where the king, who was called Samuel, hated white men and treated them all 'barbarously'. This was misinformation—King Samuel hated the French, but liked the English quite well—but because of it the *Degrave* did not put in at Port Dauphine's natural harbour and sailed south along the coast.

This mistake was, as Drury wrote, 'our utter ruin'.

Heart in a Bottle

The ship was now wallowing badly. Captain Younge realised that he would soon have to deliberately run her aground, despite the heavy surf. The sailors heaved as much overboard as they could—chests of cotton cloth, cannon, personal belongings. They even cut down the masts in attempt to lighten the vessel. Finally, the *Degrave* came to a shuddering halt on the offshore reef. A line was run to shore and Drury and some of his shipmates fashioned a small raft on which to take the two women to the beach, hauling the makeshift vessel hand over hand. But as it reached the shore-break it capsized and one of the women drowned. Drury had to swim for his life, but his practice in India kept him afloat and, dripping and exhausted, he reached the beach. Other members of the crew stumbled ashore, including the captain who, Drury noticed, was carrying his dead father's heart in a glass jar: it had been the man's dying wish that a part of him be buried in England. In all, about 150 people gathered shivering on the beach.

All around them, quick as spirits, black men issued forth from the jungle, tearing apart the chests of cloth, looking for booty. But they did not seem unfriendly, even helping pull some of the crew from the water. One of them brought a bullock for the castaways to slaughter, even loaning them his musket to do the job. The black men made a fire and helped them cook the creature, although, Drury wrote, 'it was shocking and even terrible to see the negroes cut the beast, skin and flesh together, and sometimes the guts too, then toss it into the fire or ashes … and eat it half-roasted'.

Watching them tear into the raw meat, Drury thought these people—they were the warlike Tandroy—might also eat him. His imagination ran wild: 'Everything before our eyes appeared horrid and frightful and excited most dismal thoughts and dreadful expectations.'

Nothing alarming happened immediately, although the castaways realised they had been quietly surrounded by several hundred warriors. The next morning they were surprised to see a white man walking toward them, surrounded by other warriors. This man's name was Sam; he was an English castaway enslaved to the one-eyed ruler of the Kingdom of Tandroy whose capital, Fenno-arevo, stood a few days' march away. Sam said there were other European castaways on Madagascar, a group of Scots whose ship had been taken over by a pirate, and that all were slaves of the one-eyed king, whose name was Andriankirindra.

The *Degrave* sailors were horrified to hear this, for they were now certain they would never get home. Lying that night on the beach, Drury bemoaned his 'wicked obstinacy' in ignoring the pleas of his mother not to leave home. The next day, Andriankirindra himself showed up with 200 warriors. They were not carrying guns (Drury later learned that this was because they were afraid the Englishmen might snatch them) but they all had wicked-looking 2-metre (2-yard) lances.

Andriankirindra was pleasant enough, but told them that they would have to stay in his country until a European ship came past and could take them off. Captain Younge thanked him for the courtesy, but indicated they would prefer to head north to Port Dauphine, where a ship was more likely to show up. Andriankirindra merely laughed. 'No,' he said, 'you are coming with me.'

Desperate Gambit

After a forced march of several days, they came to Fenno-arevo, where Andriankirindra announced through Sam, who was his interpreter, that he had 'a potent enemy' to the west—King Samuel, in fact—and that, since God had given him all these castaways, he was going to use them in his war against Samuel. He told Captain Younge that the next day his men and the Scottish castaways would be divided into groups and given to various of his princes.

In other words, the Europeans were to be made slaves to fight Andriankirindra's wars. The next day, Drury relates, he was 'waked in the morning by a great and sudden noise in the town'. Captain Younge, along with other members of the crew, the group of Scots, and their captain, had seized Andriankirindra and his queen, taking them hostage to safeguard the castaways' escape to the west to the land of King Samuel. Drury had not been in on the plan, but he ran to join the plotters, who had armed themselves with captured muskets and were leaving town, surrounded by a menacing, angry army of some 2000 Tandroy warriors.

It was a desperate gambit. Sam had told them a swift river divided the Tandroy kingdom from that of King Samuel and so the castaways headed for it, not realising they would first have to cross a waterless, semi-arid wasteland. Gradually some of the men fell behind, but no one dared stay with them, especially after the Tandroy 'put [one of the men] out of his pain by sticking their lances in almost every part of his body'.

They marched for four days and nights, surrounded by warriors. Exhausted and nearing breaking point, they finally made the river, where the Tandroy proposed that they release Andriankirindra for six muskets and the promise of safe passage. Captain Younge was counselled not to agree to this, but he did, another fatal mistake. As soon as his party crossed the river, the warriors fell screaming upon them. The castaways raced up a sandhill to make a final stand, blazing away until the sun set and they ran out of ammunition. That night, thirty men slipped away through the Tandroy lines, most of them making it to relative safety on the west coast. But in the morning the slaughter began.

The youthful Robert Drury watched in horror as the Tandroy rammed a lance into Captain Younge's throat and then through his side, their favoured method of dispatching an enemy. Drury and three other young crewmen were held by a group of Tandroy while the other warriors raged through the rest of the castaways, killing even those who tried to surrender. Gore ran all over the sandhill; the surviving Englishwoman was speared along with the rest. Finally it was over, and the warriors, red with blood, dragged Drury and the other three back to Fenno-arevo.

'Sons of Dogs'

Drury's life had been spared because of his youth, but he was not to be spared captivity. He was given as a personal slave to the king's grandson, Mevarrow, and put to work herding cattle. Completely isolated, he was forced to learn the Tandroy language, to eat his meat half-cooked, to dig for sweet potato-like tubers deep in the ground. Despite this, Drury became friendly with the other youths herding Mevarrow's cattle, many of them slaves like himself, with whom he ventured into the woods to steal honey from beehives, eating it wax and all. He also enjoyed hunting for what he called the tondruck (his pronunciation of the Malagasy *tandraka*), a 'wild pig' (actually a large insectivore) about the size of a cat, tailless and with feet like a rabbit—just one of the many strange animals he encountered.

Gradually, Mevarrow began to trust the young man, giving him a lance, and even leaving him to protect his wife when he went off to war. The Tandroy, it appeared to Drury, were constantly warring, and would come back in triumph (to the sound of a wailing conch shell) with processions of slaves. The common practice, he reported, was to sneak up on an enemy village with pieces of meat which were thrown to silence the dogs, then to race shouting among the huts. When the men emerged from the low-slung doorways they were lanced to death, and the women and young children carried off as slaves.

Life held unpleasant surprises for Drury as well. He had to be beaten into practising the Malagasy habit of licking his master's feet in servitude. And once, when he and some fellow slaves were herding some jointly owned cattle for several months, they secretly killed one of Mevarrow's bullocks for food. But they were discovered eating it and the cry went up: 'Kill them, sons of dogs!' His fellow slaves, who belonged to other masters, were 'mutilated' (this probably means castrated). Drury fell to his knees and licked his master's feet. Mevarrow tied his arms, placed him against a tree, walked 40 metres (44 yards) away, and fired his musket, missing narrowly.

'Whether he [missed me] on purpose, I cannot say,' Drury wrote, 'but I am apt to think he did.'

'I Broke from Her Arms'

By now ten years had passed and Drury, a man of twenty-four or so, had risen under Mevarrow's ownership to become the royal butcher, and was allowed to take up arms and go to war. During one of the endless internecine conflicts he participated in, Drury found a wounded enemy in the woods. His description of what happens next is startling: 'He looked me full in the face, with his eyes dazzling, and was going to speak, when I snatched one of the lances out of his hand, telling him it was my time now … and immediately struck him dead.'

Drury fell in love with the captive daughter of a dead chief, married her, and was given cattle and slaves of his own. Mevarrow, though he placed his trust in Drury, was careful to have a spell cast on him, which supposedly would keep him from running away. But in his heart Drury yearned to get back to England. He begged his wife to leave with him but, he writes, 'she was far too superstitious and afraid that I should be hurt by the charms' of the spell.

This was a horrible moment. 'To part with her and leave her in slavery, and perhaps to be ill-used on my account, was a mortifying stroke to me, for I loved her sincerely.' However, Drury wrote, 'My resolution was fixed.' He would escape to the west. After a last night spent with his wife, who cried and begged him to stay, 'I broke from her arms by break of day' (a nice phrase which Drury himself may not have thought of—see **A Plain Honest Narrative**, opposite) and quietly left the village.

After three weeks' arduous travel, Drury thought he had reached safety with Fiherenana, a rival of Andriankirindra who headed the Salalava tribe, which controlled most of the western half of the island. King Fiherenana accepted Drury into his army and protected him from the wrath of Mevarrow, who wanted Drury back—for this, Drury wrote, 'I licked his feet with great satisfaction'. Fiherenana called Drury 'a Mall-a-coss' (a nickname, he writes with some pride, 'which you give to the meanest of natives') and had him fight beside him in his wars, but as the years went by Drury realised that he was still a slave, albeit one who was given more freedom than most and, again, his own herd of cattle.

And so once again he became a fugitive, escaping one night to follow the Onilahy River to St Augustine's Bay on the west coast. His journey took him through 'a craggy, dismal wilderness', eating roots and some beef he had brought with him, following swarms of bees to find their hives. One night he fought off strange, fox-like creatures attempting to drag him away from his fire (there are no foxes on Madagascar and few carnivores, but these animals may have been fossa, strange, cat-like creatures which can be aggressive during the mating season).

Finally, after a month on the run, Drury came to a high hill from which he looked down at the sea and St Augustine's Bay.

'A Plain Honest Narrative'

Daniel Defoe, hounded by creditors in his lifetime, has been hounded ever since by literary sleuths who feel that the prolific author (see Alexander Selkirk, page 78) had a hand in numerous castaway stories of the period. There are some who even feel he inserted passages into the otherwise genuine memoirs of Leendert Hasenbosch (see page 48). The argument to be made for that is rather tenuous, but it can be said with reasonable certainty that Defoe had a part in helping Robert Drury write his memoir.

The Preface to the *Journal* begins with the reader addressed by an anonymous editor: 'At the first Appearance of this Treatise, I make no doubt of it being taken for another "Robinson Crusoe"; but whoever expects to find here the fine Inventions of a prolific Brain will be deceived, for so far as every Body concerned in the publication knows, it is nothing else but a plain, honest, Narrative of Matter of Fact.'

One chuckles to hear Defoe amusing himself as he tweaks the reader with 'Robinson Crusoe' and 'the fine Inventions of a prolific Brain'. The Preface does go on to say that Drury's original manuscript needed to be put 'in a more agreeable Method'; Defoe's hand can be seen in some of the descriptions, particularly of forts and grand princes, which Michael Parker Pearson's research has found to be exaggerated. Not made up entirely, of course—but one can hear Defoe nudging Drury: 'You've got to put a little pizzazz into it, kid!'

Slave trading activity in the late eighteenth century.

'How Have You Done These Many Years?'

St Augustine's Bay was the place where French and English ships moored during those countries' short-lived attempts at colonising Madagascar. There was a community of sorts here where Europeans of all stripes—castaways, slavers, pirates—lived as free men, although the Malagasy chiefs controlled the region. When Drury came down from the hills, people wondered 'what sort of white man I was without clothes'.

A white man like the others, it turned out. For while Drury would find himself belonging to another Malagasy master here, he met a Dutchman and then several Englishmen, pirates wearing braces of pistols. Drury cocked his musket when he saw this group, thinking they meant to hurt his master, but one of them said: 'Robert Drury, how have you done these many years?' The pirate turned out to be Nicholas Dove, one of the young crewmen saved from the sandhill massacre, who had been able to run away to Port Dauphine after only a few years of captivity.

Finally someone told Robert Drury's story to the captain of a slave ship, who repeated the tale when he got back to London in the very tavern owned by Drury's father, who had long since given up his son for dead. Drury senior begged another slave-trader, one Captain Mackett, to purchase his son's freedom the next time he was in Madagascar. Drury's master let him go, and this nearly 30-year-old man—now more Malagasy warrior than Englishman—found himself aboard the *Masselage* on 20 January 1718. Ironically, the ship's cargo was slaves, who were delivered in the West Indies before the *Masselage* reached London in early September.

Like many former slaves, Drury was never to find himself quite free again. By the time he returned to London, both his mother and father had died and few friends were left to him. His skills of hunting and spear-throwing were not much sought after back in civilisation. So it is not really a surprise to find that by June of the following year he was back in Madagascar, this time working as an interpreter for a slave-trader. He arrived back in London from his second voyage in 1720, and here we lose track of him for nine years until his memoirs are published and he describes himself as ready to answer all questions at Old Tom's. There is a record of him asking for, and failing to get, a berth on an Indiaman—it is possible his consolation prize was the job as porter at India House.

In any event, he lived until perhaps 1750, talking as garrulously as ever about his adventures, which some people began to think might be imagined. There is no record of Robert Drury ever marrying and having children and one wonders if he left his heart—like the heart of his first captain—back on the exotic island with the wife who remained there under a spell of enchantment.

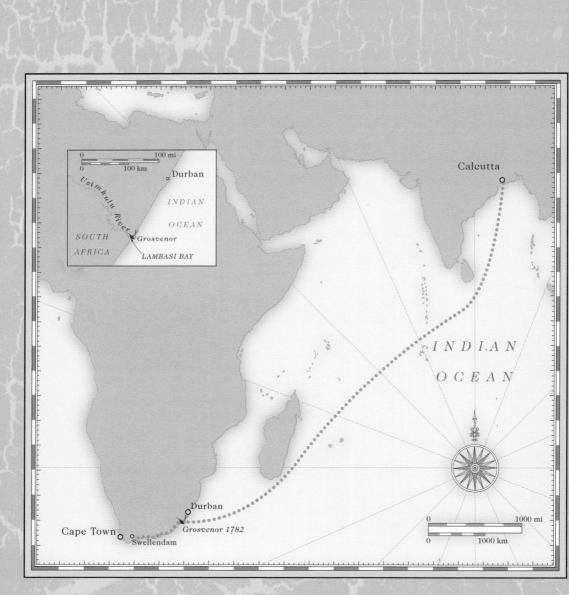

Calcutta

INDIAN

OCEAN

Durban

Grosvenor 1782

Cape Town

Swellendam

0   1000 mi
0   1000 km

The Grosvenor, 1782
Despair on Africa's Wild Coast

Of anywhere on the thousands of kilometres (miles) of the rolling east coast of Africa, the worst place you could possibly pick to be shipwrecked would be the desolate 300 kilometre (186.5 mile) stretch in South Africa known to this day as the Wild Coast. The name refers to the huge waves which gather force across the Indian Ocean and come pounding ashore in relentless succession, throwing up mountains of spray, the noise sounding, as one seventeenth century visitor wrote, 'like a fleet at sea battering each other with their guns'.

On 4 August 1782, the Pondo people who lived in the hills of the northern part of the Wild Coast set fire to huge areas of dry vegetation to burn off the underbrush and fertilise the soil. That night, only a few kilometres out to sea but a yawning cultural chasm away, the British East India merchantman *Grosvenor*, a three-masted square-rigger of 471 tons, carrying 140 men, women and children and tons of valuable cargo, was passing by on the homeward voyage from Calcutta. It was intended to round the Cape of Good Hope, avoiding the usual stop at Cape Town—for South Africa was then a Dutch possession and the Dutch and British were at war—and head north into the Atlantic.

The captain of the *Grosvenor*, John Coxon, estimated they were hundreds of kilometres from land, and had thus gone to bed on this black, windy night, leaving the helm to his sailors. Sometime after midnight, the watch noticed strange flickering lights off the starboard bow, where there should have been nothing but open sea. Like fires, the lights appeared and disappeared from view. But when the helmsman tried to turn away from the lights, Coxon came back on deck and told him to keep his course—the 'flames' were merely a hallucination, some natural atmospheric disturbance.

He went back to bed. Soon another lookout, aloft in the rigging and wiping blown spray from his face, saw a dark shape off the starboard bow. Certain that it was the coast of Africa, the terrified sailor ran to knock on Coxon's door, but this time the captain would not even come get up. He told the seaman to leave him alone—they were at least 500 kilometres (310.5 miles) off the Wild Coast.

The British East India Company

John Coxon was not much of a navigator—an odd thing in a sea captain, one might think, but not for the master of a vessel belonging to the British East India Company—an 'Indiaman', in the parlance of the day. The British East India Company, like its rival the Dutch East

Indies Company, was a huge private enterprise with quasi-governmental powers. In fact, it ruled an entire country: India. The Company was set up in 1600 when a group of English merchants consolidated and were given a monopoly on trade with India by the British government. Its fortunes rose over the next century and a half, taking advantage of the rich trade in spices, tea, precious jewels and silk, but it turned from a trading venture into a ruling enterprise in 1757, when one of its officials scored a rousing military victory over the competing French East India Company's forces at the Battle of Plassey.

The Company then acquired the rights to collect revenue in Bengal, India's richest and largest province, with the result that its officials—whom one historian has called 'a rapacious and self-aggrandising lot'—became rich through bribery and financial scheming while Bengal, and India as a whole, suffered great poverty. Despite this influx of wealth, the East India Company faltered because of the massive military operations it was forced to mount to conquer other Indian provinces. In 1773 the British government appointed the high-ranking Company administrator, Warren Hastings, as the first governor-general of India. The historian Lord Macaulay wrote of Hastings: 'His principles were rather lax. His heart was rather hard', which can be taken as an epigraph for the Company as a whole.

Dangerous Passage

The men and woman who boarded the *Grosvenor* in March 1782 were a cross-section of the British subjects who worked for the Company. William Hosea had administered one of the richest districts in Bengal and was travelling home with his wife Mary and their 18-month-old daughter Frances. Hosea had been involved in scheming against Governor-General Hastings and had decided that it was time to get out of India while his mostly-stolen fortune was intact. That fortune was a sizeable one, as evidenced by the fact that he had essentially bribed Captain John Coxon with the modern-day equivalent of of £240,000 to secure a quick passage home. Hosea also carried about £7200 worth of rough diamonds, a common practice among those who wanted to make their wealth more portable.

Others whose fates would soon be intertwined in a way none of them could have imagined included vivacious, red-headed Lydia Logie, pregnant wife of the *Grosvenor*'s chief mate, Alexander Logie; an astute young sailor named William Habberley; and several children who were being sent Home for schooling, accompanied only by a servant, among them a handsome seven-year-old Anglo-Indian boy named Thomas Law, who soon became a favourite of the crew, and Mary Wilmot and Eleanor Dennis, aged seven and three.

For those who could pay for passage in its private cabins, Hosea and other notables who wore powdered wigs and silver buckles to dinner, the *Grosvenor* was a relatively

The *Grosvenor* was laden with a rich cargo when it ran aground off the coast of South Africa.

comfortable ship, which carried over 12,000 litres (3171 gallons) of wine for its wealthy passengers. Those in steerage, including numerous Indian servants and sailors (the latter known as lascars), had a more rigorous time of it. But for rich and poor alike, a voyage on any Indiaman was perilous. This was particularly true on the passage Home, when ships typically described a west-to-east semicircle from India to the tip of Africa. Once the dangerous east coast of Africa was sighted, the ships headed south to round the Cape of Good Hope, after which the homeward leg up the Atlantic began.

The problem was that longitude—a ship's east-west position on the globe—could not be comfortably reckoned in those days. Captains heading across the Indian Ocean needed a combination of experience and gut instinct to figure out where they were relative to Africa's dangerous coastal waters. But John Coxon was not much of a captain. He was a Company man—an exalted merchant—who enriched himself by dint of charging exorbitant prices for passage to wealthy men like William Hosea, and by bringing home his own private cargoes. For the niceties of navigation he depended on his experienced chief mate, Alexander Logie.

'Horror and Apprehension'

Unfortunately, on that black and windy night of 5 August 1782, Alexander Logie lay ill, most probably with dysentery, in his cabin, and the care of the *Grosvenor* and all aborad her resided in the hands of John Coxon. While some passengers drank in the great cabin and others slept, or read quietly in their bunks, the shape on the horizon, resembling a gigantic humpback whale, grew closer and closer, and the flames of the fires—for that is the only thing they could have been, or so testified William Habberley, on deck at the time—danced brightly. Now another seaman ran to the captain's cabin and demanded his presence on deck. Coxon emerged, anger changing to fear and astonishment as he realised the *Grosvenor* was indeed heading directly for land. He immediately ordered the ship to come about and men raced up into the rigging as the helmsman spun the great wheel, trying to make the opposite tack. But it was too late. At 4.30 in the morning, the *Grosvenor* struck a hidden object with such force that the entire vessel gave a fearful shudder and passengers were hurled from their bunks.

A Narrative of the Loss of the Grosvenor, East Indiaman, written in the 1790s by British artist and author George Carter, who interviewed at least one survivor, describes the chaotic scene. 'Horror and apprehension [and] anarchy and confusion' were etched on the faces of the passengers who raced on deck and realised that the strong offshore breeze might at any moment force them off the shoal and into the open sea, where the ship with its stove-in hull would certainly sink rapidly. Captain Coxon was next to useless in this situation, at one point ordering the ship's guns to be fired—a standard distress signal, but all but useless on this remote coast. (In any event, the crewmen heading below found the powder magazine flooded.)

When the ship did come off the rocks, which had essentially been acting as a giant plug, water poured into the hull. The crew quickly dropped the mainmast with axes, the fastest way to get the sails down out of the wind, then the foremast. The *Grosvenor* lurched back against the rocks and it appeared that, for the moment, she was stable.

When first light came, it could be seen that the ship was stranded on a rocky reef perhaps 250 metres (273 yards) from shore, and the passengers gazed in astonishment as groups of black men gathered on the beach. Finally, two Italian seamen and one of the lascars, promised a huge financial reward by the captain, and possibly by William Hosea as well, attempted to swim a line to shore to secure the ship. One of them drowned, but the other two made it. About a dozen panicked sailors tried to haul themselves ashore before the line was secure, but their weight caused it to go slack in the water and all were thrown onto the wave-battered rocks, where they were knocked unconscious and drowned. Those aboard the wreck could see the tribesmen on the beach ignoring the two men tying fast the line—they were pulling in the spars and rigging which had already washed up.

Within a few hours, the great Indiaman broke in two, the passengers gathering on the stern and watching in horror as the bow drifted away. Many fell to their knees and began praying, giving themselves up as lost. But then something incredible happened. The offshore breeze shifted to an onshore direction, and the entire stern segment drifted off the rocks, through the shallows toward shore. When they realised what was happening, the men on shore took up the line they had affixed to the rock and pulled mightily. Little by little, the broken remnant of the *Grosvenor* was hauled to the beach.

By now it was almost evening. One hundred and twenty-five men, women and children had survived the wreck, an astonishing number. They crawled ashore shaking, dishevelled and frightened, all too aware that their troubles were just beginning.

Pondoland

One moment the passengers were comfortably ensconced in their cabins in the late eighteenth century's closest equivalent to a modern luxury liner, the next they were tossed ashore on a forbidding coastline. To add to the nightmarish aspect of the experience, they were surrounded by black men with hair piled high in orange, mud-daubed cones, who wore only brief loincloths and who at first completely ignored them. They were running

The Peacock Throne

Was the famous Peacock Throne aboard the *Grosvenor* when she sank in 1782? For a long time, treasure hunters were sure it was. The Peacock Throne belonged to Shah Jahan, the Mughal Emperor who built the fabulous Taj Mahal. The throne was a wonder of the East, 193 centimetres (76 inches) high, ascended by a set of silver steps, backed with reproductions of two splayed peacock tails, and gilded with silver inlaid with diamonds, rubies, emeralds and pearls. Were the throne extant today, there are estimates it would bring a billion dollars.

In the nineteenth century, a myth circulated that the *Grosvenor* was a 'treasure ship'—that it had been carrying the annual profits of the British East India Company, turned into rubies and diamonds for easy transport. Treasure hunters diving to the wreck site as recently as 2004 have found no treasure whatsoever, only fascinating artifacts.

And the truth about the Peacock Throne? When Shahanshah Nadir Shah invaded the Mughal Empire in 1738, he took the throne and brought it back to Persia, where it was almost certainly dismantled for its precious stones, although replicas were made and used until the end of the reign of the last Shah of Iran, in the 1970s.

along the shoreline collecting the wooden wreckage, burning it in one of half a dozen huge fires to pop out the iron nails and hoops, which they then doused in cold sea water.

Somehow, the way these men ignored the castaways—as if they simply did not exist—was worse than direct confrontation. William Habberley would later write that it was difficult to watch the natives expertly extracting nails (quite obviously they were used to scavenging shipwrecks) with 'our dreadful situation not apparently affecting them, as they never offered us any assistance'.

The British—and Europeans in general—were utterly ignorant about Africa and its peoples. The continent had been raided for slaves for hundreds of years, and its inhabitants derided as savages, but the people who swarmed about the wreck of the *Grosvenor* were anything but primitive. They belonged to the Pondo nation, named after a legendary chief, and had lived in the area for hundreds of years. They had almost no access to iron for their assegais, cooking utensils and hatchets, and thus the metal from the wreck was to them as valuable as gold. The Pondo had an intricate oral tradition which was later to describe the swarms of white people pouring ashore from the *Grosvenor* as being 'like an army'. For the time being, the Pondo concentrated on the immediate: gathering the precious metal and avoiding the strange invaders. When night fell on the castaways' first day on shore, the Pondo disappeared into the hills.

'Unspeakable Difficulties'

The next morning, John Coxon gathered the survivors around him, saying their best hope of salvation lay in walking the 400 kilometres (248.5 miles) south along the coast to Cape Town. There were two things wrong with this idea. One was that Cape Town was actually 650 kilometres (404 miles) away—once again, Coxon had erred in his geography. The other was that almost the entirety of the Wild Coast extended from their little beach. There were precipitous cliffs that plunged hundreds of metres (yards) into the turbulent Indian Ocean, eight rivers and a desert to cross, wild animals which included hippopotamus and lion, and tribes far more hostile than the Pondo, among them the Xhosa, Tembu and Zulu.

Because of Coxon's misunderstanding, he did not consider heading north to Delagoa Bay, about 250 kilometres (155 miles) away, where there was a Portuguese settlement. His ignorance was to prove fatal, but for the time being the survivors were happy to be given direction, and went about gathering up the meagre supplies that had washed up.

The Pondo began to swarm about them, but this time aggressively, removing jewellery from their clothes, and smashing the sea-chests that had floated in. Coxon ordered his group not to respond, a mistake, as it turned out—for the Pondo respected resistance, and the survivors' passivity only made matters worse. As the column of castaways began their march along the high ground above the shore the Pondo followed, hurling stones at them.

When the exhausted castaways lay down to rest the first night, they had only made 8 kilometres (5 miles), so difficult was the rocky landscape and so impeded was their progress by the Pondo. But the next morning, still a cohesive group, they continued on. To their surprise, they met a group from a different tribe who treated them kindly. Among them was a Dutch subject from Java (he is sometimes described as a Malay) named Trout (or Traut) who, George Carter writes, 'having committed some murders among the Dutch [at the Cape] had fled to this part of the country for refuge and concealment'.

The castaways thought that Trout would help them, but they were sorely mistaken. He refused even the most lavish bribes from Hosea and Coxon to guide them to Cape Town, saying that if he returned there his own life would be forfeit. But he did warn them of how perilous the journey they were undertaking would be, 'attended by unspeakable difficulties, with many nations [tribes] to pass ... exclusive of the difficulties from the vast numbers of wild beasts they were sure to meet with'. But Coxon refused to reconsider, and continued to urge the party on.

Confrontation

By 9 August, although continually harried by the Pondo, the castaways had found their way to Waterfall Bluff, a commanding cliff. Lydia Logie, seven months pregnant, walked beside her husband Alexander, now so ill he had to be carried in a litter. William and Mary Hosea formed a protective circle with their two Indian maids, or *ayahs*, and their daughter Frances, now nearly two years old. And several seamen were taking turns carrying young Thomas Law, who was gamely trying to keep up but kept falling behind.

From the jungle, they had heard the roar of lions and the strange barking of hyenas; crossing one river, they were startled by a hippopotamus, which seemed to them like a medieval monster. They approached the kraals and cattle pens of the Pondo, begging for milk. When it was realised they had no iron to give in return, according to Habberley the Africans 'fed the milk to their dogs' and threw stones at the survivors, driving them away.

There was cultural confusion at work here. The English could not understand why the Pondo would not help them; for their part, the Africans wanted to protect their most precious resource, their cattle, from this locust-like horde of white invaders. Inevitably, there was a confrontation. A native approached Coxon and feinted at him with his assegai; Coxon, losing his temper, grabbed it and refused to give it back. Brawling broke out, with ninety sailors fighting perhaps 400 tribesmen, in a battle which took no lives but accounted for, according to George Carter, 'a great number maimed', which included Charles Newman, a wealthy barrister who had a lance stuck in his ear, rendering him unconscious for several hours.

There was a temporary truce following this, but a few days later, after the castaways crossed the Umzimpunzi River, the Pondo attacked in force, warriors carrying rawhide shields and spears racing screaming down a hillside to surround them. It is possible they were put up to this by Trout, whose village was nearby, and whom the castaways had once again begged unsuccessfully for help. For when the Pondo came this time, they came with purpose, ripping open the pockets of the castaways' clothes and stealing their valuables.

They did not have the heart to resist. Their dissolution as a group was beginning.

'The Best of Their Way'

The advantage of being cast away with numerous of your fellows is suggested by a number of old adages—united we stand, divided we fall, being one of them. But when such a group begins to disintegrate, it is extraordinarily demoralising, for another force—survival of the fittest—comes into play. It became apparent to the seamen and soldiers of the *Grosvenor* that travelling in a group slowed down by women and children was the way to certain death. Not only were the natives getting more hostile, but the halting progress of this large contingent meant that scant supplies of food were being consumed to little advantage. As Habberley put it: 'Every person was desirous of making the best of their way, saying it was of little use to stay and perish with those they could not give any assistance to.'

And so, once the sailors helped the woman and children cross the broad Ntafufu River, the castaways split up. One group, led by the second mate William Shaw, was composed mainly of the British seamen, along with the lascars and a few passengers. This group of just over fifty was about to set off when young Thomas Law began to weep— for several of the seamen had watched over him ever since the *Grosvenor* set sail. Taking pity on the boy, four of the sailors agreed to share the burden of carrying him. This left Captain Coxon with seven seamen, among them the seriously ill Alexander Logie, and the rest of the passengers, including all the women and children, about forty-seven people in all. There is speculation that the seamen—and possibly Coxon himself—were bribed by William Hosea to remain, using his small treasure of diamonds.

Shaw's group forged slowly ahead through the dense jungles of the headlands, with the sea boiling and roaring to their left. They ate berries and whenever possible descended the cliffs to the rocky shore, where they scraped limpets and oysters off the rocks. They were terrified by the huge elephants—African elephants are far larger than the Indian variety— and by any number of other beasts in the jungle which roared, barked, hissed and slithered as they went by. They climbed mountains and by mid-August had crossed the great Umzimvubu River, though not without cost. Some had dropped out, lying quietly on the ground and promising they would catch up later. Everyone knew it was a lie; they would move on, leaving the stragglers to die of starvation or exposure and be eaten by wild beasts.

But by now Shaw's group was beginning to crumble. The lascars had already decided that they would be best served by going off on their own—probably to join native tribes. A friendly tribe had given the party their first real meal in days—a bullock slaughtered and roasted—but by 22 August the last of this meat had been eaten. At this point they had reached what George Carter calls 'a fine level country', and a dispute arose. Shaw and some of the men wanted to strike inland to seek native kraals which might provide them some sustenance, the others wanted to keep travelling by the sea. And so yet another division took place among the ever-dwindling numbers of survivors.

Diamonds and Death

Because those few who eventually survived came mainly from Shaw's original group— these included William Habberley, who wrote his own account, and John Hynes, who spoke extensively with George Carter—we know less about the fate of those, including the Hoseas, who stayed with Captain Coxon. But one of the *ayahs* did survive, and later told William Habberley as much of the story as she knew. Captain Coxon and the other seamen, having spent a few days with the passengers they had been bribed to protect, abandoned them to fend for themselves. A number straggled after Coxon's party as it disappeared into the jungle, but no one from that group was ever seen again.

Only William and Mary Hosea, their daughter Frances, Alexander and Lydia Logie, and two *ayahs* were left. Unable to think what to do, Hosea stayed where he was in what Stephen Taylor, whose book *The Caliban Shore: The Fate of the Grosvenor Castaways* is the best-researched telling to date of the story, calls 'a kind of numbed paralysis'. This lasted for about five days, and the little party then made an attempt to journey on, but with no success. Alexander Logie died and was left in the jungle. At this point, the *ayahs* decided to make their own way out of the wilderness. No one, quite, knows what happened next, but there is fascinating speculation on Lydia Logie's end (see **The Fate of Lydia Logie**, page 246). William and Mary Hosea almost certainly died of exposure. No hint was ever found of their fate until 1925, when 73-year-old Johann Bock found a few bright diamonds on his farmland near the mouth of the Kei River, about 250 kilometres (155 miles) south of the site of the *Grosvenor* shipwreck. Bock registered for prospecting rights and began to charge others for the right to mine the area, but only he found any of the precious stones—over 1000 in all. Police charged him with 'salting' the area with diamonds to lure prospectors and he was sent to prison for three years, despite the testimony of experts who said the stones were like none they had ever seen from the Cape area.

Most historians today believe that the diamonds belonged to William Hosea, but they disappeared after Johann Bock went to prison and have not been recovered.

One Last Wilderness

By October 1782, Shaw's group had re-formed when the men who had gone further into the bush decided to return to the coast. But now they were broken up into small groups staggering along, sometimes within sight of each other. The going became a little easier after the rocky coast turned into a broad beach, where the men walked day after day but found little to eat—at one point they were forced to carve up a putrefying whale carcass.

The survivors now entered a 65-kilometre (40-mile) stretch of coastline they called 'the sandy desert'. It would be their last obstacle, but of course they didn't know it. There was absolutely no fresh water and little food. In a heartbreaking moment, young Tom Law died on the beach, as did the sailor who had chiefly taken care of him. Second mate William Shaw, their leader, also died. The men in the first little group, which included John Hynes, began to drink their own urine. George Carter wrote: 'When any could not furnish himself with a draught of urine, he would borrow a shell full of his companion who was more fortunate, til it was in his power to repay it.'

It was November and the men had been struggling for three months, through incredible hardships, but now, reduced to six, they were nearing the end of their endurance. They talked about drawing lots to kill one of their number to eat. Just as it seemed this would happen, they found a freshwater spring, which gave them the strength to go on. They walked along the beach until they found green hills overlooking a small bay, where they fell asleep. In the morning, one of the group was searching for fruit when he spotted a white man walking down a track, holding a gun and smoking a pipe. He was an employee on a Dutch farm near the settlement of Swellendam, some 250 kilometres (155 miles) from Cape Town. It was 18 November 1782, and six of the survivors were saved.

The Old Woman

Despite the fact that England and the Netherlands were at war, the Dutch responded generously, and sent out search parties to look for any stragglers. William Habberley, near death from starvation, had approached a Xhosa village and begged for food. Instead of harming him, they saved his life, and for a time he became a member of the tribe, as did another seaman, Thomas Lewis. They were among the men found by the Dutch search parties, and may have owed their lives to the fact that the natives were not threatened by a lone European in the way that they were by the large group of *Grosvenor* survivors.

In all, of the 125 castaways who had begun the trek to the Cape, thirteen survived it—nine European sailors, three lascars and one of the ayahs who worked for the Hoseas. Despite further searches, none of the rest of the passengers and crew was ever found, although there is evidence that at least one sailor, John Bryan, voluntarily lived out his life among the Xhosa, taking a wife and fathering children.

The Fate of Lydia Logie

Horror, when observed from safe distance, has its titillating aspect, and one of the most titillating parts of the story of the *Grosvenor* were the rumours that spread about Lydia Logie's fate. The vivacious, red-headed 23-year-old, seven months pregnant, had been left behind in the African bush after the death of her husband, and it was at first assumed that she died. And this was as it should be, it was thought, for it would not do for a white woman to fall into the hands of black Africans—'the most barbarous and monstrous of the human species', according to one British tabloid of the time, who would certainly drag her into 'the vilest brutish prostitution'.

But then … stories spread that Logie was alive, and had probably joined a Xhosa tribe to save her life and that of her unborn child. According to author Stephen Taylor,

Robert Gordon, commander of the Cape Town garrison, heard from an African informant that a woman from the *Grosvenor* had lived with the Xhosa, a woman who 'had a child and frequently embraced the child, and cried most violently'. Supposedly this woman had married a Xhosa prince and had children by him. But by the time the news got back to the Cape, and a rescue party came looking for Lydia Logie in 1791, she had died, worn down by a life of hard work.

The rescue party missed Eleanor Dennis and Mary Wilmot both of whom lived with the nearby Pondo for years— according to the testimony of a Royal Navy lieutenant who visited the wreck site in 1823 and was told this story by the Pondo. Their eventual fate was sad—they were said to have fled into the bush to escape a Zulu invasion and starved to death.

When the survivors reached England and their story became public knowledge, it caused a sensation that lasted well into the next century—Charles Dickens would describe the story of young Tom Law and his faithful sailors as 'the most beautiful and affecting I know associated with a shipwreck'. But while many fantastic stories arose from the wreck of the *Grosvenor* and the sad journey of her castaways, the most fantastic was not known until the twentieth century. In 1905, a travelling magistrate with an interest in Pondo history spoke with an ageing trader named William Bazley. Bazley told the magistrate that forty years earlier, he had a met 'a very old white woman living exactly as a native'. This would have been between 1860 and 1870. The woman told him that she had come off the huge ship that crashed ashore, lost her family, and been saved and raised by the Pondo.

Bazley, at least, was certain that the woman was Frances Hosea, daughter of William and Mary, at two years of age left wandering alone in the wilderness after her parents lay down and died in a welter of diamonds on the high shores of the Wild Coast.

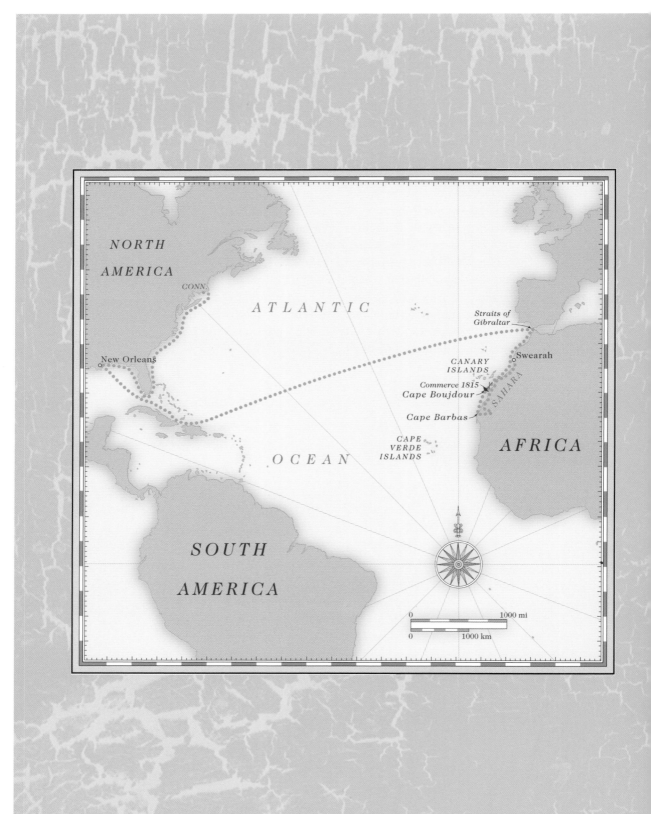

NORTH
AMERICA

ATLANTIC

CONN.

New Orleans

OCEAN

SOUTH

AMERICA

Straits of
Gibraltar

Swearah

CANARY
ISLANDS

Commerce 1815
Cape Boujdour

SAHARA

Cape Barbas

AFRICA

CAPE
VERDE
ISLANDS

0   1000 mi
0   1000 km

Shipwrecked in the Sahara, 1815
The Incredible Journey of Captain James Riley

On a September day in the year 1815, a New England sea captain, cast ashore with his crew on the northwest coast of Africa, staggered up a hill in search, he later wrote, 'of some green thing that might help to allay our burning thirst, and some tree to shelter us from the scorching blaze of the sun'.

He found instead 'a barren plain, extending as far as the eye could reach each way, without a tree, shrub or spear of grass … I had exerted myself to the utmost to get there: the dreary sight was more than I could bear; my spirits fainted within me, and I fell to the earth deprived of every sensation'.

High on a bluff above the Atlantic Ocean, Captain James Riley had found yet more of the vast Sahara Desert. Eleven of his crew—young men from his hometown in Connecticut, men whose lives he had promised to protect—had stayed behind on the beach as he climbed. They had no liquid save their own urine. They had no food except salt pork, which burned their mouths and increased their thirst. When Riley awoke from his swoon, his first reaction was to throw himself into the ocean, to commit suicide. But the thought of his crew—'men who looked up to me as an example of courage and fortitude'—stopped him, as did the image of his wife and children back home. With enormous effort, Riley, a great shambling bear of a man weighing 109 kilograms (240 pounds), turned back to the beach to rejoin his men and give them the news that before them stretched only death and misery. And that they must survive.

A Fair Voyage

Riley's journey—which would resonate in American history—began in the green hills surrounding the Connecticut River, near the village of Middletown. In May of 1815, James Riley was 37 years old and had been a seafaring man for twenty-two of those years, and a captain since the age of twenty. He had a wife, Phoebe, who was pregnant, and four children already, all under eight—but while rich in family he was poor in luck. The War of 1812 between America and Great Britain had stifled opportunities for merchant seamen like himself, and in two previous voyages before that war began his ships had been boarded and seized, either by the French or the British, themselves at war.

Unemployed for three years, he had been forced to sell his house and move into much humbler quarters, but now—with the War of 1812 newly ended by the Treaty of Ghent—

he had a command: the brand-new *Commerce*, a fine merchant vessel 26 metres long and 8 metres wide (28.5 yards long and 9 yards wide), with cargo space large enough to hold 1600 barrels of goods. The *Commerce* had a crew of eleven, almost all of whom were from the same area as Riley. The cousins Horace and Aaron Savage were the sons of the ship's owners; George Williams, chief navigator, was a local man, as were Bill Porter, James Clark and Thomas Burns, the latter a hero of the fight against the British in New York State.

It was a strong ship and a good crew and Riley was looking forward to a change of luck. His plan, as the *Commerce* slipped its moorings and headed down the Connecticut River to the ocean on 3 May, was to head south to New Orleans, there to trade its load of hay and bricks for tobacco and flour, then head across the Atlantic to Gibraltar to sell or trade those commodities.

For once in Riley's life, everything seemed to go as planned. After taking on the trade goods in New Orleans, the *Commerce* fairly sped across the Atlantic on fair breezes, arriving in Gibraltar in six weeks, on 9 August. There Riley sold his cargo and also, at the behest of the US consul, took on a impoverished American sailor named Antonio Michel, shipwrecked and wanting to work his passage home. On 24 August, Riley left Gibraltar for the second-to-last leg of the journey, south along the west coast of Africa to the Cape Verde Islands to fill the hold with salt, a commodity in high demand at home due to shortages caused by the war.

But now Riley's bad luck re-asserted itself.

'A Roaring'

The problem was Cape Bojador (today called Boujdour). Here, as at other points along Africa's northwest coast, the Sahara Desert bleeds sand far out to sea, and mariners for hundreds of years have found themselves in serious trouble as the water turns unexpectedly shallow (see **Send Christians Ashore**, opposite). Riley was aware of the danger. He steered a course that should have taken him through the centre of the Canary Islands group, well away from peril, but the powerful current that sweeps around the Canaries toward Africa pushed the ship far closer to the coast than he realised.

And visibility was bad as well, the weather being so foggy, Riley wrote, 'we could scarcely see the jib-boom'. He could not espy land, knew he should have passed through the Canaries by now—yet 'I had never passed through the Canaries without seeing them even in thick weather or in the night'. In the middle of the night of 28 August, with a stiff wind and a high sea running, his inner alarm bell began to ring uncontrollably and he ordered the helmsman to alter course. Almost as the ship began to go about, Riley heard a roaring noise—which he hoped was the sound of a squall moving in, but which in his heart he knew to be the crash of breaking waves. Foaming white water was instantly under the lee of the ship. Riley immediately ordered a dragging anchor thrown out and the sails reefed to keep the wind from carrying the *Commerce* ashore.

But it was too late—the ship 'struck with such violence as to start every man on deck'. Acting on training and adrenaline, the crew brought on deck as much water and food as possible and Riley collected his navigational books and instruments. The *Commerce* rapidly took on water as the men lowered the ship's boat and, holding a line tied to one of the masts, plunged through the surf towards shore, a dark outline some 250 metres (273½ yards) away. They came crashing and skidding onto the beach and immediately tied the line to a stake pounded into the sand, keeping at least a tenuous link to their ship, already beginning to break up on the rocks.

'Send Christians Ashore'

The people of the western Sahara—like the Pondo people of southeast Africa (see page 234) and the Irish along their stormy west coast (see page 266)—liked nothing so much as a good shipwreck. When another Yankee captain was wrecked along this coast, his captor Ahamed told him that the Arabs 'pray earnestly to the Almighty God to send Christians ashore'.

Ahamed told his new slave that Arabs believed that any type of good that came ashore after a shipwreck (including human goods) belonged to them. If any Christian resisted the local inhabitants in any way, he was slaughtered, and rightly so, the Arabs considered, for Christians were liars and infidels in any event.

Cape Bojador was notorious for its shipwrecks. Fittingly enough, the name comes from the Arab word meaning 'father of danger', for men had been wrecking their ships there since a couple of Genoan sailors first tried out the route in the late thirteenth century. Eventually Portugal's Prince Henry the Navigator sent out vessels which were able to find a route past Cape Bojador, a significant moment in navigation because it was the beginning of finding a route around Africa to the Indies.

But Allah kept smiling on the desert Arabs and the wrecks continued to pile up. Around the turn of the eighteenth century, according to one contemporary tally, around thirty known European ships ran aground at Cape Bojador in a 15-year period. Perhaps five crewmen from these wrecks ever found their way home. Undoubtedly there were other ships that vanished without a trace.

'A Most Hideous and Horrific Shape'

The seamen were painfully aware of the dangers they faced—they had entered, as Riley later wrote, a 'barren thirsty land', where water would be at an absolute premium. They knew that the nomadic inhabitants of this part of Africa were slavers who, it was rumoured, also ate human flesh. Thus, as dawn lit the scene, Riley prayed 'that we should not be discovered by any human beings on this inhospitable shore' while they hurridly repaired the ship's boat and made ready to set sail for the closest European habitation, the British-owned settlement of St Louis, some 500 kilometres (310.5 miles) to the south.

But Riley's prayer was not to be answered. As the men took stock of their provisions and began to repair the longboat (which had cracked in several places on landing), Riley looked up to see a human figure approaching along the beach, stopping to pick up various items from the shipwreck and examine them. When the man was about 100 metres (109 yards) away, Riley 'went towards him with all signs of peace and friendship', but he could see this would be of no use. For this person was terrifying. About 170 centimetres (5.5 feet) tall, he had 'a complexion between that of an American Indian and a negro'. He was an old man, yet was 'fierce and vigorous'. His coarse bushy hair, which resembled a 'pitch mop' (a stiff-bristled mop used to apply tar to ship's planking) stuck straight out for about 20 centimetres (8 inches), his eyes were 'fiery and red', and his teeth so sharp and pointed that Riley imagined they were used 'for the purpose of devouring human flesh'. All in all, this man represented 'the human face and form in its most hideous shape'.

He was soon joined by his wives, each of whose 'two eye-teeth stuck out like hogs' tusks', a rather lovely younger woman of about eighteen, and numerous children, all of them completely naked. They had knives slung on long ropes from their necks, as well as axes, which they immediately used to break into the sea-chests bobbing at the water's edge. The children found a cache of colourful lace veils and silk handkerchiefs which Riley had purchased in Gibraltar; the young nomads began dancing wildly on the beach, twirling the colourful cloths through the stiff breeze, a savage, bizarre yet strangely beautiful scene.

All of this had the air of a waking nightmare for the shattered Riley who, just the day before, had been coasting through the ocean—his natural element—and today found himself on this inhospitable shore. He knew that freedom for his sailors and himself was coming to an end. There were bound to be more of these wild tribesmen—they were probably Berbers—descending on them, and they had nothing with which to defend themselves except a number of marline spikes.

'Allah K. Beer'

That night the Berbers left them alone, but next morning the old man returned with a string of camels and carrying a huge wooden lance with a sharp metal tip. Now much more aggressive, he poked at the sailors with his spear, pointing towards the wreck and back at his camels. He wanted them to unload any goods left on board. Riley, fiercely protective, picked up a spar which he could use to parry the old man's spear, telling the men to launch the leaky longboat.

Then he got in himself and they rowed out to the wreck. Two younger Berbers appeared on the beach, waving scimitars and shouting at the Americans. The men took axes and stove-in the water barrels the crew had salvaged; now they were essentially trapped on the wreck, which was breaking up further with each pounding wave. The situation was obviously hopeless. Riley returned alone to the beach to reason with the Berbers. The old man took him by the hand, staring upwards and repeating what Riley thought was 'Allah K. Beer!' but which was probably 'Allah Akbar!' (God is great).

It became apparent that the old man thought of Riley as a gift from God when the younger men grabbed him and put their blades to his throat. Thinking quickly, Riley shouted to the crew to send a bucket of money along the line to the beach—silver Spanish dollars from Gibraltar. This momentarily satisfied the old man, but then the three Berbers stood up and, prodding at Riley with their knives, began to lead him from the beach. Moments away from enslavement, he had an odd inspiration. With signs he told the old man there was more treasure aboard the ship. When this whetted the Berber's interest, Riley called to the crew to let Antonio Michel—the old sailor who had been brought on board at Gibraltar—come ashore. There was no money left, but Riley later wrote, 'I imagined if I could get Antonio Michel on shore, I should be able to make my escape.'

Although puzzled and frightened, Michel came obediently to the beach. The Berbers searched him, finding no silver, and immediately began beating him with their fists. With his captors so occupied, Riley 'sprang out beneath their weapons', dashed for the water and dived in. The old man himself gave chase, rushing into the surf. Just as he raised his spear to impale the Yankee captain, a wave knocked him over and Riley made good his escape.

Delirious Journey

Back on the *Commerce*, Riley wrote, he watched as a Berber plunged a spear into Michel's chest, killing him—although an account penned by another member of the crew suggests that Michel was in fact taken as a slave, which would be more in keeping with Berber custom. Whatever happened, there can be no escaping the fact that Riley deliberately decided to sacrifice a member of his crew to save himself, and that it had to be Michel, the newcomer and relative stranger. It was a survivor's brutal calculation—the crew of the *Commerce* needed their captain more than they needed Michel—but Riley was to feel intense guilt over the decision, which may well be why he claimed Michel was killed on the beach rather than enslaved. Because soon Riley was to know that slavery was indeed a fate worse than death.

Knowing that the *Commerce* would shortly disintegrate beneath their feet, Riley and the crew, twelve men in all, decided that their best chance—and it was a slim one—was to attempt to make it down the coast in the leaky longboat, hoping for luck to strike in the form of a passing vessel. They spent nine days progressing just 300 kilometres (186½ miles) south. The boat 'racked [leaked] like a basket, letting in water at every seam', Riley wrote. They had to bail constantly. They were horrendously thirsty. Many of them 'by thrusting their heads into the water, endeavoured to ascertain what the pains of death were'—in other words, to get a foretaste of drowning.

By 6 September they had had enough. The only thing any of them could think about was water, and they decided to return to land, to run the risk of enslavement or death, if only they could find a drink. They came ashore at a place with high, overhanging cliffs and staggered along the beach, seeking a spot where they might climb up to see the countryside beyond. Eventually Riley climbed the bluff and found, to his despair, nothing but the Sahara Desert. Even so, he returned to his men to 'exhort and press them to go forward'.

This they did, and as they stumbled along the beach in the cool of the night, one of them cried, 'I think I see a light!' And in fact, some distance ahead, there was a campfire.

In Captivity

They got as close as they could to the fire, holding no illusion that it meant safety but desperate for water, and lay down in the sand to sleep until morning. Riley 'shut [his] eyes and prayed to be permitted to sleep, if only for an hour'. But he could not. Finally, as the sun began to rise, he woke his men and told them the name of the American consul in Tangier, should they ever have the opportunity to contact him and let him know the fate of the *Commerce* and its crew.

Then they went forward together. Topping a sand dune, they saw, about 500 metres (547 yards) away, a caravan—a very large herd of camels with 'a large company of people'. As soon as the Arabs saw them, they dropped what they were doing and ran toward them. One of the men swung a scimitar and shouted as he headed directly at Riley, who immediately bowed deeply, in 'a token of submission'. The Arab began to strip off Riley's clothing—clothes were valuable in the Sahara, since the cloth to make them was at a premium. Two women began to strip George Williams and Horace Savage.

All of a sudden, thirty or forty more men came, 'some running on foot with muskets and naked scimitars in their hands, others riding on swift camels'. A battle began over the future slaves, with scimitars whizzing just above their heads, the Arabs hacking at each other so that blood flew everywhere, although the Americans were not touched. The fighting lasted for almost an hour. The castaways were now divided among the Arabs, who had been camping around a well and were even now filling goatskin bags with water, preparing to depart. Riley begged for something to drink; he was given camel's milk, which caused a violent bout of diarrhoea, further dehydrating him.

By about ten in the morning, one group, having finished watering, headed into the desert, taking six crewmen with them, including George Williams. Riley and the rest, including Richard Delisle, the ship's cook and the only black man in the crew, were immediately put to work by their new masters drawing water for the camels and filling goatskins, which at least allowed them to satisfy their thirst.

'I Cannot Live'

Without a moment to acclimatise Riley found himself forced to drive the camels and try to keep them together. If he faltered for a moment, 'the application of a stick to my sore back' reminded him that he needed to keep going. Sinking to his knees in the sand with every step, he and his fellows staggered along while the Arab women and children, who seemed to move effortlessly across the terrain, laughed at them.

When the caravan reached the top of the dune, Riley was placed upon a camel, clinging to its hump with all his might as the animal lurched along. To understand his torment, it is important to remember that Riley was naked, and that the spine of the camel was, in his nice turn of phrase, 'as sharp as the edge of an oar's blade'. The animal's belly, 'distended with water, made him perfectly smooth, leaving no projection of the hips to keep me from sliding off'. Matters were made worse when the camels were set to a trot, and blood ran down Riley's legs from his miserably chafed thighs, while the heat of the sun raised blisters on his naked body. Eventually he slid down and tried to run alongside the camel, but the sharp stones tore so mercilessly at his bare feet that he was forced to resume his unpleasant ride.

The Arabs did not stop until midnight, at which point the new slaves were given some camel's milk and forced to sleep on the cold, stony ground. And thus, naked, blistered and utterly miserable, they attempted to pass what Riley called 'one of the longest and most dismal nights ever passed by any human beings'.

Slave trading was rife in seventeenth century Africa.

In the morning, after another draught of camel's milk, they were forced onward in the same fashion. At midday they entered a small valley where several rough tents were pitched. These belonged to a group who were friendly with Riley's captors, or so he thought at first, but soon they too were fighting, tugging the slaves this way and that.

That evening a council was held whose purpose, as far as Riley could tell, was to settle ownership of the slaves. Riley and James Clark were sold to a cruel older man who poked Riley's gaping sun-sores and blisters with a stick and forced him to march behind him and his son, carrying a shotgun whose weight was almost too much for his depleted strength. For days they trekked across the desert, or rode on the sharp backs of camels, averaging about 50 kilometres (31 miles) a day. Riley thought he was hallucinating, seeing pools of water where there were none—the famous mirages of the desert. One day he saw a man bobbing along on a camel, his body and head drooping off to the side in a strange fashion as the heatwaves shimmered around him. At first he thought it was another phantom of his imagination, but the man proved to be George Williams, close to death.

His master's wife had smeared him with animal fat, thinking it would help protect him against the sun, but instead he was being roasted alive.

'I cannot live,' he told Riley, and begged him to tell his wife that he loved her.

Then his master took him away—and Riley's master beat him for stopping.

It was around this time, the lowest point of this horrific journey, that Riley had an extraordinary dream. In it he was wandering the desert with his masters, guided by a strange 'all-seeing eye' visible in the sky, and happened upon a young man 'dressed in the English or American style' who beseeched him not to give up, telling him, 'Take courage, my dear friend, God has decreed that you shall again embrace your beloved wife and children.'

Two Traders

After ten days or so of wandering—moving ever northeast, away from the sea—Riley and Clark lay in a tent in a small valley. Clark, it appeared, was dying, 'a perfect wreck of almost naked bones ... breathing like a person in his last agonies'. They were both so dehydrated, Riley said, that if felt as if they 'were the focus of a burning glass'. The Arabs around them were short of water too, but did not suffer as did the Americans, nor did they seem to care that they were dying.

On this day in late September, two strangers rode into camp, one of them a heavyset older man with a grey beard and a turban, the other younger and thinner. Riley's master was away, but the captain was impressed by the respectful way the women treated these men. Riley had come to speak a little Arabic, and thus understood when one of the women whispered to him: 'Sidi Hamet has come from the sultan's dominions. He can buy you.'

Sidi Hamet was the grey-bearded man; the other his younger brother Seid. Riley did not really know who they were, but they did seem more prosperous than the poor Arabs he was with, and they did have water. He approached Sidi Hamet and asked for water, which the man gave him, a generous bowlful. Riley saved half the water and brought it to Clark, who drank it gratefully and said: 'This must be from a better country. If we were there and I could get one good drink of such water, I would die of pleasure.'

Riley sensed in Hamet a kindred soul, and he was right. Hamet had forged caravans across the sands for years, trying to make money to repay a debt to his father-in-law, Sheik Ali, who had taken back his daughter, and Hamet's children, until the money was repaid. Now Hamet and Seid were on their way to the town of Swearah (modern-day Essaouira), in southern Morocco, where they hoped to make enough money trading cloth and other goods to buy back Hamet's family. Riley did not then know this history but, as he later wrote, 'I found [Hamet] to be a very intelligent and feeling man.' They talked together later that day, Riley with his broken Arabic, and Hamet was brought to tears by his story of a wife and children back home. Riley pressed his advantage at this point: he told Hamet he had a rich friend in Swearah who would give Hamet large amounts of silver if he would take Riley, Clark and any other crew members they could find to Morocco. After some consultation with Seid, Hamet agreed to purchase the two men. He managed to locate three more of Riley's compatriots and purchased them as well.

This was a dangerous undertaking, for now Hamet had five American slaves, including Riley, and even though they were in terrible shape—Clark could barely stand and his sun-scalded scalp was literally an open sore—Bedouin raiders would see them as booty to be stolen. It was best not to own too much in the desert.

Of course, Riley knew no one in Swearah. Although Hamet suspected this, he was tempted by the thought of so much silver. But he told Riley that if he were lying he would slit his throat. He made Riley repeat his words aloud, just in case there was any doubt as to what his fate would be if there was no friend to greet him with piles of silver.

Just as they were about to depart, an Arab arrived with Archie Robbins, having heard that Hamet was purchasing slaves at a good price. Riley begged Hamet to buy him, but Hamet refused—his patience was almost at an end, and he warned Riley not to try him anymore. Riley tearfully left his shipmate behind, begging him not to give up hope.

'If I make it,' he told Robbins, 'I will do everything in my power to liberate you.'

Journey

Swearah was several hundred kilometres (miles) distant. On the first leg of the trip, the Americans were so thirsty they were forced to drink camel's urine, which they caught in their hands and gulped down. (Hamet and Seid did the same, telling them it was good for the stomach.) Finally, in the cleft of a cliff near the banks of a dead river, they found water. 'Sherub [Captain] Riley,' Hamet called to him, 'it is sweet.' The men drank their fill, gasping thanks to God. The entire time, Hamet quizzed Riley about his friend in Swearah, asking his name, apparently satisfied when Riley told him it was 'Consul'.

Journeying northwest now, they entered a more populous region where they needed to be on the lookout for brigands and thieves. Riley and the others were surprised when Hamet and Seid themselves committed a brazen act of thievery, rummaging through the packs on the back of a camel whose owner slept soundly nearby. What they did not understand was that thievery was a part of desert life—if you discovered goods unaccompanied by their owner, you could help yourself.

As they moved further north they began to come upon bushes and small trees, a sign, Riley thought, that 'the land was becoming more fertile and productive as we advanced on our journey and that we must shortly escape from this horrible desert'. Despite this hopeful sign, the men were growing weaker and weaker; one of the sailors, whom Riley carefully does not name, began to 'rave' at him, blaming him for their predicament. While Riley did all he could to keep the men together, he began to fear they would not make it to Swearah alive. Fortunately, in mid-October, they came upon Bedouin goatherders who were willing—with a little encouragement from Seid, who brandished his musket— to trade four goats for a lame camel.

Around the same time, off to their left they saw what they thought was a dark, smooth plain, but which on closer examination turned out to be the ocean— 'a particularly gratifying sight' for these sailors, even though it was far away and could do them little good.

The Sahara Desert

As monstrous as the men who enslaved Riley was the Sahara Desert itself, a place so fantastic that it did not seem to Riley even to be a part of the known world. Riley and his men spent weeks wandering through one of earth's most inhospitable environs—not the rolling sand dunes of popular imagination (only 25 per cent of the Sahara's is sand) but a sere and barren land of rocky and wind-blown plains. The temperature during the day could be as high as 49°C (120°F), but could drop to as low as 10°C (50°F) at night. Prolonged exposure to the sun was enough to cause blindness, in the days before sunglasses, while dust and sand storms could choke men and animals to death.

The world's largest hot desert, the Sahara is home to animals such as the desert monitor lizard, poisonous sand vipers and the extremely rare Saharan cheetah. The desert receives less than 80 millimetres (3 inches) yearly rain. It's no wonder that the men who traversed it in earlier times were as savage as the landscape, for without modern methods of communication and transport, every single instinct was focused on survival.

A ship foundering off the cost of North Africa.

Mr Willshire

Over the next month, the nearer they got to salvation the more the men wasted away. Riley, who had begun his ordeal weighing 109 kilograms (240 pounds), now weighed just under 45 kilograms (100 pounds). He was certain some of the others would not last out another week. But, staggering on, they passed through a mountain range and found green valleys on the other side. Hamet told them they were approaching Swearah. This would be Riley's most dangerous moment—for Sheik Ali, Hamet's difficult father-in-law, had joined the group and was causing problems, either demanding a share of the ransom money, or claiming that the slaves belonged to him. Hamet and Seid and others who now joined the expanding party had constantly to cajole the Sheik, assuring him he would get his share.

The poor captives, suffering from dysentery, haemorrhoids and lice, often broke down sobbing, according to Riley for no other reason than to bemoan their fate. On the outskirts of Swearah, Hamet handed Riley pen and paper and demanded that he write to his friend 'Consul'. With the quick thinking that characterised all his actions during this horrific experience, Riley addressed his note 'To the French, English, Spanish or American consuls or any Christian merchant in Mogadore or Swerah [sic].' Carefully not saying he was American—then, as now, animosity could attach to his nationality—he began: 'The brig *Commerce* from Gibraltar for America was wrecked on Cape Bajador on the 28th of August last; myself and four of my crew are here, nearly naked in barbarian slavery.'

He went on to beg the reader to ransom them for the sum of $200 for himself and two of the men, plus $160 for the other two, who were in the worst shape. He handed the note to Sidi Hamet and a companion and watched them set off along the dusty road to Swearah. After eight agonising days of waiting, Hamet's companion returned with a stranger, a man Riley described as a Moor. The Moor called out: 'How de-do, Captain!' in a most friendly manner, and handed Riley a note. Riley was shaking so hard—'my emotions were so afflicted', he wrote—that he had to hand the paper to Horace Savage to read. It began:

> *MY DEAR AND AFFLICTED SIR:*
> *I have this moment received your note from Sidi Hamet, the contents of which, I hope, you will be perfectly assured have called forth my most sincere pity for your sufferings and those of your companions in captivity.*

The note was from William Willshire, English consul in Swearah, and it was everything Riley could have hoped for. Willshire had bargained down Hamet's demands (not wanting to set a bad precedent in hostage-ransoming, a fairly common occurrence), and Hamet had accepted his offer. Now all Riley and his companions had to do was journey to Swearah, where Willshire would put them up at his own residence while he awaited reimbursement from the American consul in Tangiers.

'Tears of joy trickled down our haggard cheeks,' Riley wrote, as they realised that they were free to go. This happiness lasted only a few moments, however, for Sheik Ali was enraged that his son-in-law had been willing to take less, saying he was 'a fool and a madman'. Only after another week of bargaining would Sheik Ali let the Americans go, and they entered Swearah riding donkeys. Turning a corner they saw, as Riley writes, 'our deliverer', William Willshire. At that moment his dream of the young man 'dressed in American and English clothing' came back to him, for Willshire was the image of the figure in his dream. All of them, including Willshire, knelt on the hard-packed dirt in prayer, and then the consul took them into his home.

The once brawny Riley weighed 41 kilograms (90 pounds). As for his friends? 'The weight of my companions was less than I dare to mention, for I apprehend it would not be believed that the bodies of men retaining the vital spark, should not weigh forty pounds.'

Abraham Lincoln and the *Narrative*

Few memoirs by castaways—a genre that abounded in the seventeenth and eighteenth centuries—have been as influential as James Riley's chronicle of his experiences, entitled *Sufferings in Africa: An Authentic Narrative of the Loss of the American Brig Commerce*. The book, published in 1817, became an enormous bestseller, with new editions coming out in 1818, 1820, 1828, 1850 and 1859.

Abraham Lincoln, the 16th President of the United States, was in office during the American Civil War, which lasted from 1861 to 1865. Lincoln issued the Emancipation Proclamation abolishing slavery in 1863.

Gordon H. Evans, editor of a 1965 edition of the *Narrative*, points out that the book was popular because it presented a world alien to the everyday reader, a place few in the nineteenth century even knew existed. Riley had also had a good editor, Anthony Bleecker of New York, who forced him to tell the story in powerful, unadorned prose. Riley's description of the Arabs fighting over him with flashing scimitars, for example, is a masterpiece of verbal economy: 'They cut at each other over my head and on every side of me with the bright weapons, which fairly whizzed through the air within an inch of my body.'

But the main reason for the grip the *Narrative* took on nineteenth century America was its horrific descriptions of slavery. It helped form abolitionist thinking in men like Henry David Thoreau and was widely read in schools. Abraham Lincoln listed Riley's book, along with Aesop's *Fables*, *The Pilgrim's Progress* and Parson Weem's *Life of Washington*, as the most influential books of his childhood. In fact, there are historians who believe that Lincoln, America's Great Emancipator, formed his views against slavery in large part because of the *Narrative*.

Deliverance

In the end Captain James Riley had fulfilled his obligation to protect his crew, living mainly by his wits, for his body was a mere skeleton. When he finally looked into a mirror at Willshire's house, he became delirious, for he did not recognise the ghost staring back at him. After recovering for some weeks, the other four men took passage home, but Riley stayed in Swearah with Willshire, attempting to find Robbins and the others still lost in slavery in the desert. Two were in fact ransomed—Robbins and William Porter—but the others, including Antonio Michel, were lost forever in the sands of the Sahara.

When James Riley finally arrived home in 1816 and embraced his wife and family, he was a changed man. His experiences as a slave had made him a fervent Abolitionist. After his 1817 memoirs became extraordinarily popular (see **Abraham Lincoln and the *Narrative***, opposite), he lobbied Washington politicians on behalf of the movement to free slaves.

Riley took a job as a government surveyor in Ohio, where he founded a town called Willshire after the English consul, with whom he kept up a passionate correspondence. But the hardships of the frontier did not agree with him—like other survivors from the *Commerce*, he suffered from arthritis and depression—and finally went back to sea. In 1840, on a voyage from New York to the Caribbean, he died on board ship. The journal of his experiences lived on, reaching almost a million American readers in numerous editions, and playing an important part in swaying the minds of millions that slavery—be it in the wild Sahara or on the tamest American plantation—had no place in the world.

Part Four

NORTHERN DARKNESS

'With only a dead man as a companion,
surrounded by a sea of ice.'

Charles Francis Hall

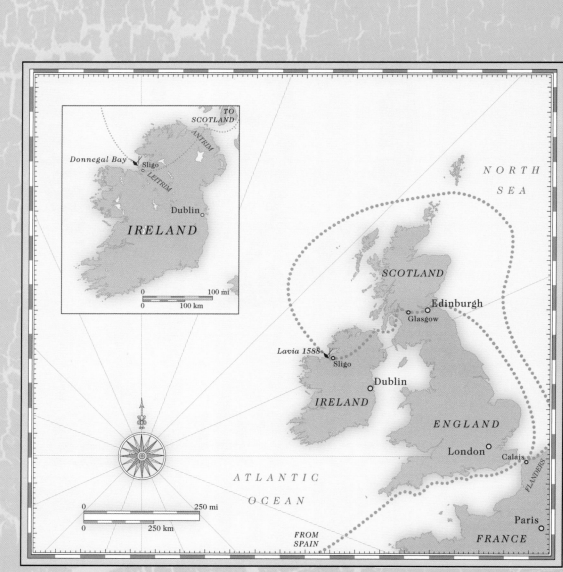

TO
SCOTLAND

ANTRIM

Donnegal Bay — Sligo
LEITRIM

Dublin

IRELAND

0   100 mi
0   100 km

NORTH
SEA

SCOTLAND

Edinburgh
Glasgow

Lavia 1588 — Sligo

Dublin

IRELAND

ENGLAND

London   Calais
FLANDERS

ATLANTIC

OCEAN

Paris

FRANCE

0   250 mi
0   250 km

FROM
SPAIN

Francisco de Cuellár, 1588–1589
Armada Castaway in Ireland

A cat has nine lives—we all know that—but what about a man? How many times can he escape the hangman's noose, the sword, the bullet, the exquisite agonies of starvation, exposure and drowning? Let's ask Francisco de Cuellár, Spanish Armada captain, who was sentenced to be hung by his own people, then wrecked on a hostile shore and cast away amid 'savages'—in other words, the Irish—but who rose from among the pale and bloodied bodies of 800 of his fellows to make a perilous trek through enemy territory, be shipwrecked again on the very edge of salvation—and survived to tell the tale in a famous letter to a friend which began, with masterful understatement: 'I believe that you will be astonished at seeing this letter on account of the slight certainty that could have existed as to my being alive.'

What he experienced during his months among those 'savages' leaves no doubt that Francisco de Cuellár would be the envy of any cat alive.

La Grande y Felicíma Armada

It was supposed to be the armada to end all armadas, the fleet that would destroy the Protestant Queen Elizabeth once and for all, an invasion force to strike London and put a Spanish pretender on the English throne. It was *La Grande y Felicíma Armada*—the great and most fortunate fleet. It contained 125 ships—thirty of them the huge many-gunned fighting galleons whose rudders alone were 9 metres (10 yards) high—which carried 23,000 infantry, artillery siege equipment, six months' worth of supplies, and vast quantities of ammunition. Admiral Medina Sidonia's orders were to head up the English Channel to Flanders, where he was to rendezvous with the Duke of Parma, leader of the Spanish forces fighting the Dutch rebels. Parma was waiting with another 25,000 men, whom the Armada would escort across the Channel to Kent, where the invasion would begin. The Spanish even brought along priests to convert the English.

Things didn't turn out quite the way they were planned. In a running battle in the Channel during July and August of 1588, a smaller English fleet led by Sir Francis Drake defeated the Spanish by dint of superior tactics and better luck. After the final English victory at the Battle of Gravelines, off Flanders, on 8 August, Medina Sidonia's hopes were dashed and he ordered the Armada's retreat to Spain. Unable to return south because of contrary winds and the presence of the English fleet in the Channel, the Spanish ran north through the North Sea, through the Shetlands, and then west into the Atlantic. But, battered by two unusually severe Atlantic storms, thirty ships—galleons, troop transports and supply vessels—were wrecked on the rocky western shores of Ireland. Aboard one of these ships, the *Lavia*, the vice-flagship of its squadron, was Captain Francisco de Cuellár.

'I Was Not in Fault'

We know very little about de Cuellár's life before this—we catch up to him in the middle of his movie, so to speak, but what an action scene! De Cuellár was a staff officer who had shipped out aboard the Castilian ship *San Pedro* and was then appointed captain of the vessel. But the ship broke strict formation as the Armada was retreating through the North Sea, and for this de Cuellár was sentenced to death, a sentence which outraged him, since 'I had served the King as a good soldier and loyal subject on all occasions'. In the letter he told his friend that the *San Pedro*, having been badly beaten up in the Battle of Gravelines, had reduced sail to allow repairs and thus had fallen behind.

For this breach of discipline, de Cuellár was to be hanged. He was transferred to the *Lavia* for execution of this sentence, where his life was saved by the Judge Advocate of the fleet, Marin de Aranda, who believed firmly that de Cuellár was innocent of any crime and refused to carry out the sentence. 'God was pleased to deliver me because I was not in fault,' de Cuellár writes.

Soon, however, God was to deliver him to a very different kind of fate. No sooner had de Cuellár breathed a sigh of relief than a storm forced the *Lavia* and two sister ships into Donegal Bay, on the west coast of Ireland, off Country Sligo. There they found some respite, but on 21 September gale-force winds rose again and drove all three vessels hard upon the sandy beaches of a 3 kilometre (2 mile) stretch of wilderness known as Streedagh Strand. The ships broke up rapidly under the pounding of the giant waves and the Spanish, the seams of their pants sewn with gold doubloons, leaped into the sea. Those who did not drown made it ashore to be met by wild Irish peasants carrying clubs and axes, and English soldiers well-armed with guns and swords and long ropes with which to hang the minions of King Philip of Spain.

The Savages

This scene was repeated up and down the west coast of Ireland, where there are twenty-three certified Armada wreck sites. Perhaps here a word is due about the chaotic scene these wretched Spanish soldiers and sailors found themselves in. In 1588, as happened so often in Ireland's history, the English had garrisoned the country and were attempting

Queen Elizabeth I (1533–1603)—The Armada Portrait.

to violently put down rebellions. One would think that normally these people would have welcomed any enemy of Queen Elizabeth gleefully and with open arms. And, in fact, a great many did. But other factors were at work here, chief among them poverty and opportunism: the Irish were poor, the Spanish castaways richly provisioned with clothing and gold—and so many of the Irish set upon the poor men crawling onto the beaches, robbing and killing.

Thus a scene of carnage greeted Francisco de Cuellár when he washed ashore on a giant hatch cover. As he wrote later:

> *The beach was full of enemies who went about jumping and dancing with delight at our misfortunes, and when any one of our people set foot on shore, two hundred savages and other enemies fell upon him and stripped him of what he had on until he was left in his naked skin …*

In an 1897 Irish edition of Francisco de Cuellár's letter to his friend, the editors explained helpfully in their introduction that 'de Cuellár's use of the term "savage" to describe the Irish should not necessarily be regarded as pejorative'.

More than 24 vessels were wrecked on the north and western coasts of Ireland. Of the fleet's initial complement of 130 vessels, about 50 failed to make it back to Spain.

Oh, but it should. As he crawled slowly across the beach, heading for the shelter of the sandhills, Francisco de Cuellár heard the screams of his countrymen being robbed and murdered by laughing clansmen, and expected to be clubbed down himself at any moment. Calling the Irish 'savages' was intended in every sense to be pejorative.

'The Crows and Wolves Devoured'

By some miracle, de Cuellár escaped detection and made it to the sandhills. 'Presently,' as he wrote, 'a gentleman came up to me, a very nice young fellow, quite naked, and he was so dazed that he could not speak, not even to tell me who he was.' De Cuellár and his mute companion lay there together; it was by this time about nine o'clock at night. After a time, two Irishmen approached, one with a gun, the other with 'a large iron axe'. Instead of murdering the two Spaniards, however, they took pity on them and covered them with large bunches of rushes and long grass.

Exhausted, de Cuellár fell asleep and was awakened at about one o'clock in the morning 'by a great noise of men on horseback'—two hundred riders, carrying torches, intent on further plunder. De Cuellár turned to speak to his quiet companion, only to discover that the man had died. De Cuellár mourned this man and all his compatriots who had been murdered on the shore, 'six hundred other dead bodies which the sea cast up, and the crows and wolves devoured'.

At daybreak, de Cuellár began to walk through the dunes. His hope was to find a monastery that might hide him, for at least the monks and he were of the same faith. At last he spied a small abbey, but to his unutterable horror he found the interior destroyed, its statues burned. Twelve Spaniards hung from the iron window gratings as a ghoulish warning. The monks appeared to have fled into the forests—it was apparent that roving English patrols had found them harbouring castaways, and so destroyed the church and executed the sailors.

De Cuellár 'sallied forth speedily' from this grotesque scene and found himself on a road going through a great forest. He had gone only a short distance when he met a woman 'of more than eighty years of age, a rough savage, who was carrying off five or six cows to hide them in the woods'.

She said to him: 'Thou Spain?'

To which he replied affirmatively, at which point she began to wail, saying that the English were beheading numerous of his companions even as they spoke.

Although his legs were painful from being struck by a piece of wood when he abandoned ship, de Cuellár decided it might be worth heading back to the beach—

perhaps he would find food and water washed ashore. Along the way he met two other Spaniards, both naked—de Cuellár was fortunate to still have his linen trousers and jacket. Nearing the beach, they came upon a trail of Spanish bodies, all run through by swords or clubbed. De Cuellár thought there might be four hundred corpses. He recognised a great captain, 'poor Don Diego Enriquez', and insisted on stopping to bury him in a shallow hole they managed to scrabble in the ground.

As the castaways searched the beach, four Irishmen turned up and tore the clothes off de Cuellár's back, then for some reason reconsidered, gave him his clothes back, and directed the Spaniards to their village. But de Cuellár soon became separated from his companions and found himself alone in a great forest.

The Savage Damsel

De Cuellár had only moved a short distance through these dark woods when 'an old savage of more than seventy years old' jumped out from behind a rock, followed by two men, one English, one French. There was also in this company (de Cuellár did not fail to notice) 'a girl of the age of twenty years old, most beautiful in the extreme'. They were on their way to take booty from the beach, but found de Cuellár a convenient target.

'Yield, Spanish poltroon,' yelled the Englishman, stabbing at de Cuellár with a knife. De Cuellár did his best to ward off the knife with a stick, but eventually received a deep slash on the back of one leg. The Englishman was going in for the kill when the ageing Irishman told him to desist, and they contented themselves with removing his clothes, which contained in a secret compartment 45 gold crown pieces. These they took. The beautiful girl made the men give de Cuellár back his clothing, although she kept some saints' relics he wore around his neck in a locket.

'These the savage damsel took,' de Cuellár writes with great sarcasm, 'saying to me that she was a Christian, which she was in like manner as Mahomet.'

Bleeding from his wound, de Cuellár staggered off through the forest, soon to be overtaken by a boy whom, it turned out, the Frenchman had sent. The boy brought him a poultice of herbs to put on his wound, and a little milk, butter and oat bread, and did de Cuellár a great service by telling him to avoid the village directly ahead, where Spaniards were being slaughtered. He should instead travel straight to the mountains, which appeared to be about 25 kilometres (15.5 miles) distant, where 'there were good lands belonging to an important savage, whose name was Senor de Ruerque [Sir Brian O'Rourke] who was very friendly to the King of Spain. With this news I took courage; and with my stick in hand, I began to walk as best I could, making for the direction of the mountains'.

'Save Yourself, Spain!'

So far de Cuellár's journey makes the wanderings of Berthold Brecht's Mother Courage during the Thirty Years' War seem like a vacation jaunt; but there was more to come. That evening he came upon a few huts in the forest where some very poor Irish people lived. One was a young man who spoke Latin (it is possible he was a priest; Irish clergy often donned secular dress so the British would not persecute them) and thus he and de Cuellár were able to converse. He sheltered the castaway in his hut, fed him and dressed his wounds; in the evening his father and brother arrived 'loaded with plunder' from the shipwrecks, but treated de Cuellár kindly and in the morning allowed him the use of a horse and a small boy to guide him as he traversed a particularly bad patch of road.

Only a short way into their journey, de Cuellár and the boy heard a great noise in front of them, and the boy yelled, 'Save yourself, Spain!' De Cuellár asked what the matter was, and the boy explained frantically, 'Many Sassana [English] horsemen are coming this way, and they will make little bits of thee if thou dost not hide thyself: come this way quickly.' They hid among rocks as the horsemen thundered by, apparently on their way to plunder the wrecks. God had delivered de Cuellár again. Or so he thought—until forty savages came behind the horsemen on foot and spotted him. They wanted to kill him, but the boy said he was a slave belonging to his master, so they contented themselves with beating de Cuellár brutally and stealing his clothes.

The boy was reduced to tears, but there was nothing he could do for de Cuellár, who wrapped some matted reeds around his waist as a kind of skirt and pressed on. Even after this, his faith in God remained undiminished—for as he walked through the foothills of the mountains he simply prayed that 'His Divine Majesty [would] fulfil His will on me'.

That evening he arrived at a lonely lake, around which there were thirty or so apparently deserted cottages. Walking through this eerie, ghostly village, he was startled by what he thought were spirits or devils—three emaciated, naked figures coming toward him in the twilight. Only after hearing them speak, beseeching God to protect them, did he realise they too were Spanish castaways. When de Cuellár identified himself, he found they were crewmen from the *San Pedro*, who had assumed him long dead. 'They came up to me and nearly killed me with embraces,' de Cuellár wrote. Happy to be with his men, the captain told them about O'Rourke and the next day they set off together to find his village, which was in modern County Leitrim, in north-central Ireland.

O'Rourke

Sir Brian O'Rourke's family had been the primary chieftains of Leitrim for centuries (the O'Rourke heraldic lion is still on the county's official shield) and Sir Brian was one of the chief rebels fighting English rule at the time. When de Cuellár reached the village he found some twenty other Spaniards being given safe harbour there. They were begging at O'Rourke's manor for food when they heard a report that a Spanish ship had come to pick up captives—in reality, merely another damaged vessel from the Armada limping along the coast—and by the time de Cuellár and eight other injured men got to the beach, she had picked up those who waiting and departed. (This turned out to be another bit of good fortune for de Cuellár, as the ship was wrecked further south.)

Returning from this failed getaway, de Cuellár and the others met a priest, again in secular garb, who spoke Latin and told them they would be safe at the castle of a great chief named MacClancy. The Spaniards stayed there for two months, each 'acting as a real savage like themselves', and de Cuellár was able to observe Irish customs. The men went on almost nightly raids, stealing the belongings of those with better fortune; the English, with whom the Irish were at 'perpetual war', would then rob the robbers. De Cuellár's portrait of this sojourn (see **Everyone Does as He Pleases**, opposite) is both frightening and amusing, for at times his observations make him sound like a rather pompous social anthropologist. Realising that these superstitious people assumed all Spaniards could foretell the future, he became a great success at palm-reading. Even MacClancy's wife (who was 'very beautiful in the extreme') took a shine to him and sat with him daily.

One day in December 1588, MacClancy, 'dishevelled hair down to his eyes', came to de Cuellár to tell him that word had reached him of a force of 1700 Englishmen sent to attack the land of any Irishman reputed to be sheltering Armada survivors. MacClancy had decided his best course was to flee with his people and their belongings into the mountains; the eight Spaniards could come with them or do as they wished. With his military eye, however, de Cuellár realised that the castle was nearly impregnable, being surrounded by marshes which meant that the English would be unable to bring up their heavy siege guns. So he told MacClancy that they elected to stay, and would defend the castle if he would provide them with food and arms.

A few weeks later the English forces showed up and demanded de Cuellár's surrender. When he refused, they hung two Spanish captives in full view of the castle, but still de Cuellár declined. The frustrated English commander made numerous threats and then switched to cajolery, saying the Spanish would be given free passage home if they surrendered. To this de Cuellár replied mockingly that he couldn't hear the man.

'Everyone Does as He Pleases'

Francisco de Cuellár's observations of how the Irish of Chieftain MacClancy lived are astute, humorous, and even empathetic:

'They live in huts made of straw. The men are all large bodied, and of handsome features and limbs; and as active as the roe-deer. They do not eat oftener than once a day, and this is at night; and that which they usually eat is butter with oaten bread. They drink sour milk, for they have no other drink; they don't drink water, although it is the best in the world. On feast days they eat some flesh half-cooked, without bread or salt, as that is their custom. They clothe themselves, according to their habit, with tight trousers and short loose coats of very coarse goat's hair. They cover themselves with blankets, and wear their hair down to their eyes. They are great walkers, and inured to toil. They carry on perpetual war with the English, who here keep garrison for the Queen, from whom they defend themselves, and do not let them enter their territory …

The chief inclination of these people is to be robbers, and to plunder each other; so that no day passes without a call to arms among them. For the people in one village becoming aware that in another there are cattle, or other effects, they immediately come armed in the night, and 'go Santiago' [attack] and kill one another, and the English from the garrisons, getting to know who had taken, and robbed, most cattle, then come down upon them, and carry away the plunder …

They sleep upon the ground, on rushes, newly cut and full of water and ice. The most of the women are very beautiful, but badly dressed. They do not wear more than a chemise, and a blanket, with which they cover themselves, and a linen cloth, much doubled, over the head, and tied in front. They are great workers and housekeepers, after their fashion. These people call themselves Christians. Mass is said among them, and regulated according to the orders of the Church of Rome. The great majority of their churches, monasteries, and hermitages, have been demolished by the hands of the English, who are in garrison, and of those natives who have joined them, and are as bad as they. In short, in this kingdom there is neither justice nor right, and everyone does as he pleases.'

When a snowstorm hit, the English retreated but promised to return. When MacClancy came back, he was quite pleased and promised always to be de Cuellár's friend—he even wanted to give him his sister in marriage. But when de Cuellár told him all he wanted was safe passage to the northern coast, the chieftain replied that such a trip was too perilous, and insisted on keeping him there—'as a friend', but mainly to act as a bodyguard. But, as de Cuellár writes wryly, 'So much friendship did not appear good to me', and he and four other Spaniards struck out for the north early one morning in January 1599.

'I Could Not Restrain Tears'

De Cuellár's last trek across Ireland was the most arduous. He had heard that there was an escape route for Spanish castaways to Scotland being run by an 85-year-old Irish chief named Sorley Boy Macdonnell, who had kinsmen in Scotland and no love for the English. De Cuellár's injuries had not healed well, and his legs were in such poor shape that he was forced to crawl much of the way 'through mountains and desolate places' and lost contact with his fellows. Some local women took pity on him and nursed him in a hut for a month until he recovered, but as he journeyed on he had to duck constantly into the woods to avoid English patrols. When he finally found Macdonnell, he discovered that the man had made peace with the English and promised 'not to keep any Spaniard in his territory'.

Resting in a hut and pondering his next move, he was appalled to see two English soldiers burst in, ready to take him prisoner. Thinking quickly, de Cuellár told them his legs were so sore he couldn't walk. Luckily they believed him, told him to stay there and began flirting with some young women outside. Hoping they were sufficiently distracted, he burst out the door 'in great haste', racing through brambles and trees until he lost sight of Macdonnell's castle. Enraged, the soldiers searched the village, but to no avail—a boy herding cows had pointed de Cuellár to the home of a bishop, some 15 kilometres (9 miles) away, who was reputed to be helping Spanish castaways.

De Cuellár arrived at the house in what is now county Antrim, ready to be disappointed again, but found that the bishop—Redmond O'Gallagher—was already harbouring twelve of his countrymen and waiting for a boat to take them to Scotland. O'Gallagher, de Cuellár writes, 'was a very good Christian, and went about in the garb of a savage for concealment, and I assure you I could not restrain tears when I approached him to kiss his ring'. Six days later, a small ship arrived, and de Cuellár and the others boarded it.

Three days after that, they were in Scotland where, to de Cuellár's scornful disappointment, the King of Scotland was unwilling to help them because he was afraid of

Queen Elizabeth I: 'The King of Scotland is a nobody: nor does he possess the authority or position of a king; and he does not move a step, nor eat a mouthful, that is not by order of the Queen.' But then, as if by magic, Queen Elizabeth granted safe conduct home for the roughly six hundred Spaniards in Scotland. They were put on four different ships and allowed to set sail for Spanish-held Netherlands, being given safe passage through English ports on the way. But it was a trap. Queen Elizabeth had promised safe passage in English waters, but not in Dutch waters. As the four ships approached the Dutch coast, the Sea Beggars—Dutch rebels—attacked. It was obvious that they had been tipped off.

Following a pitched battle, two of the ships sank off Dunkirk, drowning hundreds. The vessel de Cuellár was on managed to ground itself near shore, at which point he hung onto a piece of wood and floated ashore, wearing only his shirt. There he met some Spanish soldiers who helped him to Spanish-held Dunkirk where he collapsed. Twelve days later, having moved on to Antwerp, he picked up his pen and wrote an account of his adventure. It was 4 October 1589, and he had been among the savages for a very long time.

Armada Treasure on the Irish Coast

The Spanish Armada deposited far more than castaways on Ireland's shores—it deposited great amounts of gold and silver in the offshore shallows. The very first salvage attempts were made only a few months after the ships had careened into the western coast, with divers fortified by whiskey bringing up valuable iron cannon and a few chests of treasure.

One of the greatest hauls was raised from the great galleon *Girona*, which crashed into a reef off the shore of County Antrim on the dark night of 26 October 1588. The *Girona* was carrying survivors from five other ships which had gone down; their combined crews, a total of 1300 men, died as she sank. Nine survivors were rescued by Sorley Boy Macdonnell. Various attempts were made to salvage booty from the wreck, with little luck, until 1968, when the Belgian marine archaeologist Robert Stenuit, with a crew of experienced divers, raised 1500 gold and silver coins, precious rings and gold chains, knight's crosses, even crystal perfume vials used by Spanish officers to ward off the stench of galley slaves.

There may be numerous other treasures in the many other Spanish wreck sites along the Irish coast, but shifting sand and tides have kept them buried.

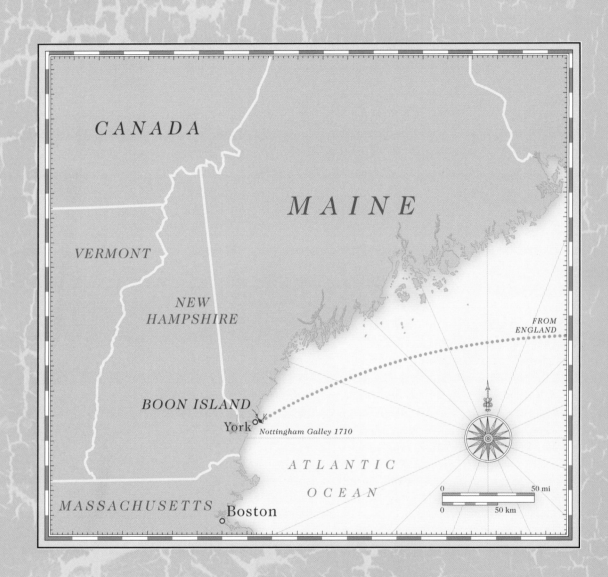

CANADA

MAINE

VERMONT

NEW
HAMPSHIRE

BOON ISLAND
York ⚓

Nottingham Galley 1710

FROM
ENGLAND

ATLANTIC

OCEAN

MASSACHUSETTS
Boston ○

0   50 mi
0   50 km

The Wreck of the Nottingham Galley, 1710–1711
Cannibalism on Boon Island

The low spit of tumbled boulders, 100 metres long and 50 wide (109 yards long and 57 wide), lies 10 kilometres (6 miles) off the rocky coast of Maine. On clear days one can see the long uneven line of the forested mainland and the low hump of Mount Agamenticus rising in the distance. The island was not discovered by Europeans until 1682 when the coastal trader *Increase* literally ran into it in a fog. Fortunately this happened in summer, but even so, it took the crew a month to attract the attention of anyone on the mainland, which they finally managed by lighting a huge fire.

When Indians came in canoes to rescue them, the grateful white men dubbed this desolate spot Boon Island, which is ironic, considering what would happen there thirty years later. A much better description is that bestowed by the nineteenth century Maine poet Celia Thaxter, who called it 'the forlornest place that can be imagined'. Boon Island is at its highest just over 4 metres (4.5 yards) above sea level, and made entirely out of geological rubble, rocks and stones of all shapes and sizes—no earth, no trees, no bushes. During the frequent storms which plague this part of New England, boulders are often picked up by the wind and hurled across the island. Waves of gargantuan size are known to wash across the entire expanse.

It's no place, in other words, to be cast away, especially in mid-winter, with no food around but your fellow human beings. But this is precisely what happened to the ocean trader *Nottingham Galley* in December 1710, in what was to become one of the most famous—and horrific—shipwreck incidents in American history.

'Impending Danger'

On 25 September 1710, the *Nottingham Galley* left London bound for Boston with a cargo of butter and cheese. The ship was a fairly typical merchantman of the day, displacing 120 tons, with a crew of fourteen and armed with ten cannon to ward off the attacks of privateers. After making port in Ireland, the vessel, piloted by Captain John Dean, headed across the Atlantic. Dean is a fascinating character. He was born in Nottingham in 1769 to a fairly well-to-do family, got in trouble as a boy for poaching deer from nearby royal estates, and escaped into the Royal Navy, where he served with distinction in the successful siege of the Spanish port of Gibraltar in 1704.

Boon Island was completely desolate—no vegetation whatsoever, just rubble, rocks and sand.

On leaving the navy, he decided to make his fortune as a merchant. He and his brother Jasper (who would go along on the fateful trip) bought a ship and named her after their home town. This trading venture to Boston was the *Nottingham Galley*'s maiden voyage. Although Dean, at 41 years of age, was an experienced skipper, he had yet to run into the kind of weather he saw on this North Atlantic crossing. Because of 'contrary Winds and bad Weather', the *Nottingham Galley* did not raise the North American coast until December, when a curtain of fog and snow opened up 'for a Quarter of an Hour' to reveal a hazy shoreline. Travelling carefully in the rough coastal waters, Dean ordered the ship to sail southwest, parallel to land, apparently thinking he had more manoeuvring room than he did.

But this was not the case. Late on the night of 11 December, Dean himself was on watch and saw white breakers ahead. He immediately ordered the ship brought hard to starboard, but claimed that his order 'was so ill-obeyed in the sudden Astonishment as to have the very reverse performed'. However, he admits a sentence or two later in the account written for him afterward that even had the order been correctly carried out, 'they were too near to avoid impending Danger [and] the ship struck with great Violence'.

'A Rock Called Boone Island'

As Dean was to relate later, with a better knowledge of the geography he had stumbled into, the *Nottingham Galley* had struck 'a Rock called Boone Island, about seven leagues eastward from the Mouth of the Piscataqua River', near the little town of York. At the time all he and the panicked crew knew was that they were hard aground, a fierce gale was blowing, and the ship was breaking up beneath them. The night was so black that Dean had no idea whether the ship had hit a lonely reef or an island which could accept the men safely. He sent two men diving overboard with ropes to try to find land and himself made belowdecks to salvage what he could in the way of firearms, brandy, ship's papers and food. But he was driven back by the chaos in the bowels of the ship—the *Nottingham Galley* was sinking fast.

The other crewmen hurriedly leaped overboard into the cold, dark waters, and so, too, did John Dean. 'He threw off his Cloaths to his Waistcoat ... and, without either Wig or Cap, cast himself with all his might from the Wreck.' Fortune favoured him in that he was able to slide along one of the masts which had fallen into the water until he came to a large rock, which he desperately attempted to climb. Wave after wave sucked him back until, bruised and bleeding, the flesh torn from his fingertips, he was eventually swept ashore.

Once he had recovered himself sufficiently, he was astonished to find that the entire crew had made it to shore and were safe. They huddled together for warmth, 'spending a Miserable night' exposed to the elements. At the grey dawn broke, Dean gathered his men and they walked around the island, discovering how extraordinarily tiny and desolate it was. To make matters even worse, the *Nottingham Galley* had utterly disappeared, broken up by the storm—almost three centuries later, nine of her cannon were found in 8 metres (9 yards) of water just offshore. Except for 'a few Fragments of Cheese beaten into uncouth Forms by the Dashing of the Sea against the Rock', there was absolutely nothing to eat.

Planks and spars, rigging and sails had washed ashore but, because everything was so wet, and they had no flint to strike a spark, the castaways were unsuccessful in starting a fire. This was especially problematic because there was frost on the ground and they began very shortly to suffer from exposure. There was only one ray of hope: the next morning the weather cleared somewhat and Dean was able to see the mainland. He realised where they were and began to encourage his men, telling them that very soon they would be discovered by a fishing sloop.

Yet the sight of the mainland would prove to be a chimera, taunting the castaways with the hope of rescue while providing no succour at all.

The Boon Island Light

After any number of wrecks on Boon Island, it was decided in 1799 to build a lighthouse to warn seamen of its dangers. This was no easy undertaking. The first Boon Island light, a wooden structure, lasted only five years before being literally knocked down by the storms that sweep the islet. A stone day-beacon, meant only to warn sailors during daylight hours, was built in 1805, but even this was marked by tragedy—three of the workers drowned when their boat capsized leaving the island.

In 1811 a proper lighthouse was built, reaching 9 metres (10 yards) above sea level. Even so, storm surges would sometimes sweep almost to the top of the light, which rocked in heavy winds. The first keeper left after two weeks, as did the second. Finally, a former mariner named Eliphalet Grover served for an astonishing twenty-two years, although storms caused such great damage to the light that it was rebuilt in 1831 to rise 21 metres (23 yards) high. The lighthouse that currently stands on the island, built in 1854, is 40.5 metres (44 yards) high, the tallest in New England.

Being lighthouse keeper on Boon was no easy duty. One keeper died and his wife, unable to summon help, kept the light working for a week while his body lay on the rocks. She was found wandering in circles and died a few weeks later. (It may be her ghost that haunts Boon—'a sad-faced young woman shrouded in white' has supposedly been seen by keepers.)

The dangers of being on Boon Island during a storm continued into contemporary times—the great New England blizzard of 1978 forced Coast Guard lighthouse keepers to take refuge in the tower as boulders were hurled about the islet like pebbles. Now, however, the light is fully automated, and humans don't have to pit themselves against the elements on this dangerous fragment of land.

'The Exquisite Torture'

'After a Shipwreck,' Dean's memoirs relate, 'all Discipline and Command ceases, and all are reduced to a State of Equality.' This sentence is not meant as a ringing declaration of human rights, for 'State of Equality', to captains who attempted to wield control over their crews after such a catastrophe, equated to 'state of chaos'. Already, Dean saw, some of the men were 'refusing to give Assistance' to others, at which point, like a wise father, he 'purposely withdrew' to allow them to elect their own leader. When he came back, he found that they had declared him their master on land as he had been at sea. Knowing that his best hope lay in keeping up morale, Dean told the men they should gather the timbers that had washed ashore so they could build a small boat to sail to the mainland in case rescue did not come.

By their fourth day on the island, Dean could see that the men were in dire condition, for several already had frostbitten feet and could not walk. The cook complained to the captain 'of a violent Illness' and was put into the makeshift tent they had made of sails and splintered timber, but died about noon. His body was placed 'at the Low-water Mark' for the tide to carry away. At this time, Dean's memoirs state, 'none so much as hinted to reserve it for Sustenance, although several afterwards confess'd they had some Thoughts of appropriating it for that Use'. The men, Dean noted, 'as yet retained some Sense of Humanity, being hitherto Strangers to the exquisite Torture of excessive Hunger'.

They would not be strangers to this torture for long. All they had to eat was cheese, about 8.5 ounces (250 grams) a day, and this would soon run out. In the meantime, Dean was everywhere, attempting to bestir them to move, to help build the boat, to try to capture seabirds. For 'a severe Frost [was] setting in with Extremities of Cold [which] so benumb'd and discolour'd the Hands and Feet of the Unactive as rendered them in manner Useless and past Sense of Feeling'. The men who had thrown boots on sockless feet in their haste to leave the ship had developed huge blisters, which Dean endeavoured to keep clean with urine or saltwater and bound up with what linen or sailcloth could be found.

They had been on the island for a week when they saw, off in the distance, three sails. Every man who could walk stumbled out and 'hallow'd as loud as possible, making every imaginable Signal', but all for naught. They were left alone under a grey winter sky with the sea roaring around them and the gulls wheeling high and out of reach.

The Boat

The ship's carpenter was quite ill, but he was able to give directions and slowly a small boat took shape. 'Slowly' is the operative word here. Only Dean and one or two others had the strength to work on a steady basis—and 'steady' meant only a few hours at a time before collapsing in the tent. Finally, on 21 December, a day when the weather had cleared somewhat, the vessel was ready to launch. There was some discussion as to who should attempt the voyage to the mainland, but it was clear that Dean, the strongest of the survivors, was the first choice. He chose four others, including his brother, to make the journey with him. The castaways prayed together, the boat was launched, but luck was not on their side. The five men were forced to wade 'far out to Sea' because the surf was running so high, and then were unable to board the rickety vessel properly. They lost control and it was dashed to pieces against the rocks.

Although all five 'narrowly escap'd Drowning', they could not rejoice. Not only was their hope of immediate rescue gone, but they lost both the axe and the hammer, still in the boat when it was launched. Without these tools they could not build another.

The island began to take on the look of a concentration camp, with skeletal figures trudging to and fro, desperately hoping to catch one of the seals that occasionally came ashore. Dean even went out at midnight, hoping to catch the creatures asleep, but the animals were far too swift for men in such an exhausted state. The cheese had run out and they were now living on kelp and what mussels they could find near the water's edge.

Strangely enough, despite their desperate shape, John Dean felt 'a Secret Persuasion of Deliverance'—he knew in his heart they would be saved. He took it as a sign from God that the first mate was, one day, miraculously able to strike down a seagull, which allowed every man a mouthful, swallowed raw. Dean claims that he exhorted the men to 'wait with Patience the appointed time of Divine Salvation'. Not surprisingly, this pious remark did not go down particularly well.

'The Bold Swede'

There was one other man on Boon possessed of Dean's inner fire, a Swedish sailor who now encouraged Dean to have the men make a raft. Although this man had lost the use of both feet from frostbite, he remained quite energetic, crawling around the rocks and pushing his cause on whoever would listen. Finally Dean agreed and the men lashed together a makeshift raft made from 'junk', as he reports—old planks and rigging, with two hammocks that had washed ashore serving as a sail. Despite his belief in their ultimate rescue, Dean declined the honour of sailing on it, and 'the bold Swede' volunteered to go, along with another man.

Preparations for launch were interrupted when another sail was spotted coming from the mainland, but this vessel did not spot the castaways either. By the time the excitement was over, night was beginning to fall. Dean urged the Swede to wait until the

The *Nottingham Galley* left London bound for Boston with a cargo of butter and cheese.

following morning, but the man refused—desperate to leave the island, he had to go *now*, while the landward wind held. In the first attempt to crest the waves, the raft capsized. Both men were recovered safely, but the Swede's companion lost heart and refused to try again. Another sailor agreed to take his place and this time the raft launched successfully, sailing over the waves towards the mouth of the Piscataqua. Dean had told the escapees to make a fire on a hill they could see from the island, to let those on Boon know they were safe, that rescue was coming

The castaways waited hopefully for days. A fire was seen in the woods near the agreed-upon hill, but when no rescue came, it was understood to be a mere coincidence. In fact, the raft was found floating near mainland two days later by fishermen who also discovered the body of the Swede's companion, with a paddle roped to his wrist. Of the Swede there was no sign. Oddly, the fishermen did not investigate further, perhaps thinking the raft was from a shipwreck far at sea.

'To Convert the Human Carcass'

And now comes the most haunting aspect of the entire story of the *Nottingham Galley*, the part that made this tale as famous in the early eighteenth century as the story of the *Bounty* was to become later in the century. John Dean relates that the ship's carpenter— 'a fat Man, naturally of a dull, heavy, phlegmatic Constitution'—had been ill since they came ashore and was now complaining of pain in his back and neck, and of his lungs filling up with fluid. He was conscious most of the last few hours of his life, although unable to talk, and died during the night.

The men were so exhausted that they could not remove his body from the tent in darkness, but in the morning Dean ordered them to take it out and did his usual lookout circuit of the island. When he returned, the body had not been moved. Somewhat irritably, Dean asked why the men hadn't complied with his order, to which they replied they were too weak.

That being the case, Dean told them—and one gets the sense that he has long been tired of these layabouts—he would do it himself, and he tied a rope around the corpse's ankles and tried to take it out himself. But 'the Decay of his Strength' was such that he was unable to budge the heavy body. Finally a few others helped, and they got the corpse outside, intending to gradually pull it down to the beach, where the tide could take it. Exhausted, the captain lay down to rest for a few moments, when he was approached by Miles Whitworth—'a young Gentleman … delicately educated, amidst so great an Affluence as to despite common Food'.

Despite this description, Whitworth was a favourite of Dean's, which is why the crew had elected him to approach their captain on the delicate matter of allowing them 'to convert the human Carcass into the matter of their Nourishment'. To eat the carpenter, in other words. This was not an unexpected development. At first Dean said no, but he knew he was swimming against the tide and eventually gave in, his only demand being that the carpenter's head, hands, feet, bowels and skin be given a proper burial at sea.

And now, hauntingly, Dean was enlisted by the exhausted men in the role of butcher, since they were simply too depleted to move. He therefore spent the better part of the day crouched in the cold wind, cutting up the body. That evening, he went down to the water, washed the sliced-up flesh in the sea, and brought it back for the crew to consume. Still without fire, they choked it down raw. Three of the men at first refused to partake, but in the morning they 'earnestly desired' to eat, and were given a share.

There is an air of great, almost religious sacrifice, in Dean's account, his belief that he was committing one transgression in order to keep from committing a greater one— failing to do everything he could to save the lives of his men. Still, he watched them carefully as they ate. It was thought at the time that eating fellow humans would turn men into 'brutes', that human flesh created an insatiable desire for more human flesh. Thus, Dean—who, after being initially reluctant, himself ate from the corpse—stood guard over the 'Remainder of the Body' the way a cook might stand guard over his pantry, making sure that no one, driven mad by blood, descended like a zombie to devour the remnants.

'A Sail! A Sail!'

Despite this sustenance, Dean writes, it was apparent that they were approaching death. His brother had begun to suffer 'convulsive fits', while Miles Whitworth could not longer walk for his frozen feet. But one morning Dean crawled out of the tent to find the deliverance he had so long believed in—a small fishing sloop was approaching.

'A sail! A sail!' he shouted.

The castaways stumbled from their tent shouting, and they could see that the men on the vessel heard them. But the surf was so high that they could not venture closer than a hundred metres (109 yards) to shore. Dean kept shouting that they needed fire, and at last a one-man canoe was launched and made it to shore. Dean asked desperately for flint, but the poor man was so aghast at the condition of these walking skeletons that he could barely speak. Here he was, a simple Maine fisherman, confronted by 'the ghastly figure of so many dismal Objects, with long Beards, nothing but Skin and Bone; wild, staring eyes and Countenances; fierce, barbarous, unwashed and infected with human Gore'.

The Controversy

In his own account of the wreck, published in 1711 and entitled *A Narrative of the Shipwreck of the Nottingham Galley, in her Voyage from England to Boston With An Account of the Miraculous Escape of the Captain and her Crew on a Rock Called Boon Island*, Captain John Dean presents himself as, if not a heroic figure, then as someone whose efforts were solely directed towards doing what was best for his men, many of whom were starting to go mad. In his telling, he is a reluctant cannibal at best, forced by the men around him to butcher the carpenter's body and even then trying to parcel out this food little by little.

Shortly after Boon's account was published, there came another one entitled *A True Account of the Voyage of the Nottingham Galley of London, John Dean Commander from the River Thames to New England, Near which Place she was castaway on Boon-Island 11 December 1710 by the captain's obstinacy, who endeavoured to betray her to the French or run her ashore*. As can be seen from the title, the authors of this account had an axe to grind. Before returning to England in 1711, three members of the crew of the *Nottingham Galley*—mate Christopher Langman, boatswain Nicholas Mellon and seaman George White—gave sworn depositions in Portsmouth, New Hampshire, which formed the basis for

the book. Langman and the others claimed that John Dean had over-insured the ship and had set out, from the very beginning of the voyage, to destroy her.

He supposedly did this by leaving the safety of a British convoy on the first leg of the trip (from England to Ireland) in the hope of being captured by privateers. When he was stopped by 'the Depondent, Christopher Langman, by whose assistance the said Ship arrived at her Port', he determined to run the ship aground in New England. When Langman attempted to stop Dean from crashing into Boon Island, Dean hit him and threatened to shoot him. After the wreck occurred, according to Langman, it was he, not Dean, who helped save everyone's lives. He also claimed that it was Dean who first brought up the idea of eating the carpenter, not the crew.

Dean's publisher (who was also his brother Jasper) called the charges 'preposterous', pointing out that Dean would have to be insane to deliberately wreck his ship in mid-winter on a place like Boon Island. 'One wou'd wonder if Malice itself cou'd invent or suggest anything so ridiculous,' he wrote. History's verdict tends to agree with this estimation—attempting to deliberately wreck a ship in a storm and then expect to survive is not something Dean, the ultimate survivor, would have bet his life on. However, given his later career as privateer and spy, one could wonder …

The man had no flint with him, so Dean insisted on boarding the canoe and paddling out to the fishing sloop with him, where he managed to secure a torch. The sloop left, the fishermen promising to return the next day, and the castaways gratefully built a roaring fire. With rescue seeming certain, the men begged Dean to 'enlarge' their portion of meat, which they roasted and ate with great relish. When they wanted more, though, Dean reverted to his role of watch-keeper, saying he would only release more if they were not rescued on the morrow.

But they were. The next morning they heard a musket shot ring out and looked to see a boat arrive with a five-man crew—'very brisk, strong Men', or so it seemed to the weak and helpless maroons—who transported them one by one to the vessel, and from thence to the mainland. It was 4 January 1711, and they had been on the island for twenty-six days. Their first bites of real food made them ill, but 'in process of time All Recovered', although many, including Dean, had permanent numbness or lost digits to frostbite.

An Adventurer's Life

When John and Jasper Dean got back to England, they published an account of the *Nottingham Galley*'s horrible adventures which would make the story famous—repeated editions were published, including one edited by Miles Whitworth in 1762, a year after John Dean's death at the venerable age of eighty-two. Although another, and very different, account of the crew's trial on Boon Island was published (see **The Controversy**, opposite), John Dean would remain a hero to most who read of his actions during that cold winter of 1710–1711. But even beyond the frostbite he had suffered, he was marked for life. Any man who ate the flesh of another and survived felt the stares of ordinary civilians everywhere he was recognised.

Perhaps this was why Dean went on to live a life of uncommon adventure. In 1714 he joined Peter the Great's Russian navy at a time when the Tsar was courting foreign officers, and fought in the Great Northern War against Sweden, capturing numerous enemy ships. At war's end he was court-martialled for failing to turn in two of his prizes (historians believe this was politically motivated—in any event, the Tsar commuted his sentence and allowed him to leave the country).

Back in Britain, Dean signed on as a spy for the British intelligence service and returned to Russia, where he reported on the disposition of the Russian Navy. As reward for this dangerous service, he was made a consul to Flanders, where he lived for seventeen years. He died in England on 18 August 1761, a day after the death of his wife, Sarah, having never once returned to the cold shores of America.

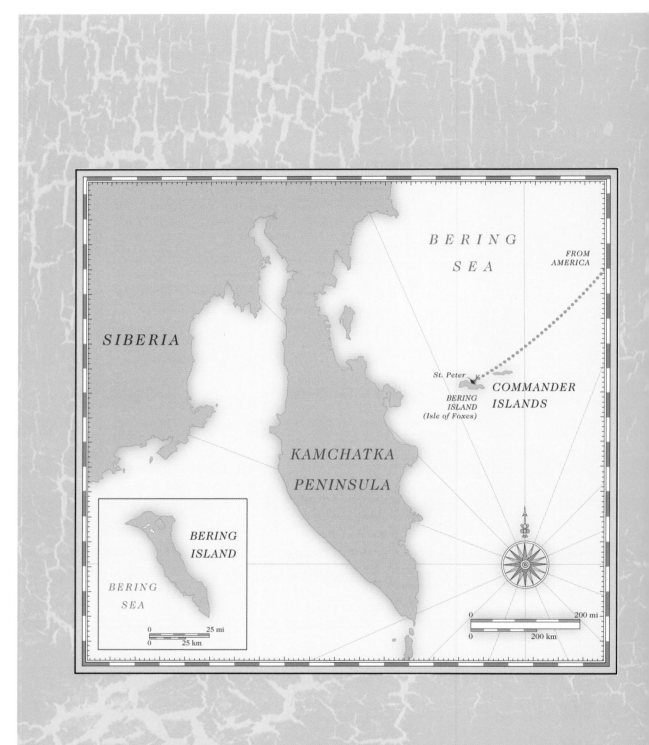

Bering in the Commander Islands, 1741–1742
Death on the Isle of the Foxes

In December of 1741, Vitus Bering lay dying on the island that was soon to bear his name. The island lies in a northern sea that would also be named after this Danish explorer, whose fame would stretch down the centuries. Right now, however, Bering's world had narrowed to a partly caved-in trench under a makeshift shelter near a high, windswept bluff. Sand covered him to his waist. When a comrade asked if he wanted to be dug out, Bering demurred with a faint smile:

'The deeper in the ground I lie, the warmer I am.'

Outside, cold winter raged across the desolate island where Bering's once-proud ship had been wrecked. Around him were men dying of exposure and scurvy—only forty-six would survive out of the seventy-five who had set off a year and a half before. And everywhere these men went they were harried by the little Arctic foxes, 'wicked' foxes which had no fear of men and were quite uncontrollable. They boldly entered the camp, rummaged through boxes, ate leather sacks and shoes (they stole one man's boots from his feet while he slept), and even 'dragged off iron and other implements that were of no use to them'.

Worse, they mutilated the unburied dead, nibbling at their fingers, until the weary living came to drive them away. Enraged, the men went after the foxes, killing scores with knives and sometimes sadistically gouging out their eyes and cutting off their tails, letting them live. Even maimed like this, the animals returned. In the midst of this hellish scene, Vitus Bering sank into a death caused by 'hunger, cold, thirst, vermin and grief', as naturalist Georg Steller, who nursed him to the end, was to write. Bering's men 'had leaned so hard on him that he himself had to go under. But he took to the grave everyone's receipted bill'.

In the Service of the Tsar

Vitus Bering was born in 1681 in Horsens, Denmark, into a poor family, and escaped an existence he later described as 'suffocating' by shipping out as a cabin boy when he was fifteen. In the next eight years he earned a formidable reputation as a navigator, sailing to India, the Dutch East Indies, and probably the West Indies and America. The stroke of fate that drove him to fame—and to the Isle of the Foxes—came in 1703, when Bering was befriended by Cornelius Cruys, an admiral in the Russian navy. Norwegian by birth, Cruys was one of the many foreign officers Tsar Peter the Great was in the process of hiring to modernise and revamp his navy.

Vitus Bering's ship wrecked in the Bering Sea, during his search for a passage from the Pacific Ocean around the top of the American continent.

Cruys, seeing promise in young Bering, recruited him. Bering got off to a fairly ordinary career transporting Russian ships during the Great Northern War with Sweden. But in 1711 he chanced to prove himself during the ill-fated conflict with the Ottoman Turks. One of the Tsar's favourite ships became trapped in the Sea of Azov and Bering bravely rescued it. Peter lauded the young man when Bering came to Moscow, and offered him an extraordinary opportunity—to explore the almost unknown regions of northeastern Russia: Siberia, the shores of the Icy Sea (the Arctic Ocean) and the Kamchatka Peninsula. And the Tsar wanted Bering to go even further—east across the northern Pacific to find a large landmass that Russian cartographers called Gamaland, supposedly spotted by a lost Spanish explorer named Juan de Gama. Peter wanted to lay claim to all this territory, to open it up to trade, to make his nation as proud a seafaring and exploring country as the Netherlands, France, England or Spain.

In 1725, with Tsar Peter gravely ill, Bering set off on his first expedition. He was 34 years old, handsome in a blunt sort of way, with dark hair, and happily married to a Swedish woman named Anna Pulse with whom he lived in St Petersburg. Bering and his party travelled overland through Siberia's barely explored regions all the way to the Arctic Ocean. After this, the Danish captain headed south for the Kamchatka Peninsula, where he established a base, constructed a ship and sailed out into what would become the Bering Sea. By now it was August 1728 and the short northern summer was coming to an end. Without having sighted the fabled Gamaland, he turned back.

Second Expedition

Bering returned to the Russian court in 1730, justifiably proud of his accomplishments in charting Siberia and the Kamchatka Peninsula. But times had changed in St Petersburg. Peter the Great and his successor Catherine I had died, as had Peter II, Peter the Great's teenage son. The new Empress was Anna Ivanovna, Peter the Great's niece, but Bering could not gain audience with her. Instead, her ministers peppered him with pointed questions. Why hadn't he kept on sailing to find Gamaland? Didn't he know how important this was? He needed to prove—or finally disprove—the story of Gamaland. And if it did exist, was it a part of the North American continent, or a separate landmass entirely?

Weary and embittered, Bering agreed to embark on a second expedition, in 1733. His new orders were unbelievably complicated. Not only was he to further chart the Siberian–Kamchatkan interior, he was to settle it, setting up iron foundries, shipyards, cattle-farming, even a postal system with the aid of thousands of soldiers, porters, Cossacks and scientists. He was to send a ship to open up trade relations with Japan, a country very little was known about at the time. Finally, he was to sail east, find out what land lay there, and chart its coastline.

A tall order. It is no wonder it was over eight years before Bering was ready to venture forth from his base in Kamchatka with two ships, the *St Peter* and the *St Paul*, each 27.5 metres long and 7 metres wide (30 yards long and 7.5 yards wide), on 4 June 1741. By this time he had undergone numerous humiliations, which included being put on half wages by the Empress Anna when the expedition ran short of money. One would think that setting sail that spring would finally bring relief from all the bureaucratic red tape Bering had been ensnared in, but it was not to be. The Russian court had reverted to the xenophobia Peter the Great had been trying to stamp out—Bering was a foreigner and not to be trusted. Thus it was decided that a 'sea council' made up of his subordinate officers—including Alexsey Chirikov, captain of the *St Paul*—could meet and overrule Bering at any time.

Voyage to America

When the *St Peter* and *St Paul* set off that summer, they had a political mission as well as a geographic one. Bering and most of his officers believed that Gamaland did not exist, but they knew they had to somehow convince the court. Therefore, instead of sailing northeast to what would become known as the Bering Strait, they would head southeast until they reached the 46th parallel, then turn north. This way they would be able to show their bosses in St Petersburg that they really had tried to locate Gamaland. What they failed to realise was that they were about to add 400 nautical miles to their trip.

One young man on the *St Peter* disagreed vehemently with the plan but since he was not an officer or even a seaman no one listened to him. His name was Georg Steller and he had joined the expedition at the last minute as scientific observer and Bering's personal physician. The journal Steller kept would become an invaluable record of the journey, and his observations of flora and fauna would earn him a lasting reputation.

Steller—one of the few who bothered to talk to the local Cossacks and the Chukchi natives of Kamchatka—had heard that there was indeed a large landmass to the northeast, that on very clear days one could see its mountains, and that sometimes natives came from there in skin boats to trade. But when he told Bering of this, the latter replied: 'Who believes Cossacks?' Bering and Steller make one of the classic odd couples in history. The stolid, sarcastic Dane was alternately irritated and bemused by this meticulous, brilliant scientist who barely had his sea legs before he was trying to tell the great captain what to do.

The *St Peter* and *St Paul* sailed in fair weather, keeping in sight of each other, on a south-southeast heading. Eight days later, the two vessels met in the open ocean and Bering and Chirikov conferred over speaker trumpets. Having reached the agreed-upon point, they decided to now head northeast, in search of the North American coastline. At this point, however, bad weather closed like a shroud around the ships and Bering and Chirikov never saw each other again.

Chirikov reached the North American coast in southeastern Alaska and set ashore two parties of men. Both groups disappeared, either drowned or killed by natives, and the *St Paul* eventually returned to Kamchatka, its crew decimated by scurvy.

'Pregnant Windbags'

Lost in bad weather, the *St Peter* wandered north until 16 July, when the clouds suddenly opened up and to the great astonishment of those on board revealed a huge, glittering, snow-covered mountain off to the east, and below it, rich forests, sparkling rivers and a shoreline dotted with capes, islands and bays. The mountain was Mount St Elias on the

North American continent, near the head of the Gulf of Alaska, a good deal further north than Chirikov's sighting.

Cheers broke out, the crew joyfully thumping each other on the back and jumping up and down. Brandy was broken out, toasts were drunk. To Steller's amazement, Bering watched these festivities disconsolately. He said to Steller: 'They are like pregnant windbags, puffed up with expectations. They don't consider where we are, how far we are from home, and what trouble we may have getting home … We don't know this country and we don't have provisions.'

Bering, ever the worrier, did have reason to be concerned. Two-thirds of their supply of fresh water was gone, and some of the men—Bering probably among them—were beginning to exhibit the first signs of scurvy. He eventually decided to sail along the coast until they found a supply of fresh water, which caused Steller to say, with great sarcasm, 'So, have we come to carry American water to Asia?' On 18 June the *St Peter* anchored off present-day Kayak Island to take on water, and Steller begged to be allowed to go ashore. Bering agreed, but on condition that he return immediately when the signal was given. Stepping ashore—the first European to do so—Steller found an Aleut campsite, its fire-rocks still warm, and earthenware jars of tasty smoked salmon, evidence that the natives had only recently fled. He wanted to stay longer, possibly to meet with them, but Bering would have none of it. As Steller later noted in his journal, with some chagrin, Bering told him 'to get his butt on board' or he would be left behind.

Heading Home

After a few weeks spent charting the complex Alaskan coastline, but refusing to land again because of rocky shoals and contrary currents, Bering turned the *St Peter* southwest, heading for Kamchatka. But their luck seemed to have turned bad. Twenty-six members of the crew had reported sick with scurvy, with five unfit for duty. Bering himself was so ill from the dread disease that he had to turn over many of his duties to Sven Waxell, his Swedish second-in-command. Now wandering through the Aleutian islands, the *St Peter* was often blanketed in fog, out of which would come the sounds of strange animals howling and birds shrieking, so often that the superstitious among the crew though they were being followed by ghosts. It rained constantly—unless the rain turned to freezing sleet.

They stopped for water at uninhabited Nagai Island where, against Steller's angry remonstrations, the crew filled the barrels from a brackish tidal pool, which would only worsen their thirst. Steller gathered antiscorbutic herbs—so-called scurvy grass, sourdock, gentian and what he called 'other cresslike plants'—which the crew, who were sick of his irascible outbursts, refused to eat. Bering accepted the herbs, which enabled him to rise from his sickbed and take a few steps, but the crew began to die one by one as the ship sailed on. Their bodies were wrapped in canvas and tipped overboard. By early November a dozen men had been given the sailor's burial.

But then a miracle occurred. On 4 November land was sighted, and to all indications it appeared they had reached the Kamchatka Peninsula. The ship anchored in what Waxell and others thought was a bay. 'It would be impossible,' Steller wrote later, 'to describe the joy created by the sight of land; the dying crawled upon the deck to see with their own eyes what they would not believe; even the feeble commander was carried out of his cabin. To the astonishment of all a small keg of brandy was taken from some hiding place and dealt out in celebration of the supposed approach to the coast of Kamchatka.'

Bering did not believe it was Kamchatka, however, and a sea council was convened in his cabin to decide the issue. The Dane wanted to keep going—even if this was northern Kamchatka, the men would never be able to travel overland down the coast to safety in the Russian port at Avacha Bay. But he was overruled by the other officers, who thought the ship was in too wretched a state to continue onward.

Bering's instincts were correct. The *St Peter* was 175 kilometres (109 miles) east of Kamchatka, in the uninhabited Commander Islands. And they were not in a bay. Two large islands close together had created an illusion, which became clear that night as a storm arose and sent the vessel crashing onto a reef. Only by good fortune was the ship pushed over the reef and nearer the shore. The hull was stove in, but the *St Peter* did not sink. The men made it to land, realising they were marooned on a large, desolate island.

The Isle of the Foxes

The Commander Islands comprise seventeen barren islands. Bering Island, as the Isle of the Foxes would come to be known, is the largest. In 1741 the group was undiscovered and uninhabited, although there is now evidence that Neolithic tribes may once have lived there (see **The Commander Islands Today**, opposite). Bering Island is 90 kilometres (56 miles) long and 25 kilometres (15.5 miles) wide, with only dwarf trees able to survive the fierce winds, and is prone to earthquakes. Despite this, its fast-moving freshwater rivers are filled with salmon, and is home to millions of seabirds, seals and other creatures, especially the white-furred Arctic fox, about the size of a small dog, which had no fear of men and a great deal of inquisitiveness. When the *St Peter*'s crew wearily pulled themselves ashore, they were immediately set upon by these animals, which they chased off time and time again, only to have them return to ravage the camp. Thus, they called the island the Isle of the Foxes, a name which encapsulated all their hatred of the desolate place.

The men found a sand bluff near a river where they could obtain fresh water, and set up sailcloth screens over holes dug in the sand. Into these dugouts they placed those who were the sickest with scurvy. Nine were too weak to survive being taken from the ship, and died almost immediately. To add to their woes, there was little firewood and most of the sick men began to suffer from exposure. Knowing that time was of the essence, Steller immediately began acting as a nurse, along with his servant Thomas Lepekhin and his artist Friedrich Plenisner. These three men brought fresh water to the sick, searched for antiscorbutic herbs and shot birds (especially ptarmigan) with which they made a soup.

Bering seemed to recover a little, but he was still weak. He lay flat on his back, and Steller confessed to his journal that he was 'amazed at his composure and strange contentment'. Steller himself railed against the sea council who had overruled Bering and insisted they land at this place, but Bering would not engage in second-guessing.

'It is the lives of the crew that matter now,' he told Steller.

The Commander Islands Today

The Commander Islands are as bleak today as they were when Vitus Bering landed there in 1741, and belong to Russia still. Bering is the only permanently populated island, with about 750 Russian and Aleut fishermen, although many others in the group support seasonal fishing camps.

The islands are still treeless, shrouded in fog, swept by gales and prone to earthquakes. Most of the area they encompass is a nature preserve and so wildlife has flourished, with over 200,000 fur seals and otters arriving each year to reproduce. Steller's sea lions also visit, although in much smaller numbers, but the immense Steller's sea cow was hunted into extinction forty years after Steller described the creature. And the wily Arctic fox survives, although its numbers, depleted by fur trappers in the eighteenth and nineteenth centuries, are far lower than when the St Peter crashed into the island.

The main visitors to Bering Island are scientists who study its ecology and history. During an excavation of the site of the castaways' camp in the 1970s, archaeologists found Neolithic tools a few levels down, indicating that all human beings, although separated by millennia, understand the value of a good campsite.

Death of Vitus Bering

As November deepened into December, the castaways found themselves fighting a deadly battle against the elements. Because of Steller's ministrations, the plague of scurvy had receded, but the men were freezing all the time, cold to their very marrow. Bering and Steller had fought in the past, but they reached a new level of respect for each other as Steller watched Bering slowly sinking, not just into his pit of sand, but into his grave. Bering confided to the younger man that he was grateful for the good fortune that had come his way in life, despite ending up here on this lonely island. Thus, 'composed and reflective', Bering died of apparent heart failure on 8 December. He was 60 years old. His body was tied to a wooden plank and taken to the grave already dug for him. Waxell, who would now act as commander in chief, said a prayer for him in a brief Lutheran service.

The fight to survive became easier. The day that Bering died, his adjutant also died and was buried near him. Four others died in December, two in January 1742. After the January deaths, no one else died, a tribute to Steller's skills as doctor and leader. His energy was incredible. He took long hikes all over the island, discovering a number of new species subsequently named after him (see **Steller's Sea Ape?**, opposite), and finding a cave which provided better shelter. On 6 February, he recorded the first earthquake they had experienced on the island, one that lasted six minutes and ended with 'a violent hissing and roaring', the shaking so strong that it buried sleeping men. Ever alert, Steller raced to the beach to watch for signs of a tsunami, but fortunately none materialised.

Most of the time, however, life was monotonous. It snowed almost every day and the men ate otter and sea lion and once had a treat when a dead whale washed ashore. Gradually the weather cleared, the days grew slightly warmer. Spring began to arrive.

The Escape

At a meeting that Sven Waxell called in April, he called on the castaways to consider 'how they might escape from this wretched place'. There was really no option but to sail off the island; the question was, in what form? Some of the men wanted to make the ship's longboat into a seaworthy craft, others to attempt to re-float the St Peter and patch her up, but the majority opted for using the timber from the shattered ship to build a new vessel.

The ship's carpenter had died of scurvy, but a Cossack among the crew had had some experience in shipbuilding and was enlisted as supervisor. The St Peter was taken apart and its timbers used to lay a keel. The new ship began to form. There were delays however.

Steller's Sea Ape?

Georg Steller discovered numerous new birds and mammals on his journey. He has many creatures named after him, including Steller's jay, Steller's eagle, Steller's sea lion, and the extinct Steller's sea cow—the enormous northern manatee of which he left the only record.

On the voyage back from Alaska, Steller noted a strange creature frolicking in the water near the ship—indeed, the animal seemed to be following the vessel. Fascinated, Steller called it 'a sea ape ... a very unusual and new animal'. Wanting a specimen, he shot at it but missed, and so had to content himself with taking notes.

The creature was about 1.5 metres (5 feet) long with 'a dog's head'. It had large, rather luminous eyes, pointed ears and floppy whiskers. Its fur was greyish on the back and reddish brown on the belly, and it had two fins on its back. Amazingly, as it watched the sailors, the animal could rise upright in the water 'like a human being'. It even juggled pieces of seaweed, seemingly for the sailors' amusement.

What was it? No doubt a seal of some type, although it was too far out at sea to be a harbour seal. His description suggests a juvenile fur seal. In any event, heading into what would soon be literally dire straits, the creature brought a lighthearted moment to those aboard the *St Peter*. 'One could not have asked for anything more comical from a monkey,' Steller wrote.

Melting ice caused the river near the camp to overflow and flood the dugouts; the men were forced to build new shelters, using salvaged timber. And food was becoming scarce— the sea lions and otters they had feasted on were now wary, and kept their distance.

In fact, meat had become such a problem that the men were trying to figure out a way to kill the northern manatees—the enormous sea cows (later named after Steller) which were up to 8 metres (9 yards) long and weighed up to 3600 kilograms (7936 pounds). They were utterly impervious to any type of clubbing, and when the men attempted to hook them in the shallows, they were dragged into the ocean. Finally, through a combination of harpooning and bayoneting, they managed to kill one, which provided not only meat but fat which was 'as pleasantly yellow as the best Dutch butter'. This they used for eating, and for caulking the seams of the vessel slowly taking shape on the beach.

A History Written in Blood

As soon as the starving remnants of Bering's crew returned to Kamchatka and related stories of islands covered with sea lions and otters, the rush to take their furs was on, resulting in a frenzy of exploitation of animal and eventually human resources one historian has called 'as brutal as any the world has known'.

The first to sail to Bering Island after the *St Peter* survivors returned—a Cossack sergeant named Basov—came back with a cargo of seal and fox furs, worth more than $1 million today. A horde of others followed in his wake. Steller's sea cow was hunted for its meat and driven into extinction within forty years. The trappers sailed further and further east, eventually stopping at each Aleutian island in turn. It was a dangerous business—their boats were leaky and unseaworthy and they had few maps—it is estimated that one out of three ships never returned.

At first the Russians did their own seal and otter hunting, but then they discovered they could get the Aleuts to do it for them for a few baubles. When the Aleuts begin to refuse their trinkets, however, the trappers would take their wives and daughters hostage and force them to comply. On the island of Attu, the trappers

murdered all the men in one village so they could rape their wives; some of the women committed suicide, and the trappers tied the hands of the rest and threw them overboard leaving no witnesses.

In 1764, the Aleuts on the island of Unalaska hit back, killing most of the hunters there. In retaliation, the Aleuts were nearly wiped out. The warfare only ceased when Russia had full control of the Aleutian Islands.

The castaways managed to kill about thirteen sea cows and, for the first time, started to thrive. With strength and energy returning, they worked with a passion on the ship, which they finished early in August. On 13 August they put together a simple wooden cross and placed it over the grave of Vitus Bering. The Isle of the Foxes was renamed Bering Island, and the entire island group named the Commander Islands.

The men climbed aboard the new *St Peter*. They left with the tide the next morning.

'God's Grace and Mercy'

That morning was bright and clear and, staring back at the disappearing island, Georg Steller wrote that 'God's grace and mercy became manifest to us all, the more brightly considering how miserably we had arrived there in November 6'. The new ship was about half the size of the old *St Peter* and leaked badly. By halfway through the next day there were 8 centimetres (3 inches) of water in the hold; the day after that she sprang a major leak that was only plugged with difficulty. Two days later the men beheld, through fog and shifting mists, the mainland of Kamchatka. Contrary winds kept their progress slow, but they finally made it to Avacha Bay on the morning of 27 August.

Their countrymen were astonished to see them. They had long been given up for dead and their belongings had been sold or given away. The castaways returned to nothing at all—but they had their lives. They were fed and given warm, dry beds, but it took them time to get used to this munificence—Steller wrote: 'We were all so accustomed to misery and wretched living that we thought the previous circumstance would always continue.'

A day or two later the survivors gathered at the local chapel, where they thanked God and commissioned a silver plaque to be hung with the inscription: 'An offering in the memory of our miraculous escape from a barren island and our return to Kamchatka.'

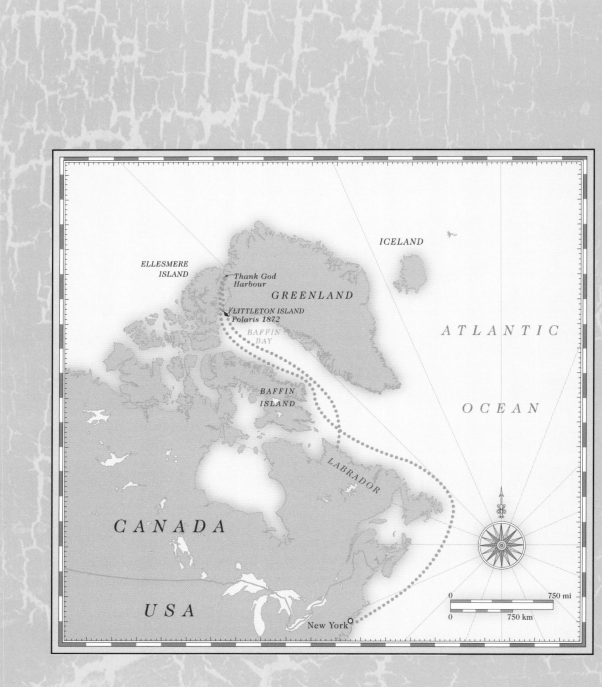

Castaways of the USS Polaris, 1871–1872
A Polar Nightmare

Despite the privation of their respective experiences—the isolation, the hunger and thirst, the longing for rescue—all our castaways so far have found themselves on solid ground. But imagine if you were cast away and the very island beneath you was careening across the ocean with the shifting winds—and you had no idea just how long your fragile haven would last before it opened up beneath you with a strange cracking roar to send you plunging into a frigid sea that would rob you of your life and breath in just under twenty seconds.

Such a situation would give fresh meaning to the word 'precarious'—and was precisely the circumstances faced by nineteen castaways of the USS *Polaris*, the proud icebreaking vessel sent in 1871 to conquer the North Pole and bring glory to America. Instead, with the expedition leader dead (and possibly murdered) these men, women and children found themselves in a race against time and weather. Could they survive until they were rescued, or would the ice floe they were on—for that is what it was—disintegrate as the winds pushed them south, at which point they would perish without a trace?

'An Earthly Heaven'

In the nineteenth century, numerous explorers led expeditions into the Arctic regions, each hoping for the honour of being the first to reach the geographic North Pole. Charles Francis Hall was one of them. Forty-nine years old in 1870, stocky of build, with a large bushy beard and a kindly manner, he was a most unlikely adventurer, a Midwestern small-town businessman—a maker of engraved plates and a newspaper publisher—who had been bitten by the Arctic bug. In 1860 he had scraped together enough money to search for survivors of the 1845 John Franklin expedition (see **The Lost Expedition**, page 304) and had spent a good deal of time on Baffin Island; a subsequent expedition in 1865–1869 saw him living among the Eskimo people on King William Island. He understood, or thought he did, how to survive the Arctic's harsh conditions, and by 1870 desperately wanted to lead the first American expedition to reach the North Pole. He went to the Congress to seek funding and told rapt lawmakers that he wanted to 'solve the Northern mystery'—whether there existed a Great Polar Sea, whether there might be land at the Pole, even an undiscovered continent. If there were, it might be possible to claim this territory for the nation.

The Lost Expedition

In 1860, Charles Francis Hall became one of numerous adventurers to seek the fate of the so-called 'lost' expedition of the British explorer Sir John Franklin, who disappeared in the Canadian Arctic with two ships and 129 men in 1845. Hall had hoped to find some of the expedition members still alive—he had heard rumours to that effect from Eskimos—but came back from King William Island with only an old watch and other items that might have come from Franklin's men.

Franklin had sailed from Greenland in 1845 in search of the Northwest Passage. His was a strong and well-provisioned group that set out with high hopes, but lost both its ships to ice near King William Island. Forced to winter there, several men, including Franklin, died. The

remnants of the expedition set out overland, striking south through the Canadian wilderness, hoping to make Hudson Bay, but disappeared. By 1849, several rescue expeditions were mounted in search of Franklin, finding clues—such as the note left behind describing the men's desperate hope of trekking safely through the frozen north—also finding horrors, for it soon became apparent from various gravesites that Franklin's men had cannibalised each other.

Rumours persisted for years that at least some of the expedition's members were alive among the Eskimos, but it seems that the local people, who were terrified of these men—some of whom carried human meat over their shoulders—had let them starve to death; they had little enough to give them anyway.

Still, no one could understand why such a large and well-equipped and well-provisioned expedition should have begun to die off so quickly. In the latter part of the twentieth century, tests conducted on bodies that had been well-preserved in graves in the Arctic permafrost revealed amounts of lead ten times higher than normal. The men had being poisoned by the lead solder used to seal their supply of tinned food—it had leached into the contents, causing fever, hallucinations and finally death.

These appeals were specifically aimed at a United States just emerging from the Civil War and seeking to grow and recover as a nation, and the appeals worked beautifully—Hall was given the grand sum of $50,000 to mount an expedition to the North Pole. However commerce, or even patriotism, were not really where his heart lay—Charles Francis Hall was a true believer and the Arctic was his one real passion. As he told a group before his expedition left: 'The Arctic region is my home. I love it dearly—its storms, its winds, its icebergs. When I am among them, it seems as if I were in an earth heaven.'

USS *Polaris*

Hall's expedition left for its momentous trip on 29 June 1871, steaming out of Brooklyn Navy Yard aboard the USS *Polaris*, a former Civil War gunboat which had been specially refitted as an icebreaker, with a reinforced hull and smooth sides. Her name had been *Periwinkle*, not exactly the moniker for a brave Arctic ship, so Hall bestowed on her the name *Polaris*, for the North Star. Aboard the *Polaris* as she chugged up the Atlantic coast that summer were thirty-three people. Chief among them were the sailing master, 47-year-old Sidney O. Budington, who had been a whaling captain for over thirty years, specialising in northern waters. Next in command was George Tyson, 42 years old, assistant navigator. Tyson, tall and lanky, was an experienced hand who had been shipwrecked in near-Arctic conditions before and was almost unflappable.

Hall considered the main purpose of his expedition to be 'geographic'—to discover what no one had ever seen before, as well as to reach the North Pole—but the influential National Academy of Sciences, concerned that he was not a scientist, put pressure on Congress to insist that he take along someone well-versed in astronomy, geology, zoology and the like. While insisting that 'science must be subordinate' to exploration, Hall finally agreed. His fateful choice as leader of the scientific team was 27-year-old Dr Emil Bessels, a proud and oversensitive German with a shock of black hair who would also be the ship's physician. With Bessels was Prussian-born meteorologist Frederick Meyer.

There were numerous nationalities aboard the *Polaris*: Germans, Swedes, English and Eskimos. These last were especially important to Hall, and included two men, two women and four children. Hall's special Eskimo friends from his previous trip to King William Island were Ebierbing (known as Joe) and Tookoolito (known as Hannah). Joe was chief hunter and dog driver, Hannah the expedition seamstress.

'A Damned Fool'

The *Polaris* stopped briefly at St Johns, Newfoundland, to take on coal and load sled dogs, sleds made by Eskimos (the only kind that Hall would use) and animal skins to be made into winter clothing by Hannah. The ship then steamed north, heading up into Baffin Bay, with Greenland to the east and Ellesmere Island to the west. The goal was to get as far north as possible before ice choked the bay, to winter on the west coast of Greenland and make their dash for the North Pole in the summer of 1872.

But trouble began brewing almost immediately. Only two days out of St Johns, George Tyson was nearly knocked over by Sidney Budington as the master clambered up the stairs from belowdecks, grabbed Tyson and took him aside.

'Tyson, we are being led by a damned fool!' he exclaimed.

Tyson asked him to lower his voice, but Budington persisted. 'When we get to Disko, I'll be heading ashore,' he said.

Tyson wrote in his journal that 'the sailing master talked of resigning'—Disko in Greenland was their last port of call before leaving human habitation—but Tyson talked him out of it. It turned out that Hall had caught Budington stealing sugar and chocolate from the ship's supplies and had lectured him, embarrassing Budington greatly.

At the time, however, the problem of Budington seemed nothing compared to the issues Hall had with Bessels and Meyer. The Germans, Tyson noted, acted as if they were superior and seemed to feel that it was not in Hall's power to command them, although he was expressly given this authority in his orders. There had been tension from the beginning with Bessels, whom Hall had not wanted in the first place and who was difficult. As they headed north, problems arose with Meyer. Hall had ordered him to keep the expedition journal, since meteorological sightings were not needed at this point, but Meyer refused. Bessels and the other Germans on board, who included several able seamen, took Meyer's part and told Hall they would leave the ship at Disko if he did not back down.

Hall was not a natural disciplinarian, preferring to lead in a more collaborative way. On the other hand, he was no pushover—on a previous expedition he had shot and killed a crewman who had taken a swing at him. Perhaps because he recognised the killing as an overreaction and felt guilty about it, he would not push things too far with the Germans. He relented, and told Meyer he would not have to write up the journal.

Now navigating the 500 kilometres (310.5 miles) of icy waterway between Greenland and Ellesmere Island—dangerous waters which had turned back previous explorers— the *Polaris* made surprisingly good time and by 30 August had travelled farther north than any previous expedition, reaching the latitude of 82° 16′. They were about 800 kilometres (497 miles) from the North Pole, all of that distance ice, although Hall did not realise this.

The wind and currents were now working against them, so Hall directed that the *Polaris* head south a short distance to winter in small bay they named Thank God Harbor. They found the stone remains of an Eskimo summer hunting camp here, but little else—the land was a low, rocky, barren expanse stretching off to the horizon under a grey sky. By mid-October the sun had almost disappeared below the horizon, resulting in 'daylight' that resembled twilight, but still light enough for Hall to make a short dog-sled expedition to chart the land to the north. While he was away, tensions escalated further when Bessels found Budington stealing his scientific supplies of ethyl alcohol. When he confronted Budington, the latter laughed at him and said he would drink it whenever he liked.

Unaware of this incident, Hall returned on 24 October. He was in a gloriously energetic mood, telling Tyson he was sure they could reach the North Pole by keeping along this shore. He entered his cabin, exchanged his wet clothing for dry garments, and accepted a cup of coffee from his steward, John Herron. Within twenty minutes, he turned pale and began vomiting. Tyson came belowdecks to speak to him and left puzzled, writing in his journal: '[Hall's] sickness came on immediately after drinking a cup of coffee. I think it must be a bilious attack but it is very sudden. I told him … I thought an emetic would do him good.'

Charles Francis Hall lived with the Eskimo people, learning their ways.

Charles Francis Hall was buried in a shallow grave on 11 November 1871. In 1968, an exhumation of Hall's corpse revealed that he died from acute arsenic poisoning.

Hall thought so too but Emil Besssels, in his role as expedition doctor, refused to administer one, even though inducing vomiting was usual in those days in cases of 'bilious' attacks or stomach complaints. Over the next few days, Hall's condition grew worse, his pulse became irregular, and he lapsed in and out of consciousness. He also became delirious. Tyson noted with concern in his journal: 'Capt. Hall very bad again. He talks wildly—seems to think some one means to poison him.'

Interestingly, during the next two weeks Hall seemed to get better when Emil Bessels stopped attending him for four days. From 29 October to 1 November, Hall banned Bessels from his bedside and became so much better that he ate a full meal and appeared on deck. (During this period he refused to eat anything but canned food and insisted that the cans be opened in front of him.) But after Bessels complained that he should look after Hall for the good of the expedition, he allowed the German to administer to him again. On 4 November, Bessels was seen injecting Hall with a syringe of white powder mixed with water, which he said was quinine for the fever.

On 8 November, raving and delirious, Charles Francis Hall died.

The Murder of Charles Francis Hall?

While a 1873 investigation by the Surgeons-General of the United States Army and Navy concluded that Charles Francis Hall died of 'natural causes', probably a stroke, and that the treatment Dr Emil Bessels provided him was 'the best possible under the circumstances', there were many people at the time who believed Hall was murdered.

Certainly there was circumstantial evidence for arsenic poisoning. The suddenness of this healthy man's falling ill immediately upon ingesting a cup of coffee (which had a strange sweet taste); the numb tongue and tingling extremities; the fierce headache, convulsions and final coma. These suspicions were given new credibility a century later, when Charles Loomis, a Dartmouth professor, visited the lonely grave at Thank God Harbor, exhumed Hall's well-preserved body from the permafrost and took tissue, hair and nail samples. Forensic examination showed elevated amounts of arsenic in Hall's hair and nails, amounts which had increased within one week before his death.

This does not mean conclusively Hall was murdered; small doses of arsenic were often used for medicinal purposes in the nineteenth century. But his sudden failing is impossible to explain by deliberate medicinal ingestion. Nor can we explain how Hall seemed to get better when Bessels was not nursing him, and worse when Bessels injected him with the white powdery substance he claimed was quinine (quinine was usually given as a liquid at the time).

If Hall was poisoned, the finger of suspicion points at Bessels, whose power struggle with Hall was well known. But Hall also feuded with Sidney Budington, whom he had reprimanded for stealing ship's stores and was on the verge of dismissing from his post. Both these men made statements after Hall's death to the effect that they were glad he was dead; it is entirely possible that, acting together, they poisoned their leader.

Ultimately, no one will ever know who did the deed, but it seems fairly certain that Charles Francis Hall met his end as a result of murder most foul.

Heading South

The suspicious circumstances under which Hall died would be debated for the next hundred years (see **The Murder of Charles Francis Hall?**, page 309) since there were at least two men aboard ship who hated him with a passion. Even before he had been buried in a shallow grave in the permafrost, Sidney Budington told a crewmember 'There is a stone off my heart', meaning that Hall was no longer around to force him to obey his orders. Frederick Meyer said something similar: 'Maybe now the officers will have something to say about this expedition.'

The day after Hall's death, Budington, reeking of alcohol, took Tyson aside and said: 'Don't you say anything about it to anybody, but that bastard little German poisoned the old man [Hall].' Tyson, who had not suspected anything so dreadful as murder, did not know how to respond, but he also knew that Budington was quite devious—it was possible *he* had murdered Hall. Although Tyson had been on numerous, dangerous expeditions into the Arctic and knew what these strange climes and the depressing dark of polar winters could do to people, he had never seen anything like this before. He decided he would say nothing, and simply watch himself carefully.

Most of the crew were aware of the tensions and divided into different factions, the Germans banding together with Bessels and Meyer, the Eskimos and other seamen quietly siding with Tyson. Budington continued to drink throughout the long winter. By the spring of 1872, he had gone through all of Bessels' alcohol and was into the liniment Hannah used for rubbing sore shoulders. When the sun returned and the ice began to break up, Bessels demanded that Budington take them further north—he apparently thought that he might make a try for the North Pole on his own—but Budington refused. He wanted to head south and, on 12 August 1872, he did.

The trip back to civilisation would prove to be a disaster, however. Continually drunk, Budington steered the vessel into the middle of pack ice, forcing Tyson and the other seamen to find clear channels through which the *Polaris* could move. Progress was painfully slow. Eventually the ship was caught in the middle of a number of icebergs and ice floes which were slowly coalescing into one enormous floe. It was now October and the danger was twofold: that they would be caught and have to spend another winter in the Arctic, this time on the ice, and that the *Polaris* might be crushed as the ice hardened.

On 15 October, the pressure of the ice finally became too much, and the *Polaris* sprang a leak. Sure she was going to sink, Budington ordered the men to throw provisions on the ice and abandon ship. Nineteen people, including Tyson and the Eskimos and their children, jumped off the vessel. Then, in a violent explosion, the ice around the *Polaris* shattered under pressure and she was momentarily free and in clear water. The ropes which had held her fast to the ice snapped and she was carried away by the current into the dark of the night.

When morning came, Tyson and the others saw that they were marooned on a huge ice floe that appeared to be drifting slowly southwest. They had assumed that the *Polaris* had sunk—but to their astonishment saw the ship steaming slowly south. Crawling and slipping to the edge of the floe, they raised a makeshift flag and shouted, but no one on board saw them, or so Budington was to claim later. In any event, the injured ship kept on going—with Emil Bessels on board as well—and its crew would eventually be rescued the next summer.

'The Fear of Death'

Tyson's first thought was to take the two ship's boats which had been left on the ice with them and set sail to try to catch up with the *Polaris*, but when he instructed the men to lighten the boats—to toss their belongings off so they might be dragged over the ice more easily—they began 'muttering and grumbling' (especially the German contingent, which included Meyer) and moved so slowly that all opportunity to catch up was lost.

After a meal of frozen meat the castaways spent the night in walrus-skin tents. In the morning they were awakened by a horrible cracking sound. Racing from his tent, Tyson saw that the ice floe had broken apart, separating them from one of their boats. There was as yet no sea running between the two sections and a determined effort could have retrieved the boat, but the men, terrified, refused to help and the two pieces drifted apart. They were now on an ice floe that was, by Tyson's reckoning 'one hundred and fifty yards [137 metres] across each way'. The next day he wrote in his journal, with a rare note of panic: 'Quite a heavy sea is running; piece after piece is broken from our floe. God grant we may have enough left to stand upon. The vessel [the *Polaris*] could now come to us in clear water if she was in condition to steam or sail.'

But the *Polaris* did not return. Resigning himself, Tyson ordered the Eskimos to hunt for seals, which in the winter came up under the ice to breathing holes and could be shot or speared by a skilled stalker. The days settled down into a routine, although not a happy one. The Eskimos hunted, either shooting seals in breathing holes or attempting to spear them in the water, using the seal-skin kayaks they had saved from the vessel. It is almost certain that this group would not have survived without the expertise of the Eskimos, who also built igloos to shelter in.

The Germans continued to complain and did very little. Everyone suffered severely from the cold. Christmas Day 1872 found Tyson sitting in his tent eating frozen seal entrails. He wrote with great irony: 'The fear of death has been starved and frozen out of me.'

Wilful Children

Tyson was amused, in a desperate sort of way, by the Germans, who generally speaking had no idea where they were. Tyson had a compass and knew that they were drifting southwest, towards Labrador. The Germans seemed to feel that they were along the coast of Greenland (the opposite direction) and would shortly be able sail their small boat to civilisation in Disko.

Despite explaining to the Germans over and over again that they were wrong, they refused to believe him. Tyson was sure they were plotting to take the boat and leave the others behind, which would greatly lessen any chance of survival—if they were not rescued before their small floe broke up, they would need the boat to survive.

In mid-January, Meyer confirmed Tyson's worst fears, saying that he and the other Germans wanted to take what few supplies remained and leave—they were only 60 kilometres (37 miles) from Disko, by his estimation. Making a desperate attempt to reason with him, Tyson told Meyer: 'Your lives depend on what I am about to say. I have sailed these waters too often to be deceived about our course. As long as we able to see land in the west, we cannot possibly be close to Greenland.' He was trying to make them understand that they were on the *west* side of Baffin Bay, which is 500 kilometres (310.5 miles) wide—and that if they got into a small boat now they would perish.

The would-be deserters stared at him, then went silently back to their igloo, apparently to discuss the matter. Shortly after this, a German seaman named John Kruger burst into the igloo Tyson shared with Joe and Hannah. He had a gun and accused Tyson of telling lies about him (Tyson had earlier had an altercation with this man when he tried to drag away a seal caught by Joe). Kruger threatened to shoot Tyson, to which Tyson responded by standing up, putting his hand on his own pistol and saying he 'was willing to afford him every facility for trying his skill in that line of business'.

At this Kruger backed down, but Tyson was very worried. 'I know not how this business will end,' he wrote, 'but unless there is some change, I fear in a disastrous manner. They are like so many wilful children.' They had been on the ice floe for over a hundred days now, and Tyson was feeling discouraged. He took heart when Meyer finally came back to him and said they would not attempt a crossing to Disko after all, but remained concerned all the same. The Germans had 'taken possession of everything from the first, and are very insolent and do as they please; I see no way to enforce obedience without shedding blood; and should I do that and live, it is easy to see that my life would be sworn away should we ever get home'.

'Fools of Fortune'

By February the sun was rising far enough above the horizon to warm the igloos a little; at one point the temperature, which had long hovered around –30°C, rose to –7°C. Tyson prepared a false keel to protect the real keel should they have to drag the boat across the ice to launch it. On 6 March, they felt a huge shaking of the ice beneath them, almost like an earthquake, but nothing else happened. But on the night of 11 March, following a fierce gale, they heard a loud explosion followed by a grinding sound, as if two icebergs were crashing together. Tyson and Joe crept out of their igloo into the darkness, but snow was blowing so hard they could barely see their hands in front of their faces. The morning revealed a horrifying sight: the floe had broken apart again, and now was only a third of its original size. The only reason they had survived was that Tyson had deliberately picked the thickest stretch of ice to make camp.

Tyson knew it was only a matter of time before they had to leave the floe, even if it remained relatively stable. Continuing to drift south, he had begun to feel more hopeful, however, for the floe would soon enter whaling lanes where they might be rescued. One night shortly afterward, he and Joe heard a commotion and looked out to sea a polar bear near one of the kayaks (polar bears are known to swim hundreds of kilometres through floating pack ice in search of seals). The bear would provide the starving castaways with badly needed meat, but Tyson had left his gun in the kayak—something they all routinely did so that the condensation of breath in the igloos wouldn't cause the guns to rust. With incredible courage, he snuck up on the 230 kilogram (507 pounds), 3 metre (3 yard) tall animal, and grabbed the gun. In doing this he made a slight noise and the bear turned on him, standing upright on its hind legs. Tyson stood too, and shot a bullet unerringly through its heart.

The bear meat gave the party much-needed food, and the strength to try something else—launch the boat and sail back to the main group of ice floes, since it was apparent the one they were on would not last much longer. 'We have been "the fools of fortune" for five months and a half,' Tyson wrote on 1 April—April Fool's Day. But now they needed to take fortune into their own hands. Taking all the supplies they dared carry, they launched the boat off the ice with Tyson at the tiller. After two days' sailing, with the vessel leaking heavily, they reached a larger floe.

Codfish and Potatoes

The castaways built igloos on the floe and were settling in when, on the night of 20 April, a huge wave swept across the floe, washing everything before it—supplies, equipment, animal skins. They were fortunate enough to reach the boat, and hung onto it with all their might to keep it from being washed away by succeeding waves. It must have been an extraordinary scene: men, women and children holding onto the boat for dear life as the waves threatened to wash it away, waves which were filled with loose blocks of ice which smote them around the legs and shoulders, bruising them badly. But they knew that if they let go, they would be letting go of their lives, so even the Germans hung on with a will.

The next day the seas subsided and they sailed to another floe which they considered safer; it was certainly luckier, for there they killed another polar bear. And now they began spotting land off to the west, appearing and disappearing in the fog. At one point they attempted to sail to it, but were pushed back to the floe by winds and currents. A few days later, to their great joy, they saw a sealing steamer working her way through the ice. Despite firing their guns and waving, they did not attract its attention.

Still, Tyson knew they had now come far enough south to be near rescue and cautioned everyone to be on vigilant lookout. And on April 26, another sealer, the *Tigress*, working its way through the ice, spotted them. The astonished crew sent out boats and brought the castaways aboard, women and children first. When Tyson boarded the *Tigress*, one of the crew asked him: 'How long have you been on the ice?'

And Tyson replied, barely believing it himself: 'Since the 15th of October.'

They had been on the ice for 197 days and drifted 2400 kilometres (1491 miles), and were now off Grady Harbor, on the coast of Labrador. Tyson's first meal was codfish and potatoes and he thought nothing could have tasted better.

Afterward two boards of inquiry were convened, mainly because George Tyson told reporters of how Charles Francis Hall might have been poisoned, but partly because he was still bitter that Sidney Budington had left them on the ice floe. 'I did not feel right about the vessel not coming for us,' Tyson said, with his usual understatement. He told the first board of inquiry—led by the Secretary of the Navy himself— that Budington was drunk almost all the time on the alcohol intended for preserving scientific specimens.

Budington appeared and denied this, claiming that he perhaps drank overmuch on one of two occasions, but no more. The result of this inquiry was a whitewash—the administration of Ulysses S. Grant had already suffered scandal after scandal and could not withstand another one involving the abandonment of half the crew of a US Navy vessel on an ice floe by a soused captain. So Budington was cleared, although he never had a sea command again. The second board of inquiry, run by the surgeons-general of both the Navy and the Army, cleared Emil Bessels of all guilt in the death of Charles Francis Hall.

And so that was it. Trying to put it all behind him, George Tyson went back to sea on another Arctic expedition, which nearly killed him and his crew, and never set foot aboard another ship. He divorced his wife, married again, but fell on hard times and only got another job at the personal intervention of President Rutherford B. Hayes—and then as a messenger at the War Department. When he died in 1906, few people knew who he was or the part he had played in keeping so many people alive for nearly seven months on a drifting ice floe. In loving remembrance, his son wrote a letter which ended: 'Peace to his ashes. He bore an honoured name. May it never perish.'

Making It?

It wasn't until forty years after the death of Charles Francis Hall that American Navy engineer Robert Peary, along with his assistant Matthew Henson and a group of Eskimos, finally made it to the North Pole. They did it with an incredible sprint across the ice, making 213 kilometres (132 miles) in only four days.

Of course, as with almost everything else about the North Pole, the Peary claim caused quite some controversy. Henson's description of their slow and torturous process over ice hummocks and pressure ridges didn't quite jibe with the speed Peary said he attained, using sleds and fresh teams of dogs. However, in 2005 the British explorer Tom Avery, using reproduction 1909 sleds, bettered Peary's time, showing that it was indeed possible (although Avery had better weather conditions).

Another bone of contention: Peary was headed for the geographic North Pole (rather than the magnetic one, where all compasses point). The two poles are 1600 kilometres (994 miles) apart. The only way to get to the geographic pole was to head straight north, which one did by celestial sightings, but there can be a large margin of error in these rough methods. It is generally assumed, however, that if Peary did not make it he got pretty close.

If one is looking for undisputed evidence of North Pole discovery, it would be the overflight of the dirigible *Norge* in 1926, carrying the explorer Roald Amundsen. So how fet foor on the Pole? Honours may go to a Soviet Russian team which traversed the territory in 1948, although that claim is disputed, or to an American group which landed their plane on the exact geographic pole in 1952.

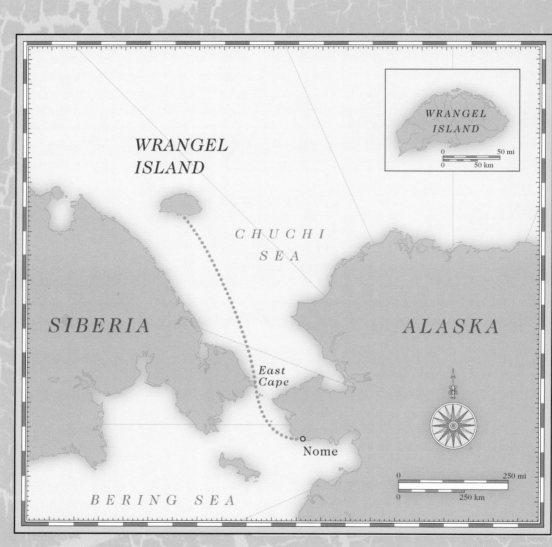

Ada Blackjack, 1921–1923
Alone on an Arctic Island

After the explorer died of scurvy in late June, Ada Blackjack walled off his body with boxes to keep wild animals from getting at it and moved from the hut to a tent, taking with her Vic, the orange tabby expedition cat. The weather was beginning to warm and polar bears roamed through the camp, pawing through the garbage, licking clean the containers she had kept seal oil in. When this happened, Ada remained very still. She was full-blooded Eskimo but she had not been raised in the wilderness, and was terrified of the great creatures. Earlier, she had shot a seal and was walking towards her kill when she saw something move against the dull grey sky, something white and huge, and realised it was a polar bear racing towards her. She turned and sprinted back to her tent. Peering out, she watched the bear and her cub tearing apart the seal the starving Ada had shot for herself.

It made her angry and she spared a precious bullet—a hollow-point, the kind you use to knock down bears—to take a shot at the animal. But the range was too far and she missed. She sat disconsolately as the sky darkened over the desolate Arctic island. She was completely alone, surrounded by wild creatures. All she had of her former life was a cat and a corpse.

I thank God for living, she told herself, over and over, trying to believe it.

Knives and Fire

Ada Blackjack was born Ada Delatuk in Solomon, Alaska, on 10 May 1898, just as the Alaskan gold rush was beginning. Solomon, once a tiny village, had swelled with five saloons and even a post office, but Ada did not stay there for long. Her father died of food poisoning when she was eight and her mother sent her to Nome to be schooled by Methodist missionaries. They gave her an elementary school education, taught her to read the Bible and sent her out into the world ready to be a seamstress. She had not learned traditional Eskimo skills like hunting or trapping, but she was still steeped in the lore of her people.

Ada was a tiny woman, less than five feet tall, who spoke little but felt deeply. She had a love of fine clothes, a taste she could rarely indulge in, and an uncanny knack for picking men who were bad for her, users and abusers. The first of a lifelong stream of these was a hunter named Jack Blackjack, whom she married when she was sixteen. He beat her, refused to give her and their three children enough food, and eventually left her in 1921, when she was twenty-three. Two of the children had already died of disease. The surviving one, five-year-old Bennett, had tuberculosis. Ada's only option, a heartbreaking one, was to put him in an orphanage while she looked for work.

There was not much of it around—sewing here and there, housecleaning. Ada was also prone to getting herself into difficulties by drinking too much and coming on to men in saloons, so when Nome's chief of police learned that there were explorers in town seeking to hire Eskimos for an expedition to remote Wrangel Island, deep in the Arctic Sea above Siberia, he suggested strongly that she consider it. Unable to decide what to do, Ada visited a shaman, who read her fortune in return for a little tobacco. He saw her sailing to this island, but told her that severe danger lay ahead, possibly even death. She must especially watch out for knives and fire.

The Friendly Arctic

Born in 1879, Vilhjalmur Stefansson was a Canadian explorer and ethnologist with a degree from Harvard who had some strange beliefs about the Arctic, one being that there existed an undiscovered continent on top of the world. He failed to find such a continent in the course of three expeditions to the Far North, from 1906 to 1918, but his adventures were many. He was the first white man to visit the famed blond Eskimos on Victoria Island (a tribe of Inuit with blond hair) and he travelled some 19 000 kilometres (11,806 miles) through polar regions by dog sled. These adventures made him famous on the lecture circuit in Canada and America—where audiences always thrilled to a good Arctic exploration tale—and in 1921 he published a book called *The Friendly Arctic*. In it Stefansson expounded on his pet theory, that the Arctic was not a terrifying and frigid desert where men died glassy-eyed from cold or with their faces stuffed down the maw of a ravening polar bear.

No, the Arctic, if you knew how to live in it, was actually quite hospitable, a beautiful place where you could hunt and enjoy the frozen stillness and awesome landscapes, far from the hustle and bustle of civilisation. Stefansson was an Arctic booster, and on his 1921 lecture tour across America, he had a secret plan in mind. He wanted to settle Wrangel Island, which is in the Arctic Ocean or, more specifically, the Chukchi Sea, some 300 kilometres (186.5 miles) north of the Siberian mainland. Although most countries agreed that the place belonged to Russia, Stefansson had the idea that he might claim it for Canada or Great Britain, colonise it, possibly place an airstrip on it, and run tourist trips there, the way one might organise safaris to Africa. Although the government of neither country was terribly encouraging about this scheme, such was Stefansson's charisma that he was able to convince four highly able young men to carry out a colonising expedition for him while he remained comfortably at home. Once they had set things up, he said, he would join them.

'The Great Silent North'

The men were Fred Maurer, E. Lorne Knight, Milton Galle and Alan Crawford. The first three were American, the fourth Canadian. All were in their twenties, young and fit, ready for adventure, although it's something of a mystery that Maurer was carried along by the idea. For he knew the Stefansson behind the public mask. He had journeyed along with the explorer on his 1913 Canadian Arctic Expedition to find the continent at the top of the world. He and twenty-five other men found themselves on a ship caught in pack ice in the Bering Strait only a month after leaving Alaska—at which point Stefansson abandoned ship and expedition and went off on a dog sled, making his own way across the pack ice to Alaska. The ship drifted northwest with the ice, broke up and finally sank; the captain led the survivors on a forced march 160 kilometres (99.5 miles) across the ice to Wrangel Island, where they were stranded for six months before rescuers reached them.

Eleven men died and yet Stefansson persisted in acting like the hero of the expedition. Maurer felt enraged at him, but agreed to go to Wrangel again in 1921, perhaps because he never got used to civilisation once he had experienced what he called 'the great silent north'. The same may have held true for Knight, who had also accompanied Stefansson on a previous expedition, on which he contracted scurvy.

On 9 September 1921, these four men sailed from Nome, Alaska, on a ship called the *Silver Wave*. With them was Ada Blackjack. Stefansson's original plan had been that a whole party of Eskimo men and women would join them, to help the men hunt and to sew and cook, but at the last moment they had backed out. Ada had intended to back out too—she didn't think it was proper to accompany four men with no other women around—but a friend of hers who knew Knight said that she would be safe with him. It's a sign of how desperate for work she was that she went along, although it also seems quite possible that she had in mind that one of the men might make her a good husband.

On 14 September, the *Silver Wave* arrived at Wrangel Island and disembarked its passengers and supplies. Another supply ship would come the following summer, Stefansson had promised, bringing him and a relief party. Until then, they were alone.

Wrangel Island

The famous American naturalist John Muir, visiting Wrangel Island in 1881, wrote that 'a land more severely solitary could hardly be found anywhere on the face of the globe'. Alone in the Chukchi Sea except for tiny Herald Island some 55 kilometres (34 miles) distant, this rugged place, icebound at least eight months out of the year, has a severe polar climate and is constantly buffeted by gales sweeping down from the Arctic. Winds

Sled dogs made exploration of the Arctic possible, with their ability to travel up to 130 kilometres (80 miles) every day.

of 80 to 95 kilometres per hour (48 to 56 mph) are common. One hundred and thirty kilometres long by 65 wide (81 miles long by 40 wide), Wrangel has two mountain ranges, fast-moving rivers, lakes, and plentiful wildlife, including so many polar bears that Muir called it 'The Land of the White Bear'.

The first thing Stefansson's expeditioners did on coming ashore was go through a ridiculous ceremony 'claiming' the island for Great Britain. Allan Crawford, though only twenty years old and the least experienced of the group, had been named team leader by Stefansson, and the others now realised why—he was a native of Canada and a British citizen, and so could make the 'claim'. After this bit of political chicanery was done, they got to work. They built the frame of a house against the side of a high hill, using driftwood since the island was treeless. When winter set in a month or so later they would cut blocks of snow to make the walls. The men went out hunting, or performed scientific experiments, while Ada sewed and cooked. She was noticeably frightened whenever a polar bear came near the camp, and firearms scared her enough to make her put her hands over her ears and turn away, but the men were happy with her work.

As October began, snow began to fall and the pack ice drifted into place against the island, roaring and cracking. The first blizzard of the year came, with 80 kilometre an hour (50 mph) winds and snow so hard it felt like needles being driven into their faces. The long winter had arrived.

Love and Madness

As the white weather set in, Ada found herself becoming more and more depressed. There seemed to be no particular reason—sadness would sweep over her, perhaps at the thought of her son in the orphanage, and she would weep. The four explorers watched her carefully, almost gingerly, at first. When she burst into tears, they would comfort her—she sometimes seemed, Knight wrote in his journal, like a child of eight or ten, not a young woman. Gradually they realised she had a crush on Crawford—she was always spending time around him, casting admiring glances his way, bringing him choice bits of food.

This caused a good deal of covert laughter among the men, and Crawford himself was quite embarrassed, something Ada apparently didn't realise right away, but resented when she did. She moved out of the hut to a small snowhouse she had built and refused to do some of her work, which angered the others. One day she was watching Knight scraping an animal skin with his knife—something she should have been doing—and grew terrified, remembering the shaman's prediction about knives. Only Crawford would protect her, she thought; she kept begging him to keep the others away. When he didn't respond, she would say to the others: 'Please get your gun and shoot me while I am asleep.'

Eventually losing their patience, the others tried to force Ada to work. They took away her dinner, made her sleep outside in the freezing cold, and at one point tied her to the flagpole. In November she tried to run away—now almost certain Knight was going to kill her with his knives—but they found her in the snow and brought her back.

No Relief

Gradually, as if she had suffered a temporary bout of insanity, Ada recovered herself, began to work again, and was restored to the others' good graces, although they were always wary of a repetition. She explained many years later that she was mainly homesick; she did, she admitted, love Crawford, but she knew it was hopeless.

As the winter of 1922 gradually turned to spring, the inhabitants of the tiny camp looked forward to summer, when the resupply ship and Stefansson would arrive. And here is where they made a fatal error, for they began to eat through their remaining supplies without rationing them. They attempted to hunt, but the game had become scarce, moving farther away from the camp—had they been experienced enough, they would have made it their first priority to lay in a stock of meat before the animals became so wary.

At first this did not seem like a crisis—Stefansson would be here, after all, in a few months. Summer arrived, the ice broke up, and each day the men gathered on the hill above the camp to watch for the relief boat. But it did not come. Stefansson had been unable to interest either the Canadians or the British in colonising the island, and thus had to hire a ship himself. Naturally, with international glory now not forthcoming, he did not accompany it. The rusty old vessel, the *Teddy Bear*, did not leave Nome until almost the end of August, too late in the season, and was turned back by pack ice and thick fog, reaching Alaska at the end of September.

On Wrangel the team waited and waited. By late September it was obvious that no ship was going to show up, and they were seriously worried. Most were suffering from one ailment or another, and Knight was feeling a stiffness in his joints which he put down to rheumatism, but was secretly afraid was scurvy—always a careful, almost fastidious eater, he turned up his nose at fresh meat and refused to eat their canned potatoes, which he thought had gone bad.

In October the pack ice, starting with small floes, began colliding with the shores of the island again. The game disappeared further into the distance, and belatedly they began to ration food. Making matters worse, they had run out of easily accessible driftwood for their all-important fire, and were forced to move camp. During this operation, Knight was short of energy and irascible, and frequently complained of being depressed. Finally, he could no longer pretend to himself that he had rheumatism or some other ailment: having suffered scurvy before, he knew the beginning signs when he saw them.

'If the Fates Favour Me'

When full winter set in, they began to realise they might not survive until the summer when, they assumed, a rescue ship must come. Ada saw Crawford and Knight, who had emerged as the two dominant figures, huddling together a great deal, and knew they were planning something. In January, they announced that a team *must* make an attempt to break out of this icebound prison. Knight was too weak to travel, so Crawford, Galle and

The Prison Island

It seems almost fitting that Wrangel Island should have been turned into a penal colony, given Ada Blackjack's experiences there.

Charles Wells and his Eskimo companions lasted only a year on Wrangel before the Red October, a Soviet patrol ship, steamed into the harbour in October 1924. The 'colonists' paddled out to meet it, thinking it was their supply boat, but when Wells saw the hammer and sickle flag he realised their days on Wrangel were over. The ship took all the men off the island, imprisoned Wells in Siberia, where he died of pneumonia, and finally released the Eskimos through intermediaries in China.

The Soviets established their own colony on Wrangel and during World War II set up a dismal prison camp for German POWs, where deaths supposedly occurred by the thousands—there is also a story of a contingent of 12 000 Polish POWs freezing to death in the prison-holds of a ship icebound near the island.

After the war the Soviets apparently established a top-secret camp for political prisoners on Wrangel—men and women whom the world thinks are dead. There were eyewitness reports that Raoul Wallenberg, the World War II hero supposedly shot by the Soviets in 1947, was spotted there as late as 1962. With the fall of the Soviet Union in the late 1980s, the camp was supposedly disbanded, but no one quite knows for sure.

Maurer would take the sled dogs, half the supplies, and attempt to make it across the ice to the Siberian coastline, some 300 kilometres (186.5 miles) away. After that, it would be another 800 kilometres (497 miles) to civilisation.

It was a desperate plan, and not a very good one. Fred Maurer, with the most experience of desolate Arctic winters, did not agree with it. Still, he acquiesced with it. He left behind a letter for his fiancée, Delphine, in which he wrote: 'The chief reason for our leaving is lack of food ... If the fates favour me, I'll have the pleasure of telling you about [our journey] in person, if against me, then someone else, no doubt, will tell you all.'

On 29 January the trio set off, promising to send help to Ada and Knight when the warmer weather arrived. All they needed to do was hold on. Once the men and the barking dogs disappeared from sight, a deep silence took hold of the camp. Ada was worried. She disliked and feared Knight, who was cool and aloof. She carefully kept a calendar, counting the days until help might return. For his part, Knight wrote in his journal: 'I wonder what people will say about my staying here alone with the female? [She seems] most anxious to "get" a white man. *No chance* as far as I am concerned.'

To their horror, on 30 January a blizzard swept over the island, one of the worst they had seen. The snow piled up so high that they were literally trapped inside their cabin with Vic the cat. When it continued the next day, and the next, they began to worry about their three companions out on the pack ice.

This odd couple spent the next months in close company, living on hard bread—six slices each per day—seal blubber and bear oil. There would be nothing else to eat until early spring, when the bears would emerge from hibernation and the seals and walruses and birds reappear. They could make it until then, they thought.

One morning Knight went out to chop wood. Ada heard the sound of the axe hitting the logs repeatedly, the dull *thunk* penetrating the snow walls of the cabin. Then it stopped. She waited for Knight to come in with an armload of firewood, but after hearing nothing for fifteen minutes, she walked outside to find him lying motionless on the ground.

'The Wosest Life I Ever Live'

Knight had fainted. After Ada revived him and helped him inside, he lay down on his bed, sure he was going to be all right—but every time he tried to get up, pain shot through him. He realised that the scurvy was farther along than he thought and that he desperately needed fresh meat to provide the vitamins necessary to cure it.

Several newspapers of the day referred to Ada Blackjack as the 'female Robinson Crusoe'.

Because Knight could not move, Ada was forced to take on the work he had been doing. She chopped wood, melted snow for drinking water, and checked the traps he had set for Arctic foxes. This terrified her, because she feared that polar bears could be out prowling the snowy wastes. But still as frightened as ever of rifles, she carried only a long knife as she made lonely treks to the spots where the traps were set, following a map sketched out by Fred Maurer.

After a good deal of trial and error, she trapped a fox, which she brought back and fed to Knight, but it did little to arrest his slide into the end-stages of scurvy. He had a sensitive stomach to begin with, and as the disease progressed his throat became quite raw and his teeth loosened, making it hard to swallow food. Desperate that he not die and leave her there alone, Ada redoubled her efforts at hunting. She swallowed her fear and learned to use the rifle, but by March had still not shot anything. One night a bear careened through the camp while they were asleep and Ada bewailed the fact that if she had been awake, she might have been able to shoot it—and provide enough meat to save them both.

Ada was feeling the first symptoms of scurvy herself, and she and Knight were acutely aware that if she came down with the disease, they would both very likely die in the cabin, unable to move from their beds. As the spring of 1923 arrived, Ada redoubled her efforts to trap foxes or shoot a bear, but by now the skin was peeling off Knight's fingers, his gums were turning black and blue, his body mere skin and bones. He was often angry with Ada and berated her, but then would turn quiet and beg her forgiveness. One day he gave her his grandfather's Bible as a gift, but the next day started 'to cruel' with her, as she wrote in a journal she began keeping. She also wrote: 'This is the wosest life I ever live in this world.' She began to prepare for her death: 'If I be known dead,' she wrote, 'I want my sister Rita to take Bennett my son … don't let his father Black Jack take him.'

'There is Nobody Here but Me'

During the night of 23 June, Lorne Knight died. Towards the end he seemed calm and told Ada what to do with his belongings, especially his journal, which he wanted preserved for his parents and posterity. Despite their arguments, Ada had grown close to him and now, looking at his still body, felt the dreadful weight of being completely alone in the wilderness. Milton Galle had left his typewriter behind and although he had warned her not to touch it, she sat down, with Knight's body on the bed nearby, and pecked out a note:

> *Wrangel Island*
> *June 23, 1923*
> *The daid of Mr Knight's death He died on June 23 I don't know what time he die though Anyway I write the daid Just to let Mr Stefansson know what month he died and what daid of the month*
> *Written by Mrs Ada B, Jack*

Not being strong enough to take Knight out and bury him, Ada left him in his bed, walled off by boxes. Then, she and the cat moved out of the hut to a nearby storage tent. Ada was terrified but she continued to function. She shored up the tent with driftwood and built a kerosene stove out of old tins flattened out and hammered together. She gathered up all Knight's possessions, including the journal so that it might be returned to his family.

Then Ada Blackjack underwent an astounding transformation. Through endless practice she became a crack shot, able to kill birds on the wing. She learned to sneak up on seals, and not to shoot one close to the water's edge, for invariably it would slide back into the ocean to die. Shooting at the polar bear that had stolen her kill seemed to give her confidence, despite the terror of the moment, and now when she went out she was able to frighten away any of the huge creatures who tried the same thing.

Before she knew it, it was early August. In July she had built a driftwood viewing platform near the beach and now spent a good part of each day peering toward the horizon with binoculars, hoping to see the ship that Galle, Crawford and Maurer must have sent by now. But it didn't come. Ada wasn't sure if she could survive another winter, not because she might not be able to shoot and trap enough food, but because the solitude had become crushing, weighing down on her with inexorable force. Sometimes she thought she would go crazy.

And then, on the morning of 20 August, as she was making tea for her breakfast, she became aware of a rumbling sound. At first it had merged into the background noises of the island and she had barely noticed it. But as it became louder and louder she realised it wasn't an island noise. In fact, she realised, as she dropped the tea and raced out the door, it was the sound of a ship's engine.

Harold Noice and Rescue

Back in America and Canada, nothing had been heard of the members of the expedition since the *Silver Wave* left them on Wrangel, and the families of Crawford, Galle, Knight and Maurer were beginning to become concerned. They begged Stefansson to mount a rescue mission, but the famed explorer, who had had the temerity to announce his retirement right around the time Crawford and his companions were caught in a gale on the pack ice of the Chukchi Sea, delayed until he could raise enough money from friends and businessmen he knew. Then he hired one Harold Noice to lead an expedition to find the men. Noice was an odd choice, an ambitious but dishonest alumnus of a past Stefansson expedition who held a grudge against Lorne Knight, one of the men he was now sworn to save.

Noice left Nome aboard his ship, the *Donaldson*, in August and found a way through the ice to within visual distance of Wrangel Island. He had a replacement party of Eskimo 'colonists' and plentiful supplies with him, and he expected to take the four men and Ada off and back to civilisation. But as he cruised the shore, he could see no one. The island seemed completely deserted.

Suddenly one of the Eskimos shouted, then others joined him, pointing over the rail. And there, on the beach, was a tiny, solitary figure, waving her arms frantically over her head. Noice immediately rowed to shore, where Ada had waded into the water to meet him.

The first thing she said was: 'Where is Crawford and Galle and Maurer? Why is not Mr Galle with you?'

But Noice, of course, thought the men were here.

'There is no one here but me,' Ada replied, beginning to cry. 'I want to go back to my mother. Will you take me back to Nome?'

The *Donaldson* stayed long enough for the crew to bury Lorne Knight's skeletal corpse and drop off the Eskimos and a lone American, Charles Wells, to keep the 'colony' going. Getting back to Nome on 31 August, Ada Blackjack had returned to civilisation, but in some ways her troubles were just beginning.

'The Heroine of Wrangel Island'

Crawford, Galle and Maurer, Ada found out, had vanished into thin air—or, more likely, into the frozen wastes of the Chukchi Sea, perhaps even in the first few days when the blizzard hit. In any event, nothing was ever heard from them again. Ada, however, found herself in the midst of an intense storm of publicity as soon as news got out that she was the sole survivor of the expedition. At first she was lauded as 'the heroine of Wrangel Island', but then, in an appalling true-life plot twist, the man who rescued her turned against her (see **Spurned Eskimo Woman**, opposite) and accused her of having starved Lorne Knight to death.

Because of the notoriety this accusation engendered, Ada Blackjack was to spend the rest of her life trying to disappear, moving back and forth between Seattle, Washington and Nome, Alaska. She rescued Bennett from the orphanage, where he had healed, had another son, Billy, and was married another three times, always to men who abused her. She was often on welfare; when she wasn't she had a series of jobs which included reindeer herding and house-cleaning. She was to die in Alaska in 1983, at the age of eighty-five; Billy, her surviving son, made sure her tombstone read: 'The Heroine of Wrangel Island'.

Spurned Eskimo Woman

In the *New York World* newspaper of 11 February 1924, an article was published with a bold headline reading SPURNED ESKIMO WOMAN BLAMED FOR ARCTIC DEATH. The subheading was *Wrangel Island Explorers Refused Proposal of Marriage, Rescuer Noice Discloses Here. When Three Left Camp, Knight Died of Hunger. Though Man's Body Was Wasted by Starvation, Ada Blackjack Was Healthy.*

This was a shocking thing to write about a plucky young woman who had only a few months before been seen as 'the heroine of Wrangel Island'. More shocking was that the story had been given to the newspaper by none other than Noice, her rescuer. On the *Donaldson*, Ada had dutifully handed over Knight's diaries when Noice asked to see them, promising to make copies and return them. But he never did. When h read the stories of Ada's infatuation with Crawford and her refusal to work, he saw something that he could turn to his advantage. Pushed on by his wife, he deliberately defaced portions of the journals, crossing them out with black pencil, then accused Ada of having done it.

And what portions might have been crossed out—portions, according to the *World* article, 'only recently deciphered by Mr. Noice and his wife'? These would be the parts, the article implied, in which Knight recorded that Ada had refused to help him as he lay dying and even hidden food from him. In fact, the article said, when she was found, Ada was fat.

When Ada, visiting in California at the time, heard what had been written, she was devastated. She had done all she could for Knight, fed him the majority of the food, and nearly died herself. She was so hounded by reporters that what was supposed to be a relaxing vacation trip turned into a nightmare and she fled to Seattle.

Fortunately, the dead men's families, especially the Knight family, who had met Ada when she returned the Bible to them, supported her staunchly in the face of these allegations. Pictures appearing in newspapers at the time she got back to Nome showed that, far from being fat, Ada was mere skin and bones. So why had Noice made up these lies? For two reasons. One, he had turned against Stefansson and wanted to blackmail him with threats of the dreadful scandals revealed in these journals—scandals that took place on an expedition organised by Stefansson, an expedition it could rightly be said that Stefansson had abandoned.

Secondly, Noice wanted to publish his own book about the castaways, and knew that this would be good publicity. But by the time the book was ready he had been revealed as a charlatan, his wife had left him, and Stefansson forced him to sign a retraction of all the untrue statements he had made about Ada and the expedition.

Bibliography

Alexander, Caroline. *The Bounty: The True Story of the Mutiny on the Bounty*. New York: Viking, 2003.

Barnard, Captain Charles. H. *Marooned: Being a Narrative of the Sufferings and Adventures of Captain Charles H. Barnard, Embracing An Account of the Seizure of his Vessel at the Falkland Islands, 1812–1816*. Syracuse, New York: Syracuse University Press, 1986.

Cabeza de Vaca, Álvar Núñez. *The Narrative of Cabeza de Vaca*. Edited, translated and with an introduction by Rolena Adorno & Patrick Charles Pautz. Lincoln, Nebraska: University of Nebraska Press, 1999.

Carter, George & Hynes, John. *A Narrative of the Grosvenor, East Indiaman*. London: J. Murray, 1791.

Cross, Wilbur & Fukami, Teiji. *The Lost Men of Anatahan*. New York: Coronet Communications, 1969.

Dash, Mike. *Batavia's Graveyard*. New York: Crown, 2002.

Druett, Joan. *Island of the Lost: Shipwrecked at the Edge of the World*. Chapel Hill, North Carolina: Algonquin Books, 2007.

Doherty, Kevin. *Sea Venture: Shipwreck, Survival and the Salvation of the First English Colony in the New World*. New York: St. Martin's Press, 2007.

Eunson, Keith. *The Wreck of the General Grant*. Wellington: A.H. & A.W. Reed, 1974.

Heffernan, Thomas Farel. *Mutiny on the Globe: The Fatal Voyage of Samuel Comstock*. London: Bloomsbury, 2002.

Henderson, Bruce. *Fatal North: Adventure and Survival Aboard USS Polaris, the First U.S. Expedition to the North Pole*. New York: NAL, 2001.

Frost, Orcutt. *Bering: The Russian Discovery of America*. New Haven: Yale University Press, 2003.

King, Dean. *Skeletons on the Zahara: A True Story of Survival*. New York: Back Bay Books, 2004.

Lummis, Trevor. *Life & Death in Eden: Pitcairn Island and the Bounty Mutineers*. London: Phoenix Press, 2000.

Milton, Giles. *Big Chief Elizabeth: The Adventures and Fate of the First English Colonists in America*. New York: Farrar, Straus, and Giroux, 2000.

Musgrave, Captain Thomas. *Castaway on the Auckland Isle: A Narrative of the Wreck of the Grafton*. Melbourne: H.T. Dwight, 1865.

Price, David A. *Love and Hate in Jamestown: John Smith, Pocohontas, and the Heart of a New Nation*. New York: Alfred A. Knopf, 2003.

Riley, James. *Sufferings in Africa: The Astonishing Account of a New England Sea Captain Enslaved*. New York: Lyons Press, 2000.

Ritsema, Alex. *A Dutch Castaway on Ascension Island in 1725*. Deventer, The Netherlands: Alex Ritsema, 2006.

Robertson-Lorant, Laurie. *Melville: A Biography*. New York: Clarkson Potter, 1996.

Severin, Tim. *In Search of Robinson Crusoe*. New York: Basic Books, 2002.

Skaggs, Jimmy M. *Clipperton: A History of the Island the World Forgot*. New York: Walker & Co., 1989.

Simmons, James C. *Castaway in Paradise: The Incredible Adventures of True-Life Robinson Crusoes*. Dobbs Ferry, NY: Sheridan House, Inc., 1993.

Smith, Barbara Darrah, ed. *Terror at Sea: True Tales of Shipwrecks, Cannibalism, Pirates, Fire at Sea, & Other Dire Disasters in the 18th and 19th Centuries*. Cape Elizabeth, ME: The Provincial Press, 1995

Souhami, Diana. *Selkirk's Island: The True and Strange Adventures of the Real Robinson Crusoe*. New York: Harcourt, Inc., 2001.

Taylor, Stephen. *The Caliban Shore: The Wreck of the Grosvenor and the Strange Fate of her Survivors*. London: Faber & Faber, 2004.

Tyson, George. *Arctic Experiences: Containing Capt. George E. Tyson's Wonderful Drift on the Ice Floe*. New York: Harper Bros., 1874.

Image Credits

Corbis: p. 5, p. 7, p. 9, p. 30, p. 39, p. 40, p. 45, p. 52, p. 62, p. 63, p. 75, p. 88, p. 95, p. 106, p. 108, p. 134, p. 147, p. 150, p. 184, p. 207, p. 213, p. 218, p. 232, p. 256, p. 262, p. 265, p. 270, p. 280, p. 282, p. 300, p. 304, p. 307, p. 308.

Courtesy of Dartmouth College Library
(item located in Rauner Special Collections Library): p. 325.

Getty Images: p. 122, p. 202, p. 292.

The Hague, Koninklijke Bibliotheek, 893 E 97: p. 67.

Photolibrary / Bridgeman Art Library: p. 8, p. 16, p. 19, p. 20, p. 25, p. 33, p. 83, p. 111, p. 112, p. 120, p. 136, p. 161, p. 164, p. 172, p. 177, p. 199, p. 206, p. 220, p. 225, p. 226, p. 237, p. 240, p. 260, p. 264, p. 269, p. 285, p. 320, p. 323.

The Granger Collection: p. 59.

Acknowledgements

I would like to thank Murdoch Books commissioning editor Diana Hill, who dreamed up this book and made sure it was Cast Away on the right shores. Thanks also to the editors Paul O'Beirne, for his skillful edits, and Anne Savage, who knows her moray eels. The great layout and design are courtesy of Hugh Ford and Anthony Vandenberg.

Index

First published in 2008 by Pier 9, an imprint of Murdoch Books Pty Limited

Murdoch Books Australia
Pier 8/9
23 Hickson Road
Millers Point NSW 2000
Phone: +61 (0)2 8220 2000
Fax: +61 (0)2 8220 2558
www.murdochbooks.com.au

Murdoch Books UK Limited
Erico House, 6th Floor
93–99 Upper Richmond Road
Putney, London SW15 2TG
Phone: +44 (0) 20 8785 5995
Fax: +44 (0) 20 8785 5985
www.murdochbooks.co.uk

Chief Executive: Juliet Rogers
Publishing Director: Kay Scarlett
Commissioning Editor: Diana Hill
Project Manager: Paul O'Beirne
Editor: Anne Savage
Design concept: Hugh Ford
Design layout: Hugh Ford and Anthony Vandenburg
Photo researcher: Samantha Bensch
Production: Nikla Martin
Cartographer: Ian F Faulkner & Associates
Text and design copyright © Joseph Cummins 2008

Quoted material appearing on page 63 has been sourced from Elizabeth Bishop's poem
Crusoe in England: From *Geography III Poems* (Farrar, Straus, and Giroux, reprinted 2008).

National Library of Australia Cataloguing-in-Publication Data:
Cummins, Joseph.
Cast Away / Joseph Cummins.
ISBN 978 1 74196 138 6 (pbk).
Includes index.
1. Shipwrecks. 2. Adventure and adventurers.
I. Title. 910.4

A catalogue record for this book is available from the British Library.

Printed by Hang Tai Printing in 2008. PRINTED IN CHINA.

NOTE: No distinction has been made between short and long tons throughout this book.